HANDBOOK OF RESEARCH METHODS AND APPLICATIONS IN ENTREPRENEURSHIP AND SMALL BUSINESS

T0329645

HANDBOOKS OF RESEARCH METHODS AND APPLICATIONS

Series Editor: Mark Casson, *University of Reading, UK*

The objective of this series is to provide definitive overviews of research methods in important fields of social science, including economics, business, finance and policy studies. The aim is to produce prestigious high quality works of lasting significance. Each *Handbook* consists of original contributions by leading authorities, selected by an editor who is a recognised leader in the field. The emphasis is on the practical application of research methods to both quantitative and qualitative evidence. The *Handbooks* will assist practising researchers in generating robust research findings that policy-makers can use with confidence.

While the *Handbooks* will engage with general issues of research methodology, their primary focus will be on the practical issues concerned with identifying and using suitable sources of data or evidence, and interpreting source material using best-practice techniques. They will review the main theories that have been used in applied research, or could be used for such research. While reference may be made to conceptual issues and to abstract theories in the course of such reviews, the emphasis will be firmly on real-world applications.

Titles in the series include:

Handbook of Research Methods and Applications in Urban Economies
Edited by Peter Karl Kresl and Jaime Sobrino

Handbook of Research Methods and Applications in Empirical Finance
Edited by Adrian R. Bell, Chris Brooks and Marcel Prokopczuk

Handbook of Research Methods and Applications in Empirical Macroeconomics
Edited by Nigar Hashimzade and Michael A. Thornton

Handbook of Research Methods and Applications in Entrepreneurship and Small Business
Edited by Alan Carsrud and Malin Brännback

Handbook of Research Methods and Applications in Entrepreneurship and Small Business

Edited by

Alan Carsrud

Visiting Research Professor and Docent, Åbo Akademi University, Finland

Malin Brännback

Vice-Rector and Chair of International Business, Åbo Akademi University, Finland and Visiting Professor in Entrepreneurship, Stockholm University School of Business, Sweden

HANDBOOKS OF RESEARCH METHODS AND APPLICATIONS

Edward Elgar

Cheltenham, UK • Northampton, MA, USA

© Alan Carsrud and Malin Brännback 2014

All rights reserved. No part of this publication may be reproduced, stored in a retrieval system or transmitted in any form or by any means, electronic, mechanical or photocopying, recording, or otherwise without the prior permission of the publisher.

Published by
Edward Elgar Publishing Limited
The Lypiatts
15 Lansdown Road
Cheltenham
Glos GL50 2JA
UK

Edward Elgar Publishing, Inc.
William Pratt House
9 Dewey Court
Northampton
Massachusetts 01060
USA

A catalogue record for this book
is available from the British Library

Library of Congress Control Number: 2013949797

This book is available electronically in the ElgarOnline.com Business Subject Collection, E-ISBN 978 0 85793 505 2

ISBN 978 0 85793 504 5 (cased)

Typeset by Columns Design XML Ltd, Reading
Printed and bound in Great Britain by T.J. International Ltd, Padstow

Contents

List of figures   vii
List of tables   viii
List of contributors   ix

1   Research in entrepreneurship: an introduction to the research challenges for the twenty-first century   1
Alan Carsrud, Malin Brännback and Richard T. Harrison

2   Thoughts on the challenge of empirical research in entrepreneurship   10
David Deeds

3   From philosophy of science to theory testing: generating practical knowledge in entrepreneurship   20
Thomas P. Kenworthy and W. Edward McMullen

4   Measuring progress in entrepreneurship research   56
Linda F. Edelman, Tatiana S. Manolova, Candida G. Brush and Scott Latham

5   Experimental methods in entrepreneurship research   88
Kelly G. Shaver

6   Looking into the future: valid multiple- and single-item measures in entrepreneurship research   112
Leon Schjoedt, Maija Renko and Kelly G. Shaver

7   Control variables: use, misuse and recommended use   136
Leon Schjoedt and Barbara Bird

8   Cross-cultural studies in entrepreneurship: a note on culture and language   156
Malin Brännback, Stefan Lång, Alan Carsrud and Siri Terjesen

9   Fighting a rearguard action? Reflections on the philosophy and practice of qualitative research in entrepreneurship   177
Richard T. Harrison and Claire M. Leitch

10 Ethnographic approaches to entrepreneurship and small-business
     research: what lessons can we learn?   201
     Karin Berglund and Caroline Wigren

11 The practice approach and interactive research in
     entrepreneurship and small-scale venturing   228
     Bengt Johannisson

Index   259

Figures

1.1 Core elements of the typical research process   5
3.1 Meehl's inferential passage from observations to substantive
    theory   29
3.2 The origins of theories used in the top three entrepreneurship
    journals   40
3.3 Most-used theories in the top three entrepreneurship journals 40
7.1 Venn diagram depicting no relationship among predictor and
    control variables   140
7.2 Venn diagram depicting relationships among predictor, criterion
    and control variables   141
7.3 Venn diagram depicting a relationship among predictor and
    control variables and no relationship among criterion and control
    variables   147
8.1 Model for integrating *emic* and *etic* perspectives in research:
    noting research-specific language   171

Tables

3.1 POS education in business doctoral programming – top 100 universities   25
3.2 Exogenous theory assessment model   42
3.3 The strength of the theory in the base discipline   43
3.4 Human capital theory variants   46
3.5 Examples of theory review studies   47
4.1 Domain of entrepreneurship: literature reviews   59
4.2 Scope of the review   62
4.3 Research methods   65
4.4 Research design   67
4.5 Research methods weighted   72
4.6 Research design weighted   73
6A.1 Items from the PSED mail questionnaire considered by Schjoedt and Shaver (2012)   135
9.1 Validation of the process of undertaking empirical interpretivist research   192
11.1 Contextual familiarity in interactive research   236
11.2 Four cases – an overview   237

Contributors

Karin Berglund, Ph.D., is Associate Professor at Stockholm University School of Business and Centre Director of Stockholm School of Entrepreneurship, Sweden. In her research, Karin has focused on how entrepreneurship has been manifested in different forms in contemporary society (e.g. in schools, in the public sector, in social and green issues, in incorporating more people in entrepreneurship, e.g. women, immigrants, young people). Her overarching research interest lies in studying the emergence of diverse entrepreneurship forms as part of an enterprise culture fostered in society. Karin has published in international journals covering different topics related to entrepreneurship such as gender, education, innovation, critical pedagogy and regional development, and now social/societal entrepreneurship. Her methodological interests lie within ethnography, discourse analysis, narrative research and participatory action research. Before entering academia Karin had a career in the private small-business sector, and also took part in starting a new venture.

Barbara Bird, Ph.D., is Professor of Management at Kogod School of Business, American University in Washington, DC. She teaches organizational behaviour and leadership courses. She holds a psychology degree from California State University, Fresno, an MA in Social Psychology from the University of Western Ontario, and a doctorate from the University of Southern California. Her research interests include entrepreneurial cognition and entrepreneurs' behaviour. Her research projects include Latino first- and second-generation immigrant entrepreneurs, as well as developing a measure of entrepreneurs' selling. She wrote *Entrepreneurial Behavior*, several scholarly journal articles in *Academy of Management Review*, *Organization Science* and *Personnel Psychology*. She is past chair of the Entrepreneurship Division of the Academy of Management and is the most senior editor of *Entrepreneurship Theory and Practice*. She has served as industry consultant to the Advanced Technology Program (NIST) and is a family business adviser.

Malin Brännback, D.Sc., B. Sc. (Pharm), is Vice-Rector and Chair of International Business at Åbo Akademi University, Finland, where she received her doctorate in Management Science in 1996. She is Visiting Professor in Entrepreneurship at Stockholm University School of Business, Sweden. She also holds a B.Sc. in Pharmacy. Before her return to Åbo

Akademi University in 2003, she served as Associate Professor in Information Systems at the University of Turku, and Professor of Marketing at Turku School of Economics. She has published widely on entrepreneurship, biotechnology business and knowledge management. She has co-authored with Alan Carsrud several books: *Entrepreneurship* (2005), *Understanding the Entrepreneurial Mind: Opening the Black Box* (2009) and *Understanding Family Businesses* (2012). She is on the review board of *Journal of Small Business Management.* Her current research interests are in entrepreneurial intentionality, entrepreneurial cognition, entrepreneurial growth and performance in technology entrepreneurship and family business.

Candida G. Brush, Ph.D., is Professor of Entrepreneurship, Chair of the Entrepreneurship Division, holds the Franklin W. Olin Chair in Entrepreneurship, and serves as Research Director of the Arthur M. Blank Center at Babson College, Wellesley, MA. She holds an honorary doctorate from Jönköping University in Sweden and she has a visiting adjunct appointment to Nordland University, Bodø Graduate School of Business, Norway. Dr Brush is a founding member of the Diana Project International, and winner of the 2007 Global Award for Entrepreneurship Research. Her research investigates women's growth businesses, angel investing and strategies of emerging ventures. She has written nine books, 120 journal articles and is the author of other publications. She serves as an editor for *Entrepreneurship Theory and Practice*, and is an angel investor and board member for several companies and organizations.

Alan Carsrud, Ph.D., Ec.D. (hc), is Visiting Research Professor and Docent at Åbo Akademi University, Finland and during 2013 Visiting Professor at Universidad del Desarrollo, Chile. In 2012 he retired as Loretta Rogers Chair of Entrepreneurship Research at Ryerson University in Canada. He served on the faculties of University of Texas at Austin, University of Southern California, Durham University, University of California, Los Angeles, Bond University and Florida International University. He has written over 200 journal articles and chapters on entrepreneurship, family business, and social and clinical psychology, as well as seven books on entrepreneurship and family business. His entrepreneurship research is in technology, cognitive factors (motivation and intentions), growth, leadership, education and family business. He co-founded *Entrepreneurship & Regional Development* and is Associate Editor of the *Journal of Small Business Management.* He is Managing Director of Carsrud & Associates, helping to create firms as diverse as biotechnology, software, wineries and airlines.

David Deeds, Ph.D., is the Schulze Chair in Entrepreneurship at the Opus College of Business at the University of St Thomas, Minneapolis, MN. Previously, he held faculty positions at the University of Texas at Dallas, Case Western Reserve University and Temple University. He received his Ph.D. from the University of Washington in 1994. He has taught courses in strategy, entrepreneurship and technology management at the undergraduate, graduate, Ph.D. and executive levels during his career. He has published numerous articles in management and entrepreneurship in journals, including *Strategic Management Journal, Journal of Business Venturing* and *Entrepreneurship Theory and Practice*. His current research interests include research alliances, entrepreneurial finance and the management of technology ventures. During his career he has worked as a consultant for a number of companies including Alcoa and Champion Technologies. Before becoming an academic, Dr Deeds was co-founder and president of Light-Speed Corporation.

Linda F. Edelman, M.B.A., D.B.A., holds her degrees from Boston University, MA. She is Associate Professor of Strategic Management at Bentley University, Waltham, MA. Before coming to Bentley she was a research fellow at the Warwick Business School, Warwick University, UK. Professor Edelman is the author of over 15 book chapters and 30 peer-reviewed journal articles. Her work has appeared in journals such as *Journal of Business Venturing, Entrepreneurship Theory and Practice, Industrial and Corporate Change* and *Organization Studies.* She serves on three editorial boards as well as on the board of reviewers for the *Frontiers of Entrepreneurship Research*. Currently, she teaches strategic management at the undergraduate, graduate and doctoral levels. Her recent research examines strategic industry dynamics, women and nascent entrepreneurs, SME internationalization and entrepreneurial finance.

Richard T. Harrison, Ph.D., is currently Professor of Entrepreneurship and Innovation at Edinburgh University, UK. He was previously Dean of Queen's University Management School in Belfast and has previously held chairs at Edinburgh, Aberdeen and Ulster universities, as well as visiting positions in China, Australia and the USA. His research into the dynamics and impact of the entrepreneurial process includes studies of entrepreneurial finance, entrepreneurial learning and leadership, technology venturing, research methods and philosophy, and economic development and public policy. Including eight books and edited conference proceedings, he has published over 150 scholarly publications on these and other topics. He is founding co-editor of *Venture Capital: An International Journal of Entrepreneurial Finance,* and sits or has sat on the editorial boards of a number of leading entrepreneurship journals.

Bengt Johannisson, Ph.D., is Professor Emeritus of Entrepreneurship at Linnaeus University and at Jönköping International Business School in Sweden. Previously he held chairs at Lund University in Sweden and at Roskilde University in Denmark. He has also been Visiting Professor at universities in the UK, Canada, Austria and Italy. During 1998–2007 he was the editor-in-chief of *Entrepreneurship & Regional Development* and has published widely on entrepreneurship, personal networking, family business and on local and regional development. In Sweden, Professor Johannisson has initiated inter-university networks on research and postgraduate studies in entrepreneurship. For 15 years he was a director of the European Doctoral Programme in Entrepreneurship and Small Business Management. Professor Johannisson is the 2008 Winner of the Global Award for Entrepreneurship Research. Recent books include Bengt Johannisson and Åsa Lindholm Dahlstrand (eds), *Enacting Regional Dynamics and Entrepreneurship* (2012) and Karin Berglund, Bengt Johannisson and Birgitta Schwartz (eds), *Societal Entrepreneurship: Positioning, Penetrating, Promoting* (2012).

Thomas P. Kenworthy, Ph.D., holds his doctorate from the University of Calgary. He is Assistant Professor of Entrepreneurship in the School of Business at the University of Dayton, Ohio. His research interests are predominantly focused on creativity, the nature and extent of scientific knowledge in the domain of entrepreneurship and entrepreneurship through acquisition.

Stefan Lång, Ph.D., holds a Lectureship in International Marketing at Åbo Akademi University in Turku, Finland, where he teaches international business, intercultural marketing management and communication. He earned his doctorate in Marketing and Strategy from Cardiff University Business School, UK, in 2009. His specific research interests relate to the role of strategic marketing, communication and semiotics in an international business context. His business expertise and consultancy activities are in the area of marketing strategy and management, branding strategy and marketing communication with a special focus on semiotics.

Scott Latham, Ph.D., holds a doctorate from the University of Massachusetts, Amherst. He is Associate Professor of Strategy and Ph.D. Director at University of Massachusetts, Lowell. His research focuses on organizational decline, environmental turbulence and innovation; it has been published in *Academy of Management Review*, *Journal of Management*, *Journal of Small Business Management*, *Journal of Business Strategy* and other outlets. He teaches strategy and entrepreneurship. In addition to his scholarship, he serves on the executive board of M2D2, the Massachusetts

Medical Device Development centre, the state's medical device incubator, where he coaches medical device start-ups.

Claire M. Leitch, Ph.D., is Professor of Management Learning and Leadership at Lancaster University Management School, UK, where she is Director of Research and Director of Doctoral Programmes. Previously she was a senior lecturer in Management at Queen's University Management School, Belfast, and was Director of Education for six years. From 2008 to 2011 she was Visiting Professor at Aarhus University Business School, Denmark and from 2005 to 2006 Visiting Fellow at the Centre for Entrepreneurship and Innovation, University of Edinburgh. Her research interests fall into three distinct but interrelated areas concentrating on the development, enhancement and growth of the individual and the organization in an entrepreneurial context. She is a researcher who investigates problems and issues from an interpretivist perspective and is particularly interested in the application of alternative research methodologies, such as critical incident technique and action research. Since 1998 she has taught research methods to undergraduate, masters and doctoral students.

Tatiana S. Manolova, D.B.A., holds a doctorate from Boston University and is Associate Professor of Management at Bentley University in Massachusetts. Her research interests include strategic management (competitive strategies for new and small companies), international entrepreneurship and management in emerging economies. During 2010–11, she was Visiting Professor at King Saud University, Riyadh, Saudi Arabia, where she conducted research on entrepreneurship in affiliation with the Prince Salman Institute for Entrepreneurship. Dr Manolova is the author of over 40 scholarly articles and book chapters. She serves on the editorial boards of *Entrepreneurship Theory and Practice*, *Journal of Business Venturing* and *Journal of Global Entrepreneurship Research*.

W. Edward McMullen, Ph.D., retired as full Professor in Management from the Haskayne School of Business at the University of Calgary, Alberta, Canada. He is widely considered to be one of the founders of entrepreneurship research in Canada. His research interests have focused on creativity, outsider assistance, the nature and extent of scientific knowledge in the domain of entrepreneurship and the efficacy of post-secondary entrepreneurial programming.

Maija Renko, D.Sc., Ph.D., holds an Associate Professorship in Entrepreneurship at the University of Illinois at Chicago. She earned her D.Sc. in International Business from the Turku School of Economics, Finland (2006), and a Ph.D. in Business Administration at Florida International University (2008). Through her research and teaching she inspires and advises budding entrepreneurs on starting up successful new businesses and social ventures, with a specific focus on market research and business planning. She has published numerous articles and book chapters on the management of technology and innovation, entrepreneurship, social entrepreneurship and marketing in outlets such as *Entrepreneurship Theory and Practice*, *Small Business Economics* and the *Journal of Small Business Management*.

Leon Schjoedt, Ph.D., received his doctorate from University of Colorado at Boulder. He is currently Associate Professor of Management with the Judd Leighton School of Business and Economics at Indiana University South Bend. His research focuses on entrepreneurial behaviour – the intersection between entrepreneurship and organizational behaviour. Dr Schjoedt's work has appeared in journals such as *Entrepreneurship Theory and Practice*, *Journal of High Technology Management Research*, *Journal of Small Business & Entrepreneurship*, *Organizational Dynamics* and *Small Business Economics*, and in numerous book chapters. He frequently presents at academic meetings, including the annual meeting for the Academy of Management and Babson College Entrepreneurship Research Conference.

Kelly G. Shaver, Ph.D., is Professor of Entrepreneurial Studies at the College of Charleston, South Carolina. His previous appointments include the College of William & Mary, Virginia, the National Science Foundation, and the Entrepreneurship and Small Business Research Institute in Stockholm. His published work includes 15 books and numerous articles, one of which is among the top quarter of 1 per cent of 'core contributions' in Entrepreneurship. He has been supported by the National Institutes of Health, the Ewing Marion Kauffman Foundation and the National Science Foundation. Dr Shaver has been editor of *Entrepreneurship Theory and Practice*, has served on the editorial boards of *Entrepreneurship & Regional Development*, *Journal of Applied Social Psychology*, *Journal of Developmental Entrepreneurship* and *Journal of Personality and Social Psychology*. He is currently an associate editor of the *Journal of Small Business Management*. Shaver is a Fellow of the American Psychological Society and past Chair of the Entrepreneurship Division of the Academy of Management.

Siri Terjesen, Ph.D., is Assistant Professor of Management and Entrepreneurship at the Kelley School of Business at Indiana University, Bloomington. She obtained a Ph.D. from Cranfield University in the UK and a Master's from Norges Handelshøyskole in Norway. Her research has been published in *Strategic Management Journal*, *Journal of Management*,

Entrepreneurship Theory and Practice, *Journal of Operations Management*, *Journal of Business Ethics*, *Strategic Entrepreneurship Journal*, *Decision Sciences* and many other outlets, and has been profiled in the *US News & World Report*, *Christian Science Monitor*, *Huffington Post* and other news media. She is co-author of *Strategic Management: Thought and Action* (2008). Her research interests are entrepreneurship, international business and strategy.

Caroline Wigren, Ph.D., obtained her doctorate in Business Administration in 2003 from Jönköping International Business School, Jönköping University in Sweden. She is currently Associate Professor in Entrepreneurship at CIRCLE and in the Sten K. Johnson Center for Entrepreneurship at Lund University, Sweden. She carries out research on entrepreneurship in different contexts, and is interested in regional development and methodological issues.

1. Research in entrepreneurship: an introduction to the research challenges for the twenty-first century

Alan Carsrud, Malin Brännback and Richard T. Harrison

1.1 INTRODUCTION

Entrepreneurship as a field of research and small business has grown exponentially for more than half a century. One of the field's leading journals *Journal of Small Business Management*, is now into its 51st volume. The field has moved from barely a handful of journals 30 years ago (*Journal of Small Business Management, American Journal of Small Business* – now *Entrepreneurship Theory and Practice* and *Entrepreneurship & Regional Development*) to over 100 in the English language alone. More importantly, articles on entrepreneurship increasingly appear in the major journals of the Academy of Management (*Academy of Management Journal* and *Academy of Management Review*) and in other disciplines that a mere ten years ago would have never published a paper on small business or new ventures (consider the creation of *Strategic Entrepreneurship Journal* by the Strategic Management Society). One has only to consider the complex survey methodologies of the Global Entrepreneurship Monitor (GEM) project or the Panel Studies on Entrepreneurial Dynamics (PSED) to appreciate how far the field has spread in the last two decades. This complexity requires researchers to be fluent in a wide range of methodologies even if they prefer one approach to another. There are many books and primers on research methodology (Gartner et al., 2004). Likewise there are workshops and articles on how to use the data from the GEM and PSED studies.

While early studies were less sophisticated in statistical analysis, researchers today use highly complex methods. In the recent Babson College Entrepreneurship Research Conference in 2013 in Lyon, a noticeable number of the papers presented included the analytical technique in the title of the paper. Two justified questions are whether it is the technique that drives the research or are the research questions motivated by researchers' curiosity to unravel some interesting phenomena within entrepreneurship.

Like many areas of research in business, entrepreneurship has had to struggle with legitimizing itself as a valid research arena. Today, it is certainly difficult to find many who would seriously doubt the relevance and importance of entrepreneurship research. Yet we still wrestle with the lack of unified definitions. However, many have begun to acknowledge that attempting to create a unified definition of entrepreneurship is not a very fruitful endeavor. What is important is to understand that entrepreneurship is contextual (Welter, 2011). Understanding the context in which entrepreneurship takes place is critical. Therefore comparative studies across different business contexts yield different research results – and there is nothing wrong with that. The world is varied!

So, why do we need yet another methods book? Handbooks on research methods, whether quantitative or qualitative, are legion. Nearly every discipline has a good set of its own. A quick search in Google Scholar proves the point: Research Methods in Entrepreneurship gives 27 7000 hits; in Management 4.8 million; in Business 2.5 million. With the prevailing publishing imperative implemented in universities worldwide, mastering research methods is a prerequisite for publishing. A primary reason for rejection of a paper is serious methodological flaws. Research questions do not match the chosen research method. The data do not offer answers to the research questions. Research questions do not reflect the contextual reality, or the focal theory does not link to the research question, or the interpretations of the results do not relate to the focal theory. And it is not just doctoral students who have problems with research methods. In 2011 the *Academy of Management Journal*, beginning with volume 54, number 3 (2011), launched an editorial series on how to publish in *AMJ*. When reading through the editorials one realizes that they give guidance not merely on how to publish in *AMJ*, but also give an excellent overview on how to conduct and write up good research (Colquitt and George, 2011; Bono and McNamara, 2011; Grant and Pollock, 2011; Sparrowe and Mayer, 2011; Zhang and Shaw, 2012; Geletkanycz and Tepper, 2012; Bansal and Corley, 2012). We do not think these editorials were written other than to emphasize that mastering research methods and being able to report what was undertaken could be substantially improved. It seems to us that research methods is an area that is challenging and difficult, yet highly rewarding when mastered.

While research methods are important in any research, the entrepreneurship field faces yet another characteristic that makes it even more important to develop an ability and competence in conducting quality research. Entrepreneurship is multidisciplinary, not merely because it includes small-business management, entrepreneurship and family business, but also because most of the field's leading scholars have been trained and educated in a wide range of disciplines other than entrepreneurship, such as management, finance, strategy, sociology, organizational behavior, social psychology, economics, anthropology, demography, political science, clinical psychology accounting, marketing and industrial engineering, to name just a few. Each of these disciples has their own perspectives – and convictions – of what constitutes appropriate research methodology and traditions. Yet they all aspire to be considered scientific in either the hard or soft sense of the term. Many of those researchers from the disciplines mentioned above come from the logical positivist tradition of empirical research.

Yet other research traditions exist in those fields as well. The wealth of theory and methods to support small business and entrepreneurial research can at times seem daunting to both appreciate and use appropriately. One telling example is the conviction that empirical research is synonymous with quantitative research conducted in the positivistic or post-positivistic research tradition. It is also the kind of research that predominantly gets published in North America (Amis and Silk, 2008). At the same time, those researchers who use qualitative research methods (case studies, ethnography, observations etc.) and follow an interpretative research tradition will argue strongly that their research is indeed empirical as well. Some researchers would call this researcher's bias. We would call it a preference to work in way that feels comfortable and is familiar. This is a perfectly valid reason by itself, but not valid as a basis for determining the quality of a study (Amis and Silk, 2008; Leitch et al., 2010).

Box 1.1 presents an outline of the core elements in any research process regardless of chosen method.

BOX 1.1 UNDERSTANDING THE RESEARCH PROCESS: THE ELEMENTS OF RESEARCH DESIGN

By Richard T. Harrison

Effective research design features a number of core elements, which are combined and integrated in different degrees and in different sequences, depending on the particular philosophical and methodological perspective taken in the research (Figure 1.1). Irrespective of the underlying philosophy of research design, effective and convincing research includes attention to a number of key elements. Background theory refers to the wider disciplinary grounding of the research, signaling what is and is not important in terms of determining the focus of the study and the domain within which a contribution will be made. Within this, focal theory refers to the establishment and analysis of the nature of the problem and sets out exactly what is to be researched, moving from the general to the specific, creating hypotheses or research propositions in the light of the arguments and work of others, and indicating how this study will develop new propositions, data and conclusions that will advance the field. All research is undertaken within specific contexts, institutionally, spatially, temporally, socially, economically and culturally, and good research recognizes and makes allowance for context in the design process. Collectively, the background theory, focal theory and research context provide the basis for establishing the specific research questions that are the primary focus of the research: using the hourglass metaphor of Figure 1.1, these research questions are the nexus of the research process. However, to address these questions it is necessary to develop a data theory that proves the relevance and validity of the data used to address the research questions, recognizing that the appropriateness of the data will vary with the nature of the research project and the underlying philosophy of research adopted. It is at this stage that choices are made, for example, among qualitative (e.g. case study, interviews, action research), quantitative (survey, secondary data, experiments, quasi-experiments) and mixed-methods research designs. These choices will in turn determine the types of analyses undertaken, on the basis of which the researcher draws out a range of interpretations and implications that define the wider contribution of the research to the research field (the focal or background theory) or to the process of undertaking research in this field (data theory and analysis).

As represented, this model of the research process is linear, implying that there is a natural progression from the general (background theory) to the specific (research questions) and back to the general (interpretation and implications). In practice, however, no research process falls neatly into this linear representation. Rather, the process evolves and is adapted to each individual research project, and frequently operates cyclically, with stages being addressed in a different order or visited and revisited at different times in the process. However, there are variations in the research process associated with different underlying philoso-phies (or ontological perspectives) of research that can be identi-fied and that introduce some additional important elements into the research process.

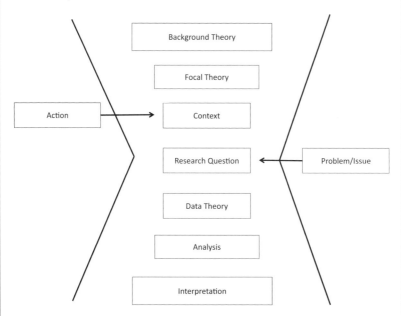

Figure 1.1   Core elements of the typical research process

Post-positivism is associated with an emphasis on explanation based on the hypothetico-deductive method, determinism, reduc-tionism, measurement and theory testing. In this, the research process set out in Figure 1.1 is followed, or represented as being followed, in a broadly linear fashion, with a review of the current state of knowledge being used to derive research questions, the answers to which provide the basis for testing theory as the basis for developing the field. Context, in this tradition, plays a minor role: in the search for generalizable knowledge, context is something to be eliminated or taken into account through, for example, the specification of a set of dummy variables in the analysis. In other words, the data theory appropriate for a post-positivist research method specifies a specific position on the role of context in the research.

Constructivism, by contrast, is focused on developing an under-standing of the research problem, through the recognition and analysis of multiple participant meanings (researcher and researched), with full account being taken of the social and histor-ical dimensions of the research in the process of theory develop-ment. In this tradition, context is everything and cannot be overlooked or downplayed. As a result, a constructivist research process will start with context, deriving from this a series of research questions that are understood, articulated and refined within the context of the researchers' understanding of the relevant focal and background theory without being directly derived from these as in post-positivist research. Subsequent analysis and interpretation are used to throw light on the research context and thereby to propose developments in the focal and perhaps also the background theory.

Research undertaken from an advocacy or participatory world-view is characterized by a commitment to political action in the realm of practice, with an orientation to issues and to empower-ment in a process that is collaborative between the researcher and the researched in a change-oriented process. This suggests an addition to the 'typical' research process elements set out in Figure 1.1. Specifically, the advocacy research worldview begins with action, defined within and defining the context for the research. This in turn defines the research questions, data theory and analysis protocols employed in the research. Typically, but not always, advocacy research engages with focal and background theory as part of the process of interpreting the findings and drawing out their implications, and in so doing contributes to the development of the field as well as the understanding of the domain of practical action.

Finally, research undertaken from the perspective of prag-matism is problem-centered, with a clear focus on identifying and understanding the consequences of actions. Philosophically and methodologically it is pluralistic, open for example to multidisciplinary research and to research drawing on diverse traditions, and it is fundamentally oriented, as is advocacy research, to understanding real-world practice. The starting point for the pragmatist research process is the problem or issue. This defines the research questions within a specific context, which are analyzed, interpreted and related back to focal and background theory in similar fashion as in advocacy research.

1.2 RATIONALE FOR THIS VOLUME

The idea for this book came from several discussions with colleagues, many of whom have contributed with chapters in this book, about problems we increasingly saw in manuscripts we were asked to review and that resulted in rejections. In essence, chapter authors were asked to develop contributions on topics that have frustrated them when reviewing submissions to journals or in directing doctoral dissertations. This book may be seen as an edited volume on research methodology and philosophy that focuses on topics often ignored or inappropriately used in research in this expansive field called entrepreneurship. Most existing methodology discussions typically focus on general issues in quantitative or qualitative approaches. This volume, however, steps back to ask more fundamental questions that every researcher in entrepreneurship, small and family business should ask before engaging in data collection. The various authors in this book address issues such as theory development, borrowing and testing in entrepreneurship, as well as determining if progress in research has been made and how to measure that progress. Many address how to make research both practical and theoretically useful. We were also very keen to ensure that this book would include scholars outside the North American research tradition, to bring out the European research tradition. We see this as important as there has for some time been an ongoing debate in Europe (RENT Conference 2012 and pre-conference to Babson College Entrepreneurship Research Conference 2013 – both held at École de Management, Lyon, France) of the state of entrepreneurship research. Are we asking the right questions? Are entrepreneurship scholars relevant to practicing entrepreneurs? Are entrepreneurship scholars using the *right* methods (italics added by authors to signify first the somewhat strange idea that there should be a *right* one and, second, evidently these questions would not be asked unless there were a collective concern)?

From a quantitative perspective the book examines experimental methods in small-business research and the issues of scale development, control variables and language issues in cross-cultural research. One chapter argues for the relevance of qualitative approaches in entrepreneurship research; one chapter takes the reader through ethnography; and the book concludes by opening up a discussion around the practice of entrepreneurship: how do we study what entrepreneurs really do? It will be clear that this book sees research on small business, entrepreneurship and family firms as an interactive, iterative process and a question of tying research to actual practice.

1.3   OVERVIEW OF THE VOLUME

The book begins with David Deeds, offering advice on how to conduct good empirical studies. While some may argue that there are other forms of empirical studies than merely quantitative studies, we specifically encouraged the author to keep this focus. This reflects a view shared by a majority of entrepreneurship scholars, yet, as the author points out, the quality is often not good, because of some serious flaws in the research process. In their chapter, Ed McMullen and Tom Kenworthy challenge the practice of borrowing theories from other disciplines without adequately understanding those theories. They see this as a growing problem. Next, Linda Edelman, Tatiana Manolova, Candida Brush and Scott Latham emphasize that researchers should consider how they are advancing work in the field. This is followed by a discussion on experimental methods by Kelly Shaver, a noted experimental social psychologist. This chapter is supported by the contribution that follows, by Leon Schjoedt, Maija Renko and Kelly Shaver on multiple and single-item measures. Concluding the focus on quantitative methods is the chapter by Leon Schjoedt and Barbara Bird. They remind readers that, in any research, qualitative or quantitative, control of extraneous variables is critical and should be rigorously performed.

The focus then turns to an issue that is critical not only in survey work, but also in international entrepreneurship work and in more qualitative approaches. In their chapter, Malin Brännback, Stefan Lång, Alan Carsrud and Siri Terjesen look at language and culture in the context of cross-cultural studies. The next chapter addresses the importance of qualitative research beyond the foundational perspective or a positivist view found in the widely cited article of Eisenhardt (1989) or in texts by Yin (1984). As this volume brings together quantitative and qualitative scholars, it is important to consider carefully the reflections offered by Richard Harrison and Claire Leitch in their chapter. This is followed by a discussion by Karin Berglund and Caroline Wigren on an investigative approach almost totally ignored in entrepreneurship, which should also be helpful in looking at entrepreneurship in emerging economies and in minority communities.

Finally, Bengt Johannisson argues that the field exists to support entrepreneurs and small firms. In his chapter he gives the researcher a participant-observer status in the research process.

In conclusion, this book is designed to be thought provoking and to build on existing research traditions that make small business, entrepreneurship and family business a resource-rich arena for research. This volume is not a substitute for in-depth knowledge of either qualitative or quantitative approaches, but should be seen as one that enriches existing knowledge.

REFERENCES

Amis, J. and Silk, M.L. (2008), 'The philosophy and politics of quality in qualitative organizational research', *Organizational Research Methods*, **11**(3): 456–80.

Bansal, P. and Corley, K. (2012), 'From the editors: publishing in *AMJ* – Part 7: What's different about qualitative research?', *Academy of Management Journal*, **55**(3): 509–13.

Bono, J.E. and McNamara, G. (2011), 'From the editors: publishing in *AMJ* – Part 2: Research design', *Academy of Management Journal*, **54**(4): 657–60.

Colquitt, J.A. and George, G. (2011), 'From the editors: publishing in *AMJ* – Part 1: Topic choice', *Academy of Management Journal*, **54**(3): 432–5.

Eisenhardt, K.M. (1989), 'Building theory from case study research', *Academy of Management Review*, **14**(4): 532–49.

Gartner, W.B., Shaver, K.G., Carter, N.M. and Reynolds, P.D. (2004), *Handbook of Entrepreneurial Dynamics: The Process of Business Creation*, Thousand Oaks, CA: Sage.

Geletkanycz, M. and Tepper, B.J. (2012), 'From the editors: publishing in *AMJ* – Part 6: Discussing the implications', *Academy of Management Journal*, **55**(2): 256–60.

Grant, A.M. and Pollock, T.G. (2011), 'From the editors: publishing in *AMJ* – Part 3: Setting the hook', *Academy of Management Journal*, **54**(5): 873–9.

Leitch, C.M., Hill, F.M. and Harrison, R.T. (2010), 'The philosophy and practice of interpretivist research in entrepreneurship', *Organizational Research Methods*, **13**(1): 67–84.

Sparrowe, R.T. and Mayer, K.J. (2011), 'From the editors: publishing in *AMJ* – Part 4: Grounding hypotheses', *Academy of Management Journal*, **54**(6): 1098–102.

Welter, F. (2011), 'Contextualizing entrepreneurship: conceptual challenges and ways forward', *Entrepreneurship Theory and Practice*, **35**: 165–83.

Yin, R.K. (1984), *Case Study Research: Design and Methods*, Beverly Hills, CA: Sage.

Zhang, A. and Shaw, J.D. (2012), 'From the editors: publishing in *AMJ* – Part 5: Crafting the methods and results', *Academy of Management Journal*, **55**(1): 8–12.

2. Thoughts on the challenge of empirical research in entrepreneurship
David Deeds

OPENING THOUGHTS

My reason for writing this chapter is that I believe entrepreneurship is one of the most important, impactful and beneficial activities being undertaken in the world today and, relative to its impact, one of the least understood. This is particularly true at the venture level. Economists are advancing our understanding of entrepreneurship at the macro level, but at the level of the venture we are still struggling. What actions increase or reduce a venture's odds of success? What type of environment nurtures ventures? How do ventures emerge? How do we prepare entrepreneurs for their career? We have a very hard time answering these basic questions. One of the reasons for this is that it is extremely difficult to design and execute a good empirical study of entrepreneurial ventures. Here I wish to provide guidance to doctoral students and young researchers about how to undertake empirical research on entrepreneurial firms, how to design an empirical research project that has the potential to provide significant insights into firm-level entrepreneurial phenomena and how to build a successful career by pursuing empirical research in entrepreneurship. I draw on over 20 years of trying and occasionally succeeding in developing credible empirical studies of entrepreneurial firms and my experience as a reviewer for numerous entrepreneurship and strategy journals. The challenges of doing good empirical research on entrepreneurial firms are daunting, which is also why there is a limited amount of good and much mediocre to bad (some of it with my name on it) empirical research on entrepreneurial ventures in print. The field is in desperate need of more and better empirical studies. This chapter is an attempt in some small way to help fill this gap.

This chapter evolved from a presentation that Dr Sharon Alvarez asked me to make for a symposium at the Academy of Management in 2009. She wanted me to help explain the challenges of research in entrepreneurship, in particular empirical research, and provide some guidance on how to overcome those challenges. What follows is one entrepreneurship scholar's opinions, thoughts and insights on empirical research in the field of entrepreneurship. First I briefly address the question of why we need to do empirical research in entrepreneurship. Then I present a detailed examination of the challenges facing those who pursue empirical research on entrepreneurial ventures. This will be followed by some guidance on how to develop a solid empirical research program on entrepreneurial ventures.

WHY UNDERTAKE EMPIRICAL RESEARCH IN THE FIELD OF ENTREPRENEURSHIP?

There are both practical and scientific reasons for undertaking empirical research. The practical side of things is pretty straightforward. As an entrepreneurship scholar you need to get published in the best journals in order to build your career, get tenured, get promoted to full professor and eventually sit in one of the numerous chairs for entrepreneurship scholars. While the calls for more and better qualitative research are numerous and valid, the reality is that qualitative research is much harder to get published in the top journals than well-executed empirical work. If you are a theoretician – and there is a huge need for better and more nuanced theory in the field of entrepreneurship, and it is theory that guides empirical research – you will make your career based on theoretical contributions. I know of only two scholars who have built their careers largely based on theoretical contributions, and they both engage in some empirical research. So the first and most practical reason to undertake empirical research as a scholar of entrepreneurship is that it is the path with the highest probability of leading to a successful academic career in the field of entrepreneurship.

The second and possibly most important reason to undertake empirical research is that the field cannot advance without significantly stronger empirical research studies. If we consider the current development of the field of entrepreneurship using Thomas Kuhn's classifications, the field of entrepreneurship is clearly pre-paradigmatic. There is no established paradigm, or overarching theory of entrepreneurship; indeed, there is no accepted definition of entrepreneurship and there is unlikely to be one until we have a substantially greater understanding of the phenomena we have chosen to study. High-quality empirical research is central to developing greater understanding, to refining theory, to guiding the next round of qualitative research and theory development. It is only through high-quality, replicable empirical research that a scientific field can advance. Those of us in the field must undertake such studies to both advance the field and institutionalize it within the broader study of economics, business and psychology. Entrepreneurs can tell plenty of war stories that are informative, entertaining and beloved by students, but these war stories are idiosyncratic and derived from a detailed study with an $n = 1$. As entrepreneurship scholars we shall never win the battle of war stories; we must bring the perspective of a scholar to the study of entrepreneurship. We shall never know more about an entrepreneur's venture than she does, but we can know more about 100, 1000 or 10 000 ventures than the entrepreneur ever can. Through high-quality empirical research we can discern best practices. We can highlight the source of novelty, sustainability and success. We can present insights based on the empirical examination of trends and patterns that cannot be found by an in-depth study with an $n = 1$.

THE CHALLENGES OF EMPIRICAL RESEARCH IN THE FIELD OF ENTREPRENEURSHIP

In comparison with research in strategic management, finance or many other business disciplines, empirical research on entrepreneurship faces unique and difficult challenges that generally revolve around two broad problems. The first is the lack of consensus within the field about definitions. The second is that, because of the nature of entrepreneurial action, it is very difficult to gather large longitudinal databases. Several consortia have attempted to address this in the past; perhaps the most prominent was the National Panel Study of US Business Startups led by Paul Reynolds. The Kauffman Foundation is also leading several efforts, and while these efforts are laudatory, the field still suffers from a dearth of solid, well-constructed databases. In sum, the challenges listed below have led to the creation and publication of a great deal of work in the field of entrepreneurship that is based on small, biased, idiosyncratic samples and employ measures that are also idiosyncratic and difficult to aggregate across studies. Samples with any of these flaws, let alone all of these flaws, reduce the perceived reliability and validity of the results and increase the difficulty of both interpreting the results and getting the work published in top-tier journals. The following subsections outline what I see as the five unique challenges for empirical research on entrepreneurial ventures.

Challenge 1: The Nature of Entrepreneurial Action

The nature of entrepreneurial action presents numerous challenges for empirical research, but two in particular are of interest. The first is that, because of the influence of founders, the environment, the lack of institutionalized routines, norms and methods and the rapidly evolving nature of entrepreneurial ventures and emerging industries, the study of entrepreneurship is a study of context-dependent idiosyncratic ventures. In these circumstances, for empirical research to be successful, measures, metrics and techniques need to be chosen, or designed, to suit the population being studied. Measures that work for emerging biotechnology ventures will not work for emerging retail ventures or emerging ventures in the gaming industry. This also means that multi-industry empirical research is likely to be difficult and produce questionable results.

The second challenge is that entrepreneurial activity is generally conducted among small groups, unnoticed by the larger part of society. It exists essentially beneath the radar of society until it becomes noteworthy because of its success or perhaps because of its massive failure. The problem for empirical research, particularly research into in nascent entrepreneurs and the emergence of ventures, is that most of these sink quietly beneath the waves of the economy without leaving a ripple, a trace or any documentary evidence. This leaves society with a highly biased view of the nature of entrepreneurship. The face of entrepreneurship is always the latest, grandest success story, not the myriad of unknown, struggling entrepreneurs attempting, usually unsuccessfully, to create a thriving, sustainable business. This condition also biases our research. In our empirical research we are almost universally sampling on our dependent variable, because those ventures that achieve enough success to be included in our samples are generally far more successful than the vast majority of nascent or recently emerged ventures. I have had great success studying biotechnology ventures, but all of my results suffer from this particular bias, as do all the results we have from such studies. Finally, because of the small numbers involved in any given venture, any empirical research, even research on OB (organizational behavior) or HR (human resource) topics, requires samples drawn from a large number of ventures. This exponentially increases the difficulty of gathering a publishable sample.

Challenge 2: The Lack of Agreed-upon Definitions in the Field

What is the age or stage of development at which an entrepreneurial venture ceases to be entrepreneurial and becomes simply another business? Under the most accepted definition a four-year-old retail venture that solidified its business model three years ago is an entrepreneurial business. In contrast, a six-year-old biotechnology company that has no products, is still fundraising and in the early stages of product development is no longer an entrepreneurial venture.

We lack an established, accepted set of criteria or even guidelines that allow us to clearly define an entrepreneurial venture, and in turn a set of criteria on which we can design a sample frame to select entrepreneurial ventures. This problem extends to definitions of nascent or emerging ventures, entrepreneurs, intrapreneurs, social entrepreneurs, social entrepreneurship and pretty much every other subset of entrepreneurial actors or organizations of interest to our field.

Challenge 3: The Lack of Established and Readily Available Outcome Variables

In strategic management research there are numerous well-established and well-reported outcome measures, such as ROE (return on equity), ROI (return on investment), net profit and so on. However, in studying three-year-old technology ventures, are profit-based measures the appropriate outcome? Growth? ROI? The first challenge, of course, is that none of these is readily available. The second is whether any of these are appropriate measures given the outcomes a three-year-old technology venture is attempting to achieve. New ventures are predominantly private companies that are not required to report significant financial data to the public at large and are generally loath to provide that information in response to survey questions. Many ventures are founded to be 'exited', that is, sold to someone else, but if sold, how can we tell if it is a success or a failure when all we know is that the venture was sold? What about the venture that was sold after three years in comparison with one that the investors have been unable to 'exit' from after seven years? In whatever research study is undertaken careful consideration of this critical issue must be at the forefront of the design. Get this wrong and your study is likely to be perceived as having a fatal flaw, but without guidance or readily available data it is not easy to get this right.

Challenge 4: The Lack of Publicly Available Databases and Secondary Data for Entrepreneurial Firms

Only in a very limited number of industries does a database of firm-level information for entrepreneurial ventures exist. Empirical research in strategy and finance has advanced by mining large, frequently longitudinal, publicly available databases. The existence of these databases has allowed the field to empirically address theoretically and practically interesting questions through statistical analysis. Unfortunately, as noted earlier, entrepreneurship suffers from a distinct lack of databases. In some industries reasonably reliable databases have been created, most notably in biotechnology, that have allowed for the examination of entrepreneurial phenomena. However, these databases have been well mined and are generally in very idiosyncratic industries, making generalizability of findings an open question. The lack of secondary data leaves us reliant on primary data collection, but as noted below we face challenges there as well.

Challenge 5: Difficult to Find/Create a Solid Sample Frame

The quality of empirical work based on primary data collection fundamentally depends on the quality of the sample frame from which the sample is drawn. Therein lies the unusual challenge of primary data collection in entrepreneurship research – much of the empirical research we undertake is not based on a solid, defensible sample frame, but rather on a convenient sample with unknown and unquantifiable biases. If you are seeking to survey all of the software ventures in the US Upper Midwest, there is no list to draw on. If you are looking for all of the retail startups, alive or dead, started within the last three years in Texas, once again there is no list to draw on. We compromise by seeking lists from industry organizations or local or regional organizations (Chambers of Commerce etc.) or we 'snowball' our sample. We often seek out groups of firms that have achieved some visibility by going public or raising venture capital, heavily biasing our sample since these firms are by definition extremely successful. Overall, the lack of solid sample frames brings our empirical results into question and makes it much more difficult to publish entrepreneurship research in the top journals.

STRATEGIES FOR SUCCESSFUL EMPIRICAL RESEARCH IN ENTREPRENEURSHIP

At this point let me reassure you that there is hope and that it is possible to do good empirical research in entrepreneurship. What is needed is thought and effort devoted to the design of your study. A good empirical research project in entrepreneurship, like a good paint job, is all about preparation. I now set out the strategies for developing a successful research program in entrepreneurship. Many of these strategies have been derived from costly errors and mistakes, mainly due to neglecting the necessary research and ground work before charging ahead and gathering data.

Strategy 1: Focus

There are many ways to focus, but the bottom line is that there are returns to specialization. As noted earlier, entrepreneurship is an idiosyncratic context-specific phenomenon. Biotechnology ventures are generally founded by people with very different experiences, skills, talents, training and background than those who found a retail business. The structure of the venture, the team, and the relationship with stakeholders and resource providers are likely to look very different. The critical processes when a nascent venture is emerging are likely to be very different than those when the venture has emerged and is attempting to access resources, grow or exit. There is a great deal to learn and leading researchers in an area must know more about their subject than anybody else. As an example, in order to understand biotechnology I had to spend a large amount of time learning the underlying science and the landscape of the scientific fields driving the research. I had to learn the language of the people I was studying. I needed to be able to establish a minimum level of credibility with them. This was time consuming and viewed by my strategy colleagues as wasted time, but without that depth of understanding I would have been unable to get some key interviews; nor would I have had the knowledge to ask the right questions in those interviews and in turn I doubt whether I would have ever had the insight necessary to build my best and most impactful papers.

I generally think about focusing along three dimensions in the entrepreneurial process. The first dimension is the level at which you are going to study: individuals, organizations/ventures or field/industry. The second is the process/stage of entrepreneurial development: are you interested in the emergent/nascent processes during which the idea emerges, the founding team is formed and the first steps of venture formation are taken? Are you interested in the organization-building and resource-gathering phase, where entrepreneurs are out raising capital, entering alliances, filling out the team and developing/refining the products, services and strategies with which they will go to market? The third is the industry, market or technology you are going to study: should you be focused on all of these? Should you define yourself as someone who focuses their research on how individual entrepreneurs' cognitive biases have impacted nascent nano-tech ventures? That is probably a good focus for a study or two, but probably not broad enough for a career.

So how do you choose a focus? I believe the best guide is to find the areas where your passion overlaps with your skills, capabilities and training. The first thing to remember is that, whatever you choose, you are going to live with it for a long time, so you must be sure of your commitment to it. I have been involved in research in the biotechnology industry since 1991. While I am active in researching other industries, I continue my work in biotech because I am passionate about understanding the commercialization process of scientific discovery through entrepreneurial action. Biotechnology allows me to develop insights into this process. You might not be passionate about an industry or technology; perhaps your passion lies in understanding the role and impact of failure in the entrepreneurial process; or perhaps you are fascinated by how industries emerge and develop norms, routines, institutions and legitimacy. Wherever your passions lead you, look for questions and areas of interest that allow you to apply the skills, knowledge and capabilities you've developed over your career.

Strategy 2: Embed Yourself in Your Chosen Area of Study

I specifically chose the term 'embed' because it implies more than just immersing yourself in the literature of your chosen area. Embedding implies not only learning, but building networks, visibility and eventually a reputation in your chosen area. The network literature is very clear that boundary spanners are generally in a superior position to develop new insights. They are able to draw on knowledge from multiple sources that provides them a unique and valuable perspective. This is one instance where, as researchers, we should take our own advice, particularly in a contextually specific, idiosyncratic area of study such as entrepreneurship. Once you have selected a focus, but before developing a detailed question, begin to build a network both within the field of the researchers working in your area and among practitioners who are trying to build ventures that fit your interests. Conferences, particularly smaller conferences with quality researchers, and consortia are invaluable in the early stages of networking. One of the great things about academics is that we all love to talk about our work and to give advice. Building a network is easy in these circumstances. Entrepreneurs can be a little more difficult, but not much. Begin by seeking interviews, not formal interviews: you do not yet know the right questions to ask or how to frame them; and seek informational interviews. Use these to begin to understand who the players are, what the entrepreneurs perceive as the problems and challenges, and to recruit a couple of practitioners who are willing to return your phone calls in the future, to help you to pilot survey or interview scripts they will provide insights into how to frame a question so that it gets the right response or can yield a valuable referral. These mentors can be highly insightful and can ask very powerful questions. In my case, one of them asked a simple question: 'How does the market value a new biotech firm?' I discovered that I had no answer for that simple question and neither did anybody else, which spurred a successful stream of research.

Strategy 3: Ask an Interesting Question

Why is this listed as the third strategy and not the first? I believe your ability to ask an interesting question is limited until you have been able to act on the first two strategies. How can you ask an interesting question if you do not have a focus and a deep understanding of your area of research? The limitations of empirical entrepreneurship research are such that we are generally at a disadvantage as regards the issue of rigor. Our samples are smaller, biased and frequently cross-sectional. Our measures are frequently idiosyncratic. Our definitions are open to debate. In order to overcome these challenges we have to ask both theoretically and practically interesting questions. We must address questions that fill gaps in relevant theories such as the resource-based view, institutional theory and agency theory, but also move the field and study of entrepreneurship forward. We must be more than simply a novel area in which to test others' theories. We must ask interesting questions that lead to the development of a robust theory of entrepreneurial action. We must also ask questions that provide interesting insights into policy makers and entrepreneurs. The balance between these various interests depends on your passions and interests, but good empirical entrepreneurship research must start with an interesting question.

Strategy 4: Look for Footprints

There are many fascinating markets in which entrepreneurial activity takes place, but they are not all created equal as research subjects. Some industries and actions leave a great many footprints; other do not. I mean by footprints a record of action such as patents, regulatory approvals, publications, membership lists, conference attendance and presentation records, industry annual reports created by accounting firms or industry publications and so on. Empirical research is much easier and more successful when secondary data are available. Biotechnology has been so well studied because there are at least three very good databases that cover biotechnology and have done so for well over a decade. Biotechnology firms patent, which leaves a record of their early-stage research products. They go through a detailed and public regulatory process that provides a record of their early-, mid- and late-stage research projects. They publish co-authored papers in the academic literature, which leaves a record of who they work with over time. The go public, which requires detailed and scrupulously honest disclosure of everything of import about the venture. They partner frequently and publicly. I know of no other industry that leaves as many, and as well-defined, footprints as biotechnology. However, every industry leaves footprints somewhere; you just have to know where to look. The SEC (Securities and Exchange Commission) is an obvious area. The EDGAR database contains a wealth of information. If you are interested in private placements, search for Form D, which will give you a list of firms that have recently either filed to issue one or completed one. Form S-1 gets every firm that files to go public. Footprints become invaluable in building defensible sample frames for primary data collection as well as sources of basic venture-specific information such as location, size, age and so on. The deeper you dig, the more knowledge you gain; the more you embed yourself, the more footprints you will discover. Learn the disclosure events that occur in your industry, such as fundraising, going public, franchising, patenting and numerous other activities that require a firm to publicly disclose something about itself.

Strategy 5: Seek out Natural Experiments

When something in the world changes, you have the basis for a natural experiment. There was a state of nature before the change and after the change, and ventures in the environment had to react to the change. Most changes make small ripples and have little impact on ventures' operations, growth and survival, but changes that matter are quite common. Regulatory changes can have dramatic impacts on ventures. Dramatic shifts in financial markets or in the economy can also provide the basis for a natural experiment. Technological shifts such as the announcement of a new gaming console or operating system can create a clean break in the environment. For a natural experiment to be successful, the two states of the environment, before and after, must have differential impacts on the phenomena under-study, so be sure you have thought through the logic and theoretical underpinnings of why the shift matters and how it should impact action, and in turn performance, growth and survival.

FINAL THOUGHTS

I end where I began by restating my reason for writing this chapter. I believe entrepreneurship is one of the most important, impactful and beneficial activities being undertaken in the world today and, relative to its impact, one of the least understood. Entrepreneurship is a field of study in need of more and better empirical research. The field cannot advance without the next generation of scholars substantially improving the empirical knowledge base of the field. As noted at the beginning of this chapter, empirical research in entrepreneurship faces some daunting and unique challenges, but these can be overcome. By focusing your efforts, embedding yourself in your chosen area of study and by asking interesting questions you can contribute to the development of the field and build a successful and rewarding career.

3. From philosophy of science to theory testing: generating practical knowledge in entrepreneurship

Thomas P. Kenworthy and W. Edward McMullen

INTRODUCTION

Prominent entrepreneurship scholars have voiced substantial concerns over the years about intellectual progress in the discipline. The purpose of this chapter is to draw attention to several fundamental aspects of social science that require greater attention. It is suggested that a greater appreciation for philosophy of science (POS), methodology, theory and theory testing, as well as the components of practical knowledge, will offer a productive way forward. The chapter begins with a brief discussion of POS and the results of an investigation into the extent of POS training in doctoral programs. The second section outlines some problems in entrepreneurship research methodology. The third section provides instruction on how practical knowledge can be generated for practitioners, educators, policy makers and scholars. The fourth section describes theory importation behavior and offers a model that aids with scrutiny of exogenous theory. The final section synthesizes the results of testing human capital theory, shedding light on theory-testing practices and the value of the theory.

THE IMPORTANCE OF PHILOSOPHY OF SCIENCE

> Much scientific thinking is of poor quality, and it could be improved by explicit metatheoretical education. (Meehl, 1993, p. 707)

Fritz Machlup (1978, p. 6), protégé of Ludwig von Mises and doctoral supervisor of Edith Penrose, regarded substitutions of the word methodology for the word method as language pollution that 'has led to a vulgar use of the word methodology in a sense violating all philosophical traditions'.
Methodology is

> the study of the principles that guide students of any field of knowledge and especially any branch of higher learning (science) in deciding whether to accept

or reject certain propositions as a part of the body of ordered knowledge in general or of their own discipline (science). (Ibid., p. 54)

Further,

> although methodology is 'about' methods, it is not 'a' method, nor a set of methods, nor a description of methods. Instead, it provides arguments, perhaps rationalizations, which support various preferences entertained by the scientific community for certain rules of intellectual procedure, including those for forming concepts, building models, formulating hypotheses and testing theories. (Ibid., p. 55)

Methodological concerns typically fall under the purview of philosophy of science (POS), a subject matter that is unavoidable in science. A POS is present every time a scientist makes a decision about scientific practice. An absence of POS education can result in a number of deleterious impacts on the way science is practiced. Furthermore, a self-developed POS that is not steeped in the masters is likely to be vague, internally inconsistent, misinformed and dated.

A leading argument for improving the social science research community's appreciation for POS can be drawn from Thomas Kuhn's work. Kuhn (1962) asserted that scientific disciplines with established scientific paradigms managed to resolve key philosophical questions, at least until the advent of another scientific revolution. Further, scientific paradigms, such as Ptolemy's geocentric theory of the universe – with its exceptionally high predictive accuracy – supplied the power of point prediction. By such standards, it is no wonder that Kuhn viewed the entirety of the social sciences as pre-paradigmatic. A notable exception may be the paradigmatic Keynesian revolution in the field of economics (Blaug, 1975). However, the rest of the social sciences are much more clearly pre-paradigmatic, and even if one or two other exceptions exist, they do not originate in the discipline of entrepreneurship.

Our current pre-paradigmatic state of affairs (Zahra, 2005) means that our philosophies of science can vary as much as our research methods across published research. In order to practice science effectively within the social sciences, we must understand how to intelligently modify our philosophies of science to fit different types of research objectives. After all, modifying one's concept of truth (e.g. consensus; correspondence), and how it is constructed, can lead to entirely different approaches to the study of a phenomenon.

It is not far-fetched to assume that productive knowledge development in the social sciences requires an extraordinary facility with the philosophy of science. John Maynard Keynes, for example, is considered to have made substantial contributions to philosophy of science (Craig, 1998). At a minimum, though, POS knowledge should make the discipline more impervious to a variety of ills attendant to the practice of modern entrepreneurship research.

A search of the top five entrepreneurship journals in the discipline (*Journal of Business Venturing, Entrepreneurship Theory and Practice, Journal of Small Business Management, Entrepreneurship & Regional Development* and *Small Business Economics*) reveals 21 hits for the term 'philosophy of science'. A review of the 21 articles indicates that the concept of philosophy of science has not as yet been used to spur debate as to how we are doing as a science. This may not be particularly surprising given that recommendations for management and entrepreneurship doctoral training programs focus on research methods rather than on methodology (cf. Summer et al., 1990; Brush et al., 2003). A research method focus, particularly on statistical data analysis, is often equated with research in the logical positivist research tradition. The result of research-method-oriented training may have prompted comments that characterize both management (cf. Cohen, 2007; Meyer, 2009) and entrepreneurship (cf. Meyer, 2009) research as logical positivistic.

Numerous philosophers have highlighted the troubles with logical positivism over a number of decades. Adherents of logical positivism railed against metaphysics, yet were never able to give their 'philosophy' anything other than metaphysical status. Moreover, the vaunted objectivity towards which logical positivists strove turned out to be extraordinarily problematic. It is rarely disputed that the nature of most social science work involves observation by an observer and, therefore, ever-present subjectivity. The essential act of interpreting collected data represents yet further subjectivity. Hence, despite the best intentions of logical positivism, metaphysics and subjectivity are seemingly unavoidable in any scientific enterprise.

The dominant replacements for logical positivism are widely considered to be the intellectual contributions of Sir Karl Popper (1963) and of Thomas S. Kuhn (1962). One might also include the work of Imre Lakatos (1978), who attempted to reconcile the works of both Popper and Kuhn. These three philosophers each worked from units of analysis more encompassing than the protocol statements emphasized by logical positivists. Popper separated relevant theory into two categories: scientific theory, which made bold/risky predictions; and pre-scientific theory, which could not claim such predictions. Kuhn developed the notions of pre-science and scientific paradigm. Lakatos emphasized research programs, which involve complex clusters of interconnected theories. Popper and Lakatos adopted the correspondence theory of truth and were decidedly prescriptive in their philosophies. Kuhn, on the other hand, adopted a consensus theory of truth and, in the process, imbued his philosophy of science with a decidedly descriptive emphasis upon the realpolitik of scientific decision-making.

For Popper's philosophy of conjecture and refutation to be meaningfully employed in an emerging applied social science such as entrepreneurship, there are two prerequisites. First, entrepreneurship researchers would need to draw a strong line between predictive, scientific theories and explanatory, pre-scientific theories. Empirical research would largely be confined to testing the former. Currently, there is little indication of such a distinction being made within the entrepreneurship discipline.

Second, research undertaken on predictive theory must strongly test the predictive relationships advocated by a theory. The extent to which such work occurs in entrepreneurship is debatable. Our recent review of tests of human capital theory – described below – suggests that strong theory testing may not be commonplace. Human capital theory (HCT) clearly predicts that financial investments in, for example, formal education and experience will yield positive financial returns over time. Researchers in entrepreneurship, unlike those in economics, chose not to measure investment costs in any of the 56 studies reviewed. Instead, entrepreneurship researchers loosely invoked HCT in order to draw linkages between human capital variables and a wide variety of other phenomena. Furthermore, failures to support hypotheses were typically treated as uninterpretable or invalid. Such pre-scientific behaviors are evidence that the discipline of entrepreneurship may not be prepared to adopt a Popperian philosophy.

Kuhn, like Popper, has much to offer, but not at this time to the discipline of entrepreneurship. A scientific field needs a paradigm in order to use Kuhn's ideas. In the 1960s, Kuhn viewed his work as contributing mainly to the hard sciences as, in his estimation, the social sciences lacked any paradigms. Although Kuhn may be debated today, there is little doubt that the discipline of entrepreneurship is pre-paradigmatic (cf. Zahra, 2005) and, therefore, not yet ready for Kuhnian analysis. Lakatos's provocative research program concept relies on the existence of at least one strongly predictive scientific theory. It involves, among other things, a number of auxiliary theories that must also be taken into consideration in order to comment on the progressive or degenerative nature of a research program. According to Blaug (1975), the notion of a Lakatosian research program has extremely limited use within the entirety of the social sciences.

The point here is that it is not enough to adopt a single philosophical position since different philosophies address a patchwork of different scientific problems. We need to understand not only the positions of prominent scholars, including an appreciation of the limitations of their thought; we also need to study those distinguished methodologists, such as

Paul Meehl, renowned psychologist and founding member of the Minnesota Center for the Philosophy of Science, who have stepped beyond the POS and into the distinctive methodological practices of particular social science fields. Similarly, we need to awaken ourselves to the methodological limitations of our own discipline.

Researchers who have not received substantial POS training may also be prone to employing suspect second-hand POS thinking from such popular works as the 1979 text by Gibson Burrell and Gareth Morgan (cf. Caruana et al., 1998; Fletcher, 2006; Fuller and Moran, 2001; Jennings et al., 2005; Johannisson et al., 2007; Sarason et al., 2010). Such researchers risk a dogmatic attachment to a philosophy with very inadequate awareness of its limits. Further, they may not appreciate that philosophies are no more than metaphysics – that is, neither demonstrably true nor false.

Scholars sometimes lean in favor of one philosophy of science over another, perhaps favoring Kuhn over Popper as if these philosophies are clearly in conflict. Certainly there are conflicts between their positions, and much may be made of these differences. Fuller (2004) went so far as to characterize the battle between Kuhn and Popper as the 'struggle for the soul of science'. This is a struggle, as Fuller points out, that is based in sizable part upon commonplace misunderstandings of both Kuhn and Popper. A more in-depth appreciation of these two figures will recognize that there is much more complementarity than conflict between their positions. Even the problems that they are addressing are distinctive. Kuhn, on the one hand, relies on a consensus theory of truth in order to help describe the actual practice of scientists. Since in everyday reality it is scientific consensus that determines what and who will be published, it is a reasonable starting-point for a philosophy. Kuhn's is a realpolitik of the scientific process. Popper, on the other hand, is attempting to develop a philosophy of how better to conduct the scientific process. His is a normative as opposed to Kuhn's descriptive approach. Popper depends on a correspondence theory of truth that seeks to find a correspondence with a 'real' world independent of our subjective sense impressions. Neither position is valid. Both need to be examined and debated.

FOCUSING ON POS AND METHODOLOGY

A social scientist must invest a substantial amount of time in order to gain an adequate knowledge of philosophy of science. A possible explanation behind limited levels of POS and methodological literacy within the entrepreneurship discipline is the extent of training in such areas at the doctoral level. As a first step in assessing the state of methodology training in business schools, we conducted a preliminary review of core curriculum requirements via business Ph.D. program websites. Table 3.1 shows the number of doctoral programs in the top 100 universities (Academic Ranking of World Universities, 2009) that provide a POS course as a core curriculum requirement.

Table 3.1   *POS education in business doctoral programming – top 100 universities*

Region	Number of institutions	Institutions with business Ph.D. programs	Business Ph.D. programs with a POS course
Australia	3	3	0 (0%)
Canada	4	4	1 (25%)
European continent	21	8	3 (37.5%)
Israel	1	0	0 (0%)
Japan	5	3	0 (0%)
UK	11	10	2 (20%)
USA	55	46	1 (2%)
Total	100	74	7

The seven business Ph.D. programs with a core-curriculum POS course referred to in Table 3.1 are offered at the following seven universities: the University of British Columbia, the University of Copenhagen, the University of Helsinki, Uppsala University, the University of Nottingham, the University of Manchester and Boston University. Many of the European universities did not offer doctoral programs in business. However, as a region, Europe appears to offer proportionally more POS courses in business doctoral programming than North America.

It should be noted that business doctoral programming varies substantially. In the UK, formal Ph.D. programming is typically light. Nevertheless, 20 percent of the UK-based universities that are referenced in Table 3.1 provide a core-curriculum POS course. In contrast to the UK management education model, American and Canadian universities tend to offer only course-based, professional MBA degrees. Hence North American business doctoral programming typically involves more coursework. A review of the 2010 *US News and World Report*'s top 100 US universities indicates that 6 percent (4 of 65 institutions that offer a Ph.D. program) require a POS course. None of the US-based universities that offer a Ph.D.-level POS course is ranked in the top 50: George Washington University (no. 53); Boston University (no. 56); the Iowa State University (no. 91); and the University of Kansas (no. 100). A review of all Canadian universities indicates that 19 percent (5 of 26 institutions that offer a business Ph.D. program) require a POS course. Ultimately, it appears that some regions or countries (e.g. Canada) are more favorably disposed towards POS course requirements in business Ph.D. programs than others (e.g. the USA).

The only comparable data available on doctoral-level POS courses in other social science disciplines are published in the field of political science. Schwartz-Shea (2003) reviewed 57 US-based doctoral programs and found that 7 institutions (12 percent) required a POS course. A total of 28 programs required some coverage of POS (i.e. stand-alone or within a research-methods-oriented course). It is quite likely that many business schools similarly provide minimal coverage of POS by briefly presenting it as part of a research-methods-oriented doctoral seminar.

If budding academics are not sufficiently exposed to POS and methodology at the doctoral level, is it not very likely that they will delve deeply into the subject matter later in their careers. It is quite likely that limited POS and methodology emphasis during doctoral training may carry over into a career-long avoidance and/or even a disdain for the subject.

PROBLEMS WITH ENTREPRENEURSHIP RESEARCH METHODOLOGY

The following five subsections examine some current methodological problems in the field of entrepreneurship: scientific theory, theory testing, variable choice, methodological aspects of statistical testing and practical requirements for scientific research. The intention here is to introduce issues and problems rather than to comprehensively review them. It is hoped that the statements will prompt readers to extend or rebut the contentions and raise additional ones with an improved science of entrepreneurship as the end goal.

1. Theory

> The critical test of any theory is its ability to predict future outcomes with accuracy.
>
> Bygrave (1993, p. 260)

Meehl (1990b) argued that the philosophy of science was, in fact, meta-theory. In order to make sense of a theory's form and function, one needs to understand it in the context of a philosophy of science. Popper's (1963) philosophy of science included methodological falsificationism as a means to distinguish between pre-scientific and scientific theory. He argued that a scientific theory makes bold predictions that are subject to falsifying evidence. This approach allowed Popper to conclude that some theories without predictive power, yet still containing academic merit, were pre-scientific and, hence, did not justify scientific testing. Theories that were true by definition could only be supported and therefore supporting evidence was not scientific. An example of a theory that is true by definition is the Marxist interpretation of history that 'cannot claim to be backed by empirical evidence in the scientific sense' (Popper, 1963, p. 38).

Entrepreneurship theories may be open to criticism as non-scientific from a Popperian perspective. Through time, renowned entrepreneurship scholars have certainly been critical of entrepreneurship theory. Amit et al. (1990, p. 1232) asserted that 'the received literature offers neither a predictive theory of the behavior of entrepreneurs nor much in the way of guidance for practice'. Bygrave and Hofer (1991, p. 13) found that entrepreneurship research 'lacks a substantial theoretical foundation'. Cooper (1993, p. 244) asserted that 'a central problem has been the lack of well-developed theories of causal relationships'. Shane and Venkataraman (2000, p. 219) have made us aware that our 'theory is underdeveloped'. Chandler and Lyon (2001, p. 107) have told us that our 'poor theory defies attempts to explain relationships with external variables'.

It is possible that our field is too young to expect much in the way of endogenous, predictive theories. It is not clear that the field has even one theory to call its own, scientific or otherwise. In this regard, Phan (2004, p. 617) stated that 'the search for a distinctive theory of entrepreneurship continues'. Our theoretical base is driven by imports. Many of our imported theories have been the subject of criticism by researchers in the originating fields. Meehl (1990b, p. 108) assessed the state of soft psychology – which includes the personality and social psychology theories that are popular in entrepreneurship – as primitive, asserting that related theory 'only rarely permits strong conjectures as to the mathematical functions'. On organizational science theories, Miner (2003) discovered that only 8 of 73 popular theories scored high on both scientific validity and usefulness.

Two of entrepreneurship's most frequently adopted theories from management/strategy, the resource-based view (RBV) and transaction cost economics (TCE), have also received seriously challenging criticism within their own disciplines. Priem and Butler (2001a, 2001b) raise numerous concerns about the scientific nature of RBV. Using a systematic quantitative analysis, David and Han (2004) dispute the claim that TCE is an 'empirical success story' (Williamson, 1999). Two popular imports from economics, agency theory and human capital theory (HCT), have also been critically attacked. Ghoshal (2005) exposed the limited explanatory and predictive power of agency theory.

Granted that all theories are flawed, some are, however, less flawed than others. For example, although Blaug (1976) and Maglen (1990) have offered various concerns with respect to HCT, most reviewers would observe that HCT has the noteworthy advantage of being boldly predictive, and of possessing substantial, relatively unequivocal, empirical support.

Strong scientific theories generate numerical point or narrow-interval predictions. Such theories are found mainly in the physical sciences, with a few exceptions. Theories of intermediate strength, according to Meehl (1990b, p. 120) are 'at least capable of deriving observational consequences about numerical agreements via qualitatively diverse observational avenues'. Intermediate-strength theories should be subject to Popperian risk or, alternatively, Salmonian 'damn strange coincidence' (Salmon, 1984) by predicting, for example, rank orderings and function forms (including specifications regarding peaks and valleys).

Most of our theory, however, is questionable. A large portion of our conceptual base might have been characterized by Imre Lakatos as vague or primitive notions underlying dubious hypotheses. Such theories are suggestive of logical positivism, in general, and of Rudolf Carnap's protocol statements, more specifically. In contrast to strong and intermediate theory described above, our weak theory (Meehl, 1990a, p. 197) can 'only predict a directional difference or an association between two things without specifying its size within a narrow range of values'. These theories tend to attract null hypothesis significance testing, a dubious testing procedure that is discussed in the following subsection.

2.   Theory Testing

> the ultimate purpose of empirical research is not to test hypotheses, but to test conceptual frameworks, models or theories!
>
> (Hofer and Bygrave, 1992, p. 99)

Hofer and Bygrave (1992) make a very important point. However, theory testing is hardly simple. According to Meehl (1990b), a common mistake across the social sciences is to conflate hypothesis testing with theory testing. Hypothesis testing relies on the application of statistical techniques that rely, in turn, on a frequency interpretation of probability. In contrast, theory testing involves the use of logical probability – an appraisal via facts that is similar to that found in a courtroom. Meehl (1990b, p. 116) distinguishes hypothesis testing from theory testing, as in Figure 3.1.

The theory-testing/hypothesis-testing distinction is crucial. In order for the field of entrepreneurship to make intellectual progress, researchers must appreciate the logical relation between observation and theory. They must

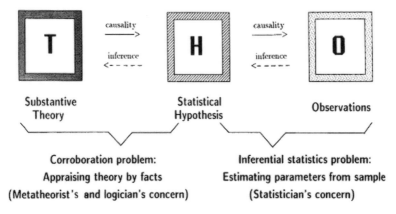

Figure 3.1   Meehl's inferential passage from observations to substantive theory

also appreciate that theories, as explained by Lakatos (1970), are intimately integrated with auxiliary theories and measurement theories, and they are not easily disentangled into single units for testing purposes – that is, the Duhem–Quine problem. The testing of theory must take into account auxiliary and measurement theories as well as experimental conditions and the implications stemming from the *ceteris paribus* assumption.

Researchers must also understand the distinction between a weak test and a strong test of a theory. Weak testing, generally the norm across the social sciences, typically entails null hypothesis significance testing (NHST – discussed below in the subsection on Problems with Statistical Testing). NHST, which amounts to little more than observing that 'the Xs differ from the Ys' (Meehl, 1978, p. 824), may appear to be the strongest tool available for evaluating weak theories. Unfortunately, NHST orients research only in the direction of theory confirmation or validation – that is, the 'normal science' that Kuhn (1962) observed, rather than towards progressive corroboration and/or refutation.

In order to avoid the problems associated with NHST, the field of entrepreneurship must develop intermediate-strength theories, as discussed in the previous subsection, to spark greater intellectual progress, at least in the near future. Although they do not offer numerical point predictions, intermediate-strength theories predict rank orderings and function forms that can provide substantial insight into entrepreneurial activity.

A number of other theory-testing issues must also be addressed. The first issue is the tendency of many researchers and reviewers to appraise theory by fit with their worldview or common-sense notions rather than by credible tests informed by evidence. Alvin Gouldner (1970, p. 29) found that, in sociology, 'A social theory is more likely to be accepted by those who share the theory's background assumptions and find them agreeable'. Such behavior does not view theory under a critical lens, is decidedly unscientific and should not have a place in any social science, including entrepreneurship.

A second theory-testing hurdle that stands in the way of intellectual progress is the ineffective use of theory. On the testing of imported theories, Zahra (2007, p. 451) finds that 'the application of these theories often lacks rigor and creativity'. The problem is illustrated below via an analysis of published tests of HCT, a theory from economics that offers impressive predictive power and substantial empirical success across time and space. The dataset, which includes 56 articles from top-ranked journals including the Cooper et al. (1994) article that initiated the HCT stream of research in entrepreneurship, shows a substantial investment in HCT-related research. However, the analysis reveals that not even one study actually tested the core hypotheses of HCT. Instead, the studies radically morphed the theory's hypotheses as if testing any relationship involving the core variables of education and experience somehow amounted to a testing of the theory.

A third issue relating to theory testing is the questionable value of narrative literature reviews (NLR). An NLR is a tool that should provide (1) an objective review of the empirical status of a theory and (2) a rationale for ongoing pursuit of knowledge in a specific theoretical direction. However, in many studies the rationale for further theory testing is often dubious for a variety of reasons. Many researchers tend to cherry-pick supportive studies to justify the use of particular theories. Some researchers appear to ignore published unsupportive findings, perhaps considering them to be bad science – that is, the confirmation bias (Nickerson, 1998). Others may find it difficult to find null or negative findings, which are harder to publish due to publication bias (cf. Sigelman, 1999). Moreover, researchers may struggle to uncover such findings because they are often downplayed or completely avoided in discussion sections of empirical articles. Additionally, researchers frequently have to cite studies that use null hypothesis significance testing, a very weak analytical technique, to establish support for their own work.

A fourth theory-testing issue is the lack of coordination in the field of entrepreneurship to enable research from solo study findings to develop into useful applied research programs. This may be driven, in part, by the remarkable transience in the field (Cornelius et al., 2006) as researchers from other fields have little informed appreciation for the problems of entrepreneurs and/or the ways of ameliorating the problems. Whatever the reason, our journals publish one solo study after another, causing the brickyard (Forscher, 1963; Platt, 1964) to accumulate more supposed bricks of knowledge with little hope for the creation of a strong wall.

3. Variables and Related Measures

The sub-disciplines of organization science generally pursue knowledge related to the maintenance and growth of large organizations. The focal organizations tend to have hundreds if not thousands of employees across numerous departments and, hence, there are hundreds of variables to consider. The field of entrepreneurship, on the other hand, is geared mainly towards opportunity identification and execution (Venkataraman, 1997; Shane 2003) of small, new ventures. The key dependent variables in entrepreneurship have the potential to be meaningfully linked to individual characteristics and behavior, as well as to entrepreneurial strategies and tactics. In this regard, cumulative knowledge creation should be less evasive here than in the other sub-disciplines of organization science.

Entrepreneurship, then, has much greater potential for becoming a harder, more credible science over time than many of its social science counterparts. Yet, in spite of the big advantage, the field of entrepreneurship is stymied by a number of key issues related to the handling of variables. There appears to be a tendency to study many variables that have only the most tenuous link to anything useful for entrepreneurs. In 1993, Cooper (p. 249) found that 'Research to date has tended to focus upon variables that are relatively easy to gather information about or to measure. This may not be the same as focusing upon the variables that most bear upon performance'. Nearly two decades later, our field continues to generate research findings based on dubious contingency and criterion variables, as well as soft measures, with questionable links to theories.

Further, we expect to publish such questionable findings when statistical significance levels below 0.10 or 0.05 are obtained. That relationships are uncovered amongst our focal variables, dubious or otherwise, should come as no surprise. It has been shown in social science research that in the presence of sufficient statistical power, everything is related to everything. The surprisingly high level of naturally occurring correlation among many phenomena in the social world is what David Lykken called the 'crud factor' (Meehl, 1990a) because such correlations are largely theoretically irrelevant and they can produce questionable inferences.

> Due to the crud factor, [an] investigator would come up with a sizable number of apparent 'substantiations' of the theories even if they had negligible verisimilitude and there were no intrinsic logical connections between the theory and the pair of variables employed for 'testing' purposes. (Meehl, 1990a, p. 124, quotation marks in original)

The field of entrepreneurship must recognize and move beyond the 'crud factor'. It must also reduce the study of marginally relevant variables, as well as the practice of dubiously linking such variables to theories. This largely descriptive research is of little value, according to Fiet (2000, pp. 11–12), who asserts that it 'often makes no effort to contribute to our understanding of the variance in dependent variables. This persistence is understandable because it is much easier to describe observations than it is to predict outcomes using theory'. Ultimately, the field is left with slow knowledge growth and research that is largely uninteresting and unhelpful to practitioners, educators and policy makers (Fiet, 2000).

4. Problems with Statistical Testing

In older, more established fields such as psychology and statistics, there has been much discussion about the substantial limitations and misleading nature of statistical significance testing (Cohen, 1990; Rosnow and Rosenthal, 1989). One key area is the problematic relationship between sample size and power, and, in turn, p value. An increase in sample size produces more power; an increase in power affects the level of significance. Awareness of the problem led journals in the field of psychology to begin requesting the reporting of effect sizes in 1994 (Thompson, 1999) or 'practically significant' findings (Kirk, 1996; Schmidt, 1996; Thompson and Snyder, 1997). It is unclear to what extent top entrepreneurship journals expect empirical research results to include effect sizes. Nevertheless, there is evidence that some researchers are reporting effect sizes (Connelly et al., 2010).

A second key problem with statistical testing is the above-mentioned 'crud factor', which denotes the inherent correlation of all things. Meehl (1990a, p. 204) states, 'Any measured trait or attribute is some function of a list of partly known and mostly unknown causal factors in the genes and life history of the individual, and both genetic and environmental factors are known from tons of empirical research to be themselves correlated'. For entrepreneurship, the crud factor results in all sorts of significant correlations among items that have little either theoretical or practical significance. The field will remain a hostage of the crud factor as long as it continues to promote atheoretical, fishing-expedition-style research and/or the testing of weak theories that do not clearly designate specific variables and the nature of the relationships among them.

A third key problem that is related to the first two is our ongoing use of null hypothesis significance testing (NHST). Taken literally, a null hypothesis is always false (Hays, 1973). Further, a directional hypothesis will be correct 50 percent of the time, assuming perfect power. Hence Lykken

(1991, p. 32) concludes: 'if the null hypothesis is always false, then refuting a null hypothesis is a very weak test of a theory and not in itself a justification for publishing a paper'.

A fourth key problem is the prevalent and questionable usage of parametric statistical data analysis techniques for new-venture performance research. Robinson (1995) and Robinson and Hofer (1997) found parametric techniques to be inappropriate and misleading for a large portion of new-venture performance research. Robinson and Hofer (1997, p. 703) state:

> This study also found that the failure to satisfy such [distributional] assumptions has a substantial impact on the number and robustness of the findings generated using parametric statistical data analysis techniques. Put differently, parametric procedures failed to identify approximately 90% of the statistically significant findings that were identified using appropriate nonparametric procedures, because the assumptions underlying the theoretical development of parametric were violated. In addition, nearly 50% of the statistically significant findings generated by parametric procedures were not consistent with the nonparametric findings, and therefore probably spurious. In short, the unquestioning (and probably unjustified) use of parametric statistical data analysis techniques may be responsible for the lack of robust findings in many of the studies done in the field of entrepreneurship.

Robinson and Hofer (1997) conclude that nonparametric statistical data analysis techniques should be embraced except in studies in which the stringent assumptions required for the use of parametric procedures are satisfied by the collected data.

5.   Practical Requirements for Research

Our field has published many non-cumulative, solo studies that more often than not invoke, rather than test, theory. Replication studies are virtually non-existent. Grounding in the philosophy of science could serve to highlight the limitations of single studies and draw attention to the need for whole programs of research around any potentially enduring practical knowledge.

In order to move toward knowledge that is useful to practitioners, educators and scholars, it is important to set out the factors upon which practical knowledge depends:

1.   Research should be replicable and replicated (Rosenthal and Rosnow, 1984) – a standard scientific requirement (Blaug, 1992) from both positivist and post-positivist (i.e. critical realist) perspectives (Tsang and Kwan, 1999). Replication work in other fields yields surprisingly

poor results (cf. Armstrong, 2003; Hubbard and Vetter, 1996). Hence we must shift focus away from seemingly endless exploratory research towards critical constructive replications.

2.   Research findings should be robust, offering general usefulness. A robust finding, such as the job-generation finding (Birch, 1979; Phillips and Kirchhoff, 1989), remains strong across research approaches, models, methods and assumptions.

3.   Research findings need to be relevant in the sense that they predict things of importance to entrepreneurs, educators and administrators – after all, this is supposed to be an applied discipline.

4.   Research findings need to be more than marginally significant; they need to be practically significant (Kirk, 1996; Schmidt, 1996; Thompson and Snyder, 1997) for entrepreneurs. We should expect studies that use statistical data analysis to report effect sizes in order to more effectively judge the relevance of independent variables.

5.   Research findings should be non-obvious or surprising, which may pose additional problems for authors. According to Armstrong (2003), surprising findings can be controversial and unpopular. They fly in the face of conventional wisdom, forcing practitioners to view their beliefs as different (and potentially incorrect) from useful, scientifically valid knowledge.

6.   Research findings need to be relevant to entrepreneurs in the sense that they involve criterion variables of interest and independent variables that can be controlled (Gouldner, 1957). The field must focus on variables that practitioners can manipulate in order to affect, for example, organizational survival and success.

7.   Research findings should provide evidence that specified, controllable independent variables provide a positive return on investment. Such costs and returns are represented by, for example, the 'capital' in human capital theory that recognizes that education and experience are not free.

8.   Research should provide a theoretical rationale for how controllable independent variables relate to important outcome variables.

9.   Research should offer evidence suggestive of a causal linkage between independent and outcome variables.

Practical knowledge thus requires large numbers of studies, informed by principles set out in this chapter, functioning as *de facto* research programs in order to develop such knowledge. At the very minimum, our academic journals need to carve out a bigger role for constructive replications. Editors and reviewers must also recognize that originality, that is, novel work, is not the same as creativity, that is, novel and useful work (Sternberg and Lubart,

1991). The field must embrace the value of surprise in research findings – of the 'damn strange coincidence' (Salmon, 1984) – that is predicted by one theory but not another. Further, we must heighten expectations regarding the predictive value of our substantive theories.

DEVELOPING PRACTICAL KNOWLEDGE

The problem that we face may be formulated in the following terms: how does a disparate group of occasionally interacting social scientists partici- pate in meaningful, cumulative programs of applied research? How does our research culture shift towards cumulative programmatic research and away from a predominant focus on single studies? Our proposed solution is for scholars to have a common understanding of the requirements of an applied research program and therefore a common knowledge development agenda.

We contend that our proposed solution is viable and achievable in part because of the existence of a few coordinated and uncoordinated applied research programs that have produced some of our most important entre- preneurship knowledge (e.g. the job generation, outsider assistance and personal creativity programs). Hence it would seem that at least some researchers are already asking the types of practical questions about research findings that we discuss here. Some questions, such as whether or not a research finding is replicable, are standard scientific concerns. Others, such as whether or not specific control variables can be manipulated in a cost-effective manner, are less standard.

It is worth pointing out that applied research program agendas are not always directed by explicit, formalized theory. This may be surprising to at least some people, who tend to see theory as the dominant research- directing mechanism (cf. Popper, 1963; Zahra, 2007). Sometimes, the types of research programs that we argue for here, for example job-generation research, occur largely in the absence of explicit theory. Of course, this is not to say that there is no relevant theory. It is simply suggested that theoretical guidance need not be driven by formally explicated theory. To be scientifically useful, theory must be used in an informed fashion and an applied research agenda (such as that which we advocate) should provide more comprehensive direction to the testing of theory.

An Applied Research Program Agenda

The construction of an applied research program (ARP) agenda involves both philosophy of science and practical concerns. As such, defining characteristics of an ARP are subject to criticism. We offer a set of eight characteristics that indicate the nature of scientific work to be included in applied research programs. Four of the characteristics are fundamental to the definition of an ARP. The other four characteristics arguably designate a desirable knowledge expansion strategy.

The four fundamental characteristics of an ARP are as follows.

Practical outcomes

In order for a set of studies to constitute an ARP, at least some of the studies need to focus on practical outcomes. A focus on practical outcomes implies that the dependent variables in tested models need grounding in practical issues typically of concern to entrepreneurs (cf. Shane and Venkataraman, 2000; Shane, 2003). Entrepreneurs are interested in investing in variables that most influence economic outcomes such as revenue and profit growth.

There can also be instances in which dependent variables in the discipline of entrepreneurship are of less concern to entrepreneurs but still of concern to scholars, educators and policy makers. Job creation (Birch, 1979), for example, is strongly associated with entrepreneurship, but is of little interest to specific entrepreneurs. Instead, the job-creation findings substantially influence government support and programming for new ventures.

Evidence of replicability

In order for a set of studies to constitute an ARP they must collectively exhibit evidence of replicability. In 2002, Dov Eden, an editor of the *Academy of Management Journal*, proclaimed that 'replication research is indispensable for scientific progress' (p. 844). His strong belief is held across the social sciences (Dewald et al., 1986; Feigenbaum and Levy, 1993; Tsang and Kwan, 1999). Unfortunately, the publication of replication studies work is uncommon across many scientific fields, including the business disciplines. According to Hubbard and Vetter (1996), replication work in leading business journals represents less than 10 percent of published empirical work in accounting, economics and finance, and 5 percent or less of published empirical work in management and marketing.

To identify a number of studies as a progressive applied research stream, many of those studies must have developed evidence of replicability. There must be credible evidence to convince scholars and practitioners that research findings will remain consistent across time, contexts and cultures, and research methodologies. Exceptions should only exist when explicitly predicted or otherwise appreciated as *ad hoc* adjustments to the generalizability of the findings.

Practical significance

In order for a collection of studies to be considered an ARP, the findings must exhibit practical significance, rather than mere statistical significance. 'Statistical significance', according to Kirk (1996, p. 746), 'is concerned with whether a research result is due to chance or sampling variability; practical significance is concerned with whether the result is useful in the real world'. Statistical significance is often investigated via null hypothesis significance testing, a technique that has been heavily criticized by leading social scientists (cf. Carver, 1978; Cohen, 1990; Meehl, 1967; Rozeboom, 1960; Schmidt, 1996).

Kirk (1996) refers to the measures of practical significance as measures of effect magnitude. The magnitude or strength of a relationship, that is, the amount of variance accounted for in the dependent variable, can be measured in a variety of ways, the most popular being Cohen's *d*.

It appears that effect sizes are already being reported to some extent in entrepreneurship studies and that they are higher than expected (Connelly et al., 2010). Such findings bode well for the development of practically significant knowledge that is useful to entrepreneurs and other relevant stakeholders.

Unexpected findings

In order for a set of studies to constitute an ARP they must provide findings that go beyond common sense:

> Surprising findings differ from current practice or current beliefs … Surprising findings may be innovative or new, although not always. When the problem is important, surprising findings are likely to be controversial or unpopular. (Armstrong, 2003, pp. 71–2)

An ARP cannot only accept findings that support existing theories and contentions. It must be open to surprising and counter-intuitive findings. Such findings can be generated from implicitly theoretical research or from strongly predictive theories that, when right, set up 'damn strange co-incidences' (Salmon, 1984), as noted above. Counter-intuitive findings, according to Lindsay et al. (1998, p. 215), 'demonstrate the superiority of science over common sense'. In the early 1960s, the field of social psychology, from which entrepreneurship research draws a number of theories, went through a transition from demonstrating the obvious to focusing on counter-intuitive effects. The shift toward non-obvious findings led to a number of productive research consequences, including increased researcher enthusiasm, unexpected research results and productive debate (Kelley, 1992).

Such a set of defining characteristics should help us recognize findings, theoretically supported or otherwise, that hold practical potential for entrepreneurs. When identifying a current research program we recommend that scholars appreciate and accommodate the factors that tend to bias published research findings (Meehl, 1990a). Most commonly, we suggest that researchers take into consideration the totality of both supporting and non-supporting findings despite some additional difficulties associated with the interpretation of non-supporting findings.

The next four agenda characteristics expand the usefulness of entrepreneurship knowledge.

Address why and how

An ARP attempts to answer the how and why questions. According to Whetten (1989), how and why are two of the essential building blocks for effective theory development. The how building block handles the manner in which factors (i.e. variables, constructs and/or concepts) are related to each other. The key relationships, and their complexities, are typically depicted graphically for purposes of presentation, testing and refinement. The why building block offers a rhetorical explanation for the underlying logic (i.e. a theory's assumptions) of the causal model. According to Sutton and Staw (1995, p. 376), good theory should be 'rich enough that processes have to be described with sentences and paragraphs so as to convey the logical nuances behind the causal arrow'.

Controllable variables

> the applied social scientist is concerned not merely with identifying predictively potent independent variables, but also with discovering some that are accessible to control. (Gouldner, 1957, p. 97)

An ARP makes an attempt to identify variables that can be manipulated by practitioners (Bauer, 1951; Gouldner, 1957). Controllable variables such as business strategies are desirable because they enable entrepreneurs to directly influence survival, growth and success.

The distinction between uncontrollable and controllable variables does not, however, imply that uncontrollable variables should be dismissed. According to Hobbs (1969, p. 243), 'uncontrollable variables are important from the standpoint that they may establish the context of change, or the limits of effect of controllable variables'.

Eliminate alternative explanations

> For those of us who grant that theory testing is meaningful ... this lack of testing
> is an undesirable state of affairs ... these tests should be comparative – that is,
> against a rival paradigm or research program (Kuhn, 1962; Lakatos, 1970;
> Pahre, 1996, p. 221.)

An ARP attempts to eliminate alternative explanations for phenomena
under observation. The ubiquitous existence of multiple explanations is
typically known as underdetermination. The process to reduce underdetermination involves strong attempts to refute rival scientific theories.
Although refutation may be a strong word, the idea is that the type of ARP
described here positions the discipline of entrepreneurship to examine
scientific evidence and weigh the relative strengths of competing theories
against each other. The outcome is stronger applied knowledge about, for
example, new-venture survival and success.

Cost-effective solutions

An ARP should uncover numerous controllable variables that vary in
magnitude and implementation costs. Hence an ARP will also undertake to
examine and compare the cost-effectiveness of the most powerful controllable variables. Cost-effectiveness analysis (cf. the field of medicine –
McClellan and Newhouse, 1997; Stinnett and Mullahy, 1998) compares
incremental cost and incremental effectiveness of existing versus new
interventions based on empirical results. The results of cost-effectiveness
analysis allow entrepreneurs to make more informed decisions about key
aspects of starting and growing new ventures.

THE IMPORTATION OF THEORY

Our recent study of explicit theory-testing practices in top entrepreneurship
and management journals uncovered 140 theories. Nearly 87 percent of the
theories are imported from five fields: strategic management (25.0 percent),
psychology (29.3 percent, including social psychology), sociology (16.4
percent), and economics (15.7 percent). Only seven theories (5.0 percent)
originated from within the field of entrepreneurship. The disciplinary
origins of the 140 theories are presented in Figure 3.2. The top ten tested
theories are shown in Figure 3.3.

All of the top ten theories originate outside the field of entrepreneurship.
The field of economics is the dominant supplier with 53.8 percent. Sociology, strategic management and biology supply 27.4 percent, 14.7 percent
and 4 percent, respectively. The main reason that scholars might want to

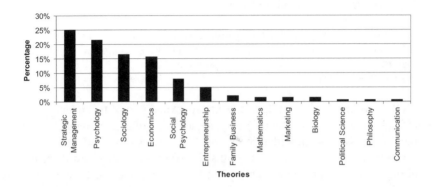

Figure 3.2   The origins of theories used in the top three entrepreneurship journals

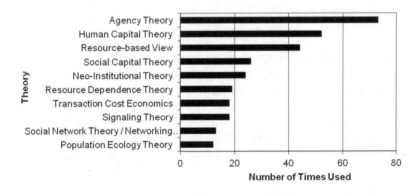

Figure 3.3   Most-used theories in the top three entrepreneurship journals

import theories from other fields ought to be based on the idea of capitaliz-ing on hard-won knowledge gained elsewhere. A social science theory 'with money in the bank' (Meehl, 1990b) is a sufficiently rare commodity that it should not be overlooked. The main questions that need to be asked are: how much money is really in the bank of the theory in question and how transferable is that value to the adopting field?

Anyone considering importing a scientific theory from another field into the field of entrepreneurship should ask: (1) does the theory have high verisimilitude and/or power in its base discipline? and (2) to what degree is the theory transferable without loss to the new field? The idea of theoretical 'verisimilitude' is important for realists (i.e. the correspondence theory of truth) who want to develop theories that accurately represent the world. The notion of theoretical 'power' is related more to the instrumentalist theory of truth, which encourages the creation of theories that are, first and foremost, pragmatically useful and/or instrumental. Both ideas of truth encourage the production of scientific theories that are testable, meaning that they can be empirically supported and possibly even refuted.

To reiterate, the first requirement of anyone choosing to import a theory is that s/he select theories that have demonstrated power (predictive and explanatory) and/or verisimilitude in their base disciplines. The second requirement is to import theories that are relevant to the field's most important problems. Ultimately, each field has its own distinctive problems that it uses theories to address and, *a priori*, there is no basis to assume that the theories of one field will be directly applicable to another field.

It requires a great deal of time, effort and journal space to intelligently vet a theory imported from another field (Meehl, 1990a). Moreover, unvetted theories may deflect a field from a more useful application of effort. In political science, Green and Shapiro (1994, pp. 5, 6) spoke about the damaging consequences of uncritical importation of rational choice theories: 'the stature of rational choice scholarship does not rest on a readily identifiable set of empirical successes' and 'the case has yet to be made that these models have advanced our understanding of how politics works in the real world'. A concerned Jeffrey Pfeffer (1995, p. 683) asked, 'Is what happened in political science being replayed in organization science?' His evidence suggests that it was.

To combat potential problems associated with foreign theory, the next section presents a model that is offered as a productive way forward. The model may facilitate vigilance and defense of the discipline of entrepreneurship.

A MODEL FOR THEORY IMPORTATION

The idea of rationalizing the process of importing theories has occurred to other scholars. Amundson (1998) developed a model to guide theory importation into the field of operations management. Our model, which builds on Amundson's, provides criteria for examining a number of important questions about the verisimilitude and power of a theory in its base discipline and the applicability of the theory to an importing discipline. It is displayed in Table 3.2. The first set of criteria is about predictive power, explanatory power and the existence of strong competing theories. Without predictive power a theory cannot be tested and it is likely to lack pragmatic

Table 3.2   Exogenous theory assessment model

Base discipline criteria	
Predictive power	• Does the theory consistently demonstrate statistically significant predictive power in its base discipline? • Does the theory have practical predictive significance in its base discipline?
Explanatory power	• Does the theory possess substantial explanatory power in its base discipline? (i.e. how much of the discipline's phenomena can it explain?)
Competing theories	• Are there strong rival theories in the base discipline?

Borrower discipline criteria	
Issue match	• Are the phenomena and problems being studied reasonably consistent between base and importing disciplines? • Are the issues central to the theory salient within the importing discipline?
Consistent concepts	• Are the concepts being used by the imported theory consistent with and meaningful in the importing discipline?
Assumptions	• Are the underlying assumptions of the theoretical perspective being employed consistent with the underlying assumptions in the importing discipline?
Knowledge fit	• Is there existing evidence in the importing discipline to support or refute the core propositions of the theory? • Is there existing evidence in the importing discipline to support or refute the peripheral propositions and logical inferences of the theory? • Is there existing theoretical support for the salience of the theory within the importing discipline?

value. Explanatory power is related to the sense-making function of theories. Theories with high explanatory power can make sense of a large amount of data from many studies. The sense of understanding a phenomenon is second only in importance to its predictive power (Popper, 1963). Furthermore, strong competing theories throw doubt on the unique explanatory power of a theory.

With regard to the importability of a theory there are a number of special concerns: the comparability of the phenomena in the two disciplines; the comparability of the issues and problems under study; the similarity of concept usage; and the fit of existing knowledge in the new field to the imported theory.

For purposes of illustration, we pilot the first portion of the model described above using peer-reviewed articles that indicate concerns with four of the top ten theories listed in Figure 3.3. The first aspect of the exogenous theory assessment model, the strength of a theory in its base discipline, is presented in Table 3.3. The citations that populate the tables represent review and critique articles. They span a number of decades, but they may not form a representative sample of relevant articles. Two terms are used in the cells of the tables. 'Issue' is used to indicate that a problem may exist, for example, with respect to the explanatory power of a theory. 'Yes' is used to indicate that a strong rival theory exists.

Table 3.3   The strength of the theory in the base discipline

Theory	Review studies	Predictive power	Explanatory power	Competing theories
Agency theory	Jensen and Murphy (1990)	Issue		
	Becker (1976)		Issue	
	Akerlof (1983)		Issue	
	Arrow (1985)		Issue	
	Sen (1986)		Issue	
	Kotowitz (1987)		Issue	
	Doucouliagos (1994)		Issue	
	Salanié (2002)		Issue	
	Donaldson and Davis (1990)			Yes
	Cornforth (2003)			Yes
	Van Essen et al. (2012)			Yes
Human capital theory	Maglen (1990)	Issue		
	Blaug (1976)	Issue		Yes
	England (1982)	Issue		
	Holst and Busch (2009)		Issue	
	Stiglitz (1975)			Yes
	Spence (1973)			Yes

Theory	Review studies	Predictive power	Explanatory power	Competing theories
Neo-institutional theory	Perrow (1985)		Issue	
	Granovetter (1985)		Issue	
	Perrow (1986)		Issue	
	Powell (1991)		Issue	
	Fligstein (1991)		Issue	
	Tolbert and Zucker (1994)		Issue	
	Tolbert and Zucker (1996)		Issue	
	Selznick (1996)		Issue	
	Barley and Tolbert (1997)		Issue	
	Hirsch and Lounsbury (1997)		Issue	
	Lewin et al. (2004)			Yes
	Donaldson (2006)			Yes
Transaction cost economics	Ghoshal and Moran (1996)	Issue	Issue	
	David and Han (2004)	Issue		
	Geyskens et al. (2006)	Issue		
	Dow (1987)		Issue	
	Langlois (1992)		Issue	
	Osterloh and Frey (2000)		Issue	
	Furubotn (2002)		Issue	
	Conner (1991)			Yes
	Poppo and Zenger (1998)			Yes

Table 3.3 indicates that concerns have been published with regard to agency theory, human capital theory, transaction cost economics and neo-institutional theory. In the following section, we review the testing of human capital theory in the field of entrepreneurship in order to gain insight into how the theory is used and what knowledge has been gained by its introduction.

TESTING HUMAN CAPITAL THEORY

At the very core of human capital theory (HCT) lies the proposition that investments in, for example, formal education and experience pay off in economic terms at both the micro (individual) and macro (societal) levels. Micro-level HCT assumes that an individual makes a rational investment decision based on expected annual return, the cost associated with an investment, the labor force time required to recoup the investment and the discount rate, that is, the value of present versus future earnings. It also assumes that there exists a curvilinear relationship between age and amount of human capital, and that individuals who expect to spend substantial time away from the labor force will invest less in human capital. Macro-level HCT contends that governments take into account human capital development costs when making decisions with respect to the sustainability and growth of gross national and domestic products.

From 1994 until the end of 2008, entrepreneurship scholars generated 52 human-capital-related articles in three of the journals in the field of entrepreneurship: the *Journal of Business Venturing*, *Entrepreneurship Theory and Practice* and the *Journal of Small Business Management*. Four additional articles linking human capital to entrepreneurship were published in the following leading management journals: *Academy of Management Journal*, *Administrative Science Quarterly* and *Strategic Management Journal*.

The analysis of each article in the dataset revealed how HCT is being used in the top entrepreneurship and management journals. The research uncovered 10 variants of HCT. Each is presented in Table 3.4, with the number of related hypothesis and articles.

Two key observations can be drawn from Table 3.4. The first is that none of the hypotheses is categorized under HCT or HCT with diminishing returns. None of the articles in the dataset is concerned with measuring the costs and benefits in financial terms or in calculating the rate of return on investments in formal education or experience over time, despite the fact that many of the authors appear to recognize the economic origins of the theory. An analysis of reference sections reveals that 26 articles (46.4 percent) cite Gary S. Becker's work (1957 [1971], 1964 [1975, 1993]). Further, seven articles (12.5 percent and five articles (8.9 percent) cite works by Jacob Mincer (1974, 1986) and Theodore W. Schultz (1959, 1961), respectively.

The second observation is that 78 (17.8 percent) of the hypotheses in 15 articles (26.8 percent) fall into the increasing human experience model (IHEM), which suggests that more formal education and experience should increase entrepreneurial performance.

Table 3.4   Human capital theory variants

Theory variants	Number of hypotheses	Number of articles
Human capital theory	0	0
Human capital theory with diminishing returns	0	0
Increasing human experience models	78	15
No effect and decreasing human experience models	7	3
Curvilinear models	3	1
Moderator effects models	58	12
Gender differences	19	8
Mediator effect models	48	17
Moderator/mediator combination effects models	9	2
Outsider participation effects model	10	4
Team models	121	11
Difficult to classify	86	23

The empirical findings provide several discussion points. The first point is the vast diversity of implicit theories that are actually tested. The 10 new theory variants indicate that researchers imagine an incredible array of competing theories that involve education, experience and entre-preneurship. Most of the theories are largely unrecognizable as HCT. It is unclear why researchers choose not to test the theory in its original form. It is also unclear why so many variations exist. One possibility is that researchers believe that if they try enough different permutations and combinations of data they will eventually discover something. This behavior fits Paul Feyerabend's 'anything goes' anarchist approach to science. It could even be called dust-bowl empiricism. It certainly is not theory-driven research demanded by top journals.

The second discussion point speaks to the usefulness of HCT in the field of entrepreneurship. It appears that the theory is not being tested properly. The costs of formal education and work experience are not included in empirical research. However, if the indirect tests return extremely strong results for formal education and work experience, a stronger rationale exists for remaining positive about HCT.

The indirect test of formal education does not, however, promote the efficacy of formal education. Entrepreneurship success is not indicated by increases in formal education. Nineteen of the hypothesis tests (73 percent) find no relationship. There is also evidence for a negative relationship.

The indirect test of experience is not quite so straightforward. Thirteen hypotheses support a positive relationship at or beyond the 0.01 level. However, 29 of the hypothesis tests (62 percent) do not indicate a relationship. Five hypotheses (10 percent) at or below the 0.05 level indicate a weak relationship. Ultimately, the evidence is still far from strongly supportive. In addition, there remains the problem of untangling which specific types of experience significantly impact new-venture outcomes.

The third point is that several published review studies have found questionable support for other popular theories such as transaction cost economics and agency theory. Table 3.5 displays some of the results.

Table 3.5   Examples of theory review studies

Theory and review Article	Type of analysis	Support for theory
Transaction cost economics (David and Han, 2004)	Systematic and quantitative narrative review (63 articles)	Mixed support: 'Of 308 tests of core TCE, 144 (47%) were statistically supported, 133 (43%) produced statistically nonsignificant results, and 31 (10%) were statistically significant in the opposite direction to the theory' (p. 44).
Theory of generic competitive Strategy (Campbell-Hunt, 2000)	Meta-analysis (10 articles)	No support: 'there is no clear evidence here that no-distinctive-emphasis designs are any more or less capable of above-average performance than other archetypes' (p. 149).
Agency theory and stewardship theory (Dalton et al., 1998)	Meta-analysis (85 articles)	No support for either theory
Structural contingency theory (Ketchen et al., 1997)	Meta-analysis (33 articles)	Limited support
Leader–member exchange theory (Schriesheim et al., 1999)	Narrative review (147 articles)	The 'support for LMX theory as a dyadic or within-group portrayal of leadership processes is substantially less than it should be' (p. 102).

There is little doubt that the confirmation and refutation of social science theories are more problematic than in disciplines that rely on point prediction. However, there must be a point at which scientists drop a focal theory in favor of another. For the field of entrepreneurship, HCT may no longer be a useful lens.

A fourth point is that many observers could have doubted the applicability of the human capital thesis within an entrepreneurial context given the large number of famous entrepreneurs who have built business empires without the benefit of either much formal education or much prior business experience. Others, who have been afflicted by dyslexia (e.g. Richard Branson and Henry Ford), and were unable to effectively learn in most formal education environments, have been also very effective as entrepreneurs.

Interestingly, in spite of the widespread evidence of counter-examples, not one entrepreneurship researcher in the sample studied questioned the applicability of HCT to entrepreneurs or the field of entrepreneurship. To find that formal education has a negligible effect on entrepreneurial success may not be surprising, but it is materially important. To find that experience may weakly impact entrepreneurial performance depending on the concept of experience employed is equally unsurprising, given how hard it is to learn from experience (cf. Fischhoff, 1982; Alpert and Raiffa, 1982; Thompson, 1990, 1991).

CONCLUSION

Entrepreneurship researchers regularly offer reminders of the embryonic nature of our applied social science discipline (cf. Cornelius et al., 2006); yet, despite our youth, it still is a time to address key concerns about intellectual development. We must ensure that future researchers are trained in philosophy of science and methodology. We must carefully consider the usefulness of exogenous theory. We must also make great efforts to properly test theory. Such efforts will facilitate the development of practical knowledge for entrepreneurs, educators, policy makers and scholars.

REFERENCES

Akerlof, G. (1983), 'Loyalty filters', *The American Economic Review*, **73**(1): 54–63.
Alpert, M. and Raiffa, H. (1982), 'A progress report on the training of probability assessors', in D. Kahneman, P. Slovic and A. Tversky (eds), *Judgment under Uncertainty: Heuristics and Biases*, Cambridge: Cambridge University Press, pp. 294–305.
Amit, R., Glosten, L. and Muller, E. (1990), 'Entrepreneurial ability, venture investments, and risk sharing', *Management Science*, **36**(10): 1232–45.
Amundson, S.D. (1998), 'Relationships between theory-driven empirical research in operations management and other disciplines', *Journal of Operations Management*, **16**(4): 341–59.
Armstrong, J.S. (2003), 'Discovery and communication of important marketing findings: evidence and proposals', *Journal of Business Research*, **56**(1): 69–84.

Arrow, K. (1985), 'The economics of agency', in J. Pratt and R. Zeckhauser (eds), *Principal and Agents: The Structure of Business*, Boston, MA: Harvard Business School Press, pp. 37–51.

Barley, S.R. and Tolbert, P.S. (1997), 'Institutionalization and structuration: studying the links between action and institution', *Organization Studies*, **18**(1): 93–118.

Bauer, C. (1951), 'Social questions in housing and community planning', *The Journal of Social Issues*, **7** (1/2): 1–34.

Becker, G.S. (1957, 1971), *The Economics of Discrimination*, 2nd edn, Chicago, IL:University of Chicago Press.

Becker, G.S. (1964, 1975, 1993), *Human Capital: A Theoretical and Empirical Analysis, with Special Reference to Education*, Chicago, IL: University of Chicago Press.

Becker, G.S. (1976), 'Altruism, egoism, and genetic fitness: economics and sociobiology', *Journal of Economic Literature*, **14**(3): 817–26.

Birch, D.L. (1979), 'The job generation process', unpublished report prepared by the Massachusetts Institute of Technology Program on Neighborhood and Regional Change for the Economic Development Administration, US Department of Commerce, Washington, DC.

Blaug, M. (1975), 'Kuhn versus Lakatos, or paradigms versus research programmes in the history of economics', *Hope*, **7**(4): 399–433.

Blaug, M. (1976), 'The empirical status of human capital theory: a slightly jaundiced view', *Journal of Economic Literature*, **14**(3): 827–55.

Blaug, M. (1992), *The Methodology of Economics: Or How Economists Explain*, New York: Cambridge University Press.

Brush, C.G., Duhaime, I.M., Gartner, W.B., Stewart, A., Katz, J.A., Hitt, M.A., Alvarez, S.A., Meyer, G.D. and Venkataraman, S. (2003), 'Doctoral education in the field of entrepreneurship', *Journal of Management*, **29**(3): 309–31.

Burrell, G. and Morgan, G. (1979), *Sociological Paradigms and Organizational Analysis: Elements of the Sociology of Corporate Life*, London: Heinemann.

Bygrave, W.D. (1993), 'Theory building in the entrepreneurship paradigm', *Journal of Business Venturing*, **8**(3): 255–80.

Bygrave, W. and Hofer, C. (1991), 'Theorizing about entrepreneurship', *Entrepreneurship Theory and* Practice, **16**(2): 13–22.

Campbell-Hunt, C. (2000), 'What have we learned about generic competitive strategy? A meta-analysis', *Strategic Management Journal*, **21**(2): 127–54.

Caruana, A., Morris, M.H. and Vella, A.J. (1998), 'The effect of centralization and formalization on entrepreneurship in export firms', *Journal of Small Business Management*, **36**(1): 16–29.

Carver, R.P. (1978), 'The case against statistical significance testing', *Harvard Educational Review*, **48** (3): 378–99.

Chandler, G.N. and Lyon, D.W. (2001), 'Issues of research design and construct measurement in entrepreneurship research: the past decade', *Entrepreneurship Theory and Practice*, **25**(4): 101–13.

Cohen, J. (1990), 'Things I have learned (so far)', *American Psychologist*, **45**(12): 1304–12.

Cohen, M.D. (2007), 'Administrative behavior: laying the foundations for Cyert and March', *Organization Science*, **18**(3): 503–6.

Connelly, B.L., Ireland, R.D., Reutzel, C. and Coombs, J. (2010), 'The power and effects of entrepreneurship research', *Entrepreneurship Theory and Practice*, **34**(1): 131–49.

Conner, K.R. (1991), 'A historical comparison of resource-based theory and five schools of thought within industrial organizational economics: do we have a new theory of the firm?', *Journal of Management*, **17**(1): 121–54.

Cooper, A.C. (1993), 'Challenges in predicting new firm performance', *Journal of Business Venturing*, **8**(3): 241–53.

Cooper, A.C., Gimeno-Gascon, F.J. and Woo, C.J. (1994), 'Initial human and financial capital as predictors of new venture performance', *Journal of Business Venturing*, **9**(5): 371–95.

Cornelius, B., Landstrom, H. and Persson, O. (2006), 'Entrepreneurial studies: the dynamic research front of a developing social science', *Entrepreneurship Theory and Practice*, **30**(3): 375–98.

Cornforth, C. (2003), 'Introduction. The changing context of governance – emerging issues and paradoxes', in C. Cornforth (ed.), *The Governance of Public and Non-profit Organizations: What Do Boards Do?*, London: Routledge, pp. 1–20.

Craig, E. (1998), 'Keynes, John Maynard (1883–1946)', in E. Craig (ed.), *Routledge Encyclopedia of Philosophy: Irigaray to Lushi Chunqiu*, Vol. 5, London: Routledge, pp. 233–5.

Dalton, D.R., Daily, C.M., Ellstrand, A.E. and Johnson, J.L. (1998), 'Meta-analytic reviews of board composition, leadership structure, and financial performance', *Strategic Management Journal*, **19**(3): 269–90.

David R. and Han, S. (2004), 'A systematic assessment of the empirical support for transaction cost economics', *Strategic Management Journal*, **25**(1): 39–58.

Dewald, W.G., Thursby, J.G. and Anderson, R.G. (1986), 'Replication in empirical economics: the *Journal of Money, Credit, and Banking* project', *American Economic Review*, **76**(4): 587–603.

Donaldson, J. and Davis, P. (1990), 'Business ethics? Yes, but what can it do for the bottom line?', *Management Decision*, **28**(6): 29–33.

Donaldson, L. (2006), 'The contingency theory of organizational design: challenges and opportunities', in M. Burton, B. Erikson, D.D. Hakonsson and C.S. Snow (eds), *Organizational Design: The Evolving State-of-the-Art*, New York: Springer, pp. 19–40.

Doucouliagos, C. (1994), 'A note on the evolution of Homo Economicus', *Journal of Economic Issues*, **28**(3): 877–83.

Dow, Gregory K. (1987), 'The function of authority in transaction cost economics', *Journal of Economic Behavior and Organization*, **8**: 13–38.

Eden, D. (2002), 'Replication, meta-analysis, scientific progress, and *AMJ*'s publication process', *Academy of Management Journal*, **45**(5): 841–7.

England, P. (1982), 'The failure of human capital theory to explain occupational sex segregation', *The Journal of Human Resources*, **17**(3), 358–70.

Feigenbaum, S. and Levy, D.M. (1993), 'The market for (ir)reproducible econometrics', *Social Epistemology*, **7**(3): 286–92.

Fiet, J.O. (2000), 'The theoretical side of teaching entrepreneurship', *Journal of Business Venturing*, **16** (1): 1–24.

Fischhoff, B. (1982), 'Latitudes and platitudes: how much credit do people deserve?', in G. Ungson and D. Braunstein (eds), *Decision Making: An Interdisciplinary Inquiry*, New York: Kent, pp. 116–20.

Fletcher, D.E. (2006), 'Entrepreneurial processes and the social construction of opportunity', *Entrepreneurship & Regional Development*, **18**(5): 421–40.

Fligstein, N. (1991), 'The structural transformation of American industry: an institutional account of the causes of diversification in the largest firms, 1919–1979', in W.W. Powell and P.J. DiMaggio (eds), *The New Institutionalism in Organizational Analysis*, Chicago, IL: University of Chicago Press, pp. 311–36.

Forscher, B.K. (1963), 'Chaos in the brickyard', *Science*, **142**(3590): 339.

Fuller, S. (2004), *Kuhn vs. Popper: The Struggle for the Soul of Science*, New York: Columbia University Press.

Fuller, T. and Moran, P. (2001), 'Small enterprises as complex adaptive systems: a methodological question?', *Entrepreneurship & Regional Development*, **13**(1): 47–63.

Furubotn, E. (2002), 'Entrepreneurship, transaction-cost economics, and the design of contracts', in Eric Brousseau and Jean-Michel Glachant (eds), *The Economics of Contracts*, Cambridge: Cambridge University Press, pp. 72–98.

Geyskens, I., Steenkamp, J. and Kumar, N. (2006), 'Make, buy, or ally: a transaction cost theory meta-analysis', *Academy of Management Journal*, **49**(3): 519–43.

Ghoshal, S. (2005), 'Bad management theories are destroying good management practices', *Academy of Management Learning & Education*, **4**(1): 75–91.

Ghoshal, S. and Moran, P. (1996), 'Bad for practice: a critique of the transaction cost theory', *Academy of Management Review*, **21**: 13–47.

Gouldner, A.W. (1957), 'Theoretical requirements of the applied social sciences', *American Sociological Review*, **22**(1): 92–102.

Gouldner, A.W. (1970), *The Coming Crisis in Western Sociology*, London: Heinemann.

Granovetter, M. (1985), 'Economic action and social structure: the problem of embeddedness', *American Journal of Sociology*, **91**: 481–510.

Green, D.P. and Shapiro, I. (1994), *Pathologies of Rational Choice Theory: A Critique of Applications in Political Science*, New Haven, CT: Yale University Press.

Hays, W.L. (1973), *Statistics for the Social Sciences*, 2nd edn, New York: Holt, Rinehart & Winston.

Hirsch, P.M. and Lounsbury, M. (1997), 'Ending the family quarrel: towards a reconciliation of "old" and "new" institutionalism', *American Behavioral Scientist*, **40**: 406–18.

Hobbs, D. (1969), 'A comment on applied sociological research', *Rural Sociology*, **34**(2): 241–5.

Hofer, C.W. and Bygrave, W.D. (1992), 'Researching entrepreneurship', *Entrepreneurship Theory and Practice*, **16**(3): 91–100.

Holst, E. and Busch, A. (2009), 'Glass ceiling effect and earnings: the gender pay gap in managerial positions in Germany', SOEP paper No. 201; DIW Berlin Discussion Paper No. 905.

Hubbard, R. and Vetter, D.E. (1996), 'An empirical comparison of published replication research in accounting, economics, finance, management, and marketing', *Journal of Business Research*, **35**(2): 153–64.

Jennings, P.L., Perren, L. and Carter, S. (2005), 'Guest editors' introduction: alternative perspectives on entrepreneurship research', *Entrepreneurship Theory and Practice*, **29**(2): 145–52.

Jensen, M.C. and Murphy, K.J. (1990), 'Performance pay and top management incentives', *Journal of Political Economy*, **98**(2): 225–64.

Johannisson, B., Caffarena, L.C., Discua-Cruz, A.F., Hormiga-Perez, E., Kapelko, M., Murdock, K., Nanka-Bruce, D., Olejarova, M., Sanchez-Lopez, A., Sekki, A., Stoian, M.C., Totterman, H. and Bisignano, A. (2007), 'Understanding the industrial district: contrasting conceptual images as a road to insight', *Entrepreneurship & Regional Development*, **19**(6): 527–54.

Kelley, H.H. (1992), 'Common sense psychology and scientific psychology', *Annual Review of Psychology*, **43**: 1–23.

Ketchen, D. Jr, Combs, J.G., Russell, C.J., Shook, C., Dean, M.A., Runge, J., Lohrke, F.T., Naumann, S.E., Haptonstahl, D.E., Baker, R., Beckstein, B.A., Handler, C., Honig, H. and Lamoureux, S. (1997), 'Organizational configurations and performance: a meta-analysis', *Academy of Management Journal*, **40** (1): 223–40.

Kirk, R.E. (1996), 'Practical significance: a concept whose time has come', *Educational and Psychological Measurement*, **56**(5): 746–59.

Kotowitz, Y. (1987), 'Moral hazard', in J. Eatwell, M. Milgate and P. Newman (eds), *The New Palgrave: A Dictionary of Economics*, London: Macmillan, pp. 549–51.

Kuhn, T.S. (1962), *The Structure of Scientific Revolutions*, Chicago, IL: The University of Chicago Press.

Lakatos, I. (1970), 'Falsification and the methodology of scientific research programmes', in I. Lakatos and A. Musgrave (eds), *Criticism and the Growth of Knowledge*, Cambridge: Cambridge University Press, pp. 91–196.

Lakatos, I. (1978), *The Methodology of Scientific Research Programmes: Philosophical Papers*, Vol. 1, Cambridge: Cambridge University Press.

Langlois, R.N. (1992), 'Transaction cost economics in real time', *Industrial and Corporate Change*, **1**(1): 99–127.

Lewin, A.Y., Weigelt, C.B. and Emery, J.D. (2004), 'Adaptation and selection in strategy and change: perspectives on strategic change in organizations', in M.S. Poole and A.H. Van de Ven (eds), *Handbook of Organizational Change and Innovation*, New York: Oxford University Press, pp. 108–60.

Lindsay, D.S., Read, J.D. and Sharma, K. (1998), 'Accuracy and confidence in person identification: the relationship is strong when witnessing conditions vary widely', *Psychological Science*, **9**(3): 215–18.

Lykken, D.T. (1991), 'What's wrong with psychology anyway?', in D. Cicchetti and W.M. Grove (eds), *Thinking Clearly about Psychology Volume 1: Matters of Public Interest*, Minneapolis, MN: University of Minnesota Press, pp. 3–39.

Machlup, F. (1978), *Methodology of Economics and Other Social Sciences*, New York: Academic.

Maglen, L.R. (1990), 'Challenging the human capital orthodoxy: the education–productivity link re-examined', *The Economic Record*, **66**(4): 281–94.

McClellan, M. and Newhouse, J.P. (1997), 'The marginal cost-effectiveness of medical technology: a panel instrumental-variables approach', *Journal of Econometrics*, **77**: 39–64.

Meehl, P.E. (1967), 'Theory testing in psychology and physics: a methodological paradox', *Philosophy of Science*, **34**(2): 103–15.

Meehl, P.E. (1978), 'Theoretical risks and tabular asterisks: Sir Karl, Sir Ronald, and the slow progress of soft psychology', *Journal of Consulting and Clinical Psychology*, **46**: 806–34.

Meehl, P.E. (1990a), 'Why summaries of research on psychological theories are often uninterpretable', *Psychological Reports*, **66**(1): 195–244.

Meehl, P.E. (1990b), 'Appraising and amending theories: the strategy of Lakatosian defense and two principles that warrant it', *Psychological Inquiry*, **1**(2): 108–41.

Meehl, P.E. (1993), 'Philosophy of science: help or hindrance', *Psychological Reports*, **72**: 707–33.

Meyer, G.D. (2009), 'Commentary: on the integration of strategic management and entrepreneurship: views of a contrarian', *Entrepreneurship Theory and Practice*, **33**(1): 341–52.

Mincer, J. (1974), *Schooling, Experience and Earnings*, New York: Columbia University Press.

Mincer, J. (1986), 'Wage changes and job changes', in R.G. Ehrenberg (ed.), *Research in Labor Economics*, Vol. 8, Greenwich, CT: JAI Press, pp. 171–97.

Miner, J.B. (2003), 'The rated importance, scientific validity, and practical usefulness of organizational behavior theories: a quantitative review', *Academy of Management Learning and Education*, **2**(3): 250–68.

Nickerson, R.S. (1998), 'Confirmation bias: a ubiquitous phenomenon in many guises', *Review of General Psychology*, **2**(2): 175–220.

Osterloh, M. and Frey, B. (2000), 'Motivation, knowledge transfer and organizational form', *Organization Science*, **11**: 538–50.

Pahre, R. (1996), 'Patterns of knowledge communities in the social sciences', *Library Trends*, **45**(2): 204–25.

Perrow, C. (1985), 'Review essay: overboard with myth and symbols', *American Journal of Sociology*, **91**(1): 151–5.

Perrow, C. (1986), *Complex Organizations: A Critical Essay*, New York: Random House.

Pfeffer, J. (1995), 'Mortality, reproducibility, and the persistence of styles of theory', *Organization Science*, **6**(6): 681–6.

Phan, P.H. (2004), 'Entrepreneurship theory: possibilities and future directions', *Journal of Business Venturing*, **19**(5): 617–20.

Phillips, B.D. and Kirchhoff, B.A. (1989), 'Formation, growth, and survival: small firm dynamics in the U.S. economy', *Small Business Economics*, **1**(1): 65–74.

Platt, J.R. (1964), 'Strong inference', *Science*, **146**(3642): 347–53.

Popper, K.R. (1963), *Conjectures and Refutations: The Growth of Scientific Knowledge*, London: Routledge.

Poppo, L. and Zenger, T. (1998), 'Testing alternative theories of the firm: transaction cost, knowledge-based, and measurement explanations for make-or-buy decisions in information services', *Strategic Management Journal*, **19**: 853–77.

Powell, Walter W. (1991), 'Expanding the scope of institutional analysis', in Walter W. Powell and Paul J. DiMaggio (eds), *The New Institutionalism in Organizational Analysis*, Chicago, IL: University of Chicago Press, pp. 183–203.

Priem, R.L. and Butler, J.E. (2001a), 'Is the resource-based theory a useful perspective for strategic management research?', *Academy of Management Review*, **26**(1): 22–40.

Priem, R.L. and Butler, J.E. (2001b), 'Tautology in the resource-based view and implications of externally determined resource value: further comments', *Academy of Management Review*, **26**(1): 57–66.

Robinson, K.C. (1995), 'Measures of entrepreneurial value creation: an investigation of the impact of strategy and industry structure on the economic performance of independent new ventures', unpublished doctoral dissertation, Athens, GA: University of Georgia.

Robinson, K.C. and Hofer, C.W. (1997), 'A methodological investigation of the validity and usefulness of parametric and nonparametric statistical data analysis techniques for new venture research', in P.R. Reynolds, W.D. Bygrave, N.M. Carter, P. Davidsson, W.B. Gartner, C.M. Mason and P.P. McDougall (eds), *Frontiers of Entrepreneurship*, Wellesley, MA: Babson College Press, pp. 692–705.

Rosenthal, R. and Rosnow, R.L. (1984), *Essentials of Behavioral Research: Methods and Data Analysis*, New York: McGraw-Hill.

Rosnow, R.L. and Rosenthal, R. (1989), 'Statistical procedures and the justification of knowledge in psychological science', *American Psychologist*, **44**(10): 1276–84.

Rozeboom, W.W. (1960), 'The fallacy of the null hypothesis significance test', *Psychological Bulletin*, **57**: 416–28.

Salanié, B. (1997), *The Economics of Contracts: A Primer*, Cambridge, MA: MIT Press.

Salmon, W.C. (1984), *Scientific Explanation and the Causal Structure of the World*, Princeton, NJ: Princeton University Press.

Sarason, Y., Dillard, J.F. and Dean, T. (2010), 'How can we know the dancer from the dance? Reply to entrepreneurship as the structuration of individual and opportunity: a response using a critical realist perspective (Mole and Mole, 2008)', *Journal of Business Venturing*, **25**(2): 238–43.

Schmidt, F. (1996), 'Statistical significance testing and cumulative knowledge in psychology: implications for the training of researchers', *Psychological Methods*, **1**(2): 115–29.

Schriesheim, C.A., Castro, S.L. and Cogliser, C.C. (1999), 'Leader–member exchange (LMX) research: a comprehensive review of theory, measurement, and data-analytic practices', *The Leadership Quarterly*, **10**(1): 63–113.

Schultz, T.W. (1959), 'Investment in man: an economist's view', *The Social Service Review*, June: 109–17.

Schultz, T.W. (1961), 'Investment in human capital', *American Economic Review*, **51**(1): 1–17.

Schwartz-Shea, P. (2003), 'Is this the curriculum we want? Doctoral requirements and offerings in methods and methodology', *PS: Political Science and Politics*, **36**(3): 379–86.

Selznick, Philip (1996), 'Institutionalism "Old" and "New"', *Administrative Science Quarterly*, **41**: 270–77.

Sen, A.K. (1987), *On Ethics & Economics*, Oxford: Blackwell.

Shane, S. (2003), *A General Theory of Entrepreneurship: The Individual–Opportunity Nexus*, Cheltenham, UK and Northampton, MA, USA: Edward Elgar Publishing.

Shane, S. and Venkataraman, S. (2000), 'The promise of entrepreneurship as a field of research', *Academy of Management Review*, **25**(1): 217–26.

Sigelman, L. (1999), 'Publication bias reconsidered', *Political Analysis*, **8**(2): 201–10.

Spence, M. (1973), 'Job market signaling', *The Quarterly Journal of Economics*, **87**(3): 355–74.

Sternberg, R.J. and Lubart, T.I. (1991), 'An investment theory of creativity and its development', *Human Development*, **34**(1): 1–31.

Stiglitz, J.E. (1975), 'The theory of "screening," education, and the distribution of income', *The American Economic Review*, **65**(3): 283–300.

Stinnett, A.A. and Mullahy, J. (1998), 'Net health benefits: a new framework for the analysis of uncertainty in cost-effectiveness analysis', *Medical Decision Making*, **18**(2): S68–80.

Summer, C.E., Bettis, R.A., Duhaime, I.H., Grant, J.H., Hambrick, D.C., Snow, C.C. and Zeithaml, C.P. (1990), 'Doctoral education in the field of business policy and strategy', *Journal of Management*, **16**(2): 361–98.

Sutton, R.I. and Staw, B.M. (1995), 'What theory is not', *Administrative Science Quarterly*, **40**(3): 371–84.

Thompson, B. (1999), 'If statistical significance tests are broken/misused, what practices should supplement or replace them?', *Theory & Psychology*, **9**(2): 165–81.

Thompson, B. and Snyder, P.A. (1997), 'Statistical significance testing practices in the *Journal of Experimental Education*', *Journal of Experimental Education*, **66**(1): 75–83.

Thompson, L. (1990), 'The influence of experience on negotiation performance', *Journal of Experimental Social Psychology*, **26**: 528–44.

Thompson, L. (1991), 'Information exchange in negotiation', *Journal of Experimental Psychology*, **27**: 161–79.

Tolbert, P. and Zucker, L. (1994), 'Institutional analyses of organizations: legitimate but not institutionalized', ISSR Working Papers in the Social Sciences, **6**(5).

Tolbert, P. and Zucker, L. (1996), 'The institutionalization of institutional theory', in S. Clegg, C. Hardy and W. Nord (eds), *Handbook of Organizations Studies*, London: Sage Publications, pp. 175–90.

Tsang, E.W.K. and Kwan, K.M. (1999), 'Replication and theory development in organizational science: a critical realist perspective', *Academy of Management Review*, **24**(4): 759–80.

Van Essen, M., Otten, J. and Carberry, E.J. (2012), 'Assessing managerial power theory: a meta-analytic approach to understanding the determinants of CEO compensation', *Journal of Management*, **38**(3): 396–423.

Venkataraman, S. (1997), 'The distinctive domain of entrepreneurship research', in J. Katz and R. Brockhaus (eds), *Advances in Entrepreneurship, Firm Emergence and Growth*, Vol. 3, Greenwich, CT: JAI Press, pp. 119–38.

Whetten, D.A. (1989), 'What constitutes a theoretical contribution?', *Academy of Management Review*, **14**(4): 490–95.

Williamson, O.E. (1999), 'Strategy research: governance and competence perspectives', *Strategic Management Journal*, **20**(12): 1087–108.

Zahra, S.A. (2005), 'Disciplinary research and entrepreneurship scholarship', in S.A. Alvarez, R. Agarwal and O. Sorenson (eds), *Handbook of Entrepreneurship Research*, 2nd edn, New York: Kluwer, pp. 253–68.

Zahra, S.A. (2007), 'Contextualizing theory building in entrepreneurship research', *Journal of Business Venturing*, **22**(3): 443–52.

4. Measuring progress in entrepreneurship research

Linda F. Edelman, Tatiana S. Manolova,
Candida G. Brush and Scott Latham

INTRODUCTION

During the past ten years there have been significant developments in the field of entrepreneurship. Increased attention to a variety of new topics such as opportunity recognition (Eckhardt and Shane, 2003; Alvarez and Barney, 2010), growth (Delmar et al., 2003), entrepreneurial cognition (Baron, 2007), entrepreneurial orientation (Wiklund and Shepherd, 2003), venture capital (Hsu, 2004), nascent entrepreneurs (Gartner et al., 2004; Brush et al., 2008); social networks and social capital (Aldrich and Kim, 2007; Aldrich et al., 2004; Davidsson and Honig, 2003) has led to communities of scholars coalescing around these topical areas (Gartner, 2001). Since 2000, the number of entrepreneurship scholars and journals publishing entrepreneurship research has also increased dramatically. For example, in 2013 the Entrepreneurship division of the Academy of Management had 2738 registered members (Academy of Management, 2013). In 2002, Katz and Boal classified 44 English-speaking entrepreneurship journals by quality into three levels. Since then, the number has almost tripled, so that at the time of writing (2013) there are more than 116 entrepreneurship journals (http://www.slu.edu/x17970.xml). Taken together, the four top journals[1] in the Katz and Boal (2002) classification published over 150 academic articles per year, providing entrepreneurship researchers with many opportunities to disseminate their scholarship. Notably, these journals also rose in the SSCI rankings and acceptance rates declined, indicating improved quality and impact of these journals. Clearly, the field of entrepreneurship enjoys significant growth in terms of number of topics studied, the number of scholars attracted to the field and the number of publication outlets. In sum, entrepreneurship has blossomed into a legitimate and popular field of study.

Several current reviews of the field have considered theory development (Gartner, 2001; Brush et al., 2003; Dean et al., 2007), the distinctiveness of the domain of entrepreneurship (Sorenson and Stuart, 2008), the distinctiveness of the European tradition in studying entrepreneurship (Down,

2013), or the future of entrepreneurship research (Wiklund et al., 2011; Zahra and Wright, 2011). While these reviews cover aspects of theory and methodology, the question remains as to whether the field is converging on a single phenomenon, or whether it is becoming fragmented into a variety of smaller subfields. For instance, some authors argue that there are umbrella topics that define the field and research directions such as opportunity recognition (Shane and Venkataraman, 2000); creation (Brush et al., 2003); cognition (Mitchell et al., 2004) modes of organizing (Busenitz et al., 2003; Gartner, 2004); and effectuation (Sarasvathy, 2001). Others argue that building communities of scholarship allows for deeper study of narrower topics or phenomena (Gartner, 2001). Alternatively, Low and MacMillan (1988) propose that entrepreneurship is inherently multifaceted; thus theory is just one of six key design specification decisions that researchers must make as they begin to assemble a research program. They argue that scholars must additionally consider the purpose of the research, the phenomena of interest, level of analysis, the time frame of the study and the methodology to be adopted.

Other recent reviews examine methodologies used in entrepreneurship. Chandler and Lyon (2001) considered whether methodologies and measures used in the 1990s contributed to progress in the field, while Grant and Perren (2002) applied a meta-theoretic analysis to 36 top articles in the field of small business and entrepreneurship to assess perspectives and concluded that a functionalist perspective dominates research. More recently, Mullen et al. (2009) examined four journals in relation to aspects of construct, and internal and external validity.

While current assessments of the field focus primarily on theory development (Gartner, 2001; Brush et al., 2003; Grant and Perren, 2002), research design (Chandler and Lyon, 2001; Mullen et al., 2009), or on data analytic trends (Davidsson and Wiklund, 2001; Dean et al., 2008), more than ten years have passed since Aldrich and Baker (1997) systematically compared the methodology used in entrepreneurship scholarship to benchmark journals in the field of management. As the numbers previously cited suggest, the past ten years arguably reflect the greatest advancement in breadth and scope of entrepreneurship research. In light of the vigorous research activity within the field of entrepreneurship, the field is ripe for an extension of Aldrich and Baker's original treatment. That is the purpose of our study. Our question is whether or not the expansion of research and subsequent debate about single- versus multiple-paradigm approaches are leading to progress in the field of entrepreneurship. This is an important question when we consider the expansion of the field in terms of country context (emerging, developing and industrialized countries), firm context (corporate, social, family or *de novo* startups), and overall heterogeneity of entrepreneurial activity in venture creation and development (Short et al., 2010; Davidsson, 2007).

More specifically, we followed the approach used by Aldrich and Baker (1997), who assessed progress of the entrepreneurship field starting with the foundations of normal science. Kuhn (1962) put forth the notion of normal science to describe the manner in which scientific progress is achieved. Derived from positivism, in normal science, scientific inquiry is guided by an explicit research question, grounded in established theory, and conducted using rigorous methods (Aldrich et al., 1994). Replication, confirmation and extensions of previous studies are encouraged, as this is the means to incremental knowledge accumulation (Chua, 1986). Over time, convergence around the appropriate phenomenon of study, as well as consensus around the appropriate methods of inquiry, will prevail. Aldrich and Baker (1997) also considered two other contrasting views, one that supports diversity of theories and methods, and advocates a multi-paradigm perspective (Low and MacMillan, 1988), and another view that they refer to as a pragmatic approach, focusing on the importance of issues addressed, where topicality, uniqueness and usefulness are central rather than continuity (Mone and McKinley, 1993). In this chapter, we examine three years of current scholarship in six entrepreneurship-specific journals; three published in the USA and three published in Europe, and compare these with the research published in two benchmark journals. We then compare our findings with the previous review by Aldrich and Baker (1997), which allows us to assess progress in entrepreneurship research over time. We consider our findings in relation to the normal science perspective first, and then draw implications for current and future scholarship in the field of entrepreneurship. In the following sections, we provide a brief overview of normal science, present our methodology and findings, and then discuss the implications of our findings from the normal science perspective. We conclude by challenging many of the tenets of the normal science approach and offering suggestions for future research.

BACKGROUND

Taking stock of progress in a domain of study requires an understanding of the nature of assumptions that underlie the paradigms in social science (Burrell and Morgan, 1979). Assumptions about the nature of knowledge, what is true or false, whether knowledge is acquired or experienced, and the methodological approach used to measure knowledge form the underpinning of social science perspectives and paradigms (Burrell and Morgan, 1979). The dimensions of a domain can be distinguished by the fundamental image of the subject and include key topics such as what and who are studied, what is the appropriate unit of analysis or analyses, what research questions are asked and how they are asked (i.e. theories), and what methods are used to interpret the answers (Ritzer, 1975).

Since 1988, at least 16 major reviews of the entrepreneurship field have been published in entrepreneurship journals. Table 4.1 presents a summary of articles on the domain of entrepreneurship research.

Table 4.1 Domain of entrepreneurship: literature reviews

Author(s)	Year	Journal/book	Title
Aldrich and Baker	1997	*Entrepreneurship 2000*	'Blinded by the cities? Has there been progress in entrepreneurship research?'
Brush, Duhaime, Gartner, Steward, Katz, Hitt, Alverez, Meyer and Venkataraman	2003	*Journal of Management*	'Doctoral education in the field of entrepreneurship'
Busenitz, West, Shepard, Nelson, Chandler and Zacharakis	2003	*Journal of Management*	'Entrepreneurship research in emergence: past trends and future directions'
Chandler and Lyon	2001	*Entrepreneurship Theory and Practice*	'Issues of research design and construct measurement in entrepreneurship research: the past decade'
Davidsson	2004	*Researching Entrepreneurship*	'Researching entrepreneurship'
Davidsson and Wiklund	2001	*Entrepreneurship Theory and Practice*	'Levels of analysis in entrepreneurship research: current research and suggestions for the future'
Dean, Shook and Payne	2007	*Entrepreneurship Theory and Practice*	'The past, present and future of entrepreneurship research: data analytic trends and training'
Forbes	1999	*International Journal of Management Reviews*	'Cognitive approaches to new venture creation'
Gartner	2001	*Entrepreneurship Theory and Practice*	'Is there an elephant in entrepreneurship? Blind assumptions in theory development'

Author(s)	Year	Journal/book	Title
Grant and Perren	2002	*International Small Business Journal*	'Small business and entrepreneurial research: meta-theories, paradigms and prejudices'
Low	2001	*Entrepreneurship Theory and Practice*	'The adolescence of entrepreneurship research: specification of purpose'
Low and MacMillan	1988	*Journal of Management*	'Entrepreneurship: past research and future challenges'
Mitchell, Busenitz, Lant, McDougall, Morse and Smith	2004	*Entrepreneurship Theory and Practice*	'The distinctive domain of entrepreneurship cognition research'
Mullen, Budeva and Doney	2009	*Journal of Small Business Management*	'Research methods in the leading small business-entrepreneurship journals: a critical review with recommendations for future research'
Venkataraman	1997	*Advances in Entrepreneurship, Firm Emergence and Growth*	'The distinctive domain of entrepreneurship research'

The implicit question that is behind all of these reviews of the field is: Are we making progress in the field of entrepreneurship? But the definition of progress is not always clear. An earlier review by Aldrich (1992) notes that the field had expanded its repertoire of research designs and analytical techniques, and proposed that research directions depend on the assumptions we make about the scientific and normative structure of the field. On one hand, the unified or normal science view holds that progress is achieved when there is an accumulation of empirically tested hypotheses and well-grounded generalizations, developed through quantitative data, rigorous design and statistical techniques (Kuhn, 1970). This view derives from positivism, where there is one assumed, identifiable reality that can be evidenced through the cause-and-effect examination with a reductionist approach (Chua, 1986; Guba and Lincoln, 1994). In contrast, post-positivism values replication but examines findings relative to fit with pre-existing knowledge using triangulation as a way to falsify hypotheses (Guba and Lincoln, 1994). Researchers test theories using hypotheses to replicate and confirm previous findings, working to achieve continuity and an accumulated body of work. Sampling issues are of high priority in normal science, as researchers are interested in the unit of analysis studied as well as the generalizability of their sample across the population of interest (Aldrich and Baker, 1997).

In this chapter, we frame our discussion within the lens of normal science and ask: From a normal science perspective, are we making progress in entrepreneurship research? We looked at this question in two ways: (1) over time by comparing our findings with the 1997 findings of Aldrich and Baker (1997); and (2) more contemporaneously by splitting our sample and comparing the findings from the US journals with those from the UK journals and the two benchmark journals. We discuss the implications of our findings through the lens of normal science; however, we also expose some of the challenges involved when a field adopts only a normal science approach. The following sections describe our methodology and findings.

METHODOLOGY

Data Collection

We systematically read and classified every article published between 2003 and 2005 (three years) in six entrepreneurship-only journals, three published in the USA and three published in Europe.[2] We also read and classified every article published between 2003 and 2005 in two benchmark journals, both published in the USA. To examine entrepreneurship research we looked at *Journal of Business Venturing*, *Entrepreneurship Theory and Practice*, *Journal of Small Business Management*, *International Small Business Journal*, *Small Business Economics* and *Entrepreneurship & Regional Development*. For benchmark journals we examined *Administrative Science Quarterly* and the *Academy of Management Journal*, the same two journals identified by Aldrich and Baker (1997) in their study. The eight journal mission statements are presented in Appendix 2. We chose these journals because they are well-regarded outlets for entrepreneurship publication or highly esteemed management journals. Specifically, according to the 2011 Social Science Citation Index, *Journal of Business Venturing* has an impact factor score[3] of 3.062, *Entrepreneurship Theory and Practice* has an impact factor score of 2.542 and *Journal of Small Business Management* has an impact factor score of 1.392. At the time of the study, they were the three highest-ranked US entrepreneurship-specific journals. *Small Business Economics* has an impact factor score of 1.549, *International Small Business Journal* is ranked at 1.492 and *Entrepreneurship & Regional Development* has an impact factor score of 0.943, indicating that they are well-regarded European-based entrepreneurship journals. Finally, *Administrative Science Quarterly* has an impact factor score of 4.212 and the *Academy of Management Journal* has an impact factor score of 5.608, suggesting that they are appropriate journals to use when benchmarking other scholarly research. In all, the eight journals we tracked over the 2003–05 period yielded a total of 1046 articles, of which 674 came from the entrepreneurship journals and the remaining 372 came from the leading management journals.

Following Aldrich and Baker's classification system (1997, p. 382, Table 17.2.), we excluded from the initial dataset any literature reviews, methods topics, articles on entrepreneurship education, journalistic and armchair theorizing pieces. In addition, we excluded articles that presented other forms of scholarship (e.g. book reviews, editorials, opinion pieces, introductions to special issues, teaching case studies and accompanying teaching notes). This selection process reduced our initial dataset of 1046 articles by 391 articles (37.38 percent), rendering a dataset of 655 empirical articles, which formed the basis for our subsequent exploration. Of these, 449 came from the entrepreneurship journals and thus comprised our usable study sample, and 206 came from the benchmark journals and thus comprised the 'control group' for the study. Table 4.2 illustrates the scope of the review.

Table 4.2   Scope of the review

Journal	Number of articles (2003–05)			
	Total	%	Empirical	%
Journal of Business Venturing	123	11.8	80	12.2
Entrepreneurship Theory and Practice	77	7.4	27	4.1
Journal of Small Business Management	87	8.3	76	11.6
Small Business Economics	187	17.9	157	24.0
International Small Business Journal	128	12.2	54	8.2
Entrepreneurship & Regional Development	72	6.9	55	8.4
Academy of Management Journal	194	18.5	161	24.6
Administrative Science Quarterly	178	17	45	6.9
Total	1046	100	655	100.0

Data Coding

To ensure comparability of results, we followed the classification scheme developed by Aldrich and Baker (1997, Tables 17.3 and 17.4, respectively). More specifically, we coded for *research method used* (survey, public database, ethnography, simulation, case study or other empirical method); *research design* (longitudinal data collection, more than one nation studied, whether or not the study includes a nation besides the USA, whether or not the study identifies a homogeneous population, explicitly samples from an identifiable sampling frame); *topic area* (hypothesis testing, negative findings and reliability assessment); *sample response rate*; *sample size*; and *statistical method* implemented. Because of the active conversation in the entrepreneurship field around the appropriate unit of analysis (Brush et al., 2008; Davidsson and Wiklund, 2001), we included an additional coding category, *unit of analysis*.

The four principal investigators were assigned to code two journals each. To ensure coding reliability, we trained three research assistants, who independently coded all 674 articles from the six entrepreneurship journals comprising the initial study sample. We then calculated inter-rater reliability, implementing the kappa procedure in STATA, and utilized the linear weighted Cohen's kappa statistics for the ordinal categories.[4] The percentage agreement across 13 of the 14 coding categories ranged between 75.89 percent and 93.63 percent, well above the recommended 0.70 threshold (Stemler, 2004). In only one of the 14 categories, whether or not the study identifies a homogeneous population, the percentage agreement between the principal investigators and the secondary coders was below 70 percent, at 62.97 percent. The results in this category, therefore, need to be interpreted with caution.

Analytical Procedure

We started by calculating the frequencies of different research methods, research designs, topic areas, response rates, sample sizes, statistical methods and units of analysis, as reported in the 655 articles comprising our dataset. To address the first part of our research question we compared the frequencies for the three US-based entrepreneurship journals in the 2003–05 period with the frequencies reported by Aldrich and Baker (1997, tables 17.3 and 17.4) for the 1991–95 period. We next compared the frequencies for the two benchmark journals in the 2003–05 period with the frequencies reported by Aldrich and Baker (1997). For each comparison, we ran a two-sample test of proportions, implementing the *prtesti* procedure in STATA. To address the second part of our research question, we cross-tabulated the frequencies for different research methods, research designs, topic areas, response rates, sample sizes, statistical methods and units of analysis by source (e.g. US-based entrepreneurship journals, European entrepreneurship journals and benchmark journals) and ran chi-square tests for all our cross-tabulations, implementing the SPSS procedure.

Sample Description

As noted in the previous section, we investigated the universe of empirical research published in six entrepreneurship and two leading management scholarly journals over three years (2003–05), with the number of articles per year increasing over time in both types of sources. More specifically, 29.2 percent of the entrepreneurship articles we reviewed were published in 2003, 32.7 percent were published in 2004 and 38.1 percent were published in 2005. Similarly, in the leading management journals, 29.6 percent of the articles were published in 2003, 34.5 percent in 2004, and 35.9 percent in 2005. Out of the 449 empirical articles that constituted our final sample, *JBV* provided 12.2 percent, *ETP* provided 4.1 percent, *JSBM* provided 11.6 percent, *ISBJ* and *ERD* provided 8.2 percent and 8.4 percent, respectively, while *SBE* provided the remaining 24.0 percent (see Table 4.2). The disproportionate representation of the six journals in the sample raises questions about the effects of publishing frequency and journal editorial foci on our results. We explore this issue through sensitivity analysis, reported at the end of the results and discussion section.

RESULTS AND DISCUSSION

Research Method

From a methodological perspective, entrepreneurship empirical research did not change substantially over the ten-year period between 1995 and 2005, as reported in Table 4.3. Of note is the decrease in the proportion of survey research methodology, which dominated the 1991–95 time period at 74.6 percent, and remains the most popular research methodology, but accounts for a significantly lower 54.1 percent in the 2003–05 period. The only other significant change in proportions came from the increased percentage of simulations (a statistically significant, but not substantively significant change, since the percentage increased from 0 percent to a still very low 0.5 percent, or two studies in six journals over three years). There is a significant shift in research methods over the same period in the benchmark journals. While survey-based methodology retained its popularity at exactly the same level (43.7 percent in both periods), in 2003–05 the leading management journals published significantly fewer studies based on public databases, ethnography or simulations, while significantly increasing the proportion of case studies. In fact, Aldrich and Baker (1997) reported no case studies published in *AMJ/ASQ* over the 1991–95 period, while we identified 22 such studies over the 2003–05 period (10.7 percent of the total 206 *AMJ/ASQ* empirical articles).[5]

Table 4.3 Research methods

Methodology†	US entrepreneurship journals 2003–05	European entrepreneurship journals 2003–05	Benchmark journals 2003–05	US entrepreneurship journals‡ 1991–95	Benchmark journals‡ 1990–95	Two-sample test of proportions US journals 1990–95 2003–05	Two-sample test of proportions Benchmark journals 1990–95 2003–05
	%	%	%	%	%	z-score	z-score
Survey	54.1	40.6	43.7	74.6	43.7	3.44**	0.00
Public database	20.2	30.8	33.5	14.1	44.7	–1.3	2.15*
Ethnography	4.9	4.5	0.0	3.9	2.9	–0.39	2.46*
Simulation	0.5	1.1	2.4	0.0	7.7	–2.33*	2.35*
Case study	10.4	15.8	10.7	7.8	0.0	–0.73	–4.13***
Other empirical	9.8	7.1	9.7	n.a.	n.a.		
Total %	99.9	99.9	100.0	100.5	99.0		
	(n = 183)	(n = 266)	(n = 206)	(n = 105)	(n = 150)		

Notes:

† Pearson chi-square test for differences in research methods (df = 10) = 28.272**.

* Significant at $p < 0.05$, ** significant at $p < 0.01$, *** significant at $p < 0.001$.

‡ Data from Aldrich and Baker (1998, table 17.3); percentages recalculated after excluding the 'journalistic' and 'armchair' categories, which we coded as 'nonempirical'.

While there was little change in the preferences for particular types of research methodologies across the ten years of our study, the methodologies used within the entrepreneurship field remain relatively diverse. Our findings indicate that there are highly significant differences in the categories of research methodologies across journal types (Pearson chi-square test for differences in research methods across the three journals sources in the 2003–05 period = 28.272, p < 0.01). Even though survey-based research continues to dominate empirical scholarship, this prevalence is more pronounced in the US-based journals, while European outlets publish higher percentages of case studies and studies based on secondary sources (public databases).

Research Design

Research design issues involve decisions such as those that are made about the population of interest, data collection tradeoffs and sampling. When we compare research designs between 1995 and 2005 (see Table 4.4), we see a significant increase in the proportion of longitudinal studies (from 5 percent to 27.9 percent), identification of a homogeneous study population (from 16 percent to 53 percent), explicit hypothesis testing (from 48 percent to 60.7 percent), reporting of negative findings (from 17 percent to 34.4 percent), utilizing sample sizes of over 1000 observations (from 7 percent to 26.2 percent), and the use of more sophisticated statistical analysis procedures, such as complex regression, event history or formal network models (from 14 percent to 28.4 percent and from 1 percent to 10.4 percent, respectively).

Compared to the progress in the benchmark journals over the same period, the only area in which entrepreneurship appears to be under-performing is reliability assessment. In the 1991–95 time period, reliability assessments were reported in 31 percent of the empirical articles published in entrepreneurship journals and 42 percent of the articles published in leading management journals. Ten years later, the gap widened even further. Reliability assessments were included in only 24 percent of the entrepreneurship papers (a significant decrease) compared with 62.6 percent of the articles published in leading management journals. Such a finding is likely consistent with the decline in survey-based methods.

Sample response rates are another area of mixed results. While only 2.2 percent of entrepreneurship research articles in 2003–05 reported response rates in the 0–4 percent category, down from 32 percent in the 1991–95 time period (a highly significant decrease), response rates above 50 percent also decreased significantly (from 16 percent to 6 percent in the 50–74 percent category and from 11 percent to 2.7 percent in the 75–100 percent category). For survey-based research, in particular, the comparison with the

Table 4.4 Research design

Methodology	US entrepreneurship journals 2003–05	European entrepreneurship journals 2003–05	Benchmark journals 2003–05	US entrepreneurship journals[‡] 1990–95	Benchmark journals[‡] 1990–95	Pearson chi-square test (df)	Two-sample test of proportions	
							US journals 1990–95 2003–05	Benchmark journals 1990–95 2003–05
	%	%	%	%	%		z-score	z-score
Research design								
Longitudinal data collection	27.9	42.1	37.4	5.0	25.0	9.535** (2)	−4.72***	−2.47*
More than one nation studied	12.0	12.8	8.7	14.0	8.0	2.028 (2)	0.49	−0.24
Includes a nation besides USA	43.2	83.1	24.8	40.0	18.0	169.873*** (2)	−0.53	−1.53
Identifies a homogeneous population	53.0	47.4	68.0	16.0	46.0	20.526*** (2)	−6.18***	−4.16***
Explicitly samples from an identifiable sampling frame	47.5	50.4	51.9	62.0	87.0	0.767 (2)	2.37*	6.94***
Topic area								
Hypothesis testing?	60.7	22.6	87.9	48.0	83.0	204.059*** (2)	−2.09*	−1.31

Methodology	US entrepreneurship journals 2003–05	European entrepreneurship journals 2003–05	Benchmark journals 2003–05	US entrepreneurship journals[‡] 1990–95	Benchmark journals[‡] 1990–95	Pearson chi-square test (df)	Two-sample test of proportions	
							US journals 1990–95 2003–05	Benchmark journals 1990–95 2003–05
	%	%	%	%	%		z-score	z-score
Negative findings?	34.4	12.8	52.9	17.0	17.0	87.765*** (2)	–3.16**	–6.90***
Reliability assessment	24.0	8.3	62.6	31.0	42.0	168.008*** (2)	1.29	–3.85***
Sample response rate						66.214*** (8)		
0–4	2.2	1.9	0.5	32.0	8.0		6.77***	3.43***
5–49	39.9	26.3	18.0	42.0	32.0		0.28	2.19*
50–74	6.0	3.0	13.1	16.0	34.0		2.38*	3.51***
75–100	2.7	3.8	14.1	11.0	26.0		2.59**	2.06*
n.a.	49.2	65.1	54.4	n.a	n.a.			
Sample size						44.236*** (12)		
1–4	4.4	5.3	1.9	11.0	7.0		2.14*	2.38*
5–24	8.2	10.9	4.4	6.0	8.0		–0.69	1.4
25–99	13.1	12.4	15.5	21.0	22.0		1.76	1.53
100–249	18.0	12.0	29.6	31.0	30.0		2.53*	0.08

250–999	24.6	16.9	22.8	25.0	24.0		0.08	0.26
1000+	26.2	35.3	23.3	7.0	10.0		−3.98***	−3.15**
n.a.	5.4	7.1	2.4	n.a.	n.a.			
Statistical methods						67.390*** (12)		
None	14.2	18.8	4.4	17.0	1.0		0.65	−1.87
Simple percentagess or raw numbers	5.5	9.4	4.4	18.0	5.0		3.45***	0.27
Chi-square	4.9	3.4	0.5	8.0	3.0		1.09	1.89
T-tests, ANOVA, factor analysis	15.8	10.9	5.3	24.0	10.0		1.76	1.69
Ordinary least squares	20.8	22.2	23.8	17.0	16.0		−0.81	−1.8
Other regression, discriminant analysis	28.4	22.9	35.0	14.0	49.0		−2.88**	2.65**
Nonrecursive, event history, or formal network models	10.4	12.4	26.7	1.0	8.0		−3.14**	−4.46***
Other statistical methods	n.a.	n.a.	n.a.	2.0	8.0			
Unit of analysis						95.532*** (8)		
Individual	29.5	24.1	27.2	n.a.	n.a.			
Team	2.7	0.4	12.6	n.a.	n.a.			
Firm	60.7	65.0	33.5	n.a.	n.a.			
Industry	0.0	0.4	2.4	n.a.	n.a.			

Methodology	US entrepreneurship journals 2003–05	European entrepreneurship journals 2003–05	Benchmark journals 2003–05	US entrepreneurship journals[‡] 1990–95	Benchmark journals[‡] 1990–95	Pearson chi-square test (df)	Two-sample test of proportions	
							US journals 1990–95 2003–05	Benchmark journals 1990–95 2003–05
	%	%	%	%	%		z-score	z-score
Other	7.1	10.2	24.3	n.a.	n.a.			

Notes:

* Significant at $p < 0.05$, ** significant at $p < 0.01$, *** significant at $p < 0.001$.
‡ Data from Aldrich and Baker (1998, table 17.4).

benchmark journals is quite revealing. Over two-thirds (68.7 percent) of the entrepreneurship studies in 2003–05 reported response rates in the 5–49 percent category, compared with one-third (33.3 percent) of the studies published in benchmark journals, and only 4 percent of the entrepreneurship studies reported response rates in the 75–100 percent category, compared with over a quarter (25.6 percent) of the benchmark studies.

The field is similarly diverse in its approaches to research design. In fact, the chi-square tests revealed significant differences across the types of journal sources in every category except 'more than one nation studied' and 'explicitly samples from an identifiable sample frame'. In particular, entrepreneurship research has been and continues to be significantly 'less parochial' (e.g. less US focused) than research published in the leading management journals.

Focusing on the differences between US-based and European-based entrepreneurship research over the 2003–05 period, we note that, understandably, European-based research tended to focus much more on nations outside the USA (83.1 percent of all studies, compared with 43.2 percent of the articles published in US journals). US-based entrepreneurship research tended to be much more hypothesis-driven (60.7 percent versus 22.6 percent, respectively). At the same time, empirical research appeared to converge around the firm at the primary level of analysis (60.7 percent of the articles published in the US journals and 65 percent of the articles published in the European journals) and in the use of increasingly sophisticated statistical tools (close to 40 percent of the articles published in US journals and over one-third of the articles published in European journals implemented complex regression, event history or formal network models).

Sensitivity Analysis

As reported in our Sample Description section and Table 4.2, the six entrepreneurship journals and the two benchmark journals were not equally represented in our sample in terms of number of articles. Thus *Small Business Economics*, an entrepreneurship journal that tends to publish articles based on secondary data sources and to implement econometric modeling techniques, accounted for over a quarter of all entrepreneurship research articles in our dataset, whereas the *Academy of Management Journal* provided over three-quarters of the benchmark articles. To better understand our findings, we reran the frequency analysis on a weighted sample, which assumed equal distribution of the articles from all sources.[6] For the entrepreneurship journals, the respective weights were calculated using the formula *Wt Journal*$_i$ = 1/6 * 449/N_i, where 449 is the total number of entrepreneurship empirical articles in our dataset and N_i is the number of

Table 4.5 Research methods weighted

Methodology	US entrepreneurship journals 2003–05	European entrepreneurship journals 2003–05	Benchmark journals 2003–05
	%	%	%
Survey	55.5	44.5	35.2
Public database	16.4	22.6	37.4
Ethnography	3.9	3.3	0.0
Simulation	0.4	0.6	1.6
Case study	9.6	22.5	11.6
Other empirical	14.1	6.4	14.2
Total %	99.9	99.9	100.0
	(n = 183)	(n = 266)	(n = 206)

Table 4.6   Research design weighted

Methodology	US entrepreneurship journals 2003–05 %	European entrepreneurship journals 2003–05 %	Benchmark journals 2003–05 %
Research design			
Longitudinal data collection	25.6	32.5	43.1
More than one nation studied	14.3	13.2	9.6
Includes a nation besides USA	45.8	86.5	23.8
Identifies a homogeneous population	52.5	51.4	62.7
Explicitly samples from an identifiable sample frame	49.6	38.4	58.0
Topic area			
Hypothesis testing?	60.3	21.5	82.6
Negative findings?	38.0	13.2	46.7
Reliability assessment	25.4	9.9	64.9
Sample response rate			
0–4	2.5	2.7	0.3
5–49	40.4	28.9	18.7
50–74	5.5	3.3	11.6
75–100	2.1	5.3	13.0
n.a.	49.4	59.8	56.4

Methodology	US entrepreneurship journals 2003–05 %	European entrepreneurship journals 2003–05 %	Benchmark journals 2003–05 %
Sample size			
1–4	3.4	6.5	2.8
5–24	7.2	15.7	4.4
25–99	11.9	13.4	13.1
100–249	15.6	12.4	29.4
250–999	24.1	18.0	19.4
1000+	28.0	26.8	28.5
n.a.	9.9	7.2	2.4
Statistical methods			
None	15.1	27.3	3.6
Simple percentages or raw numbers	4.3	12.5	8.4
Chi-square	4.7	4.3	0.3
T-tests, ANOVA, factor analysis	16.6	12.2	3.4
Ordinary least squares	18.7	14.5	17.6
Other regression, discriminant analysis	30.2	19.7	37.6
Nonrecursive, event history, formal network models	10.4	9.4	29.1
Other statistical methods			

Unit of analysis

Individual	25.0	20.0	25.4
Team	2.9	0.2	12.1
Firm	64.2	65.6	34.2
Industry	0.0	0.6	5.6
Other	7.9	13.7	22.7

articles coming from *Journal_i*. Similarly, for the benchmark journals, the weights were calculated using the formula $Wt\ Journal_j = 1/2 * 206/N_j$, where 206 is the total number of benchmark empirical articles in our dataset and N_j is the number of articles coming from *Journal_j*. The results for research methodologies and research design on the weighted sample are presented in Tables 4.5 and 4.6, respectively.

We note that, in the 'weighted' dataset, surveys remain the most popular research method followed in both the US and European entrepreneurship journals. However, the European entrepreneurship journals exhibited higher reliance on the case study method (22.5 percent of all studies), suggesting that qualitative methods are more popular in Europe than in the USA. Consistent with this finding, in the area of research design we found that US journals relied more on statistical methods while in the European journals over a quarter of all studies had no statistical inference procedures.

In other words, when controlling for the editorial focus and publishing frequency of the journals, we find that the realm of entrepreneurship empirical research is even more diverse than is indicated by the raw numbers. In addition, while those researchers who implement statistical methodologies tend to use increasingly sophisticated statistical procedures, there is a substantial body of empirical entrepreneurship research that does not rely on statistical inferences at all.

IMPLICATIONS

In this chapter, we were particularly interested in exploring the research question: From a normal science perspective, are we making progress in entrepreneurship research? To do this, we first compared our US and benchmark findings with those of Aldrich and Baker (1997), and then we split our sample and compared research in US journals with research in UK journals and with the benchmark journals.

With respect to our first set of tests, our research suggests that over the 1995–2005 time period empirical research in US entrepreneurship journals appears to have made progress towards a normal science approach. This is in line with the progress made in empirical research published in the leading management journals. Recall that a normal science perspective calls for cumulative findings over time, which are generated when a group of scholars comes to accept as a worldview the research paradigm that defines both the questions that are being asked and the methods that are used to answer those questions. Our findings indicate that there is some convergence around a dominant paradigm in the entrepreneurship literature, and that, as social scientists, entrepreneurship scholars in the USA are occupied with testing the tenets of the existing paradigm.[7] This implies that at least for scholarship that is published in US journals, as a field of research, entrepreneurship is making progress on normal science dimensions using hypothesis testing, replications, rigorous design, statistical techniques and empirical data.

However, when we compare the US journals and the European journals we find a significant amount of methodological diversity. Data from the weighted sample indicate a greater use of case study methodology coupled with a lower sample size and a reduced reliance on statistical analytical techniques. This suggests that while there is convergence towards a standard set of methodological norms in the research published in the USA, there is less convergence in the research published in Europe.

We were curious as to why there is some convergence towards a normal science perspective in research published in the USA, but much less convergence in research published in Europe. We suggest several possible explanations. One possibility may be that a substantial sub-disciplinary specialty of entrepreneurship faculty members in the USA is strategy, which tends to emphasize empirical/quantitative methodologies. This would suggest that researchers in entrepreneurship are simply using the empirical techniques with which they are most familiar. Therefore adherence to a normal science perspective in the USA may be less a function of the state of the field, and more a function of the training of the scholars who are engaged in research in the field.

Another possible explanation for the shift towards normal science is that, at least in the USA, institutional norms may be more likely to reward promotion and tenure based on research that utilizes normal science methodologies. With institutions developing journal ranking lists, faculty have greater incentives to try to publish papers in top peer-reviewed journals that arguably publish a preponderance of empirical and quantitative papers. Studies based on large datasets of secondary data are easier to analyze, easier to generalize, and more likely to be published in the top-tier management journals. This would suggest that institutional standards are influencing researchers in entrepreneurship and might be pushing the field towards a normal science perspective. This raises a question: to what degree are schools encouraging faculty to base their research on large-sample empirical surveys as a pathway to tenure and promotion? And, if this trend continues, what is the implication for our field?

While these explanations offer ideas as to why there is convergence around the normal science perspective, we suggest that there may also be fundamental differences in the types of research valued across various research traditions that might help to explain the methodological differences in entrepreneurship research in Europe and the USA. Positivism, which has its roots in the natural sciences and is based on the existence of *a priori* fixed relationships within phenomena, is more widely received in the USA than in other research traditions. In contrast, interpretivism, which assumes that people create their own subjective meanings as they interact with the world around them, is a research perspective that is more popular outside of the USA. For example, Down and Cope (2010) explained the European tradition in entrepreneurship research. Given the large amount of work in European journals with foundations in the interpretive tradition, it is not surprising that there are differences in the methodologies employed in the USA and Europe. This raises a question of whether US entrepreneurship is overly biased towards theory testing while European entrepreneurship research may be biased towards theory development. If so, and if this trend continues, what would be the implications for our understanding of entrepreneurial processes and behaviors?

In a classic critique of strategic management research, Bettis (1991) suggested that strategic management is stuck in a normal science 'strait-jacket'. Bettis's commentary offers a strong basis for extending our findings. Specifically, he argued (1) that strategic management is conducting research based on the use of dated concepts, (2) that there was an ethnocentric focus to strategic management research, (3) that a focus on methods dominates theory, (4) that strategic management is merely second-class economics research, and (5) that there is a lack of prescription in strategic management research, making the research irrelevant for industry and government. On the one hand, if the above trends continue, it is possible that entrepreneurship will fall into the same trap as strategic management. On the other hand, when we take a broader look at the field of entrepreneurship, we find the existence of multiple paradigms that suggests the existence of multiple communities of scholars who are committed to different streams of research. This is not unusual given the adolescence of the field where multiple paradigms are common (Ritzer, 1975; Low, 2001). We are encouraged by these multiple communities of scholars as the social phenomena studied in entrepreneurship are quite complex and a plurality of perspectives allows the exploration of pressing entrepreneurship questions from diverse frames of reference, each with their own theoretical assumptions, methodologies and devoted adherents (Gartner, 2001, Gartner et al., 2006). There is an increasing number of specialized conferences examining populations of entrepreneurs (e.g. family businesses, women entrepreneurs) or focusing on particular topics (e.g. social entrepreneurship, cognition). Alternatively, when we look at the researchers who are attracted to the field of entrepreneurship, we find a thoughtful but independent group of scholars who, given the field's history and struggles for legitimacy, tend to be less well socialized into mainstream academia. So if academia does not accept the unique contributions of entrepreneurship scholars, these scholars are likely to move in new directions, creating new ideas and developing new models (Baker and Pollock, 2007). This suggests that entrepreneurship may be better positioned than strategic management to resist the temptation to succumb to one dominant theoretical paradigm, and therefore may continue to offer many lenses, based in multifarious academic traditions. Because of that, we do not believe that the entrepreneurship scholarship runs the risk of being similarly 'straitjacketed' by normal science.

Another question has to do with the increasing emphasis on large-sample, empirical statistical method driven studies and how this relates to current definitions and theories of entrepreneurship. If we consider the current definitions and trends in entrepreneurship that differentiate the field from other domains, such as creation (Brush et al., 2003), cognition (Mitchell et al., 2004), modes of organizing (Busenitz et al., 2003; Gartner, 2004) and effectuation (Sarasvathy, 2001), we wonder if theory-testing empirical approaches are best for understanding these aspects of entrepreneurship? Or, are we better served by theory-building, qualitative or other approaches in order to garner a more specific and insightful understanding? Arguably, studies of different manifestations of entrepreneurship may beg for the utilization of experimental designs (Chandler and Lyon, 2001) in order to infer causality, or more case studies (Perren and Ram, 2004) and narratives (Gartner, 2007) that render 'thick' descriptions (Geertz, 1973) of the phenomena of interest.

Even within the realm of empirical studies that use primarily statistical methods and study the firm as a unit of analysis, our findings found few instances of replication of studies, reliability assessment or consistent operationalization of measures. These findings are echoed in other recent reviews of research designs in entrepreneurship (e.g. Mullen et al., 2009). So, on the one hand, the field appears to follow the more established strategy paradigm in approach, but on the other hand, the convergence of research findings is minimal. Does this paradox represent a fractionation of the field or does it reflect the heterogeneity of the field, the variety of contexts, forms, levels and pathways to entrepreneurship?

Finally, how relevant is current entrepreneurship research to practitioners and entrepreneurs? Considering the perspective that topical relevance should guide the field, a focus on firm-level questions and performance may be less important to entrepreneurs struggling to assess opportunities, transform family enterprises or create social value in emerging economies. Around the world countries are creating policies to stimulate entrepreneurship as a means out of poverty, or as a vehicle for economic growth. As Zahra and Wright (2011, p. 80) argued, '[e]ntrepreneurship researchers focused on publishing in leading academic journals need to have an incentive to engage in research that speaks directly to public policy agendas'. A bias toward firm-level entrepreneurial study leaves out the self-employed individuals and 'entrepreneurial households' who are creating value for themselves and society (Davidsson and Wiklund, 2001; Carter, 2011).

In sum, in their 1997 review, Aldrich and Baker noted that '[m]ultiple voices, expressing multiple points of view and methods, contribute to the body of work reaching the outlets that were examined' (1997, p. 396). Ten years later, our statistical examination leads us to a similar conclusion. Our research suggests that progress is being made in the field of entrepreneurship from a normal science perspective; however, there are many communities of scholars within the domain of entrepreneurship who each have their own unique voice. Therefore overall entrepreneurship research remains highly methodologically diverse, with axes of convergence shaping along the level of analysis and the use of formal statistical methods.

LIMITATIONS AND CONCLUSIONS

While our study critically assessed a comprehensive number of scholarly articles in six premier journals for entrepreneurship research and in two benchmark journals over three years, as well as comparing those findings with similar research conducted approximately ten years ago, it is not without limitations, which need to be kept in mind when interpreting these findings.

While our study aims to explore the entrepreneurship research that is currently being published in the field, this review does not necessarily present a comprehensive picture of all of the current research in the field of entrepreneurship. Notably, research published in non-English-language outlets was beyond the scope of our review. Given the large amount of entrepreneurship activity in non-English-speaking transitional economies such as China, it is reasonable to assume that a great deal of entrepreneurship research is being published in languages other than English.

In addition, while our research suggests that for scholarship published in the USA, progress is being made on normal science dimensions, our analysis cannot determine whether or not these studies are cumulative or accumulating. The extent to which researchers are testing and/or retesting theories on different samples, and/or systematically linking research, cannot be determined from our investigation.

However, our study does suggest that the nature of paradigmatic debates has changed over time. In their 1997 review Aldrich and Baker noted the debate between 'traits versus non-traits' research as an example of the tension between studies using multiple paradigms. Given the focus on the firm as a unit of analysis, this debate seems to be less relevant today. A more current tension in the field is between social science and economic paradigms (Brush et al., 2003). An example of this is Alvarez and Barney's (2010) recent work, which articulates the central assumptions and themes in opportunity discovery theory rooted in economics (Shane, 2003; Kirzner, 1973) and opportunity creation theory which draws from the social sciences (Aldrich and Kenworthy, 1999; Gartner, 1985).

In conclusion, our chapter illustrates that, to date, the field has not become 'so exclusionary and paradigm driven that we kill the energy that has made this field so exciting' (Low, 2001, p. 23). However, from a normal science perspective there is some progress in scholarship that is published in the USA, suggesting that the field is converging around a dominant set of ideas.

Aldrich and Baker (1997, p. 398) argue that 'the field will be shaped by those who produce research that interests and attracts other to build on their work … not by repetitive calls to do "more ethnographic work" or "more longitudinal studies"'. They argue not for one perspective over another, but instead for a field that is known for its exemplary research. The field of entrepreneurship is gaining in popularity and legitimacy, and that suggests that as an area of inquiry it will continue to attract more exciting and more rigorous research conducted by increasingly talented and dedicated scholars.

ACKNOWLEDGMENTS

The authors would like to thank Howard Aldrich and Ted Baker for their helpful comments on an earlier version of this chapter.

NOTES

1. The four top journals are *Journal of Business Venturing*, *Small Business Economics*, *Entrepreneurship Theory and Practice* and *Journal of Small Business Management*.
2. While our objective was to replicate Aldrich and Baker's (1997) methodology, we chose not to include full-length papers published in the *Frontiers of Entrepreneurship* as we reasoned that many of these papers ultimately appear as articles in the entrepreneurship journals.
3. The journal impact factor is a measure of the frequency with which the 'average article' in a journal has been cited in a particular year. The impact factor helps in evaluating a journal's relative importance, especially when compared with other journals in the same field (ISI Web of Knowledge, 2013).
4. The linear-weighted Cohen's kappa specifies weights $1 - | i - j |/(k - 1)$, where i and j index the rows and columns of the ratings by the two raters and k is the maximum number of possible ratings (www.stata.com/help/kappa). It takes into consideration the distance

between the assigned categories, for example the degree of disagreement between the raters, and because of this property is used customarily when the categories are ordered.

5. In this study we did not elaborate on the progress of statistical methodologies. A recent paper by Dean et al. (2007) focuses on this topic and our results corroborate their findings.
6. Aldrich and Baker (1997) did not report weighted statistics so we are unable to compare our findings with theirs.
7. A discussion of the paradigms tested in entrepreneurship research is beyond the scope of this chapter.

REFERENCES

Academy of Management (2013), http://aom.org/Divisions-and-Interest-Groups/Entrepren eurtship/Entrepreneurship.aspx.
Aldrich, H.E. and Baker, T. (1997), 'Blinded by the cites? Has there been progress in entrepreneurship research?', in D.L. Sexton and R.W. Smilor (eds), *Entrepreneurship 2000*, Chicago, IL: Upstart Publishing, pp. 377–400.
Aldrich, H.E. and Kenworthy, A. (1999), 'The accidental entrepreneur: Campbellian antinomies and organizational foundings', in Joel A.C. Baum and Bill McKelvey (eds), *Variations in Organization Science: In Honor of Donald T. Campbell*, Thousand Oaks, CA: Sage, pp. 19–33.
Aldrich, H.E. and Kim, P. (2007), 'Small worlds, infinite possibilities? How social networks affect entrepreneurial team formation and search', *Strategic Entrepreneurship Journal*, **1**(1–2): 147–66.
Aldrich, H.E., Carter, N. and Reuf, M. (2004), 'Teams', in W.B. Gartner, K.G. Shaver, N.M. Carter and P. Reynolds (eds), *Handbook of Entrepreneurial Dynamics: The Processes of Business Creation*, Thousand Oaks, CA: Sage, pp. 299–310.
Alvarez, S.A. and Barney, J.B. (2010), 'Entrepreneurship and epistemology: the philosophical underpinnings of the study of entrepreneurial opportunities', *The Academy of Management Annals*, **4**(1): 557–83.
Baker, T. and Pollock, T.G. (2007), 'Making the marriage work: the benefits of strategy's takeover of entrepreneurship for strategic organization', *Strategic Organization*, **5**(3): 297–312.
Baron, R. (2007), 'Behavioral and cognitive factors in entrepreneurship: entrepreneurs as the active element in new venture creation', *Strategic Entrepreneurship Journal*, **1**(1)2: 167–83.
Bettis, R. (1991), 'Strategic management and the straightjacket: an editorial essay', *Organization Science*, **2**: 315–19.
Brush, C.G., Duhaime, I.M., Gartner, W.B., Steward, A., Katz, J.A., Hitt, M.A., Alvarez, S.A., Meyer, G.D. and Venkataraman, S. (2003), 'Doctoral education in the field of entrepreneurship', *Journal of Management*, **29**(3): 309–11.
Brush, C.G., Edelman, L.F. and Manolova, T.S. (2008), 'Properties of emerging organizations: an empirical test', *Journal of Business Venturing*, **23**(5): 547–66.
Burrell, G. and Morgan, G. (1979), *Sociological Paradigms and Organisational Analysis: Elements of the Sociology of Corporate Life*, London: Heinemann.
Busenitz, L.W., West, G.P., Shepard, D., Nelson, T., Chandler, G.N. and Zacharakis, A. (2003), 'Entrepreneurship research in emergence: past trends and future directions', *Journal of Management*, **29**(3): 285–308.
Carter, S. (2011), 'The rewards of entrepreneurship: exploring the incomes, wealth, and economic well-being of entrepreneurial households', *Entrepreneurship Theory and Practice*, **35**(1): 39–55.

Chandler, G.N. and Lyon, D.W. (2001), 'Issues of research design and construct measurement in entrepreneurship research: the past decade', *Entrepreneurship Theory and Practice*, **25**(4): 101–13.

Chua, W.F. (1986), 'Radical developments in accounting thought', *The Accounting Review*, **61**: 601–32.

Davidsson, P. (2004), *Researching Entrepreneurship*, New York: Springer.

Davidsson, P. (2007), 'Strategies for dealing with heterogeneity in entrepreneurship research', paper presented at the Academy of Management 2007 Annual Meeting: Doing Well By Doing Good, 3–8 August, Philadelphia, USA.

Davidsson, P. and Wiklund, J. (2001), 'Levels of analysis in entrepreneurship research: current research practice and suggestions for the future', *Entrepreneurship Theory and Practice*, Summer: 81–99.

Davidsson, P. and Honig, B. (2003), 'The role of social and human capital among nascent entrepreneurs', *Journal of Business Venturing*, **18**(3): 301–31.

Dean, M.A., Shook, C.L. and Payne, G.T. (2007), 'The past, present and future of entrepreneurship research: data analytic trends and training', *Entrepreneurship Theory and Practice*, July: 601–18.

Delmar, F., Davidsson, P. and Gartner, W. (2003), 'Arriving at the high growth firm', *Journal of Business Venturing*, **18**(2): 189–216.

Down, S. (2013), 'The distinctiveness of the European tradition in entrepreneurship research', *Entrepreneurship & Regional Development*, **25**(1–2): 1–4.

Eckhardt, J.T. and Shane, S.A. (2003), 'Opportunities and entrepreneurship', *Journal of Management*, **29**(3): 333–49.

Forbes, D.P. (1999), 'Cognitive approaches to new venture creation', *International Journal of Management Reviews*, **1**(4): 415–25.

Gartner, W.B. (1985), 'A conceptual framework for describing the phenomenon of new venture creation', *Academy of Management Review*, **10**(4): 696–706.

Gartner, W.B. (2001), 'Is there an elephant in entrepreneurship? Blind assumptions in theory development', *Entrepreneurship Theory and Practice*, **25**(4): 27–39.

Gartner, W.B. (2007), 'Entrepreneurial narrative and a science of the imagination', *Journal of Business Venturing*, **22**(5): 613–27.

Gartner, W.B., Shaver, K.G., Carter, N.M. and Reynolds, P. (2004) (eds), *Handbook of Entrepreneurial Dynamics: The Processes of Business Creation*, Thousand Oaks, CA: Sage.

Gartner, W.B., Davidsson, P. and Zahra, S.A. (2006), 'Are you talking to me? The nature of community in entrepreneurship scholarship', *Entrepreneurship Theory and Practice*, May: 321–31.

Geertz, C. (1973), *The Interpretation of Cultures*, New York: Basic Books.

Grant, P. and Perren, L. (2002), 'Small business and entrepreneurial research: meta-theories, paradigms and prejudices', *International Small Business Journal*, 20(2): 185–211.

Guba, E.G. and Lincoln, Y.S. (1994), 'Competing paradigms in qualitative research', in N.K. Denzin and Y.S. Lincoln (eds), *Handbook of Qualitative Research*, Vol. 2, London: Sage, pp. 163–94.

Hsu, D.H. (2004), 'What do entrepreneurs pay for venture capital affiliation?', *Journal of Finance*, **59**(4): 1805–6.

ISI Web of Knowledge (2013), Thomson Reuters.

Katz, J. and Boal, K. (2002), http://www.marketingtechie.com/articles/mtart20020307.pdf. 2002.

Kirzner, I. (1973), *Competition and Entrepreneurship*, Chicago, IL: University of Chicago Press.

Kuhn, T.S. (1962), *The Structure of Scientific Revolutions*, Chicago, IL: University of Chicago Press.

Kuhn, T.S. (1970), *The Structure of Scientific Revolutions*, at http://en.wikipedia.org/wiki/The_Structure_of_Scientific_Revolutions.

Low, M.B. (2001), 'The adolescence of entrepreneurship research: specification of purpose', *Entrepreneurship Theory and Practice*, Summer: 17–25.

Low, M.B. and MacMillan, I.C. (1988), 'Entrepreneurship: past research and future challenges', *Journal of Management*, **14**(2): 139–61.

Mitchell, R.K., Busenitz, L.W., Lant, T., McDougall, P.P., Morse, E.A. and Smith, J.B. (2004), 'The distinctive and inclusive domain of entrepreneurial cognition research', *Entrepreneurship Theory and Practice*, Winter: 505–18.

Mone, M.A. and McKinley, W. (1993), 'The uniqueness value and its consequences for organization studies', *Journal of Management Inquiry*, **2**(3): 284–96.

Mullen, M.R., Budeva, D.G. and Doney, P.M. (2009), 'Research methods in the leading small business-entrepreneurship journals: a critical review with recommendations for future research', *Journal of Small Business Management*, **47**(3): 287–307.

Perren, L. and Ram, M. (2004), 'Case-study method in small business and entrepreneurship research: mapping boundaries and perspectives', *International Small Business Journal*, **22**(1): 83–101.

Ritzer, G. (1975), 'Sociology: a multiple paradigm science', *American Sociologist*, **10**: 156–67.

Sarasvathy, S. (2001), 'Causation and effectuation: toward a theoretical shift from economic inevitability to entrepreneurial contingency', *Academy of Management Review*, **26**(2): 243–62.

Shane, S.A. (2003), *A General Theory of Entrepreneurship: The Individual–Opportunity Nexus*, Cheltenham, UK and Northampton, MA, USA: Edward Elgar Publishing.

Shane, S. and Venkataraman, S. (2000), 'The promise of entrepreneurship as a field of research', *Academy of Management Review*, 25(1): 217–26.

Short, J., Ketchen, D., Coombs, J. and Ireland, D. (2010), 'Research methods in entrepreneurship: opportunities and challenges', *Organizational Research Methods*, **13** (1): 6–15.

Sorenson, O. and Stuart, T.E. (2008), 'Entrepreneurship: a field of dreams?', *Academy of Management Annals*, **2**(1): 517–43.

Stemler, S.E. (2004), 'A comparison of consensus, consistency, and measurement approaches to estimating interrater reliability', *Practical Assessment, Research and Evaluation*, **9**(4). Retrieved 11 April 2006, http://PAREonline.net/getvn.asp?v=9&n=4.

Venkataraman, S. (1997), 'The distinctive domain of entrepreneurship research', in J. Katz (ed.), *Advances in Entrepreneurship Research, Firm Emergence and Growth*, Vol. 3, Greenwich, CT: JAI Press, pp. 119–38.

Wiklund, J. and Shepherd, D. (2003), 'Knowledge-based resources, entrepreneurial orientation, and the performance of small and medium-sized businesses', *Strategic Management Journal*, **24**(13): 1307–14.

Wiklund, J., Davidsson, P., Audretsch, D.B. and Karlsson, C. (2011), 'The future of entrepreneurship research', *Entrepreneurship Theory and Practice*, **35**(1): 1–9.

Zahra, S.A. and Wright, M. (2011), 'Entrepreneurship's next act', *Academy of Management Perspectives*, **25**(4): 67–83.

APPENDIX 1 DESCRIPTION OF RESEARCH METHODOLOGY CATEGORIES*

Survey: Survey sampling of larger populations based on questionnaires, tests, interviews or a combination thereof.

Public databases: Analysis of data from public or private archival sources, e.g. Dun & Bradstreet credit files and industry databases.

Ethnography (field study): Direct and indirect observation of phenomena in natural settings that is longitudinal in nature.

Computer simulation or modeling: Mathematical theory-building allowing manipulation of variables in a non-experimental way.

Case study: An intensive but non-ethnographic study of a single organization, a set of organizations or an industry.

Other empirical: Empirical studies not included in the categories above.

APPENDIX 2 JOURNAL MISSION STATEMENTS†

Academy of Management Journal

The *Academy of Management Journal* (*AMJ*) is the flagship empirical journal in management, and has been indispensable reading for management scholars for more than five decades. *AMJ* articles test, extend or build theory and contribute to management practice using a variety of empirical methods (e.g. quantitative, qualitative, field, laboratory, meta-analytic and combination). *AMJ* articles are regularly cited in the major business media, including *The New York Times*, *The Economist*, *The Wall Street Journal*, *The Washington Post*, *Business Week* and *Fortune*.

Administrative Science Quarterly

Administrative Science Quarterly (*ASQ*) has been at the cutting edge of organizational studies since the field emerged. This top-tier journal regularly publishes the best theoretical and empirical papers based on dissertations and on the evolving and new work of more established scholars, as well as interdisciplinary work in organizational theory, and informative book reviews.

---

* Adapted from Aldrich and Baker (1997).
† Based on the mission statement (description and/or aims and scope) as stated on the journal website (accessed January 24, 2013).

Entrepreneurship & Regional Development

Entrepreneurship & Regional Development is unique in that it addresses the central factors in economic development – entrepreneurial vitality and innovation – as local and regional phenomena. It provides a multidisciplinary forum for researchers and practitioners in the field of entrepreneurship and small-firm development and for those studying and developing the local and regional context in which entrepreneurs emerge, innovate and establish the new economic activities that drive economic growth and create new economic wealth and employment. The journal focuses on the diverse and complex characteristics of local and regional economies that lead to entrepreneurial vitality and endow the large and small firms within them with international competitiveness.

Entrepreneurship Theory and Practice

Entrepreneurship Theory and Practice is a leading scholarly journal in the field of entrepreneurship studies and the official journal of the US Association for Small Business and Entrepreneurship (USASBE). The journal's mission is to publish original conceptual and empirical papers that contribute to the advancement of the field of entrepreneurship. Topics include, but are not limited to: national and international studies of enterprise creation; small business management; family-owned businesses; minority issues in small business and entrepreneurship; research methodologies; venture financing; corporate and non-profit entrepreneurship.

International Small Business Journal

The *International Small Business Journal* (*ISBJ*) publishes the highest-quality original research papers on small business and entrepreneurship. The *ISBJ* attracts submissions from international academics focusing upon theoretical, empirical, policy and practitioner issues within the fields of small business and entrepreneurship. Articles published in the *ISBJ* are of importance to academics, policy makers, practitioners and analysts in government and organizations seeking to understand small businesses, entrepreneurial processes and outcomes.

Journal of Business Venturing

The *Journal of Business Venturing: A Journal Dedicated to Entrepreneurship* provides a scholarly forum for sharing useful and interesting theories, narratives and interpretations of the antecedents, mechanisms, and/or consequences of entrepreneurship.

This multidisciplinary, multifunctional, and multicontextual journal aspires to deepen our understanding of the entrepreneurial phenomenon in its myriad of forms. The journal publishes entrepreneurship research from

(1) the disciplines of economics, psychology and sociology, and welcomes research from other disciplines such as anthropology, geography, history and so on, (2) the functions of finance/accounting, management, marketing and strategy, and welcomes research from other functions such as operations, information technology, public policy, medicine, law, music and so on, and (3) the contexts of international and sustainability (environmental and social), and welcomes research from other contexts such as high uncertainty, dynamism, time pressured, emotional and so on.

Journal of Small Business Management

The primary purpose of the *Journal of Small Business Management* (*JSBM*) is to publish scholarly research articles in the fields of small-business management and entrepreneurship. As the official journal of the International Council for Small Business (ICSB), the *JSBM* is recognized as a primary instrument for projecting and supporting the goals and objectives of this organization, which include scholarly research and the free exchange of ideas. The journal, which is circulated in 60 countries around the world, is a leader in the field of small-business research.

Small Business Economics

Entrepreneurship is becoming increasingly important as a scholarly field. *Small Business Economics* provides an invaluable forum for research and scholarship focusing on the role of entrepreneurship and small business. The journal has a broad scope and focuses on multiple dimensions of entrepreneurship, including entrepreneurs' characteristics, new ventures and innovation, and firms' life cycles, as well as the role played by institutions and public policies within local, regional, national and international contexts. *Small Business Economics* publishes theoretical, empirical and conceptual papers and encourages interdisciplinary and cross-disciplinary research from a broad spectrum of disciplines and related fields, including economics, finance, management, psychology, regional studies, sociology and strategy.

5. Experimental methods in entrepreneurship research

Kelly G. Shaver

> Speculation is valuable and may provide good hunches, but hunches are still hunches and must be regarded as tentative answers. Theory is also valuable in raising hypotheses or tentative answers to problems. Tentative answers can become definitive answers, however, only when tested by empirical research ...
> Experiments are particular ways of making observations.
>
> Edwards (1954, pp. 259–60)

In the early 1990s Ray Bagby, then the publisher of *Entrepreneurship Theory and Practice*, organized an 'Interdisciplinary Conference on Entrepreneurship Theory' that was co-sponsored by Baylor University and the University of Baltimore. The purpose of the conference was to bring various disciplinary perspectives to the study of entrepreneurship. Results of the conference were published in two special issues of the journal, with Lanny Herron, Harry Sapienza and Deborah Smith-Cook as issue editors. The first special issue (1991, Vol. 16, No. 2) included a paper about theorizing in entrepreneurship and articles from the disciplinary perspectives of psychology, sociology, anthropology and economics. The second special issue (1992, Vol. 16, No. 3) concentrated on approaches from the business disciplines of organization behavior, marketing, finance and strategic management, concluding with a paper on the process of researching entrepreneurship.

In that last paper, Hofer and Bygrave (1992, p. 93) presented a set of characteristics of the entrepreneurial process. In part they argued that (a) the process 'is initiated by an act of human volition', (b) 'involves a change of state', (c) 'is a dynamic process' and (d) 'involves numerous antecedent variables'. Together these elements suggest the benefits of longitudinal designs that include relatively detailed qualitative and quantitative information on the psychological characteristics of the target entrepreneurs. Although Hofer and Bygrave included experimental designs in a list of possible research methods, they noted that 'the numerous antecedent variables associated with entrepreneurial processes make it difficult to employ matched pair or controlled variable [experimental] comparisons' (ibid., p. 94).

Much the same conclusion would seem to follow from the work of Chandler and Lyon (2001). These authors set out to review the research designs employed in nine entrepreneurship journals from 1989 through 1999. Most of the studies reviewed were published either in *Entrepreneurship Theory and Practice* (*n* = 137) or the *Journal of Business Venturing* (*n* = 210), with all others contributing the remaining 69. Two raters judged whether each article was empirical or conceptual, what data sources were used, what reliability and validity procedures were used, what statistical designs were used, whether the effects were direct or contingent, and whether the studies were longitudinal or cross-sectional. Roughly 70 percent of the studies considered reported some empirical component. Among these, roughly 300 studies, nearly two-thirds, used paper surveys, another quarter used interviews, but only nine studies used experiments.

A more recent review of entrepreneurship research reinforces the impression that experimentation is rarely the method of choice for entrepreneurship researchers. Brush et al. (2008) examined every article appearing between 2003 and 2005 inclusive in two journals published in the USA (*Entrepreneurship Theory and Practice* and *Journal of Business Venturing*) and two published in Europe (*International Small Business Journal* and *Small Business Economics*). There were 389 articles in the final sample. The primary goal of the review was to compare articles on the nature of the independent variable, the unit of analysis for the dependent variable, whether the dependent variable was performance based, the sample size, data collection method and analysis procedures. Results showed that studies at the firm level predominated (roughly one-third of all articles) with individual-level studies constituting only 11 percent of the total. Among the individual-level studies, only one of 28 included some measure of performance as one of the dependent variables. More important for our present purposes, only two of the 389 were experiments.

Another review at approximately the same time covered all 665 articles published in *Entrepreneurship Theory and Practice*, the *Journal of Business Venturing* and the *Journal of Small Business Management* between 2001 and February 2008 (Mullen et al., 2009). This review organized its conclusions around the four kinds of validity outlined by Cook and Campbell (1979). The first of these is statistical conclusion validity, the sensitivity of the procedures to unearth a real covariation between two variables of interest. The second is construct validity, which involves testing for convergence between two measures of 'the same thing' and divergence between measures of related but conceptually different underlying constructs. Next is internal validity, the freedom from artifacts; and external validity, the ability to generalize across individuals and settings. Following the lead of Chandler and Lyon (2001), Mullen et al. found 478 empirical papers. Across the three journals there were 273 studies reporting primary data (as opposed to data from secondary sources). Of these 273, there were only 13 experiments published (2 in *JSBM*, 8 in *JBV* and 3 in *ET&P*) during the more than seven years of articles examined.

When the data in entrepreneurship research are derived from secondary sources, dependent variables are specified at the level of the firm, or when there is no strong theory being tested, experimentation is neither possible nor wise. On the other hand, in studies where the individual is the unit of analysis and there is a strong guiding theory that can be tested, experimentation can be an extremely valuable addition to the field's research armamentarium. The present chapter was designed to provide an introduction to experimental methods for entrepreneurship scholars whose disciplinary training did not routinely include these techniques among the research methods taught.

As rare as experimentation has been in entrepreneurship research, it has been a staple of research on other forms of social behavior for more than a century. The social facilitation experiment by Triplett (1897) actually preceded the first social psychology textbook (McDougall, 1908) by a decade. One of the first well-known introductions to experimentation in social psychology is the chapter by Edwards in the first *Handbook of Social Psychology*, edited by Lindzey (1954), from which the opening quote is taken. Similar treatments of experimentation can be found in subsequent volumes of the *Handbook* (Lindzey and Aronson, 1969; 1985; Gilbert et al., 1998). Experimentation is so pervasive in social psychology that at least one section on the method has been a staple in most introductory textbooks on social psychology, even when popular demand by students relegates the topic to a methodological appendix (Shaver, 1987). Cook and Campbell's book (1979) on quasi-experimentation is a frequent reading in social research methods courses, the *Journal of Experimental Social Psychology* has been published since 1966, and one of two premier disciplinary organizations in the field is the Society of Experimental Social Psychology. This chapter will review important aspects of experimentation, providing illustrations of how the various techniques have already been applied in the study of entrepreneurial action.

Experimental methods designed to examine the causes of social behavior are particularly appropriate for the study of entrepreneurship. Whatever else they might or might not be, entrepreneurs are social beings. More specifically, entrepreneurship is most definitely a form of social behavior, as it involves social cognition, attitudes, self-evaluation and interpersonal action (Shaver, 2010). In the 1954 *Handbook* (Vol. 1), Edwards provided one of the first comprehensive descriptions of the experimental approach to investigations concerning human social behavior. As noted, that chapter followed by 50 years what is frequently regarded as the first experiment on social behavior (Triplett, 1897). It precedes this submission by more than another

50 years. Central features of experimentation, however, are very much the same as they have always been.

OPERATIONALIZATION, MEASUREMENT, VALIDITY

Experimental investigations of entrepreneurial behavior necessarily reduce the richness of an entrepreneurial narrative, but they provide a corresponding increase in precision. In part, this is accomplished by the way in which entrepreneurial behavior is *operationalized*. For example, we may believe that persistence is the key to entrepreneurial success. This makes intuitive sense. Indeed, it is difficult to imagine that a business can be successfully organized (let alone sustained and grown) without tremendous persistence on the part of the entrepreneur. But persistence is a conceptual variable. The real issue is what operations are performed in order to turn that conceptual variable into something that can be measured, and replicated, by others. Is persistence defined by hours per day spent on the business? By the number of times the 'road show' has been presented? By the number of identifiable obstacles that have been overcome? By the number of friends who have been ignored? By the number of vacations not taken? By the number of people persuaded to join the venture's team? By the technical skill or financial wherewithal of those individuals? As Gartner (1989) pointed out with respect to assessment of the personal characteristics of entrepreneurs, what appear to be inconsistencies in research conclusions may be nothing more than differences in the operationalization of core concepts. For present purposes, it is worth noting that of all the research methods available, experimentation focuses the brightest light on what the investigator is actually doing, down to the last detail.

Experimentation also requires that researchers pay closer attention to how one actually measures the effects of the operations performed. In large-scale survey research samples, only those who participate in the construction of the items have the chance to consider issues of reliability and validity. Those who subsequently use the databases are at the mercy of the original designers. By contrast, any experimenter is virtually forced to consider how the variables of interest are to be measured. There are at least two reasons why this is the case.

First, the experimenter designs the entire procedure from scratch. This includes the choice of topic, the selection of variables to include, the particular methods to be employed, and the dependent variables most appropriate for assessing the research outcomes. Occasionally, especially when engaging in empirical replication of prior research, the dependent variables are 'given' at the outset. More often, however, the specific procedures must be followed by equally specific dependent measures.

Sometimes those will be rating scales of one sort or another, sometimes they will be behaviors that the respondent performs, and sometimes they will be 'behavioroid' measures that ask for a respondent's likelihood of engaging in a particular action.

The second reason has to do with the relatively small size of the respondent pool in a typical experiment. In social psychological research, a popular rule of thumb is that each experimental condition should have a minimum of 10 respondents. For example, in a 2×3 factorial design, the total number of respondents should be at least 60. Researchers accustomed to databases containing hundreds or thousands of participants often believe this to be a very small number. And indeed, if the dependent variable of interest were dichotomous, 10 respondents per cell would likely be insufficient. At the other extreme, a dependent variable expressed as a true ratio scale would provide excellent levels of precision. In between these two extremes are some of the interval scales often found in social psychological research. Many of these follow the principles first outlined by Likert (1932) for the measurement of attitudes (but now adapted to assess behaviors as well). Rather than asking respondents to indicate simple agreement/disagreement with an attitude item, Likert also asked for the degree of each (strongly, moderately, slightly), thus creating six response alternatives (typically scored on a 7-point scale because the respondent is prevented from giving an answer of 'neither agree nor disagree', which would fall between the two 'slightly' responses). Whatever their format might be, rating scales need to have enough divisions to be capable of reflecting any real differences produced by the experimental manipulations.

Finally, with regard to validity, Cook and Campbell (1979) have identified four questions that must be satisfactorily answered before one can reasonably conclude that variations in independent variable *A* have caused the observed changes in dependent variable *B*. Very briefly, these can be summarized as:

- Is there a relationship (at all) between the two variables? This is 'statistical conclusion validity', influenced by the sensitivity of the measures and the power of the statistical tests, and is part of the rationale for highly standardized experimental procedures and the inclusion of variance estimates for outcomes.
- Assuming that there is a relationship, is it causal? This is 'internal validity', the ability to rule out alternative explanations for the relationship. When the 'independent' variables and the 'dependent' variables are measured at the same time, as in much archival and survey research, high degrees of internal validity are difficult to achieve. By contrast, the particular contributions of experimentation are that the

time sequence is known, and that alternative explanations have been ruled out by virtue of random assignment of respondents to experimental conditions. A detailed discussion of ways to increase internal validity in entrepreneurship experiments has been provided by Patel and Fiet (2010).

- Assuming that the relationship is causal, what are the particular cause and effect constructs involved? This is 'construct validity', reflected in the absence of confounding by other variables at the same level of reduction. For example, if an entrepreneur's stated confidence increases following an infusion of cash for the business, is the confidence a product of the cash alone, the venture's perceived value in the eyes of the investor, or a combination of the two? Issues of construct validity are discussed in more detail in the Schjoedt, Renko and Shaver chapter in the present volume (Chapter 6). Here we need only remind readers of the convergent and divergent validity mentioned earlier. In an experiment, conditions can be created that allow direct tests of convergent and divergent validity, typically by including dependent variables on which the predicted results are expected and other dependent variables on which no differences are expected.
- Assuming there is a causal relationship from construct *A* to construct *B*, how widely can it be expected to hold? This is the issue of 'external validity', which involves the possibility to generalize across persons, settings and target populations. Experimental methods are least effective in establishing external validity, as the respondent samples are often haphazardly chosen before being randomly assigned to conditions. (It should be noted that convenience samples of any sort also present challenges to external validity.)

At this point, skeptics might point out that the methodological precision of experiments is achieved at the expense of a rich qualitative description of entrepreneurs and their achievements. It is certainly true that 'What do Sergey Brin (Google), Jeff Bezos (Amazon), Howard Schultz (Starbucks), and Fred Smith (Fedex) have in common?' is not a question that can be answered with experimental methods. Yes, of course, the financial performance of their companies can be compared, but an equally straightforward means of assessing either the founders' personal characteristics or their entrepreneurial actions remains outside the reach of experimentation, despite the historical significance of the stories. In reply, proponents of experimentation would note that no single research method would accomplish all of the discovery goals that might be desired. What experiments can do very effectively is test theoretically derived causal hypotheses.

REACTIVITY IN EXPERIMENTAL RESEARCH

Even if researchers (a) carefully state their conceptual variables, (b) describe their operations in sufficient detail to permit replication, (c) assign respondents randomly to experimental conditions, (d) exercise a level of control that will rule out extraneous variables and (e) measure their dependent variables with precision, there is one complicating factor that can only be minimized – not ruled out altogether. That factor is reactivity, the generic descriptor for biases that arise when one human being asks another human being for information.

Whether the data are gathered from survey research, personal interviews or experimental procedures, the fact remains that entrepreneurs are thinking people with their own impressions, which they may or may not be willing to share. In a survey of MBA alumni, for example, what percentage of people contacted wonder whether the requested data on personal or company performance will eventually find their way into the hands of the university development office? Does this concern affect only the response rate, or does it also affect the answers of those who do respond? In an 'in-depth interview' about venture performance, how much of the respondent's reply is influenced by his or her (a) past success or failure, (b) emotional connection with the interviewer or (c) expectations about what the 'correct' answers might be? In an experiment, how much will the respondent's answers be affected by the feeling of being a 'guinea pig'? These examples capture some of the well-known sources of reactivity in research: self-presentation, defensiveness, social desirability and what has been called 'evaluation apprehension' (Rosenberg, 1965).

If the respondent biases were not a sufficient problem in and of themselves, there are – in any face-to-face data collection procedure – important sources of invalidity brought into the situation by the researcher. Perhaps the most prominent of these is 'experimenter expectancy' (Rosenthal, 1966). Despite its label, this problem is even more likely in face-to-face interview settings than in experimentation (where elements of the experimental procedure can be altered to minimize expectancy effects). It is important to note at the outset that the potential for expectancy effects cannot be discovered by examining a written record of what the researcher said. Try this out on one of your classes: After a weekend on which your students might have been especially tempted to overindulge in alcohol, enter the classroom and immediately send half of the students out into the hallway. Next, with the inflections that might be used by a curious close friend, say to the remaining students, 'Now tell me the truth, how many of you had too much to drink over the weekend?' Count the hands. Bring the rest of the students back into the room. Ask them exactly the same words, only this time look each student in the eyes and use the inflections of a stern and disapproving parent. Again, count the hands, and be prepared for the numbers to be much lower. When your behavior implies the answer you desire, that will be the answer you receive.

In experimental methods there are several accepted ways of reducing the effects of experimenter expectancy, a few of which can also be used profitably in face-to-face interview settings. One of the obvious choices is to keep the experimenter ignorant of the particular condition to which the respondent has been randomly assigned. Specifically, for example, an experimenter could describe the research to a group of respondents by saying, 'This study deals with the ways in which entrepreneurs make decisions important for the future of their firms. You will be given a scenario to follow, and we expect you to do the best job you can to reach the goals identified in the scenario. Once we begin, I will not be able to answer any questions.' Each respondent then picks a paper containing detailed instructions out of a box. All papers ask the respondent to make a series of choices about his or her business, choices that have been structured to operationalize 'confidence in the future of the business'. Half of the papers say that the company has received an infusion of $100 000 in unexpected cash, half do not mention cash. Because the crucial variable was delivered in written form, to a group of respondents that includes people who have been told about the cash and people who have not, the experimenter's expectancy about what difference the cash infusion might make has effectively been eliminated.

Keeping a researcher ignorant of the specific conditions to which respondents have been assigned works well in an experimental setting, but not well in face-to-face interviews. A solution that can work in both instances is for the researcher to train one group of previously naive experimenters (or interviewers) to expect one sort of outcome and train another set of naive experimenters (or interviewers) to expect the opposite sort of outcome. Then both sets of assistants are sent to the lab or the field (with opposing expectations) and the data collected are averaged across the two groups of experimenters. Needless to say, the use of multiple experimenters or interviewers dramatically raises the costs associated with collecting the data.

Especially in experimental research, the key to avoiding both respondent biases and experimenter biases is to recognize their existence and plan the research in a way that minimizes their effects. As Aronson et al. (1985) suggested years ago, part of the experimenter's job is to create conditions with so much impact that they lead participants to put aside the knowledge that they are participants in favor of responding as people. This involves carefully setting the stage, so that everything that happens in the experiment seems both real and expected. Good experiments have both 'experimental realism' (the procedures are personally involving) and 'mundane realism' (what respondents are asked to do is not much different from what they might be asked to do in the world outside the laboratory).

In addition to providing a convincing and realistic situation for the respondent, other features of the design can further reduce the effects of biases. For example, experimenters should make certain that all conditions are represented in every data-collection session. Not only does this dramatically reduce experimenter effects; it also removes the confounding of conditions with sessions. As another example, questions should be asked that require contemporaneous, not retrospective, answers. Dependent variables that are closed-ended (thus forcing respondents to conform their answers to what the scales say) are preferable to open-ended dependent variables later to be combined and categorized by a researcher who knows 'the right answer'. Response scales should use labels rather than numbers to help minimize the respondent's natural curiosity about which answers are 'more important' than which others. If possible, use unobtrusive dependent variables, or dependent variables that are normally not under conscious control. Above all, standardize the research procedures as much as possible.

One example that involves substantial standardization is a Web-based study by Gatewood et al. (2002). These investigators were interested in the relationship between expectancies for entrepreneurial success and subsequent persistence on venture-related tasks. A total of 179 undergraduate business students were asked to complete an online experiment in which they were told that their entrepreneurial potential would be assessed (more about this particular design feature in a moment).

Respondents completed three tasks. First, they answered a measure of their entrepreneurial beliefs and attitudes, the Entrepreneurial Attitude Questionnaire (EAQ; Shaver et al., 1996), which included a number of subscales related to entrepreneurial performance and was later used as a covariate in the statistical design. Second, they read a business case involving two entrepreneurs who desired to start and grow a business (Vesper, 1966). After working their way through the case, by selecting Web pages each of which provided a piece of the relevant information, students were asked to say how profitable the venture might be, to identify the most important assumptions that must hold for the venture to succeed, to indicate how well suited to the venture were the entrepreneurs and their board, what the reasons for failure might be if the venture were to fail, and whether (and why) they would choose to invest their own money in the venture. Finally, students were asked to answer a questionnaire that included items assessing their own expectancies for future business success.

Three aspects of the methodology are important for present purposes. First, there is the EAQ-based "feedback" respondents received about their entrepreneurial potential. A randomly selected half of the respondents were told that their entrepreneurial potential was high, the other half were told that theirs was low. This is an experimental deception – a feature used to influence motivation in some social-psychological research but very rare in entrepreneurship research. We shall return to a detailed discussion of this technique in the next section.

The second element of the study that is relevant here is the use of a Web-based design to accomplish a number of objectives usually elusive in face-to-face experimentation. Because the manipulation of entrepreneurial potential (low or high) was accomplished by randomly determined computer-delivered feedback, experimenter effects were completely removed from the procedure. Because the number of Web pages visited, and the time spent on each, were recorded, it was (at least in theory) possible to make educated guesses about how much effort was being put into obtaining the information needed to answer the case questions. As it happens, because the procedure neglected to prevent the printing of pages, the time-on-page numbers were uninformative. Finally, because the case questions were open-ended, it was possible to collect overall word counts (as an unobtrusive measure of effort devoted to the task).

The third design feature included was what is known as an 'independent check on the manipulations'. When an experimental design fails to produce the predicted results, there are at least two obvious explanations. The uninteresting one is that the manipulations simply failed to materialize as intended: the particular operationalization used was ineffective in capturing the essence of the conceptual variables being tested. The interesting explanation is that, although the operationalization produced the psychological states intended, those states for some reason had no effect on the dependent variables. Obviously, the only way to disentangle these two explanations is to have some way to verify that the manipulations 'worked'. In this study, the independent check on manipulations was included as part of the final questionnaire. The six expectancy items included in the Panel Study of Entrepreneurial Dynamics (PSED I) were among the questions included as part of the third task respondents performed. A good thing they were: the initial manipulation of presumed entrepreneurial potential did produce differences in expectancies for business success, but none of the predicted effects on effort expended or quality of work. Thus the design created the anticipated psychological states, but these were not reflected in the respondents' behavior.

RESPONSIBLE CONDUCT OF RESEARCH

Research that involves human participants is regulated by federal laws translated into policies available from the Department of Health and Human Services (DHHS) Office for Human Research Protections (OHRP), located at http://www.hhs.gov/ohrp/policy/. Every institution that receives any federal funding is required to have an Institutional Review Board (IRB) charged with reviewing any research involving human participants. For purposes of review, 'research' is defined as systematic investigation designed to develop or contribute generalizable knowledge. By this definition data collection (either by students or faculty) designed as part of class projects and not intended for publication is typically not considered 'research'. However, any data collection for undergraduate and graduate theses, or data collection by students or faculty that is intended for conference presentation or publication, is typically considered 'research' that must be reported to the IRB. (Most institutions have electronic forms for submission of protocols.)

When registering a project as research, the investigator must provide his/her name, institutional address, date of last CITI (Collaborative Institutional Training Initiative) certification, a brief description of the rationale for the research and the methods to be employed. If the research will used data collected through interaction (including surveys) with living individuals, investigators are required to describe the participants, the way in which they will be recruited, the time commitment expected of them, and the risks and benefits associated with the research. If the participants are identifiable in any way (as would be the case in nearly all primary data collection within entrepreneurship), additional material must describe the procedures to maintain confidentiality of the data and to obtain informed consent from the participants. Normally, informed consent is obtained in writing, although in some cases verbal consent is an acceptable substitute. Whether the research is found to be 'exempt' from formal IRB review, eligible for 'expedited' review, or required to undergo 'full board review' depends on factors such as the nature of the respondent group, the presumed ability of respondents to freely give informed consent, the benefits to participants and science, and the risks associated with taking part in the research.

If the research involves deception (as did the Gatewood et al., 2002 study described above) – or even withholding information from the participants – there are additional layers in the process of obtaining IRB approval. Specifically, researchers need to (a) make a convincing case that the particular question cannot be investigated in some other way, (b) describe the information being withheld from respondents, (c) employ the least intense deception possible, (d) provide a thorough description of the debriefing to be conducted following the conclusion of the experiment, (e) indicate how participants will be given the opportunity to withdraw their consent after having heard the debriefing, and (f) detail the level of risk to participants inherent in the procedures. All of these things were done by Gatewood et al. (2002). Given the additional requirements that accompany a design involving deception, it is not surprising that most of the recent experimental work in entrepreneurship investigates cognitive processes that can be studied without deception (e.g. Burmeister-Lamp et al., 2012; Haynie et al., 2012; Welpe et al., 2012) or by asking respondents to imagine themselves in a setting designed to evoke one sort of emotion or another (e.g. Foo, 2011). One very interesting exception is the recommendation by Aguinis and Lawal (2012) to conduct field experiments involving deception using the Elance Web site for hiring freelancers of all sorts. Despite the recommendation to follow local IRB regulations and the external validity advantages provided by 'hiring' respondents from across the globe, this suggestion has two inherent problems. First, because the respondents are truly hired for a 'project', they must be paid, placing the cost of the project (at least a few thousand dollars) beyond the reach of most investigators. Second, using members of an e-commerce site as research subjects may lead members of the online community to view the research enterprise with a level of distaste now reserved for annoying pop-up advertisements.

RANDOM ASSIGNMENT

Whether a particular research question is theory driven or phenomenon driven, the crucial feature of an experimental design is the comparison of the behavior of people in at least one group with the behavior of people in at least one other group (Shaver, 2007). Comparisons are, of course, found in research methods other than experimentation. A detailed case study of one entrepreneurial company is just that – a case study. A detailed analysis of at least two such cases that attempts to identify similarities and differences between the two is a comparison. A research procedure that assesses central characteristics of an entrepreneurial company during its organizational phase, returns for a second assessment after the company is established and returns again at some later time also contains comparisons.

What sets experiments apart is that the groups involved in the comparisons are not pre-existing. Rather, in experimental designs the research participants are randomly assigned to conditions. One fairly recent article in entrepreneurship found it necessary to devote space to the process of random assignment (Fiet et al., 2007), and experience suggests that it might be useful to do so here as well. Remember what is the objective of experimental research: the testing of causal statements about the relationships between two or more variables. One or more of these will be true independent variables (*A*), manipulated by the experimenter. One or more will be true dependent variables (*B*), assessed at some time following manipulation of the independent variables. The time order by itself rules out one potential alternative explanation: the possibility that *B* actually caused *A*. What the experimental procedures by themselves cannot rule out is the possibility that pre-existing individual differences produced the observed variations in the dependent variables. It is to rule out the influence of these pre-existing personal characteristics that participants are randomly assigned to experimental conditions. With random assignment, the various pre-existing differences will – in principle – add to the error variance, but will not be related in any systematic fashion to the dependent variables.

A few cautions are in order concerning what random assignment is *not*. First, flipping a coin to assign the first few people in a list to conditions, then placing every *k*th person into the corresponding conditions, is not random assignment. True random assignment requires that each succeeding person have an equal chance of being in any treatment group, regardless of the choices that have been made for the preceding individuals in the list. Neither 'haphazard' assignment of people to treatments, nor alternating assignment (person 1 to treatment *A*, person 2 to treatment *B*, person 3 to treatment *C*, with the series repeated for the remaining individuals) is true random sampling. Before the advent of spreadsheets with RANDOM functions, experimenters used flipped coins, rolled dice and the extensive tables of random numbers found in statistics texts to ensure that condition assignments were random.

Second, even true random assignment across the board is not a panacea for pre-existing individual differences. If a sample is 80 percent of one social or demographic characteristic, and 20 percent of another, the fact that random assignment works 'in the long term' may not be sufficient for the subset of respondents who constitute the 20 percent. In a sample 80 percent of whom are founders, and 20 percent of whom are owner–managers, there is a measurable probability that most of the 20 percent could find themselves unevenly distributed across conditions. Even without such obvious demographic splits, random assignment corrects for pre-existing differences with a high and measurable probability, not with certainty.

Third, some individual differences really need to be considered before random assignment. For example, although it is trite to say so, women and men are different. Randomly assigning a group of people to conditions without regard to their sex will have the effect of putting all variability associated with sex differences into the error term of the statistical design.

Assuming that the statistical tests will be done with analysis of variance, the consensus choice for experiments, the general form of the test is:

$$\frac{\text{Treatment effects} + \text{error}}{\text{Error}}$$

with the null hypothesis being that the numerical value of the fraction will be 1.0. In this model, failure to consider the two sexes separately will have all of the sex-based variation placed in the denominator. By contrast, if respondent sex is considered a separate factor in the design, and random assignment to conditions is accomplished within the two sexes, the component that previously increased error will now be a form of 'treatment effect', thus raising the likelihood that the research will produce statistically discoverable differences. The general point is that random assignment, like other features of an experimental design, has to be done thoughtfully.

FACTORIAL DESIGNS

Let us consider in more detail what it means to say that a variable is 'a factor in the experimental design'. As students back in our elementary methods courses, we were introduced to experimentation by a simple two-group design: one treatment group and one 'control' group that received no treatment. This simple design is probably adequate when the research subjects are laboratory animals specifically bred to have about as few real individual differences as possible. When the research participants are complex human beings, however, the 'control group' really becomes an 'individual differences group' with all the attendant variability in background, perspective, desires, expectations and motives that characterize us. Outside the experimental laboratory our differences make us interesting; inside the lab they are little more than a nuisance. Why bother to create very carefully constructed laboratory situations when only one of the two groups is subject to any real control?

For social psychologists, and by implication for entrepreneurship researchers as well, it is preferable to have *some* treatment in each experimental condition. The real issue is what that treatment should be. The answer lies in what I would call an ability to 'dimensionalize' a variable of either theoretical or practical interest. Suppose that the research question deals with the percentage of equity in an entrepreneurial company that the founder is willing to trade away for a needed investment. The two-group version of this experiment would be to offer the treatment group some stated (but arbitrary) amount of financing, while offering the control group no specific amount, and then to ask each group for its trade percentage. This particular experiment is neither interesting nor likely to be informative. A better question is how much an entrepreneur is willing to trade away given a particular amount of investment – turning the amount from one point into a dimension of possible amounts. (To keep the rest of the example 'simple', let's assume that there are only three different amounts.)

What the entrepreneurs believe to be a fair trade of equity for investment is one thing; what angel investors might think could be something else. So, in addition to a respondent sample of entrepreneurs, we could enlist a respondent sample of investors. As people are not randomly assigned to the role of entrepreneur or investor, this particular variable is an *organismic* one (as would be respondent sex). Nevertheless, it enters as a separate factor, turning the experiment into a 2×3 (status $\times$ cash amount) factorial design. Statistically, such a design will produce a main effect for status (factor A, with two 'levels'), a main effect for cash amount (factor B, with three levels), and an interaction between the two ($A \times B$). Following the rule of thumb for number of participants in each cell, the design now requires 60 participants, 30 entrepreneurs and 30 investors with the cash amount conditions assigned randomly within participant type.

Suppose we also believed that the equity/cash trade might be different depending on the stage of development of the business (e.g. seed, first round, mezzanine). Adding this factor creates a $2 \times 3 \times 3$ design with 18 treatment combinations, now requiring 90 entrepreneurs and 90 investors. There would be three main effects (A, B and C), three two-way interactions (A–B, A–C and B–C), and one three-way interaction ($A \times B \times C$). Suddenly the design seems out of control and with more factors it becomes unmanageable. One solution is to change one of the manipulated factors from being a 'between-subjects' variable to be a 'within-subjects' variable. As is the case with other aspects of experimentation, which variable should be changed to within-subjects is a decision that has to be made by the investigator (with the rationale available for scrutiny by readers of the paper). For example, an investigator might well argue that respondents would be less surprised to find different amounts of money in the experiment than to find different stages being considered. If that were true, then money would be less 'reactive' than stage, so stage should remain a between-subjects variable and money could be the within-subjects variable. This would bring the number of respondents needed back down to 60 participants and would have the added advantage of reduced variance for the within-subjects factor because each person is serving as his or her own control.

There is, however, one additional complication in a within-subjects design: order of presentation of materials. We know from research on anchoring (see Kahneman et al., 1982), that a person's judgment of several 'later' numbers will be affected by the first number the person has heard or read. So rather than put all of the small amounts first, all of the medium amounts second, and all of the large amounts last, the number amounts (*S, M, L*) should be arranged in all possible orders: *SML, SLM, MSL, MLS, LSM, LMS*. And because it is rarely a good idea to have order of presentation completely confounded with person, there should be at least two respondents who receive each order. Thus the six within-subjects orders dictate that each of the between-subjects variables should have 12 people per cell rather than the 10 specified by the rule of thumb. Moreover, the random assignment will now need to be two-phase: first to stage of venture; then within stage of venture to one of the six orders of monetary amount.

The complexity that can successfully be built into factorial designs in entrepreneurship is illustrated in a study by Patzelt et al. (2007). This research investigated the factors that might lead an entrepreneurial firm to seek strategic alliances with others, specifically with new potential partners with whom there was no prior history. Using a sample of biotechnology entrepreneurs, three primary factors were considered: the entrepreneurial firm's capabilities (comparable to 'resources'); the external context (environmental demands and opportunities); and the high-discretion financial slack available to the venture (cash and receivables). It is important to note that financial slack was expected to be a moderating variable, of interest for its interactions with other factors, not for its sole contributions to alliance-seeking.

The study involved eight attributes, each of which was described by two levels. The capabilities factor was represented in four attributes: number of early-stage product candidates (few or many); number of late-stage product candidates (few or many); quality of the scientific team (low versus high); and the venture's network size (limited versus extended). The external context was represented in three attributes: patent position (weak versus strong); level of industry competition (low versus high); and munificence of the financing environment (low versus high). Finally, the presumed moderating variable of high-discretion financial slack was represented as a single variable (low versus high).

As a completely between-subjects design, this experiment would have required almost a cast of thousands. Three two-level capabilities attributes ($3 \times 2 = 6$); four two-level context attributes ($4 \times 2 = 8$); one financial slack variable with two levels (2). In a between-subjects format, this would have been a 96-cell design ($6 \times 8 \times 2$), calling for a minimum of 960 respondents. However, as the investigators had no interest in any of the higher-order interactions, they were able to employ a 'conjoint analysis' procedure in which several attributes were combined into one scenario, and then respondents were asked to state how desirable an alliance would be under the circumstances described by the attribute combination. In other terms, the conjoint analysis procedure is a *fractional* factorial design, one that in this case involved only 16 attribute combinations. To permit checks on test–retest reliability, there was a full replication for each of the 16 attribute combinations. Thus, in all, each respondent was asked to make 32 decisions. As the authors note, these 32 decisions were then nested within respondents (in other words, the design was entirely within-subjects), resulting in 1632 data points across the 51 participants in the research. Because of this nesting, the results were analyzed with hierarchical linear modeling (HLM; Bryk and Raudenbush, 1992). Although this sort of conjoint analysis experiment is prevalent in topic areas that call for decisions or preferences (e.g. Mitchell and Shepherd, 2010), it is less common in topic areas for which the higher-order interactions are valuable sources of information.

PROCEDURES AND RESERVATIONS

It is sometimes claimed that experimentation is appropriate only for testing tightly constructed theories, not for examining the possible causes of phenomena. At one level, it is certainly true that when it comes to theory-testing, experimentation is the method of choice. On the other hand, there are instances in social psychology where experimentation was employed to test propositions that were more like the investigator's hunch than like fully specified theoretical ideas. One of the more prominent of these – now so well known that it appears in classes taught in high schools – is the area of bystander intervention into emergency situations. This entire line of research began with the tragic death of a young woman in New York, a death caused by multiple knife attacks inflicted over the space of half an hour and witnessed by 38 observers, none of whom so much as called the police. No detailed theory here, only a tragic phenomenon that demanded explanation. But the response of the two social psychologists whose work is the foundation for our understanding of bystander intervention (or, more appropriately, non-intervention) was a series of experimental studies that over time allowed the development of a multi-step theory of the intervention decision process (Latané and Darley, 1970). For present purposes, however, the point is that a phenomenon, even one like entrepreneurship with a relatively low base rate of occurrence, can profitably be examined through experimentation.

Whether designed to test theoretical propositions or to identify the possible causes of phenomena, there are several important aspects of experimentation that must not be overlooked. The internal validity that can be derived from an experiment requires (a) an understanding of the differences between conceptual replication and empirical replication, (b) a careful operationalization of the independent variables of interest, (c) control over the situation that is sufficient to rule out potential confounds, (d) dependent variable measures with sufficient reliability, and (e) appropriate statistical designs. Convenience samples, fuzzy definitions of central concepts, non-random assignment of individuals to experimental conditions, imprecise dependent variables and the wrong statistical tests will all reduce the value of any conclusions reached. In a special issue on experimentation, Patel and Fiet (2010) suggest statistical procedures designed to improve the quality of information obtained from entrepreneurship experiments.

Whatever might be done with statistical analysis, one methodological pitfall that is likely to be especially problematic in the study of entrepreneurial behavior is a version of Gergen's (1973) view of 'social psychology as history'. Specifically, knowing the outcomes of research is likely to make it more difficult to find the same outcomes again. Everyone who has passed through an Introductory Psychology course knows about the Milgram (1963) experiment testing the limits of obedience to authority. Now when a participant is told to provide an increasing level of electric shock to a person in order to 'teach' that person to memorize word pairs, the answer is apt to be 'You've gotta be kidding! I'm outta here.' It is worth noting that Gergen made this argument more than 20 years before the World Wide Web. At that point in time it might have been possible to claim that potential research participants had to do some serious digging through past issues of printed journals in order to discover what social psychologists believe they have learned about human behavior. In the present era of Web 2.0, Google™ and YouTube™ it is hard to believe that there are many secrets left. Gergen's position is that social reality is constructed, using all that the individual knows. Although the argument between constructionistic and positivistic views of human behavior continues (see Vol. 6, No. 3 of the *Personality and Social Psychology Review*, 2002), one of the signal characteristics of entrepreneurs is claimed to be their eagerness to learn from experience – their own or that of others. Consequently, it is reasonable to believe that entrepreneurs will be especially likely to be aware of – and affected by – the results of research on entrepreneurial behavior.

One reason that the last 20 years of social psychological experimentation has concentrated on topics of social cognition is that doing so does not ask research participants to admit having socially disapproved motives, or performing socially disapproved actions. Study of these processes often requires deception such as that described above, an experimental method that makes many investigators queasy. But as we have known for years, even positive social behavior can be exaggerated either for purposes of establishing self-worth or for responding to the expectations of the investigator (Rosenthal, 1966). The latter, of course, are even more prevalent in research designs involving 'in-depth interviews' than in experimental designs.

There are procedures for examining socially disapproved behavior without having to resort to deception, and as noted earlier there are other procedures for guarding against experimenter expectancy effects. But one limitation of the experimental method will remain despite the investigator's best efforts. Experiments are, by both method and philosophy of science, designed to discover differences between treatment groups. By themselves, experiments are unable to provide information about the prevalence of any social behavior.

This point often requires further comment. In the past, a good deal of research in human behavior has been criticized as 'the psychology of the college sophomore'. True, many psychological studies rely on the assistance of the large numbers of students who pass through Introductory Psychology courses. But whether this is, or is not, a fatal flaw depends on the specific research objectives. An attempt to describe and measure most behaviors associated with creating a new venture should really use people who are engaged in the process. On the other hand, some elements of the entrepreneurial process can be studied quite effectively in research on college students.

SO WHAT? (OR, 'SO HOW?')

As noted earlier, experiments are especially useful tools for testing theoretically derived causal hypotheses. For example, consider the process of opportunity recognition. In their description of the field, Shane and Venkataraman (2000) stated that entrepreneurship involves 'the processes of discovery, evaluation, and exploitation of opportunities ...'. Obviously, research with college students is not likely to help illuminate the 'exploitation' part of this triad. Discovery and evaluation, however, might be a completely different matter. If, as Lumpkin et al. (2004) have argued, opportunity recognition is a creative process – read, a cognitive process – then an experimental approach using college students might well be appropriate. The social cognition literature is replete with examples of 'hot' cognitive processes – cognitive activities that can be affected by motivation. One of these is the hedonic principle that people are motivated to seek pleasure and avoid pain. Specifically, Higgins (1998) has argued that there are two distinct motivational orientations toward cognitive activity. One of these, a 'promotion' focus, leads decision makers to concentrate on making correct positive decisions (in terms of signal detection theory these are 'hits') while ensuring against omitting a correct negative decision (in signal detection theory these are 'misses'). The other orientation is the 'prevention' focus, which leads decision makers to concentrate on ensuring the rejection of wrong choices ('correct rejections') while avoiding false positives ('false alarms'). The two foci have been related to business by Brockner et al. (2004), who argued that the promotion focus would be advantageous for generating business ideas.

Thus the conceptual chain is (a) a central element of entrepreneurship is the identification of opportunities, (b) this identification process is akin to cognitive processes involved in creativity, and (c) the promotion focus is more likely than the prevention focus to undergird the creative process (including the creative process of generating new business ideas). Although the prevention and prediction foci are often considered individual difference variables, it is entirely possible that the situation in which one finds oneself will also influence which focus is adopted. An entrepreneur is in a situation where more promotion is good; an investor is in a situation where more prevention is good.

All of these ideas were combined into an experimental design by Monllor et al. (2007). Specifically, undergraduate business students were primed either for a promotion focus or a prevention focus, and were then asked to generate ideas for a new business based on an existing patent. Respondents were first asked to generate as many ideas as possible, then to elaborate on the 'best' of those ideas. Outside judges then rated the novelty and usefulness (Amabile, 1983) of the ideas produced. Dependent variables included the number of ideas generated, the average rated novelty and usefulness of those ideas, and the novelty and usefulness of the idea finally selected. Following the advice discussed above, respondent sex was included as a factor in the experimental design, thus producing a $2 \times 2 \times 5$ design with the 5 (the number of dependent variables) being treated as a within-subjects variable.

For present purposes, the critical point made by this experiment is that theory that attempts to account for differences in entrepreneurial behavior can be tested using undergraduate students as respondents. Nobody believes that the number of ideas generated by undergraduates is a good proxy for the number of ideas that might be generated by a group of experienced entrepreneurs. Similarly, nobody believes that the research shows whether entrepreneurs have a promotion focus as opposed to a prevention focus. In neither case does the research provide an estimate of the prevalence of particular cognitive styles among entrepreneurs. Rather, what the research does is attempt to show whether a factor thought to be involved in entrepreneurial opportunity recognition can create statistically significant differences between conditions in an experiment conducted with undergraduate respondents. In short, if the research objective is to examine the operation of a process rather than the prevalence of an outcome, the experimental method applied to undergraduates can add substantial value to our level of understanding.

As a discipline, entrepreneurship has freely imported theory from other disciplines. Economics, psychology and sociology have been especially prominent sources of theoretical insight into entrepreneurial behavior. Now that the field has a better grasp on the 'what' of entrepreneurial action, it is appropriate to turn to the 'how' and the 'why'. It is for these latter two tasks that experimentation is particularly appropriate, especially when competing theoretical views can be brought to bear on the same problem.

For example, let us return to the nature of entrepreneurial opportunity. In a comparison of several views of opportunity, Sarasvathy et al. (2010) have noted that there are three useful views of opportunity – the allocative view, the discovery view and the creative view. Further, they have argued that 'the key issue is not which of the three views is *right*, but rather which view is more useful under what conditions of uncertainty' (p. 145, emphasis in original). Their summary comparison of the three views is presented as a table intended to identify the conditions under which each perspective might be most appropriate. Presented in this form, the table is a conceptual analysis of the consequences of each view. But described another way, many elements of the table sound like the theoretical basis for experiments. The allocative view is said to apply when both supply and demand are known, the discovery view applies when only one or the other is known, and the creative view applies when neither supply nor demand is known. However, if it were possible to identify which dependent variables would successfully operationalize the allocative process, the discovery process, and the creative process, then a joint manipulation of supply and demand could be tested to determine which view emerges under which conditions.

Experimentation is a method that, as we have seen, requires attention to any number of procedural details. On the other hand, some of the issues that arise in the course of doing an experiment (such as reactivity) should be a concern in other forms of research as well. With careful operationalization of independent variables, dimensionalization of the dependent variables, standardization of procedures, random assignment to minimize the influence of pre-existing individual differences and factorial designs that capture some of the complexity inherent in the 'real world', experimentation can and should play a larger role in the study of entrepreneurship.

REFERENCES

Aguinis, H. and Lawal, S.O. (2012), 'Conducting field experiments using eLancing's [sic] natural environment', *Journal of Business Venturing*, **27**: 493–505.

Amabile, T.M. (1983), *The Social Psychology of Creativity*, New York: Springer-Verlag.

Aronson, E., Brewer, M.B. and Carlsmith, J.M. (1985), 'Experimentation in social psychology', in G. Lindzey and E. Aronson (eds), *Handbook of Social Psychology*, 3rd edn, Vol. 1, New York: Random House, pp. 441–86.

Brockner, J., Higgins, E.T. and Low, M.B. (2004), 'Regulatory focus theory and the entrepreneurial process', *Journal of Business Venturing*, **19**: 203–20.

Brush, C.G., Manolova, T.S. and Edelman, L.F. (2008), 'Separated by a common language? Entrepreneurship research across the Atlantic', *Entrepreneurship Theory and Practice*, **32**: 249–66.

Bryk, A. and Raudenbush, S.W. (1992), *Hierarchical Linear Models for Social and Behavioral Research: Applications and Data Analysis Methods*, Newbury Park, CA: Sage.

Burmeister-Lamp, K., Lévesque, M. and Schade, C. (2012), 'Are entrepreneurs influenced by risk attitude, regulatory focus or both? An experiment on entrepreneurs' time allocation', *Journal of Business Venturing*, **27**: 456–76.

Chandler, G.N. and Lyon, D.W. (2001), 'Issues of research design and construct measurement in entrepreneurship research: the past decade', *Entrepreneurship Theory and Practice*, **25**: 101–13.

Cook, T.D. and Campbell, D.T. (1979), *Quasi-experimentation: Design and Analysis Issues for Field Settings*, Chicago, IL: Rand McNally.

Edwards, A.L. (1954), 'Experiments: their planning and execution', in G. Lindzey (ed.), *Handbook of Social Psychology*, Vol. 1, Cambridge, MA: Addison-Wesley, pp. 259–88.

Fiet, J.O., Norton, W.I. and Clouse, V.G.H. (2007), 'Systematic search as a source of technical innovation: an empirical test', *Journal of Engineering and Technology Management*, **24**: 329–46.

Foo, M. (2011), 'Emotions and entrepreneurial opportunity evaluation', *Entrepreneurship Theory and Practice*, **35**: 375–93.

Gartner, W.B. (1989), 'Some suggestions for research on entrepreneurial traits and characteristics', *Entrepreneurship Theory and Practice*, **14**(1): 27–38.

Gatewood, E.J., Shaver, K.G., Powers, J.B. and Gartner, W.B. (2002), 'Entrepreneurial expectancy, task effort, and performance', *Entrepreneurship Theory and Practice*, **27**(2): 187–206.

Gergen, K.J. (1973), 'Social psychology as history', *Journal of Personality and Social Psychology*, **26**: 309–20.

Gilbert, D.T., Fiske, S.T. and Lindzey, G. (eds) (1998), *The Handbook of Social Psychology*, 4th edn, Vols 1–2, New York: McGraw-Hill.

Haynie, J.M., Shepherd, D.A. and Patzelt, H. (2012), 'Cognitive adaptability and an entrepreneurial task: the role of metacognitive ability and feedback', *Entrepreneurship Theory and Practice*, **36**, 237–65.

Higgins, E.T. (1998), 'Promotion and prevention: regulatory focus as a motivational principle', in M.P. Zanna (ed.), *Advances in Experimental Social Psychology*, Vol. 30, New York: Academic Press, pp. 1–46.

Hofer, C.W. and Bygrave, W.D. (1992), 'Researching entrepreneurship', *Entrepreneurship Theory and Practice*, **16**(3): 91–100.

Kahneman, D., Slovic, P. and Tversky, A. (eds) (1982), *Judgment under Uncertainty: Heuristics and Biases*, New York: Cambridge University Press.

Latané, B. and Darley, J.M., Jr (1970), *The Unresponsive Bystander: Why Doesn't he Help?*, New York: Appleton-Century-Crofts.

Likert, R. (1932), 'A technique for the measurement of attitudes', *Archives of Psychology*, **22**(140): 5–53.

Lindzey, G. (ed.) (1954), *Handbook of Social Psychology*, Vol. 1, Cambridge, MA: Addison-Wesley.

Lindzey, G. and Aronson, E. (eds) (1969), *The Handbook of Social Psychology*, 2nd edn, Vols 1–5, Reading, MA: Addison-Wesley.

Lindzey, G. and Aronson, E. (eds) (1985), *The Handbook of Social Psychology*, 3rd edn, Vols 1–2, New York: Random House.

Lumpkin, G.T., Hills, G.E. and Shrader, R.C. (2004), 'Opportunity recognition', in H.P. Welsch (ed.), *Entrepreneurship: The Way Ahead*, London: Routledge, pp. 73–90.

McDougall, W. (1908), *Introduction to Social Psychology*, London: Methuen.

Milgram, S. (1963), 'Behavioral study of obedience', Journal of Abnormal and Social Psychology, **67**: 371–8.

Mitchell, J.R. and Shepherd, D.A. (2010), 'To thine own self be true: images of self, images of opportunity, and entrepreneurial action', *Journal of Business Venturing*, **25**: 138–54.

Monllor, J., Hansen, D.J., Sullivan, D. and Shaver, K.G. (2007), 'Regulatory focus, opportunity recognition and creativity: an experimental investigation'. Babson College Entrepreneurship Research Conference, Madrid, Spain.

Mullen, M.R., Budeva, D.G. and Doney, P.M. (2009), 'Research methods in the leading small business–entrepreneurship journals: a critical review with recommendations for future research', *Journal of Small Business Management*, **47**(3): 287–307.

Patel, P.C. and Fiet, J.O. (2010), 'Enhancing the internal validity of entrepreneurship experiments by assessing treatment effects at multiple levels across multiple trials', *Journal of Economic Behavior and Organization*, **76**: 127–40.

Patzelt, H., Shepherd, D.A., Deeds, D. and Bradley, S.W. (2007), 'Financial slack and venture managers' decisions to seek a new alliance', *Journal of Business Venturing*, **23**: 465–81.

Rosenberg, M.J. (1965), 'When dissonance fails: on eliminating evaluation apprehension from attitude measurement', *Journal of Personality and Social Psychology*, **1**: 28–42.

Rosenthal, R. (1966), *Experimenter Effects in Behavioral Research*, New York: Appleton-Century-Crofts.

Sarasvathy, S., Dew, N., Velamuri, S.R. and Venkataraman, S. (2010), 'Three views of entrepreneurial opportunity', in Z.J. Acs and D.B. Audretsch (eds), *Handbook of Entrepreneurship Research*, 2nd edn, New York: Springer, pp. 77–96.

Shane, S. and Venkataraman, S. (2000), 'The promise of entrepreneurship as a field of research', *Academy of Management Review*, **26**: 217–26.

Shaver, K.G. (1987), *Principles of Social Psychology*, 3rd edn. Hillsdale, NJ: Lawrence Erlbaum Associates.

Shaver, K.G. (2007), 'C2D2: psychological methods in entrepreneurship research', in J.R. Baum, M. Frese and R.A. Baron (eds), *The Psychology of Entrepreneurship*, Mahwah, NJ: Lawrence Erlbaum Associates, pp. 335–46.

Shaver, K.G. (2010), 'The social psychology of entrepreneurial behavior', in Z.J. Acs and D.B. Audretsch (eds), *Handbook of Entrepreneurship Research*, 2nd edn, New York: Springer, pp. 359–86.

Shaver, K.G., Gartner, W.B., Gatewood, E.J. and Vos, L.H. (1996), 'Psychological factors in success at getting into business', in P. Reynolds, S. Birley, J.E. Butler, W.D. Bygrave, P. Davidsson, W.B. Gartner and P.P. McDougall (eds), *Frontiers of Entrepreneurship Research 1996*, Babson Park, MA: Babson College, pp. 77–90.

Triplett, N. (1897), 'The dynamogenic factors in pacemaking and competition', *American Journal of Psychology*, **9**: 507–33.

Vesper, K.H. (1966), *New Venture Experience*, Seattle, WA: Vector Books.

Welpe, I.M., Spörrle, M., Grichnik, D., Michl, T. and Audretsch, D.B. (2012), 'Emotions and opportunities: the interplay of opportunity evaluation, fear, joy, and anger as antecedent of entrepreneurial exploitation', *Entrepreneurship Theory and Practice*, **36**: 69–96.

6. Looking into the future: valid multiple- and single-item measures in entrepreneurship research

Leon Schjoedt, Maija Renko and Kelly G. Shaver

As a discipline, entrepreneurship has grown dramatically in recent years. This coming of age is reflected in both substantive and measurement developments (Schwab, 1980). The former refer to studies addressing the nature of the relationships among constructs – independent and dependent variables. The latter refer to the operationalization of those theoretical concepts. Conclusions drawn in the entrepreneurship literature are only as robust as the methods employed in conducting the research (e.g. design, sampling, measurement, analysis and interpretation of results). Although methodological progress has been made, developments in measurement have lagged the substantive developments in entrepreneurship. This is troublesome because accurate and well-tested measures are essential for replicable substantive developments. Nowhere is the problem clearer than in the body of research on traits in entrepreneurship, and in the calls for abandonment of this line of research. To lay the groundwork for future development of this area, the present chapter offers guidance on measurement development and validation in entrepreneurship research.

Assessing measurement validity in entrepreneurship research is a problematic issue as, for example, observed in recent reviews of the literature on entrepreneurs' behaviors (Bird and Schjoedt, 2009; Bird et al., 2012). There are four particular concerns: (1) use of *ad hoc*, or one-time, measures; (2) use of global measures to assess specific constructs, such as using a global measure (e.g. general self-efficacy) to assess a specific construct (e.g. entrepreneurial self-efficacy); (3) use of specific measures (e.g. task-specific self-efficacy such as self-efficacy with new product development, finance) in a summated form to make claims about a higher-level construct (e.g. entrepreneurial self-efficacy) without conceptual justification for how or why the specific measures combined should constitute the higher-level construct; and (4) use of multidimensional measures to assess one-dimensional constructs.

These are not new problems. Peter (1979) illustrates the critical role of measurement validity in the research process when noting:

> Valid measurement is the *sine qua non* of science. In a general sense, validity refers to the degree to which instruments truly measure the constructs which [sic] they are intended to measure. If the measurements used in a discipline have not been demonstrated to have a high degree of validity, that discipline is not science. (Peter, 1979, p. 6)

Placing Peter's comment in a broader context means that assessing or establishing measurement validity is fundamental to the interpretation of substantive relationships in entrepreneurship. Measurement validation is central to the accurate interpretation of data that stem from the measurement (Cook and Campbell, 1979) and the generalizability of results (Cronbach et al., 1972). In effect, measurement validity is a necessary condition for substantive and theory developments (Bagozzi, 1980; Churchill, 1979; Peter, 1981); thus entrepreneurship 'cannot progress any faster than the measurement of important variables in the field' (Aguinis et al., 2001, p. 28).

We hope this chapter will serve as a stimulus for entrepreneurship scholars to develop and employ more valid single- and multi-item measures. We address measurement validity from a psychometric perspective. In the space available, we focus on presenting a brief overview that provides the basics for scale development. We recognize that the real-world exigencies of entrepreneurship research often preclude use of very long scales, but hope to illustrate how more concentrated attention to measurement issues might improve both multiple-item and single-item measures in entrepreneurship research. Overall, we hope this chapter will encourage greater attention to measurement validity in future research.

MEASUREMENT VALIDITY AND VALIDATION

Psychometric theorists (e.g. Cronbach, 1971; Nunnally, 1978) argue that constructing new measures for every situation is wasteful. However, given the conceptual developments and practical realities in entrepreneurship research, scholars in the area are often faced with the need to develop a new measure or to revise an existing measure. This requires careful observation of key aspects of measurement validity and the validation process.

Before turning to measurement validity, it is necessary to clarify various types of validity. Our focus in this chapter is on the measurement of constructs. A construct is not a fact that can be independently verified. A construct is designed to represent or describe something that exists in nature that cannot be observed directly. Constructs can also be used to organize knowledge. When placed in the context of theories, constructs are 'judged by their adequacy or usefulness in making observable predictions' (Peter,

1981, p. 134). Some central constructs in entrepreneurship that have prompted recent measurement efforts include entrepreneurial passion (Cardon et al., 2013), entrepreneurial leadership (Renko et al., forthcoming), effectuation (Chandler et al., 2011) and locus of control (Schjoedt and Shaver, 2012), to which we will return later in this chapter.

In empirical studies that test theory and its inherent constructs, we use proxies. That is to say, measurement models are based on relationships among sets of variables, which serve as proxies for constructs; or, phrased differently, a construct is the conceptual equivalent of a variable (Schwab, 1980). Whether a measure is single-item or multiple-item, if it is an appropriate representation of the construct, we refer to the measurement as valid (Cattell, 1966). Accordingly, measurement validity here refers to the degree to which a measurement captures only the construct it is intended to measure. This is also referred to as 'construct validity' (Cook and Campbell, 1979; Cronbach and Meehl, 1955; Peter, 1981). To avoid confusion we use the term 'measurement validity' because 'construct validity' at times refers to the validity of the 'construct' per se (e.g. 'valid construct'; Peter, 1981).

CHARACTERISTICS OF VALID MEASUREMENTS

What characterizes a valid measure? Simply put, such a measure assesses the direction and magnitude of all the characteristics and only the characteristics of the construct it is intended to measure. A measure is said to be valid when variations in the construct are reflected in the observed scores despite the fact that the observed score contains the true score and an error (Churchill, 1976). In effect, validity refers to the utility of inferences made from scores of a measure based on the degree of how well a measure assesses the intended construct (Aguinis et al., 2001).

Another way to understand measurement validity is to look at its various components. Because a plethora of different types of validity exist, the American Psychological Association (APA) formed a committee on validity to introduce a degree of order among the competing taxonomies of validity (American Psychological Association, 1954, 1966). These efforts led to some debate (e.g. Campbell and Fiske, 1959; Cronbach and Meehl, 1955) and to the now classical forms of validity (Campbell, 1976). To establish measurement validity, four types of validity combined with two types of operationalization consistency are necessary. None of these alone, or in combinations of two or three, is enough to illustrate measurement validity. The four types of validity are *content*, *convergent*, *discriminant* and *nomological* (*predictive*). The two types of internal consistency are *unidimensionality* and *reliability*. Before investigating each of these, it should be noted that even though numbers are used to indicate validity, unidimensionality or reliability, they are in fact estimates or approximations of validity (Cook and Campbell, 1979).

Content validity concerns the extent to which a set of measurement items reflects a specific content domain (item sampling adequacy). For example, a key aspect of entrepreneurial passion according to Cardon and colleagues (2013) is that such passion involves the experience of intense positive feelings. Hence the items they use to measure such passion ask respondents to rate their level of excitement, enjoyment and liking of certain entrepreneurial tasks. Content validity should be assessed as a first step in the measurement development and validation process (i.e. before measure refinement).[1] Content validity is initially assessed by 'experts'. Once data are available, the consistency among the items of a scale can be evaluated by factor analysis (Campbell, 1976).

Convergent validity is illustrated when a measure is highly correlated with other measures designed to assess the same construct (Churchill, 1979); or when correlations of a construct measure are similar across different established measures of a theoretically related construct (Aguinis et al., 2001; DeVellis, 2003). As an example, Renko and colleagues (forthcoming) discuss how entrepreneurial leadership and entrepreneurial orientation are separate constructs, yet they share some important theoretical similarities. The significant positive correlation between the two scales, then, suggests that there is convergent validity (Renko et al., forthcoming). In general, convergent validity is typically illustrated by correlations or using structural equation modeling (Aguinis et al., 2001; Bagozzi, 1980; Churchill, 1979; Peter, 1981). Alternatively, but less often (in part due to the critiques, e.g. Lumsden, 1976), the multitrait–multimethod matrix (MTMM) is used to illustrate convergent validity of a measure (Campbell and Fiske, 1959).

Discriminant validity can also be illustrated using the MTMM (Campbell and Fiske, 1959) and with correlations or using structural equation modeling (Aguinis et al., 2001; Bagozzi, 1980; Churchill, 1979; Peter, 1981). Unlike convergent validity, discriminant validity is evident when a measure is not correlated significantly or is only weakly correlated with measures of other constructs that are not theoretically related (Aguinis et al., 2001; Bagozzi, 1980; Churchill, 1979; Peter, 1981). In line with the MTMM (Campbell and Fiske, 1959), it is strongly encouraged that convergent validity and discriminant validity be assessed by diverse methods.

The preceding paragraphs pertain to trait validity, which can, largely, be assessed in a context free of theory (Campbell, 1960). Trait validity is a necessary but not a sufficient condition for measurement validity. *Nomological validity* (e.g. Cronbach and Meehl, 1955) is needed too (Campbell,

1960). Nomological validity refers to the degree to which a construct measure behaves as expected within a system of related construct measures; or the construct measure behaves as prescribed by theory with respect to assessments of different but conceptually related constructs (Peter, 1981). Correlations, regression coefficients, structural equation modeling and causal modeling can provide evidence of nomological validity if the results are in line with the conceptual relationships prescribed by theory (Aguinis et al., 2001; Churchill, 1979; Peter, 1981). For example, Brettel and colleagues (2012) and Chandler et al. (2011) first develop measurements for effectuation and then provide empirical support for conceptual relationships between effectuation, assessed by their new instruments, and theoretically relevant outcomes (R&D output and R&D efficiency; and uncertainty).

These two groups of validity – trait and nomological validity – collectively indicate whether a measure provides a valid assessment of a construct. Still another form of validity needs to be considered: *external validity*. External validity concerns the degree to which results hold across time, settings and individuals (Cook and Campbell, 1979).

Understanding the within-individual variation across times and settings is particularly important in entrepreneurship. Entrepreneurship is often defined as new business activity that some people are involved in at certain times during their careers (Gartner, 1988). Consequently, entrepreneurship research designs often compare those involved in entrepreneurship with those who are not (Gartner et al., 2004; Reynolds, 2000). To distinguish among entrepreneurs and non-entrepreneurs, the measurements should be developed for the entrepreneurship domain. Global, or general, measures and task-specific measures (based on tasks that are not unique to venture creation) may not be useful in comparing entrepreneurs with non-entrepreneurs, as such measures have external validity specifically with regard to external validity across individuals (Cook and Campbell, 1979). Consequently, in entrepreneurship research there is a need for measures that are valid across time but not individuals. After all, someone may qualify as an entrepreneur today but not five years from now (Gartner, 1988). When measures are developed and validated based on samples of individuals who are not entrepreneurs, external validity may be achieved (particularly across individuals), but predictive validity with regard to entrepreneurship may be limited. Careful consideration regarding samples and their effects on predictive and external validity is necessary. For example, the use of undergraduate or graduate students in development and validation of measures for the entrepreneurship domain (e.g. undergraduate students in an introductory accounting course: Cassar and Friedman, 2009; MBA students:

Chen et al., 1998) may be problematic. In particular, the resulting measurements may have external validity (across individuals) at the expense of limited predictive validity.

DIMENSIONALITY AND RELIABILITY

Besides the various dimensions of validity discussed above, measurement validity also requires the assessment of two types of operationalization consistency: unidimensionality and reliability. Unidimensionality refers to the extent that items reflect one construct; and reliability indicates the absence of error in the measurement score.

Factor analysis is used to determine the *dimensionality* of a measure. Exploratory factor analysis provides the basis for the assessment of dimensionality (Nunnally, 1978) and a number of techniques can be used. Perhaps the most widely known method is the K1 rule (eigenvalue-greater-than-one rule: Kaiser, 1960). A lesser-known method is the minimum average partial (MAP) approach provided by Velicer (1976). Because the K1 rule tends to overestimate and the MAP tends to underestimate the number of factors inherent in the data (Fabrigar et al., 1999; Zwick and Velicer, 1986), it is recommended that these methods be used in combination. Further, an analysis of a scree plot (Cattell, 1966) and parallel analysis (Horn, 1965) can be used. Although the scree plot is considered more accurate than the K1 and MAP, it is somewhat more subjective when determining the number of factors. As a standalone method, the parallel analysis (Horn, 1965) is considered superior to any of the other three approaches, especially when the 95th percentile eigenvalues are used (Glorfeld, 1995). Yet scholars recommend that all four methods (K1, MAP, scree plot and parallel analysis) be employed when assessing dimensionality (Fabrigar et al., 1999; Zwick and Velicer, 1986).

After the dimensionality of the measure has been determined using exploratory factor analysis, confirmatory factor analysis (CFA) should be employed to corroborate the findings. When a construct is not unidimensional but, instead, has multiple dimensions, a composite measure is necessary. This composite measure of a multidimensional construct consists of as many unidimensional measures as the construct has dimensions. In this case, the CFA should verify that the items load on the appropriate factors (dimensions). For example, consistent with their theoretical considerations, Cardon and colleagues (2013) develop and validate a multidimensional measurement model for entrepreneurial passion. CFA is used to show that the measurement model captures the two dimensions of entrepreneurial passion – intense positive feelings and identity centrality –

across the three domains of inventing, founding and developing a firm (Cardon et al., 2013).

Reliability is defined as the correlation between a measure and itself (Peter, 1979, 1981). Reliability[2] is based on an assumption that the observed measurement score includes a true score – the accurate degree of an individual's level of a construct (Aguinis et al., 2001) – and an error (e.g. Aguinis et al., 2001; Campbell, 1976; Churchill, 1979; Peter, 1979). A measure is reliable when it is stable across time (Aguinis et al., 2001) and variation in the score is relatively free of errors (Churchill, 1979). Errors may stem from random effects or chance in the response options, item ordering, situational conditions (physical or psychological conditions, like room temperature or experienced stress) or measurement mode (e.g. computer-based, online, paper-and-pencil, verbal over the phone or in person). There are several kinds of reliability (e.g. parallel/alternative forms reliability, interrater reliability) (for a comprehensive review, see the work by Peter, 1979). Various types of reliability should be considered in the measurement validation process (Campbell, 1976). In this chapter, we focus on two types: test–retest reliability and internal reliability.

Test–retest reliability, also referred to as a coefficient of stability, assesses the error in scores across time (Aguinis et al., 2001; DeVellis, 2003). It can be assessed by analyzing the correlation of the measurement scores from the same group of individuals at two points in time. This estimate of reliability applies to both single- and multi-item measures. Three issues pertain to test–retest reliability: length of time between measurements one and two; change in the construct over time (e.g. learning may occur); and the correlation between the measurement scores at times one and two may partly depend on the correlation between different items in the measure (Peter, 1979). It is recommended that the time between measurements should be two to eight weeks, but no longer than six months, to reduce the potential for changes in the construct being measured (Aguinis et al., 2001; DeVellis, 2003; Peter, 1979). In entrepreneurship research one must attend to events as well as time: in a measure of entrepreneurial self-efficacy, if the test immediately precedes a success in raising capital and the retest follows that success, differences in the scores may not indicate lack of reliability. Considering the definition of reliability, test–retest reliability may be higher than the correlation among multiple items that constitute a measure (Nunnally, 1978). Even though the correlation between test and retest of the measure provides useful information regarding the reliability of a measure, it is recommended that an estimate of test–retest reliability be supplemented by an estimate of internal reliability (Peter, 1979).

Internal reliability (more specifically, internal consistency reliability) refers to the degree to which various items of a measure correlate with each other. High item-to-item correlations demonstrate internal reliability because error is defined as item heterogeneity, and a measure is reliable when variation in the score is free of errors (Churchill, 1979). High internal reliability is critical to measurement validity when the measure is used to assess a unidimensional construct (Peter, 1981). Internal reliability can be estimated only for multi-item measures.

Internal reliability is typically estimated by two methods: split-half and coefficient alpha (e.g. Cronbach, 1951; Kuder and Richardson, 1937). The split-half method is based on the premise that an item or a group of items should be equivalent to any other item or group of items of the measure. In practice, the items of a measure are divided into two halves (the method cannot be used for measures with an odd number of items). Then, correlation between the scores of the two groups of items is calculated to provide the internal reliability estimate (Aguinis et al., 2001; DeVellis, 2003; Peter, 1979). The items may be split based on a random basis.

A slightly different use of the split-half method can be used to estimate reliability for single-item measures (also referred to as parallel or alternative forms reliability). Here, the same individuals should provide scores at two different points of time on two single-item measures that are worded differently but are not considered conceptually different. The correlation between the two single-item measures provides a reliability estimate (Aguinis et al., 2001). Peter (1979) specifically notes there should be two weeks between the measurements; whereas Aguinis et al. (2001) note the purpose of the time separation is to avoid ordering bias.

Internal consistency reliability may also be estimated by the coefficient alpha. For detailed considerations regarding coefficient alpha and its assumptions, issues and use, see the review by Cortina (1993). The most widely known estimation method for coefficient alpha is Cronbach's alpha (Cronbach, 1951); this is also the most widely used estimate of internal reliability in entrepreneurship research (cf. Bird et al., 2012). Following the logic of the split-half method, coefficient alpha is based on the average correlation of all the possible split-halves of a measure (Aguinis et al., 2001). More specifically, Cronbach's alpha is a function of the ratio of the sum of inter-item covariances to the variance of the total score (Campbell, 1976; Cronbach, 1951). Because the estimation of coefficient alpha is a function of the number of items in the measure, it may over- or under-estimate reliability (Campbell, 1976; Cortina, 1993; Cronbach, 1951; Raykov, 1998). In effect, Cronbach's alpha will be larger for a measure with more items, given that the items assess the same unidimensional construct. Consequently, recent recommendations emphasize the use of composite reliability instead of Cronbach's alpha (Graham, 2006). Although detailed consideration of composite reliability is beyond the scope of this chapter, readers are encouraged to review the literature on composite reliability as it overcomes some of the challenges facing coefficient alpha in over- and underestimation, especially for measures with few items.

DEVELOPING A MEASURE: A BRIEF OVERVIEW

Thus far, we have described the traditionalist approach in considering measures and their assessment. There is, however, a place where the traditionalist approach has been supplanted in the development of a measure. The traditional procedure for measurement development, as advocated by Churchill (1979), suggests that internal reliability (Cronbach's alpha) should be estimated first to qualify the measure and a factor analysis should be employed later. However, this suggested order has changed. The (revised) traditional procedure now employs the factor analysis (exploratory factor analysis) before the estimation of internal reliability to ensure that the measure is unidimensional (Aguinis et al., 2001; DeVellis, 2003; Netemeyer et al., 2003).

The first step in measurement development (and validation) is to determine the purpose of the measure (the construct it is supposed to measure) (Aguinis et al., 2001; DeVellis, 2003). The intended purpose of the measure will influence other factors in measurement development, such as construct definition specificity or numbers and types of items for the measure. The definition of the construct needs to be carefully considered (Schwab, 1980). Construct definitions indicate the level of specificity of the measure. For example, if the construct has multiple facets that collectively comprise the construct, then multiple unidimensional measures are needed, each of which becomes a subscale. Or, if the construct is very complex (and facets cannot be determined or are too numerous to be assessed individually), then a single-item measure may be appropriate. As an example, consider the 'success' of a new venture. Is continued existence sufficient? Must there be sales? Is revenue or employment growth required? What about a 'dot-com bubble' company that had 'eyeballs' but no sales, no revenues, and only one employee (the founder) that was sold for millions to a larger firm? In this case a single-item measure of the founder's satisfaction might well suffice. We shall return to a detailed consideration of single-item measures later in this chapter.

The second step is to generate a pool of items (DeVellis, 2003). It is critical to develop items that reflect the construct, as well as the purpose, of the measure. DeVellis (2003) advises that redundancy is desirable at this stage because some items will be discarded later in the development process. Exceptionally lengthy items and items that are hard to understand should be avoided. This means that items should be simple and clear, should not be vague or ambiguous, and should not contain double negatives (Aguinis et al., 2001; DeVellis, 2003). Nor should items be 'double-barreled' by including two clauses joined by 'and'. Depending on the construct, it may be appropriate to include both positively and negatively worded items. Based on the recommendations by Nunnally (1978), it appears that at least 60 items should be developed for the item pool. However, recent scale development studies in entrepreneurship – including some of our own – have fallen short on this threshold. For example, Cardon and colleagues (2013) initially test a pool of 22 to 24 items for entre-preneurial passion; Chandler and colleagues (2011) first develop eight items for the measurement of effectuation and nine items for the measure-ment of causation; Schjoedt and Shaver (2012) start with an item pool of 11 items for entrepreneurial locus of control; and Renko and colleagues (forthcoming) use experts to pre-screen an initial item pool of 63 items into a smaller pool of 18 items, which are then subjected to empirical testing.

The focus of step three is determination of the measurement format (DeVellis, 2003). Format has been shown to affect responses and, in effect, the validity of the measure. Thus careful consideration of the format is needed. Formats come in a large variety, including Likert scaling (Likert, 1932), Thurstone scaling (Thurstone and Chave, 1929), Guttman scaling (1950), semantic differential scaling (Osgood et al., 1957) and Stevens scaling (nominal, ordinal, interval and ratio scales: Stevens, 1951). Also, response alternatives need to be considered at this stage. If an item consists of a stem that is a declarative statement and response options expressing degree of disagreement or agreement with the statement, particular adverbs need to be used as modifiers. Also, whether the number of response options is even or odd matters; this depends on the type of stem and the purpose of the item and measure. If a scale asks for a judgment, it is important to consider whether the response scale is unipolar or bipolar. As an example of the latter, much research on entrepreneurial orientation has adopted the scale of nine semantic differential items developed by Covin and Slevin (1989). The use of visual analog scales has not been commonplace in entrepreneurship research, but recent advances in methodologies for Internet-based questionnaires will probably lead to a more widespread use of this response scale type. Currently, perhaps the two most widely used response option scales are the Likert scale and the binary scale. For example, the four recent entrepreneurship scale development studies men-tioned earlier in the chapter use Likert scales (Cardon et al., 2013; Chandler et al., 2011; Schjoedt and Shaver 2012; Renko et al., forthcoming).

In step four, content validity is assessed. According to DeVellis (2003), the item pool should be reviewed by experts, that is, people who are knowledgeable about the topic of interest. This provides an opportunity to revise item wording in light of the construct definition and clarity, to assess item relevance, to reduce the number of items and to identify relevant items not included in the item pool. The resulting, improved item pool provides the basis for content validity of the measurement. Alternatively, Aguinis and colleagues (2001) recommend a different approach to this step: a pilot study and item analysis. Based on this, items are selected for the measurement and the data pertaining to the selected items are used to refine the measure (enhance reliability and validity using statistics). This psychometric approach may result in measures with inappropriate items but high internal reliability (Rossiter, 2002). Thus in this chapter we focus on the process advocated by DeVellis (2003) and others (e.g. Netemeyer et al., 2003; Peter, 1981), which is less driven by psychometrics.

Including validation items constitutes step five (DeVellis, 2003). Validation items provide an opportunity to assess whether respondents answer the items of interest for the same reasons as presumed by the measurement developers. For example, the ten-item social desirability measure provided by Strahan and Gerbasi (1972) could be included when the scale items of interest are administered to a development sample or in a pilot study. The use of a development sample is step six in the process. A variety of recommendations have been made for an adequate size of the development sample: Nunnally (1978) recommends a sample size of 300. Others recommend a ratio between sample size and variables. The recommended ratios include 20:1 (Hair et al., 2006), 5:1 (e.g. Bryant and Yarnold, 1995; Everitt, 1975) and 1.3:1 for samples with fewer than 100 (Arrindell and van der Ende, 1985). It should be noted that, based on their results, Guadagnoli and Velicer (1988) pointed out that absolute sample size is more important than ratios, and that sample sizes of 100 to 200 are adequate. Step six is similar to the pilot study and item analysis using psychometric statistics advocated by Aguinis et al. (2001). It is critical that an exploratory factor analysis is conducted to determine the dimensionality and the underlying factor structure before undertaking the item analysis. This means that exploratory factor analysis is employed to determine the unidimensionality of the measure. And this is done before estimation of coefficient alpha and item analysis.[3] As part of the item analysis, reverse-scored items are evaluated together with item correlations, item means, item variances and coefficient alpha for the purpose of identifying the items that provide the best assessment of the unidimensional construct. Aguinis et al. (2001) provide an overview of how to enhance the psychometric properties and to optimize the measure. This optimization constitutes the final step, step seven, in the measurement development process. This step, along with data from the development sample, also begins the measurement validation process since content validity, unidimensionality and coefficient alpha have been assessed. As an alternative to the desirable multitrait-multimethod approach (Campbell and Fiske, 1959), the limited version – multitrait-monomethod – may be employed to assess convergent, discriminant and nomological validity with data from the development sample.[4]

Before we move on, to a practical example of measurement development and validation, it should be noted there are alternative approaches to measurement development, including the C-OAR-SE procedure (Rossiter, 2002). It is beyond the scope of this chapter to detail this procedure; however, it is worth observing the basis for Rossiter's (2002) rationale for departing from the traditional measurement development procedure. Rossiter observes that the traditional procedure for measurement development is based on the emphasis on factor analysis and internal reliability; and this has been furthered by the use of structural equation modeling. This emphasis has led to unusual results in the development of measures, such as elimination of conceptually necessary items in pursuit of unidimensionality, addition of conceptually inappropriate items, and use of high estimates of internal reliability (alphas) as the singular evidence of measurement validity. The issue of using Cronbach's alpha as the only psychometric property indicating measurement validity is also widespread in the entrepreneurship literature (cf. Bird and Schjoedt, 2009; Bird et al., 2012).

An important observation by Rossiter (2002) is that content validity – '*a priori* evidence that the items are a good representation of the construct (from expert judges)' (Rossiter, 2002, p. 311) – is often confused with face validity, which is a *post hoc* claim that measurement items assess the construct (Nunnally, 1978). Face validity is an inadequate assessment of validity because only the final, purified scale items are assessed. This means that illustration of content validity requires that all items considered to represent the construct will have to be included in the journal article, which may not be possible due to page limitations of journal submissions. While this is an issue, the more profound issue in presenting face validity only is that, in many cases, face validity is the only means of purification employed. In addition to face validity, item analysis is used to increase coefficient alpha. Consequently, this may result in a measure with a high coefficient alpha but limited construct validity. This issue is evident when some researchers use only selected items from an established scale based on face validity as their measure. This emphasis on face validity, while disregarding construct validity, is also prevalent in entrepreneurship research as only the wording of the final items included in the measurement scale is often presented (cf. Bird and Schjoedt, 2009; Bird, et al., 2012).

Reflecting on the process approach described above, but at the same time recognizing the limitations sometimes imposed by the real world, we next present a practical example of scale development by two of the authors of this chapter. Reader alert: we consider what follows to be a less-than-perfect exemplar of the process approach. It is, however, one with which we are intimately acquainted.

DEVELOPING A MULTI-ITEM MEASURE: A PRACTICAL EXAMPLE

Locus of control refers to the extent to which individuals believe that their desired outcomes depend on their own actions (Rotter, 1966; 1975). Several different approaches have been taken in assessing locus of control in entrepreneurship research, including the use of general locus of control measures (e.g. Chen et al., 1998) and task-specific locus of control measures (e.g. Bonnett and Furnham, 1991). However, no domain-specific locus of control measure has been available. This is unfortunate as the general locus of control measures lack specificity and the task-specific measures may be too narrow, hence ignoring some important aspects of the construct. In our recent article, we set out to develop a locus of control measure for the entrepreneurship domain (Schjoedt and Shaver, 2012). In developing this measure, we followed the traditional development and validation procedure (DeVellis, 2003; Netemeyer et al., 2003) using two separate studies.

As a first step, we carefully considered the level of specificity of locus of control for the entrepreneurship domain. One good way to stay connected to the domain is to develop a measure constructed from items answered by a sample of nascent entrepreneurs from the first Panel Study of Entrepreneurial Dynamics (PSED I). The PSED studies are publicly available from the University of Michigan (www.psed.isr.umich.edu) and PSED has been described in detail by Gartner et al. (2004). Beginning with a sample of nascent entrepreneurs has the advantage of ensuring that the particular items are relevant to the ultimate target population. Once a set of items had been identified, the focus changed to establishing the convergent and discriminant validity of the measure using a separate sample of undergraduate students, half of whom were enrolled in entrepreneurship courses.

Items that might pertain to locus of control were identified from the PSED I mail survey. These included the three items originally intended to assess locus of control based on two separate kinds of control from Paulhus's (1983) spheres of control scale and items originally intended to assess other constructs related to locus of control, such as entrepreneurial intensity and entrepreneurial expectancy. This resulted in the item pool of 11 items shown in the Appendix to this chapter; all based on a 5-point Likert-type response format. Obviously this is a substantially smaller number than the 60 items often recommended (e.g. Nunnally, 1978), just one way in which the study is a real, if imperfect, example. Using the responses from the 463 nascent entrepreneurs in PSED I, we identified three factors inherent in the data. The three factors were identified using the following approaches: K1, scree plot and MAP (Cattell, 1966; Kaiser, 1960; Fabrigar et al., 1999; Zwick and Velicer, 1986). One factor included the following items:

1.   I have no trouble making and keeping friends.
2.   When I make plans I am almost certain to make them work.
3.   When I get what I want it is usually because I worked hard for it.
4.   I can do anything I set my mind on doing.

The first three items were from the Paulhus (1983) scale, so it is reasonable to claim that the four together represent locus of control. Because (1) deals with friendship ties indicating a separate dimension, confirmatory factor analysis was used to check whether the data fit the three- or four-item measure better. The results from the confirmatory factor analyses supported the three-item (items 2, 3 and 4) measure. Data from the 301 respondents constituting the control group (non-entrepreneurs) for PSED I were also used to assess the appropriateness of the three-item measure using confirmatory factor analysis.

Next, the reliability of the three-item unidimensional measure of locus of control was estimated using Cronbach's alpha. It was expected that Cronbach's alpha would have a low value because it is susceptible to the number of items and the measure had only three items. Cronbach's alpha of the measure was compared to Cronbach's alpha of the three items (from Paulhus's spheres of control scale) intended to assess locus of control in the PSED I. The coefficient alphas were tested for difference; the difference was significant, with the developed locus of control measure having a higher Cronbach's alpha than the intended measure of locus of control. Additionally, by comparing Cronbach's alpha for the sample of nascent entrepreneurs ($\alpha = 0.59$) with that of the control group ($\alpha = 0.54$), we were able to show that the developed measure was stable across samples.[5] Lastly, using the PSED I data we assessed the nomological validity of the developed measure: we inspected the correlations between the developed measure and measures of job stress ($r = 0.13$, $p \leq 0.01$) and life satisfaction ($r = 0.24$, $p \leq 0.0001$), which were as expected from other research studies (cf. Schjoedt and Shaver, 2012).

The PSED I data did not provide an opportunity to assess convergent and discriminant validity. Thus we gathered data from 119 undergraduate university students participating in a senior-level business course from a mid-western public university for Study Two. The survey instrument included the 11 items considered for the item pool in Study One and several widely used measures of conceptually related and unrelated constructs (e.g. general locus of control, general self-efficacy, self-esteem, neuroticism and social desirability). In addition to providing further evidence of the uni-dimensionality and reliability of the developed (three-item) measure, the study provided evidence of convergent and discriminant validity. In sum, paying careful attention to the measurement development and validation process described in this chapter, we developed and validated an efficient, reliable, valid and unidimensional three-item measure of locus of control for the entrepreneurship domain. Although it is recommended that scales are multi-item – the more items, the better (Cronbach, 1951; Nunnally, 1978), at times scales with few items provide a valid measure of the construct, as shown in the practical example above. Some constructs may be assessed by single-item measures that are valid measures.

A CONTROVERSY: SINGLE- VERSUS MULTI-ITEM MEASURES

Construct definition plays a major role in determining whether to use a single- or multiple-item measure to assess the construct. It is a widely accepted practice to employ single items to measure facts, such as age or the number of previous jobs (Wanous and Reichers, 1996; Wanous et al., 1997). Even if the predictive validity of single-item and multi-item measures is the same (Bergkvist and Rossiter, 2007), latent constructs, such as job satisfaction (e.g. Schjoedt, 2002, 2009), are predominantly measured using multi-item scales. In fact, the use of single-item measures is often perceived as a 'fatal error' that can result in rejection for publication (Bergkvist and Rossiter, 2007; Wanous et al., 1997). This perception may be, in part, for one of three reasons. The first reason rests on a comment from Nunnally (1978), who states: 'others things being equal, a long test is a good test' (p. 243). This comment is based on the reduction in standard error that accompanies the use of increasing numbers of items. Another strike against the use of single-item measures is that structural equation modeling, which has been increasingly used in recent years, requires an estimation of reliable variance, thus requiring multiple items. Third, internal reliability cannot be estimated for single-item measures (Wanous et al., 1997).

Despite these shortcomings, single-item measures have some attractive features and may be more appropriate than multiple-item measures when assessing certain latent constructs (such as global job satisfaction). The use of multi-item measures is costly in terms of money, time and information, and places a heavy burden on the respondent in terms of time and effort.

This may result in respondent refusal, fatigue and information inaccuracy. Drolet and Morrison (2001) note a trade-off between the quality of information and reliability: 'mindless response behavior' (p. 200) may result especially when respondents are asked the same question more than once (in different wordings). Multi-item measures may produce high reliabilities, but that may be at the expense of response quality, adding very little information over single-item measures. A single-item measure may be particularly useful when the construct is narrow or unambiguous to the respondent (Sackett and Larson, 1990). Nunnally (1978) notes that, if a measure assesses a simple, unidimensional construct, single-item measures are acceptable. This is countered by Peter's observation that 'most constructs by definition are too complex to be measured effectively with a single item' (1979, p. 16). Combined, these observations by Nunnally (1978) and Peter (1981) indicate that, when a unidimensional construct is assessed, it may be acceptable to do so using a single-item measure; and, when a multidimensional construct is assessed, it may also be acceptable to measure it using multiple single-item measures (e.g. Hackman and Oldham, 1975; Quinn and Staines, 1979). While these combined observations are employed in many studies, the overall sentiment among researchers and journal editors is still found in the comment by Nunnally (1978) that a long test is better. However, at least one group of investigators has noted that single-item measures are superior to summated facet measures (e.g. Ironson et al., 1989). This is because single-item measures are holistic and respondents consider what is important to them as they provide their response, whereas summated facet measures are based on researchers' *a priori* selection of facets that may or may not be the facets important to the respondents. Let us illustrate this with an example: job satisfaction.

In 1969, Locke defined job satisfaction as 'overall job satisfaction is the sum of the evaluations of the discrete elements of which the job is composed' (p. 330). This definition clearly indicates that job satisfaction is a combination (additive, multiplicative or some other formula) of facets, such as satisfaction with pay or satisfaction with supervisor. We will call such measures composite measures of the general construct. However, in 1976, Locke provided a different and widely used definition of job satisfaction: 'a pleasurable or positive emotional state resulting from the appraisal of one's job or job experiences' (p. 1300). This later definition indicates that job satisfaction is a singular (unidimensional) construct. These two definitions illustrate the importance of a clear definition of the construct to be assessed in terms of its dimensionality. They have also led to a debate in the job satisfaction literature on whether job satisfaction should be assessed using single-item measures or multi-item composite measures (e.g. Scarpello and Campbell, 1983). Thus the dimensionality inherent in the definition of the job satisfaction construct influences the mode of measurement. Considering that the 1976 definition by Locke is a widely used definition and illustrates that job satisfaction is a unidimensional construct, researchers may choose a single-item measure or a composite multi-item measure to assess job satisfaction.

In choosing whether to use a single-item or a composite multi-item job satisfaction measure, researchers need to consider the following. Research shows that, regardless of whether composite job satisfaction measures are based on addition, multiplication or some other formula, there is little difference in the assessment (Aldag and Brief, 1978; Ferratt, 1981). However, there is non-equivalence among single-item measures and composite measures of job satisfaction (Ironson et al., 1989). Multi-item composite measures may omit areas that are important to the respondent (Nagy, 2002; Scarpello and Campbell, 1983; Wanous et al., 1997) and may include areas that are not important to the individual (Ironson et al., 1989). Also, the method of combining the items (e.g. addition, multiplication) does not account for the unique individual composition of job satisfaction (Ironson et al., 1989), resulting in an error. Compounding the issue of measurement error is respondent fatigue. Collectively, this suggests that single-item job satisfaction measures may be superior to composite job satisfaction measures due to their effectiveness of assessment, consideration of respondent uniqueness, lesser bias and higher efficiency in assessment (less respondent fatigue, cost and time) (Bergkvist and Rossiter, 2007; Drolet and Morrison, 2001; Nagy, 2002). With that said, we recognize that the choice of measurement is to be made within the context of the research purpose and the need for level of specificity in the construct assessment.

As we have pointed out, single-item measures have their time and place; yet many researchers still routinely employ multi-item measures to avoid rejection of publication even though single-item measurements may be more appropriate (Bergkvist and Rossiter, 2007; Wanous et al., 1997). This avoidance of single-item measures is based on a widely held notion: 'single item measures are notoriously unreliable' (Peter, 1981, p. 138). However, there is no evidence indicating that single-item measures are not reliable (Holmes and Anderson, 1980). Thus it is worthwhile to consider briefly how to estimate the reliability of single-item measures. In addition to test–retest reliability for a single-item measure (Aguinis et al., 2001),[6] there is a procedure based on a well-known formula for the correction for attenuation that may be used for estimating reliability of single-item measures (Wanous and Reichers, 1996; Wanous et al. 1997).[7] This formula is found in many texts on psychometrics and is most commonly employed in situations where data are available on two variables representing two different constructs (e.g. job satisfaction and job performance):

$$\text{T}r_{xy} = r_{xy} / (r_{xx} \, r_{yy})^{1/2}$$

where r_{xy} is the correlation between variables x and y; r_{xx} is the reliability of variable x; r_{yy} is the reliability of variable y; and $\text{T}r_{xy}$ is the assumed true underlying correlation between x and y if both are measured perfectly (Wanous et al., 1997, p. 248). When this formula is applied in situations in which the measured variables assess the same construct, then, according to Nunnally (1978 in Wanous et al., 1997, p. 248), $r_{xy} = (r_{xx})^{1/2} (r_{yy})^{1/2}$. This provides an opportunity to assess reliability for single-item measures. Wanous et al. (1997), in their estimation of minimum reliability, assumed a true r-score of, first, 1.00 and then 0.90. They found that single-items are reliable and that the response format had effectuated differences in the results, which is similar to the findings by Gardner et al. (1998). Wanous and Reichers (1996) conclude that the 'rejection of single-item measures does not seem warranted' (p. 634). When considering this conclusion, it should be observed that Wanous and Reichers (1996) and Wanous et al. (1997) used the construct of job satisfaction for their examination. As noted earlier, job satisfaction is one of the constructs that may be better assessed using single-item measures than summated facet satisfaction scales (Nagy, 2002; Scarpello and Campbell, 1983).

As noted earlier, many hold that single-item measures are not appropriate for assessing constructs. We have illustrated that single-item measures may be appropriate for assessing the general level of unidimensional constructs, and that there are two methods for estimating the reliability of single-item measures. In addition to the advantages we have already noted in terms of being efficient and effective, single-item measures have additional benefits. Single-item measures have been shown to have the same predictive validity as multi-item measures (Bergkvist and Rossiter, 2007); be temporally stable and have concurrent, convergent and divergent validity (e.g. Abdel-Khalek, 2006); be more robust (Nagy, 2002); and may even be psychometrically superior to multi-item measures (e.g. Holmes and Anderson, 1980; Scarpello and Campbell, 1983; Wanous and Reichers, 1996; Wanous et al., 1997). While we are not advocating a reversal of the practice of employing multi-item measures, we suggest that there is a time and a place for using single-item measures in entrepreneurship research; and this time and place depend upon construct definition, construct complexity and research purpose (especially in terms of level of measurement detail).

MOVING FORWARD: A CALL FOR IMPROVED MEASUREMENT

Entrepreneurship research has advanced substantially over the years. Increasingly, entrepreneurship researchers have employed the practice of providing evidence of the validity of their measures (cf. Chandler and Lyon, 2001). This is something that the journals in the field are also demanding. In particular, researchers provide item wordings from surveys used and increasingly also include estimates of Cronbach's alpha for multi-item measures (cf. Bird et al., 2012). However, there is still considerable room for improvement. Given that substantive and measurement developments are interrelated (Schwab, 1980), there is a pressing need to enhance measurement in entrepreneurship research. As Cook and Campbell (1979) note, the ability to make causal statements about the relationship between two constructs begins with unambiguous and nonconfounded measurement of each construct separately. This requires that we carefully consider the measures employed, whether single- or multi-item measures, and their validity. Alternatively, we run the risk of being held back and not advancing our collective understanding of entrepreneurship. As we look into the future, we call for better illustration of measurement validity in entrepreneurship research. Also, regardless of past practices and norms, we encourage researchers to use both single- and multi-item measures, depending on the construct being assessed. Lastly, we call for entrepreneurship scholars to assess and report the psychometric properties of all measures employed in their research.

NOTES

1. Content validity should not be confused with face validity. Face validity is not concerned with what the items actually measure, but what they appear to measure (superficially) (Anastasi, 1988).
2. An alternative to classical reliability theory – the traditional psychometric approach to reliability presented here – is provided in the generalization theory (Cronbach et al., 1972). For more information on the generalization theory see Cronbach et al. (1972) and other works (e.g. Finn and Kayande, 1997).
3. We advocate this contemporary approach over the traditional approach advocated by Churchill (1979) based on using coefficient alpha as the first 'purifying tool' to optimize the measure.
4. For an example of the multitrait-monomethod see Schjoedt and Shaver (2012).
5. While Cronbach's alpha is lower than what could be desired, it should be observed that Cronbach's alpha is influenced by the number of scale items and constitutes the lower bound of the internal reliability estimate (Hair et al., 1998; Miller, 1995).
6. However, test–retest reliability has been criticized for the following reasons: learning may take place from time one to time two; situational factors are not identical; the

magnitude of test–retest reliability cannot be specified *a priori*; and it does not estimate internal reliability.

7. It should be observed that parallel/alternative forms of reliability may also be estimated in place of coefficient alpha. Using a sample of entrepreneurs and small-business managers, Schjoedt (2002) assessed job satisfaction using two distinct single-item measures (Ganzach, 1998; Trevor, 2001) and Minnesota Satisfaction Questionnaire (MSQ: Weiss et al., 1967). He found that the coefficient alpha for the two-item job satisfaction measure using the two single-item measures was 0.94 and the coefficient alpha for the two single-item measures and MSQ items was 0.91.

REFERENCES

Abdel-Khalek, A.M. (2006), 'Measuring happiness with a single-item scale', *Social Behavior and Personality*, **34**(2): 139–50.

Aguinis, H., Henle, C.A. and Ostroff, C. (2001), 'Measurement in work and organizational psychology', in N. Anderson, D.S. Ones, H.K. Sinangil and C. Viswesvaran (eds), *Handbook of Industrial, Work, and Organizational Psychology*, Vol. 1, Thousand Oaks, CA: Sage, pp. 27–51.

Aldag, R.J. and Brief, A.P. (1978), 'Examinations of alternative models of job satisfaction', *Human Relations*, **31**(1): 91–8.

American Psychological Association (1954), *Technical Recommendations for Psychological Tests and Diagnostic Techniques*, Washington, DC: American Psychological Association.

American Psychological Association (1966), *Standards for Educational and Psychological Tests and Manuals*, Washington, DC: American Psychological Association.

Anastasi, A. (1988), *Psychological Testing*, New York: Macmillan.

Arrindell, W.A. and van der Ende, J. (1985), 'An empirical test of the utility of the observations-to-variables ratio in factor and component analysis', *Applied Psychological Measurement*, **9**: 165–78.

Bagozzi, R.P. (1980), *Causal Models in Marketing*, New York: Wiley.

Bergkvist, L. and Rossiter, J.R. (2007), 'The predictive validity of multiple-item versus single-item measures of the same constructs', *Journal of Marketing Research*, **44**: 175–84.

Bird, B. and Schjoedt, L. (2009), 'Entrepreneurial behavior: its nature, scope, recent research and future research', in A.L. Carsrud and M.E. Brännback (eds), *Understanding the Entrepreneurial Mind: Opening the Black Box*, New York: Springer, pp. 327–58.

Bird, B.J., Schjoedt, L. and Baum, J.R. (2012), 'Entrepreneurs' behavior: elucidation and measurement', *Entrepreneurship Theory and Practice*, **36**(5): 889–913.

Bird, B.J., Schjoedt, L. and Hanke, R. (forthcoming), 'Research on behavior in small and entrepreneurial firms', in E. Chell and M. Karatas-Ozkan (eds), *Handbook of Research in Small Business and Entrepreneurship*, Edward Elgar.

Bonnett, C. and Furnham, A. (1991), 'Who wants to be an entrepreneur? A study of adolescents interested in a young enterprise scheme', *Journal of Economic Psychology*, **12**: 465–78.

Brettel, M., Mauer, R., Engelen, A. and Küpper, D. (2012), 'Corporate effectuation: entrepreneurial action and its impact on R&D project performance', *Journal of Business Venturing*, **27**(2): 167–84.

Bryant, F.B. and Yarnold, P.R. (1995), 'Principal-component analysis and exploratory and confirmatory factor analysis', in J.J. Grimm and P.R. Yarnold (eds), *Reading and Understanding Multivariate Statistics*, Washington, DC: American Psychological Association, pp. 99–136.

Campbell, D.T. (1960), 'Recommendations for APA test standards regarding construct, trait, or discriminant validity', *American Psychologist*, **15**: 546–53.

Campbell, J.P. (1976), 'Psychometric theory', in M.D. Dunnette (ed.), *Handbook of Industrial and Organizational Psychology*, Chicago, IL: Rand McNally, pp. 185–222.

Campbell, D.T. and Fiske, D.W. (1959), 'Convergent and discriminant validation by the multitrait–multimethod matrix', *Psychological Bulletin*, **56**(2): 81–105.

Cardon, M.S., Grégoire, D.A., Stevens, C.E. and Patel, P.C. (2013), 'Measuring entrepreneurial passion: conceptual foundations and scale validation', *Journal of Business Venturing*, **28**(3): 373–96.

Cassar, G. and Friedman, H. (2009), 'Does self-efficacy affect entrepreneurial investment?', *Strategic Entrepreneurship Journal*, **3**: 241–60.

Cattell, R.B. (1966), 'The scree test for the number of factors', *Multivariate Behavioral Research*, **1**: 245–76.

Chandler, G.N. and Lyon, D.W. (2001), 'Issues of research design and construct measurement in entrepreneurship research: the past decade', *Entrepreneurship Theory and Practice*, **25**(4): 101–13.

Chandler, G.N., DeTienne, D.R., McKelvie, A. and Mumford, T.V. (2011), 'Causation and effectuation processes: a validation study', *Journal of Business Venturing*, **26**(3): 375–90.

Chen, C.C., Greene, P.G. and Crick, A. (1998), 'Does entrepreneurial self-efficacy distinguish entrepreneurs from managers?', *Journal of Business Venturing*, **13**: 295–316.

Churchill, G.A. (1979), 'A paradigm for developing better measures of marketing constructs', *Journal of Marketing Research*, **16**: 64–73.

Cook, T.D. and Campbell, D.T. (1979), *Quasi-Experimentation: Design & Analysis Issues for Field Settings*, Boston, MA: Houghton Mifflin.

Cortina, J.M. (1993), 'What is coefficient alpha? An examination of theory and applications', *Journal of Applied Psychology*, **78**: 98–104.

Covin, J.G. and Slevin, D.P. (1989), 'Strategic management of small firms in hostile and benign environments', *Strategic Management Journal*, **10**: 75–87.

Cronbach, L.J. (1951), 'Coefficient alpha and the internal structure of tests', *Psychometrika*, **16**(3): 297–334.

Cronbach, L.J. (1971), 'Test validation', in R.L. Thorndike (ed.), *Educational Measurement*, 2nd edn, Washington, DC: American Council on Education, pp. 443–507.

Cronbach, L.J. and Meehl, P.E. (1955), 'Construct validity in psychological tests', *Psychological Bulletin*, **52**: 281–302.

Cronbach, L.J., Gleser, G., Nanda, H. and Rajaratnam, N. (1972), *The Dependability of Behavioral Measurements: Theory of Generalizability of Scores and Profiles*, New York: Wiley.

DeVellis, R.F. (2003), *Scale Development: Theory and Application*, 2nd edn, Newbury Park, CA: Sage.

Drolet, A.L. and Morrison, D.G. (2001), 'Do we really need multiple-item measures in service research?', *Journal of Service Research*, **3**(3): 196–204.

Everitt, B.S. (1975), 'Multivariate analysis: the need for data, and other problems', *The British Journal of Psychiatry*, **126**: 237–40.

Fabrigar, L.R., Wegener, D.T., MacCallum, R.C. and Strahan, E.J. (1999), 'Evaluating the use of exploratory factor analysis in psychological research', *Psychological Methods*, **4**: 272–99.

Ferratt, T.W. (1981), 'Overall job satisfaction: is it a linear function of facet satisfaction?', *Human Relations*, **34**(6): 463–73.

Finn, A. and Kayande, U. (1997), 'Reliability assessment and optimization of marketing measurement', *Journal of Marketing Research*, **34**: 262–75.

Ganzach, Y. (1998), 'Intelligence and job satisfaction', *Academy of Management Journal*, **41**(5): 526–39.

Gardner, D.G., Cummings, L.L., Dunham, R.B. and Pierce, J.L. (1998), 'Single-item versus multiple-item measurement scales: an empirical comparison', *Educational and Psychological Measurement*, **58**(6): 898–915.

Gartner, W.B. (1988), '"Who is an entrepreneur?" is the wrong question', *American Journal of Small Business*, **12**(Spring): 11–32.

Gartner, W.B., Shaver, K.G., Carter, N.M. and Reynolds, P.D. (2004), *Handbook of Entrepreneurial Dynamics: The Process of Business Creation*, Thousand Oaks, CA: Sage.

Glorfeld, L.W. (1995), 'An improvement on Horn's parallel analysis methodology for selecting the correct number of factors to retain', *Educational and Psychological Measurement*, **55**(3): 377–93.

Graham, J.M. (2006), 'Congeneric and (essentially) tau-equivalent estimates of score reliability', *Education and Psychological Measurement*, **66**(6): 930–44.

Guadagnoli, E. and Velicer, W.F. (1988), 'Relation of sample size to stability of component patterns', *Psychological Bulletin*, **103**: 265–75.

Guttman, L. (1950), 'The basis for scalogram', in S.A. Stouffer et al. (eds), *Measurement and Prediction*, Vol. IV, New York: Wiley, pp. 60–90.

Hackman, J.R. and Oldham, G.R. (1975), 'Development of the Job Diagnostic Survey', *Journal of Applied Psychology*, **60**: 159–70.

Hair, J.F., Anderson, R.E., Tatham, R.L. and Black, W.C. (1998), *Multivariate Data Analysis*, 5th edn, Upper Saddle River, NJ: Prentice Hall.

Hair, J.F., Black, W.C., Babin, B.J., Anderson, R.E. and Tatham, R.L. (2006), *Multivariate Data Analysis*, 6th edn, Upper Saddle River, NJ: Pearson/Prentice Hall.

Holmes, C.B. and Anderson, D.J. (1980), 'Comparison of four death anxiety measures', *Psychological Reports*, **46**: 1341–2.

Horn, J.L. (1965), 'A rationale and test for the number of factors in factor analysis', *Psychometrika*, **30**: 179–85.

Ironson, G.H., Smith, P.C., Brannick, M.T., Gibson, W.M. and Paul, K.B. (1989), 'Construction of a job in general scale: a comparison of global, composite, and specific measures', *Journal of Applied Psychology*, **74**(2): 193–200.

Kaiser, H.F. (1960), 'The application of electronic computers to factor analysis', *Educational and Psychological Measurement*, **20**(1): 141–51.

Kuder, G.F. and Richardson, M.W. (1937), 'The theory of the estimation of test reliability', *Psychometrika*, **2**: 151–60.

Likert, R. (1932), 'A technique for the measurement of attitudes', *Archives of Psychology*, **22**(140): 5–53.

Locke, E.A. (1969), 'What is job satisfaction?', *Organizational Behavior and Human Performance*, **4**: 309–36.

Locke, E.A. (1976), 'The nature and causes of job satisfaction', in M.D. Dunnette (ed.), *Handbook of Industrial and Organizational Psychology*, Chicago, IL: Rand McNally, pp. 1297–349.

Lumsden, J. (1976), 'Test theory', *Annual Review of Psychology*, **27**: 251–80.

Miller, M.B. (1995), 'Coefficient alpha: a basic introduction from the perspectives of classical test theory and structural equation modeling', *Structural Equation Modeling*, **2**(3): 255–73.

Nagy, M.S. (2002), 'Using a single-item approach to measure facet job satisfaction', *Journal of Occupational and Organizational Psychology*, **75**: 77–86.

Netemeyer, R.G., Bearden, W.O. and Sharma, S. (2003), *Scaling Procedures: Issues and Applications*, Thousand Oaks, CA: Sage.

Nunnally, J.C. (1978), *Psychometric Theory*, 2nd edn, New York: McGraw-Hill.

Osgood, C.E., Suci, G.J. and Tannenbaum, P.H. (1957), *The Measurement of Meaning*, Urbana, IL: University of Illinois Press.

Paulhus, D. (1983), 'Sphere-specific measures of perceived control', *Journal of Personality and Social Psychology*, **44**: 1253–65.

Peter, J.P. (1981), 'Construct validity: a review of basic issues and marketing practices', *Journal of Marketing Research*, **18**(2): 133–45.

Peter, J.P. (1979), 'Reliability: a review of psychometric basics and recent marketing practices', *Journal of Marketing Research*, **16**(1): 6–17.

Quinn, R.E. and Staines, G.L. (1979), *The 1977 Quality of Employment Survey: Descriptive Statistics, with Comparison Data from the 1969–1970 and 1972–1973 Surveys*, Ann Arbor, MI: Institute for Social Research.

Raykov, T. (1998), 'Coefficient alpha and composite reliability with interrelated nonhomogeneous items', *Applied Psychological Measurement*, **22**(4): 375–85.

Renko, M., Tarabishy, A., Carsrud, A. and Brännback, M. (forthcoming), 'Understanding and measuring entrepreneurial leadership style', *Journal of Small Business Management*.

Reynolds, P.D. (2000), 'National panel study of U.S. business startups: background and methodology', in J.A. Katz (ed.), *Advances in Entrepreneurship, Firm Emergence, and Growth*, Stamford, CT: JAI Press, pp. 153–227.

Rossiter, J.R. (2002), 'The C-OAR-SE procedure for scale development in marketing', *International Journal of Research in Marketing*, **19**: 305–35.

Rotter, J.B. (1966), 'Generalized expectancies for internal versus external control of reinforcement', *Psychological Monographs*, **80**(609): whole number.

Rotter, J.B. (1975), 'Some problems and misconceptions related to the construct of internal versus external control of reinforcement', *Journal of Consulting and Clinical Psychology*, **43**(1): 56–67.

Sackett, P.R. and Larson, J.R. (1990), 'Research strategies and tactics in industrial and organizational psychology', in M.D. Dunnette and L.M. Hough (eds), *Handbook of Industrial and Organizational Psychology*, 2nd edn, Vol. 1, Palo Alto, CA: Consulting Psychologists Press, pp. 419–89.

Scarpello, V. and Campbell, J.P. (1983), 'Job satisfaction: are all the parts there?', *Personnel Psychology*, **36**: 577–600.

Schjoedt, L. (2002), *Entrepreneurial Job Satisfaction: An empirical investigation of the situational, dispositional and interactional approaches to entrepreneurs' job satisfaction*, doctoral dissertation, University of Colorado at Boulder, CO.

Schjoedt, L. (2009), 'Entrepreneurial job characteristics: an examination of their effects on entrepreneurial satisfaction', *Entrepreneurship Theory and Practice*, **33**(3): 619–44.

Schjoedt, L. and Shaver, K.G. (2012), 'Development and validation of a locus of control scale for the entrepreneurship domain', *Small Business Economics*, **39**(3): 713–26.

Schwab, D.P. (1980), 'Construct validity in organizational behavior', *Research in Organizational Behavior*, **2**: 3–43.

Stevens, S.S. (1951), 'Measurement, statistics, and the schemapiric view', *Science*, **161**: 849–56.

Strahan, R. and Gerbasi, K.C. (1972), 'Short, homogeneous versions of the Marlow–Crowne social desirability scale', *Journal of Clinical Psychology*, **28**: 191–3.

Thurstone, L.L. and Chave, E.J. (1929), *The Measurement of Attitude*, Chicago, IL: University of Chicago Press.

Trevor, C.O. (2001), 'Interactions among actual ease-of-movement determinants and job satisfaction in the prediction of voluntary turnover', *Academy of Management Journal*, **44**(4): 621–38.

Velicer, W.F. (1976), 'Determining the number of components from the matrix of partial correlations', *Psychometrika*, **41**(3): 321–7.

Wanous, J.P. and Reichers, A.E. (1996), 'Estimating the reliability of a single-item measure', *Psychological Reports*, **78**: 631–4.

Wanous, J.P., Reichers, A.E. and Hudy, M.J. (1997), 'Overall job satisfaction: how good are single-item measures?', *Journal of Applied Psychology*, **82**(2): 247–52.

Weiss, D.J., Dawis, R.V., England, G.W. and Lofquist, L.H. (1967), *Manual for the Minnesota Satisfaction Questionnaire*, Minnesota Studies in Vocational Rehabilitation, XXII, Minneapolis, MN: SVR.

Zwick, W.R. and Velicer, W.F. (1986), 'Comparison of five rules for determining the number of components to retain', *Psychological Bulletin*, **99**(3): 432–42.

APPENDIX

Table 6A.1   *Items from the PSED mail questionnaire considered by Schjoedt and Shaver (2012)*

No.	Item	PSED item no.
1	I have no trouble making and keeping friends.	QL1h
2	**When I make plans, I am almost certain to make them work.**	QL1i
3	**When I get what I want, it is usually because I worked hard for it.**	QL1j
4	If I work hard, I can successfully start a business.	QK1a
5	If I start a business, it will help me achieve other important goals in my life.	QK1c
6	Overall, my skills and abilities will help me start a business.	QK1d
7	My past experience will be very valuable in starting a business.	QK1e
8	I am confident I can put in the effort needed to start a business.	QK1f
9	**I can do anything I set my mind on doing.**	QL1a
10	There is no limit as to how long I would give maximum effort to establish my business.	QL1e
11	My personal philosophy is 'do whatever it takes' to establish my own business.	QL1f

Notes: All the items considered are from the PSED mail questionnaire. This questionnaire and the 501-page codebook for the project can be found at http://www.psed.isr.umich.edu.

Items 2, 3 and 9, which comprise the Locus of Control scale developed by Schjoedt and Shaver (2012) are in bold.

7. Control variables: use, misuse and recommended use

Leon Schjoedt and Barbara Bird

When investigating entrepreneurial phenomena, scholars are frequently interested in understanding causal relationships. Conducting an experiment provides better insights into causal relationships than many other research strategies (Schwab, 2005). This is because researchers are better able to eliminate alternative explanations among the predictor and criterion variables by randomly assigning individuals to experimental conditions and manipulating the variables. For several reasons (e.g. an experiment may not be feasible), researchers frequently use a nonexperimental research design (Austin et al., 2002; Stone-Romero, 2007). However, nonexperimental research does not benefit from the control of variables possible in experimental research.

Because extraneous nuisance variables – variables that influence the variables of interest in a study but are not central to the study – are correlated with the variables of interest, the use of nonexperimental research design makes drawing causal inferences difficult. These nuisance variables offer alternative explanations for the relationship among the variables of interest – the predictor and criterion variables. To limit such alterative explanations, researchers often attempt to measure extraneous nuisance variables presumed to be associated the variables of interest in the relationship investigated. These extraneous nuisance variables are, then, controlled for in correlational research, such as multiple regression analysis, to rule out alternative explanations or to reduce error variance (Becker, 2005; Schwab, 2005).

Inclusion of control variables in nonexperimental research is widespread in management research, as evidenced by several authors (e.g. Atinc et al., 2012; Becker, 2005; Breaugh, 2006, 2008; Carlson and Wu, 2012; Spector and Brannick, 2011). For example, a recent review of the management literature shows that control variables were included in 812 of the 1199 articles published from 2005 to 2009 in the *Academy of Management Journal*, *Journal of Applied Psychology*, *Journal of Management* and *Strategic Management Journal* (Atinc et al., 2012). In preparing this chapter, we reviewed the little more than 140 works published in 2012 in four prestigious entrepreneurship journals – *Entrepreneurship Theory and*

Practice, Journal of Business Venturing, Journal of Small Business Management and *Strategic Entrepreneurship Journal*. In line with published reviews, our review also revealed a widespread use of control variables in nonexperimental entrepreneurship research. For example, 13 of the 20 quantitative nonexperimental studies published in *Strategic Entrepreneurship Journal* included control variables. Thus an important aspect of nonexperimental entrepreneurship research is control variables and their use, misuse and recommended use.

A number of methodologists (e.g. Spector and Brannick, 2011; Stone-Romero, 2007) have noted that, when researchers blindly include control variables in an effort to enhance the casual inference in nonexperimental research, it constitutes a methodological urban legend. In our review of the empirical entrepreneurship research published in 2012 and in our work as editors, reviewers and readers of entrepreneurship research, we have also noted a tendency to include control variables without theoretical justification, even without empirical support from previous research and, at times, without any justification at all. There are several reasons for inclusion of control variables; however, their use is often less than fruitful in generating valid research findings (Spector and Brannick, 2011; Stone-Romero, 2007). First, researchers are seldom aware of all the relevant control variables. Second, even if all the relevant control variables were known, it would rarely be possible to measure more than a few. Spector and Brannick (2011) found an average of 7.7 control variables in macro-organizational and 3.7 control variables in micro-organizational research. Third, unless the measures of control variables are reliable and valid, their use (as with measures of independent and dependent variables) is problematic, which may invalidate the research findings. Fourth, controlling for the confounding effect of the extraneous nuisance variables on the predictor variables does not control for the confounding effect of the control variables on the criterion variable (and vice versa). Fifth, control variables are most often used with limited theoretical consideration or rationale. Sixth, when control variables are included in statistical analysis, researchers *de facto* statistically correct the sample to make an idealized sample or, phrased differently, use a sample of 'fictional people assigned fictional scores' (Meehl, 1970, p. 401). Results based on these 'fictional people' do not generalize and are, consequently, of little interest in contributing to advancement of the field (Cohen and Cohen, 1983; Hunter and Schmidt, 2004; Meehl, 1970).

Our review of entrepreneurship research published in 2012, as well as our review of the methods literature, gives us grounds to state that there may be three over-arching motivations for the (mis)use of control variables in nonexperimental entrepreneurship research. First, there may be a well-intentioned interest to control the variance explained, even if it is sometimes poorly executed. Second, there may be social norms of what multivariate studies look like: 'If previous studies include these controls, so should I.' Third, there may be a well-meant interest to 'purify' results without careful attention to what the specific study requires in terms of control variables. For example, in our review of entrepreneurship research published in 2012, we found research that included control variables that were not conceptually or empirically associated with either the criterion or predictor variables in the study.[1]

The purpose of this chapter is to draw attention to the issue of control variables in nonexperimental entrepreneurship research and to enhance the appropriate use of control variables in future entrepreneurship research. By drawing attention to the issue of control variables, their use, misuse and recommended use, we are confident that entrepreneurship researchers will seek to reduce, or even eliminate, the problematic issues surrounding the current use of control variables to improve future entrepreneurship research. Such improvements will help advance the field of entrepreneurship since greater confidence in research findings will be gained from more appropriate use of control variables (Hunter and Schmidt, 2004; Meehl, 1970, 1971).

To draw attention to the issue of control variables in nonexperimental entrepreneurship research, we will next address statistical control to illustrate that control variables constitute a separate and important research consideration. We follow up on this by addressing three particular issues in the current use of control variables in empirical entrepreneurship research: (1) lack of theoretical justification for inclusion of control variables; (2) the purification principle; and (3) the potential for lack of generalizable results when using control variables. While drawing attention to these issues is important, it is equally important to provide recommendations for how to use control variables in future research to enhance validity of the findings and advance the entrepreneurship literature. We do so by providing ten recommendations for best practice in using control variables before offering our concluding remarks.

STATISTICAL CONTROL

Entrepreneurship researchers are generally interested in understanding causal relationships among a set of variables – criterion and predictor variables (Hunter and Schmidt, 2004). Nonexperimental research design best addresses causality with longitudinal studies, whether it is based on primary or secondary data. Empirical studies, based on either cross-sectional or longitudinal data, are often based on a statistical approach (e.g. multiple regression analysis, structural equation modeling) to control for confounding effects of extraneous nuisance variables when examining a focal relationship between the variables of interest. This is done to rule out alternative explanations (Becker, 2005; Schmitt and Klimoski, 1991) and to reduce error variance (Schwab, 2005). It is also done when researchers do not appreciate that their use of statistical control may be inconsistent with the theoretical foundation of the study (Breaugh, 2008) or done blindly, out of habit, with minimal consideration of why the control variables were included. We noticed these less mindful uses of statistical control when reviewing the literature of entrepreneurs' behavior (Bird and Schjoedt, 2009; Bird et al., 2012). We have also noticed, as editors and reviewers for entrepreneurship journals, these uses of control variables. Statistical control is broadly defined as

> the use of statistical methods to identify, isolate, or nullify variance in a dependent variable that is presumably 'caused' by one or more independent variables that are extraneous to the particular relation or relations under study. (Pedhazur, 1997, p. 157)

Statistical control is a complex matter that depends on the particular theoretical foundation and specific methods of a study. In the remainder of this section, we will focus on what statistical control encompasses. While there is little new information in the remainder of this section, it seems pertinent to briefly address what statistical control involves, because several methodologists (Atinc et al., 2012; Becker, 2005; Breaugh, 2006, 2008; Meehl, 1970; Spector and Brannick, 2011; Spector et al., 2000; Stone-Romero, 2007) have noted that statistical control is often used inappropriately.

Many entrepreneurship researchers, as well as other management and social science researchers, attempt to control for confounding effects through the use multiple regression analysis (Austin et al., 2002; Stone-Romero, 2007). Typically, researchers use a hierarchical approach in which control variables are entered first, followed, in second separate step, by the predictor (typically referred to as independent) variables. Researchers typically examine the incremental change in R^2, between the regression model with control variables only and the regression model with the control and predictor variables. This provides an estimate of the not-confounded effect of the predictor variable. Our hypothetical example below illustrates the issue of statistical control.

A researcher interested in examining a hypothesized relationship between parental role models (X) – the causal predictor variable – and student intentions to start a new business venture (Y) – the criterion variable. Given a nonexperimental research design in which the researcher cannot manipulate variable X and the researcher also collected data on student major (*Z*) – an extraneous nuisance variable that might confound the relationship between variables *X* and *Y*. The researcher faces one of the situations depicted in Figures 7.1 and 7.2.

In Figure 7.1, the area labeled *a* represents the unique variance accounted for in student intentions to start a new business venture (*Y*) by parental role models (*X*). Similarly, the area labeled *b* represents the unique variance accounted for in student intentions to start a new business venture (*Y*) by a potentially confounding variable, student major (*Z*); or, stated differently, the squared zero-order correlation between variables *Z* and *Y*. Since there is no correlation between parental role models (*X*) and student major (*Z*), there is no overlap between variables *X*, *Y* and *Z*. In effect, there is no confounding effect of student major (*Z*) on the relationship of interest between parental role models (*X*) and student intentions to start a new business venture (*Y*).

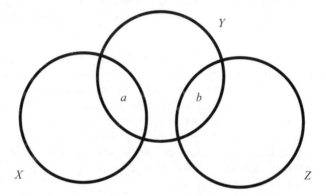

Figure 7.1   Venn diagram depicting no relationship among predictor and control variables

In Figure 7.2, parental role models (*X*) and student major (*Z*) are correlated as shown by the overlapping areas labeled *c* and *d*; in effect student major (*Z*) is a confounding variable. In this figure, the proportion of variance accounted for in student intentions to start a new business venture (*Y*) by parental role models (*X*) is represented by the areas labeled *a* and *c*: the squared zero-order correlation among variables *X* and *Y*. By using a statistical control approach, the effect of student major (*Z*) can be removed from the effect of parental role models (*X*) to determine the unique variance accounted for by parental role models (*X*) in student intentions to start a new business venture (*Y*) represented by the area labeled *a*. Also illustrated in Figure 7.2, the squared zero-order correlation among variables *X* and *Y* represented by the areas labeled *a* and *c* is larger than the unique variance accounted for by parental role models (X) or by student major (Z) alone in student intentions to start a new business venture (Y): each of the areas labeled *a* and *c*.

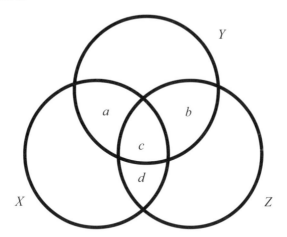

Figure 7.2   Venn diagram depicting relationships among predictor, criterion and control variables

It is also worth noting that the situation displayed in Figure 7.1 rarely occurs and that the overlapping areas labeled *a*, *b*, *c* and *d* in Figure 7.2 vary. To illustrate the varying degrees of overlap and make the illustration more concrete, let us compare two numerical examples (provided by Breaugh, 2008, pp. 283–4). Given that the correlation between X and Y is 0.50, the correlation between Y and Z is 0.40, and the correlation between X and Z is 0.30, the predictor variable (X) accounts for 25 percent of variance in the criterion variable (Y), which is indicated by areas *a* and *c* in Figure 7.2. This also means that the unique variance accounted for by the predictor variable (X), controlling for the confounding variable (Z), is 16 percent, illustrated by the area *a* in Figure 7.2. On the other hand, given the same correlations as in the previous example except that the correlation between the predictor variable (X) and the confounding variable (Z) is 0.60 (instead of 0.30), we find that the predictor variable (X) accounts for only 11 percent of unique variance in the criterion variable (Y). As this comparison shows, when a researcher controls for confounding variables it should be expected that the predictor variable of interest (X) will account for less variance in the criterion variable (Y) when a control variable (in our example variable Z) is included. It also shows that the magnitude of the relationship – the correlation – among the predictor and control variables matters. Note that the example presented here is based on just one control variable, whereas most researchers include multiple control variables that further reduce the unique variance accounted for by the predictor variable (X) in the criterion variable (Y) given that the control variables are correlated with both the predictor (X) and criterion (Y) variables and the control variables were not perfectly correlated with each other. Carlson and Wu (2012) also point out that combining multiple control variables with moderate correlations may have large effects on regression coefficients. This is especially so if the magnitudes of the correlations among the control and criterion variables are close to or exceed the correlations among the criterion and predictor variables. While this brief section on statistical control illustrates the principles of statistical control, it is far from exhaustive. Interested readers may benefit from reading more detailed works, such as Cohen et al. (2003).

THREE ISSUES IN USING CONTROL VARIABLES

Perusing the entrepreneurship literature, one is inclined to gain the same impression as Becker (2005) did with regard to the industrial and organizational psychology literature. This impression is that the theoretical reasons for inclusion of control variables are often neglected and the choice of control variables is explained to a limited extent, or even unexplained, in the study. An example of the limited justification for inclusion of control variables is provided in a quote from one of the entrepreneurship publications we reviewed in preparing this chapter: 'To rule out the possibility that the current findings were due to a spurious relationship, we included the demographic control variables, age and gender.' To examine whether his impression was appropriate, Becker (2005) examined a stratified random sample of 60 research studies published from 2000 to 2002 in *Academy of Management Journal, Journal of Applied Psychology, Administrative Science Quarterly* and *Personnel Psychology*. His findings are interesting because they confirm the impression that the use of control variables is problematic in published research. Among Becker's findings is that in more than 50 percent of the studies an explanation for the inclusion of one or more control variables was not provided; in more than 68 percent of the articles no evidence or citation was provided in support of one or more of the control variables; and in more than 63 percent of the research one or more of the control variables were not described or the description was unclear. Other researchers report similar findings (e.g. Breaugh, 2008; Spector and Brannick, 2011).

A more recent study on the use of control variables in empirical studies published in four leading journals, which was mentioned in the introduction, also confirms the findings by Becker (2005). Atinc et al. (2012) report that 18 percent of the studies did not include any rationale for inclusion of control variables and that only 48 percent of the studies provided conceptual reasoning or empirical evidence from prior research as justification for the use of control variables. Also troubling, Atinc et al. found that in more than 91 percent of the studies no prediction was made in regard to the direction of the relationship among the criterion and control variables and that in less than 4 percent of the studies were the control variables included in the stated hypotheses. Surprisingly, Atinc et al. (2012) found that 68 percent of the published studies included control variables and that the control variables in general accounted for more variance than the main effects. Unlike the results by Atinc et al. (2012), Carlson and Wu (2012) note that, in their study of relationships among control variables and predictor variables, control variables 'are frequently weakly related to focal variables'; these authors continue by stating that, 'as a result, current practice offers an illusion of statistical control when in fact little control actually occurs' (p. 413). Despite the limited attention given to control variables in published research, the results provided by Atinc et al. (2012) and the comment by Carlson and Wu (2012) that control variables need to be meaningful in the context of a study clearly illustrate the importance of control variables in empirical nonexperimental research.

Our review of the more than 140 works published in four prestigious entrepreneurship journals during 2012 showed that the use (and description) of control variables is also often problematic in the entrepreneurship literature. Even though the majority of publications included a brief description of the control variables, and many of these also provided citations as support for the control variable, its definition, prior use and/or measurement, it is disturbing that several studies did not include this information for *all* the control variables and that many studies did not include any explanation for the choice of control variables. With these observations in mind, it is worth noting that we observed a few studies in which the citations were used as support for the empirical association among the variables of interest and the control variables (e.g. Semrau and Werner, 2012). In several studies, the correlation table showed that the control variables were not related with any other variable considered, whether dependent, independent or other control variables; yet the control variables were still included as control variables in the principal method of analysis, for example multiple regression analysis. We observed only a very few studies that included considerations in regard to directionality of the relationship among the control variables and variables of interest. One of these is provided by Delgado-García, Rodríguez-Escudero and Martín-Cruz (2012). Unfortunately, we found no published research study in which the control variables were included in the stated hypotheses. This practice is unfortunate because without control variables included in the hypotheses and the control variables included in the statistical analyses researchers should not draw conclusions regarding whether the stated hypotheses are supported or not as these were not tested empirically. The omission of control variables in the stated hypotheses occurs even though some authors include conceptual considerations and citations to empirical evidence regarding the relationships among the control and criterion variables as part of their methods section in justifying the inclusion of the control variables (e.g. Delgado-García et al., 2012; Patel and Conklin, 2012). In effect, these scholars have done the work necessary, but would have done well to include these conceptual and empirical considerations regarding the control variables in the hypothesis development and, thus, include the control variables in the stated hypotheses.

Based on the empirical studies on the use of control variables (Atinc et al., 2012; Becker, 2005) and our review, it is clear that the number one issue in the current use of control variables is the failure to provide theoretical justification for inclusion of control variables. Methodologists have pointed out that the inclusion of control variables should rest upon theoretical considerations of the relationships among the control variables on the one hand and the criterion and predictor variables on the other (e.g. Meehl, 1970; Pedhazur, 1997; Spector and Brannick, 2011). These methodologists also emphasize that expectations in regard to the relationships among the control and criterion variables – the directionality of the relationships – should be clearly stated and based on conceptual considerations *and* prior empirical research. Based on our considerations here, it appears that in entrepreneurship research there is room for improvement in how control variables are used.

While the previous issue is the too often inadequate rationale for the inclusion and consideration of control variables, the second issue we address is the 'purification principle' (Spector and Brannick, 2011), namely, efforts focused on enhancing the explanatory power of the predictor variables on the criterion variable by purifying the correlational results using extraneous variables. Noted methodologists (Meehl, 1970; Pedhazur, 1997) caution against the use of the purification principle and the automatic, or blind, use of statistical control in correlational research (e.g. in multiple regression analysis). This is because it may inadvertently limit the validity of the results and findings of a study. Unfortunately, in our review, we found several examples of the use of the purification principle, and even more studies in which we believe the purification principle was employed, knowingly or not. In one study, it is abundantly clear that the purification principle was employed, as the authors write: 'None of the control variables were significant and the inclusion of the variables did not affect the results.

Therefore, the control variables were removed from the model for parsimony and the results do not include these variables for clarity.' These authors followed the typical approach described in the section on statistical control: enter a block of control variables in step one and then the variables of interest, the predictor variables, as a block of variables in step two. Despite its widespread use, this is only part of the analytical process. Methodologists (Carlson and Wu, 2012; Pedhazur, 1997; Spector and Brannick, 2011) advocate that the zero-order correlations should be carefully considered before the relationship of interest is analyzed using the principal method of analysis. This is to determine if the situation is as depicted in Figure 7.1 or in Figure 7.2 that represents the relationship among the predictor and control variables. These methodologists further advocate that results generated by the principal method of analysis regarding the relationship among the predictor and criterion variables (without any control variables) should also be carefully considered before inclusion of control variables. Thus the above quote shows a situation in which the zero-order correlations and results of the principal method of analysis pertaining to the relationship of interest (without inclusion of control variables) were not carefully considered before inclusion of control variables in the principal method of analysis. Consequently, the quote illustrates evidence of the 'purification principle' for two reasons. First, the inclusion of control variables was not meaningful (Carlson and Wu, 2012); and second, the control variables were included in the principal statistical analysis before examining the zero-order correlations, and the results from the principal method of analysis of the relationship among the criterion and predictor variables only. Again, there seems to be room for improvement in how control variables are used in entrepreneurship research.

Contamination of the criterion and predictor variables is an issue. Given interest in the relationship among criterion and predictor variables, a concern exists that an extraneous nuisance variable may affect the relationship of interest. This nuisance effect may occur in a number of ways. The nuisance variable may be associated with both the predictor and criterion variables, as depicted in Figure 7.2. If this is the case, contamination from the nuisance variable is much like method variance in which an extraneous aspect of the method produces variance in the observed variables (Campbell and Fiske, 1959). It also means that the effect of the nuisance variable may be controlled for in a study; however, it also means that indiscriminate use of control variables can increase Type II error – the failure to reject a false null hypothesis – by partialling out true variance from the relationship of interest when attempting to control for the nuisance variable effect.

Contamination may also occur when a nuisance variable influences either the predictor or the criterion variable but not both (Breaugh, 2006). As depicted in Figure 7.1, when the nuisance variable contaminates the criterion variable but not the predictor variable, variance in the criterion variable is accounted for, in part, by the nuisance variable (the area labeled *b* in Figure 7.1). This means that the relationship among the criterion and predictor variables exists (it is not due to random effects) but the magnitude of the relationship is smaller because the nuisance variable is an extraneous independent factor that 'consumes' some of the total variance available in the criterion variable. This situation is evident in studies in which the zero-order correlation among the criterion and predictor variables is significant but, when controlling for the nuisance variable, the regression coefficient is not. On the other hand, as shown in Figure 7.3, if the nuisance variable affects the predictor variable but not the criterion variable, both the nuisance variable and the predictor variable account for variance in the relationship among the criterion and predictor variables (shown in Figure 7.3 by the area labeled *d* that is part of variable *X*). Consequently, when it appears that the predictor variable is associated with the criterion variable, it may, in fact, be due to a random association among the nuisance and criterion variables. This means that indiscriminate use of control variables can increase Type I error – the incorrect rejection of a true null hypothesis. As this shows, inclusion of control variables has different effects depending on whether the control variables influence either the criterion variable or the predictor variable(s) but not both. The different effects that nuisance (control) variables may have on criterion or predictor variables are rarely considered in published research, which may be because many scholars – as authors, editors and reviewers – implicitly assume that control variables only contaminate the predictor variable. Thus the inclusion of control variables may be an issue *per se* as it may pose a threat to the validity of findings if the inclusion of control variables is not carefully considered in terms of how they are associated with the criterion and predictor variables individually (e.g. Meehl, 1970). In our review of the research published in 2012, we observed only a few publications in which consideration of the impact of the control variables was explicitly addressed (e.g. Parida et al., 2012). This also means that there is room for improvement in entrepreneurship research in the area of using control variables.

The third and last issue we consider in this chapter is generalizability of the results. When examining a hypothesized relationship empirically, researchers who use statistical control may face the issue that the results may not be generalizable (Breaugh, 2006). While the issue of partial (and semi-partial) correlations between variables has already been addressed in this chapter, the issue of generalizability needs individual attention because if results do not generalize, it is difficult to claim that a study advances our

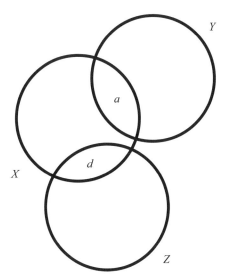

Figure 7.3 Venn diagram depicting a relationship among predictor and control variables and no relationship among criterion and control variables

understanding of entrepreneurship (Breaugh, 2006; Pedhazur, 1997; Spector and Brannick, 2011; Stone-Romero, 2007). Recall that, when statistical controls are used, it generates a sample of 'fictional people assigned fictional scores' (Meehl, 1970, p. 401). This issue may undermine the generalizability of study results. This is especially so if such an idealized sample has limited representation of people in the real world. For example, controlling for sex removes consideration of a smaller subset of either men or women. Similarly, controlling for firm size makes all firms equal when important differences might exist. Stating the issue in more general terms, phenomena in the real world are correlated. Because the use of statistical control allows for the creation of a residual predictor that is free from the contaminating effects of extraneous nuisance variables, great care should be taken in claiming valid generalizable results from a study in which control variables were employed (Breaugh, 2008; Newcombe, 2003).[2] In our review of the more than 140 works published in entrepreneurship journals in 2012, we observed only a very limited number of studies (e.g. Seghers et al., 2012) that included a robustness check as part of the analysis (e.g. by determining if the results were similar with and without control variables). We also noticed that many researchers who considered generalizability of the study findings did so merely as part of their considerations of the study limitations (e.g. a geographically focused sample), and no one considered the use of control variables as a potential limitation to the generalizability of the results. As a field, we need to move beyond the current approach to demonstrate empirically that our research results are robust and the findings can be generalized. Therefore considerations of the generalizability of results based on employing control variables is the third area in which there is room for improvement in entrepreneurship research.

The considerations above – lack of theoretical justification, the purification principle and generalizability – are not exhaustive in covering issues pertaining to the use control variables in entrepreneurship research. They illustrate that the use of control variables in nonexperimental entrepreneurship research remains problematic and there is a need to consider the best practices for using control variables in future entrepreneurship research.

BEST PRACTICES

In the preceding two sections we drew attention to the issue of statistical control and three potential problems in using control variables in nonexperimental entrepreneurship research. This fulfilled the first of the two purposes of this chapter. The second purpose is to provide recommendations on how to enhance entrepreneurship research through improving the use of control variables. Therefore this section will outline the best practices in use of control variables in nonexperimental empirical research. In doing so, it echoes other authors' recent recommendations (e.g. Antic et al., 2012; Becker, 2005; Breaugh, 2006, 2008; Carlson and Wu, 2012; Spector and Brannick, 2011). Specifically, we offer ten recommendations, followed by our concluding remarks.

Selection of Control Variables

First, use theory to justify inclusion of control variables. The best scenario is when the control variables are considered in the development of the hypotheses and, in turn, included in the hypotheses. This should include how the control variables are related to the variables of interest in the study; why the control variables are considered a biasing or substantive factor; and the direction of the relationship among the control variables and the criterion variable. At a minimum, a brief explanation should be provided for why each control variable was included and provide empirical and/or conceptual evidence supported by citations to works that illustrate the appropriateness of each control variable in the context of the present study (Atinc et al., 2012; Becker, 2005; Breaugh, 2006, 2008; Carlson and Wu,

2012; Gordon, 1968; Meehl, 1970, 1971; Spector and Brannick, 2011; Spector et al., 2000).

Second, avoid impotent control variables. Be careful not to over-control by including control variables that are unrelated conceptually or empirically with the criterion variable. Only if a control variable is believed to act as a suppressor should it be included in the study. Avoid inclusion of multiple control variables to cover all eventualities. Inclusion of many impotent control variables could lead to Type II error (e.g. conclusion that there is no effect when there is, in fact, an effect). There should be a reason and/or empirical or conceptual evidence for the inclusion of control variables in a study. Inclusion of more control variables comes at a price: reduction of statistical power and potential for reduced generalizability of the findings (Bandura, 1997; Becker, 2005; Carlson and Wu, 2011; Cohen and Cohen, 1983; Cohen et al., 2003; Pedhazur, 1997; Pedhazur and Schmelkin, 1991). This is perhaps best said by Carlson and Wu (2012): 'When in doubt, leave them out' (p. 413).

Measurement and Use of Control Variables

Third, describe in a clear and concise manner how each control variable was measured and how it was used (e.g. explain differences between analyses with one set versus another set of control variables; Becker, 2005).

Fourth, do not use demographic variables as proxies for the real variable to be controlled for in a study. The problem with statistical control using proxy variables is that the relationship between a proxy variable and the underlying real nuisance variable is generally unknown. It is not clear to what extent the proxy variable truly controls for the nuisance variance. For example, in entrepreneurship research, a person's age has been used as a proxy for many nuisance variables, including industry experience, level of ambition and level of satisfaction. Instead of using proxies, entre-preneurship researchers should measure the actual nuisance variable that is to be controlled for in a study, if at all possible (Breaugh, 2006, 2008; Carlson and Wu, 2011; Meehl, 1970, 1971; Spector and Brannick, 2011; Pedhazur, 1997).

Fifth, run the analyses with and without the control variables. To deter-mine if the impact of the control variables is meaningful in the principal analysis (e.g. regression analysis), run the principal analysis with the criterion and predictor variables without inclusion of any control variables; then, as a second step, introduce control variables into the analysis (Carlson and Wu, 2012). If the results do not differ, the control variables do not account for the findings. If they do differ, this indicates that the study manuscript should include examination of how the controls influence the variables of interest (Becker, 2005; Meehl, 1971).

Reporting

Sixth, provide descriptive statistics (i.e. means and standard deviations) for all continuous control variables. Provide summary descriptive statistics for categorical control variables (e.g, percentage of observations for each category; Atinc et al., 2012; Becker, 2005; Breaugh 2006, 2008; Gordon, 1968).

Seventh, provide evidence of reliability and validity of all measures including controls when possible (Becker, 2005; Breaugh 2006, 2008; Pedhazur, 1997; Stone-Romero, 2007). If the measurement validity of the control variables is questionable, so are the findings based on results generated with the control variables assessed on those questionable measures.

Eighth, present all correlations among all continuous or dichotomous variables, whether control, criterion or predictor variables. For categorical variables, provide a summary of the relationships with other variables, especially the criterion variable. Reporting all correlations helps to identify discrepancies between results of multiple regression analysis and zero-order correlations, which may be indicative of variable suppression leading to issues in the interpretation of the regression results (Atinc et al., 2012; Becker, 2005; Breaugh, 2008; Carlson and Wu, 2011; Spector and Brannick, 2011).

Ninth, when reporting the results of the analyses, treat the control variables with the same attention given to the predictor variables; after all, both the control and predictor variables have independent effects on the criterion variable. For example, when using regression analysis, as part of the results section include the same results (e.g. beta, significance level, variance explained) for the continuous and dichotomous control variables as are typically provided for the predictor variables (Atinc et al., 2012; Becker, 2005; Meehl, 1970, 1971; Breaugh, 2008; Carlson and Wu, 2011; Spector et al., 2000).

Interpretation of Results

Tenth, and finally, the vast majority of authors do not include control variables in the stated hypotheses. Recall that, in our review of entrepreneurship research published in 2012, we found no study in which the control variables were included in the stated hypotheses. This effectively means that the vast majority of entrepreneurship researchers do not include control variables in their hypotheses; yet, based on results from analyses that include control variables, they provide findings by claiming that the stated hypotheses were supported or not by the results.[3] In effect, such authors claim support for *X*, as stated in the hypothesis, by providing empirical support for *Y*, which constitutes support for an unstated hypothesis that includes control variables. Thus authors are encouraged to include control variables in their hypothesis development and stated hypotheses whereby they provide a rationale for the inclusion of control variables and will be able to claim support for *X* when the empirical results also support *X*. While we did not observe any hypotheses that included control variables, some scholars included a theoretical justification including citations of empirical support for the control variables (e.g. Delgado-García et al., 2012; Patel and Conklin, 2012). Given this, it should not take too much additional effort to include such theoretical justification and empirical support in the hypothesis development and include the control variables in the stated hypotheses in future entrepreneurship research. As an alternative, results will have to be reported with and without the control variables, including the incremental variance in the explained variables that stems from the control variables. This approach at least gives readers an opportunity to assess the robustness of the results and, independently of the authors, assess whether the hypotheses are supported by the results (Atinc et al., 2012; Becker, 2005; Carlson and Wu, 2012; Spector and Brannick, 2011).

CONCLUDING REMARKS

The purpose of this chapter was to draw attention to the issue of control variables in nonexperimental entrepreneurship research and to illustrate how researchers may enhance future entrepreneurship research by appropriate use of control variables. We fulfilled this dual purpose by addressing statistical control and illustrating three issues in the current use of control variables in entrepreneurship research. The three issues we considered may result in inappropriate, if not invalid, research findings that may not be generalizable. This, in turn, limits advancement of theory and our understanding of entrepreneurship. We also fulfilled the purpose of this chapter by providing ten specific recommendations for best practices in using control variables in nonexperimental research. Our intention behind providing the recommendations for (more appropriate) use of control variables in entrepreneurship research is to improve future research findings. This is because if we reduce, or eliminate, the problematic issues surrounding the current use of control variables and, in turn, their effects, the field of entrepreneurship would benefit from greater confidence in the findings generated from nonexperimental research.

One limitation to our considerations on the use of control variables is our bias in favor of multiple regression analysis as the principal method of statistical analysis. Because multiple regression analysis is inherently correlational, similar issues pertain to the use of control variables in other correlational-based methods of analysis, such as structural equation modeling. However, consideration of this or other methods of data analysis is beyond the scope of this chapter. As the use of structural equation modeling is expanding, it seems pertinent to address the use, misuse and recommended use of control variables in structure equation modeling, as well as for other forms of correlation-based data analysis, in another chapter in another book.

An alternative to the traditional use of statistical control in multiple regression analysis, and in other forms of correlational analysis, is to control for nuisance variables using a matched-groups research design (Cohen et al., 2003; Schwab, 2005). This approach is based on matching the individuals or firms – the unit of analysis – on one or more nuisance variables when examining causal relationships. As with the selection of control variables, the matching should also be driven by theory (Meehl, 1970, 1971). The matching may be based on identical scores or similar scores and on a one-on-one or group basis (Campbell and Kenny, 1999; Shadish et al., 2002). The nuisance variables upon which the matching is based may be the very same nuisance variables already considered in entrepreneurship research, for example age of the entrepreneur or venture, venture size, industry and venture performance. This method of controlling nuisance variables has received little attention from entrepreneurship researchers and methodologists. For example, Schwab (2005) allocated less than one page on matching in his methods book. While Breaugh and Arnold (2007) point out that there are three major limitations to this method of controlling for nuisance variables – regression towards different means, systematic unmatching and generalizability of results – they, in concert with Schwab (2005), emphasize that matched-groups research design provides a powerful method of controlling for nuisance variables.

Before we end this chapter, we want to reiterate that the major issue in the current use of control variables is not the inclusion of control variables; it is that they are often used inappropriately. Research based on the 'purification principle' unfortunately results in a mismatch between the stated hypotheses and statistical analyses. This is because the inclusion of the control variables in the statistical analyses means that the stated hypotheses are not being tested; a different, not necessarily theory-driven, hypothesis is *de facto* being tested, which includes control variables. The widespread use of the purification principle may be due to convenience. It allows researchers to avoid careful considerations of the role control variables play in their research, both conceptually and empirically (Spector and Brannick, 2011). This is especially evident in publications in which considerations of the zero-order correlations are limited and the patterns among the zero-order correlations and the results of the principal method of analysis (e.g. multiple regression analysis; SEM) lack consistency (Breaugh, 2008). With this in mind and in concert with many authors (e.g. Atinc et al., 2012; Becker, 2005; Breaugh, 2008; Meehl, 1970, 1971; Spector and Brannick, 2011), we re-emphasize that use of control variables should be theory-driven. Perhaps a better way to emphasize this is to ask two questions posed by Breaugh (2008):

- Is the use of control variables consistent with the theory being tested?
- What variables does the theory suggest should be controlled in testing the hypotheses?

Lastly, we want to emphasize that control variables deserve the same level of attention and respect as the criterion and predictor variables because they are equally important in generating the results, and, similar to predictor variables, control variables are also independent variables (Becker, 2005).

NOTES

1. Note that out of professional courtesy, we have chosen not to identify publications that include problematic issues. We will, however, identify publications that illustrate features we consider best practice.
2. Authors usually cover issues of generalizability in the limitations discussion in most manuscripts. This important topic of generalizability is for another chapter in another volume.
3. Of course, many authors, editors and reviewers do not seem to hold to this standard, which may explain why we did not find any study in which the stated hypotheses included control variables.

REFERENCES

Atinc, G., Simmering, M.J. and Kroll, M.J. (2012), 'Control variable use and reporting in macroand micro management research', *Organizational Research Methods*, **15**: 57–74.
Austin, J.T., Scherbaum, C.A. and Mahlman, R.A. (2002), 'History of research methods in industrial and organizational psychology: measurement, design, analysis', in S.G. Rogelberg (ed.), *Handbook of Research Methods in Industrial and Organizational Psychology*, Malden, MA: Blackwell, pp. 3–33.
Bandura, A. (1997), *Self-Efficacy: The Exercise of Control*, New York: W.H. Freeman.
Becker, T.E. (2005), 'Potential problems in the statistical control of variables in organizational research: a qualitative analysis with recommendations', *Organizational Research Methods*, **8**(3): 274–89.

Bird, B. and Schjoedt, L. (2009), 'Entrepreneurial behavior: its nature, scope, recent research and future research', in A.L. Carsrud and M.E. Brännback (eds), *Understanding the Entrepreneurial Mind: Opening the Black Box*, New York: Springer, pp. 327–58.

Bird, B.J., Schjoedt, L. and Baum, J.R. (2012), 'Entrepreneurs' behavior: elucidation and measurement', *Entrepreneurship Theory and Practice*, **36**(5): 889–913.

Breaugh, J.A. (2006), 'Rethinking the control of nuisance variables in theory testing', *Journal of Business and Psychology*, **20**: 429–43.

Breaugh, J.A. (2008), 'Important considerations in using statistical procedures to control for nuisance variables in non-experimental studies', *Human Resource Management Review*, **18**: 282–93.

Breaugh, J.A. and Arnold, J. (2007), 'Controlling nuisance variables by using a matched-groups design', *Organizational Research Methods*, **10**(3): 523–41.

Campbell, D.T. and Fiske, D.W. (1959), 'Convergent and discriminant validation by the multitrait–multimethod matrix', *Psychological Bulletin*, **56**(2): 81–105.

Campbell, D.T. and Kenny, D.A. (1999), *A Primer of Regression Artifacts*, New York: Guilford.

Carlson, K.D. and Wu, J. (2012), 'The illusion of statistical control: control variable practice in management research', *Organizational Research Methods*, **15**(3): 413–35.

Cohen, J. and Cohen, P. (1983), *Applied Multiple Regression/Correlation Analysis for the Behavioral Sciences*, Mahwah, NJ: Lawrence Erlbaum Associates.

Cohen, J., Cohen, P., West, S.G. and Aiken, L.S. (2003), *Applied Multiple Regression/Correlation Analysis for the Behavior Sciences*, Mahwah, NJ: Lawrence Erlbaum Associates.

Delgado-García, J.B., Rodríguez-Escudero, A.I. and Martín-Cruz, N. (2012), 'Influence of affective traits on entrepreneur's goals and satisfaction', *Journal of Small Business Management*, **50**(3): 408–28.

Gordon, R.A. (1968), 'Issues in multiple regression', *American Journal of Sociology*, **73**: 92–616.

Hunter, J.E. and Schmidt, F.L. (2004), *Methods of Meta-analysis*, Thousand Oaks, CA: Sage.

Meehl, P.E. (1970), 'Nuisance variables and the ex post facto design', in M. Radner and S. Winokur (eds), *Analyses of Theories and Methods of Physics and Psychology*, Minneapolis, MN: University of Minnesota Press, pp. 373–402.

Meehl, P.E. (1971), 'High school yearbooks: a reply to Schwarz', *Journal of Abnormal Psychology*, **77**: 143–8.

Newcombe, N.S. (2003), 'Some controls control too much', *Child Development*, **74**: 1050–52.

Parida, V., Westerberg, M. and Frishammar, J. (2012), 'Inbound open innovation activities in high-tech SMEs: the impact on innovation performance', *Journal of Small Business Management*, **50**(2): 283–309.

Patel, P.C. and Conklin, B. (2012), 'Perceived labor productivity in small firms: the effects of high-performance work systems and group culture through employee retention', *Entrepreneurship Theory and Practice*, **36**: 205–35.

Pedhazur, E.J. (1997), *Multiple Regression in Behavioral Research*, Fort Worth, TX: Harcourt Brace & Company.

Pedhazur, E.J. and Schmelkin, L.P. (1991), *Measurement, Design, and Analysis: An Integrated Approach*, Hillsdale, NJ: Lawrence Erlbaum Associates.

Schmitt, N.W. and Klimoski, R.J. (1991), *Research Methods in Human Resources Management*, Cincinnati, OH: South-Western.

Schwab, D.B. (2005), *Research Methods for Organizational Studies*, Mahwah, NJ: Lawrence Erlbaum Associates.

Seghers, A., Manigart, S. and Vanacker, T. (2012), 'The impact of human and social capital on entrepreneurs' knowledge of finance alternatives', *Journal of Small Business Management*, **50**(1): 63–86.

Semrau, T. and Werner, A. (2012), 'The two sides of the story: network investments and new venture creation', *Journal of Small Business Management*, **50**(1): 159–80.

Shadish, W.R., Cook, T.D. and Campbell, D.T. (2002), *Experimental and Quasi-experimental Designs for Generalized Causal Inference*, Boston, MA: Houghton Mifflin.

Spector, P.E. and Brannick, M.T. (2011), 'Methodological urban legends: the misuse of statistical control variables', *Organizational Research Methods*, **14**(2): 287–305.

Spector, P.E., Zapf, D., Chen, P.Y. and Frese, M. (2000), 'Why negative affectivity should not be controlled in job stress research: don't throw out the baby with the bath water', *Journal of Organizational Behavior*, **21**: 79–95.

Stone-Romero, E.F. (2007), 'Non-experimental designs', in S. Rogelberg (ed.), *The Encyclopedia of Industrial and Organizational Psychology*, Beverly Hills, CA: Sage, pp. 519–21.

8. Cross-cultural studies in entrepreneurship: a note on culture and language

Malin Brännback, Stefan Lång, Alan Carsrud and Siri Terjesen

INTRODUCTION

The field of international business (IB) emerged after World War II to capture phenomena in international trade and foreign direct investments. During the 1950s, the IB field added the cross-cultural perspective to its repertoire as it was widely recognized that national cultures differ and thus could impact management processes (Brannen and Doz, 2010). Early cross-cultural studies primarily studied demographic and economic variables and how these differed on a national level. Later cross-cultural issues on an organizational level became interesting with the conceptualization of multinational corporations (MNCs). These studies were primarily concerned with issues related to cross-cultural psychology and intercultural communication that management had to deal with. One of the best-known studies on how cultures vary across nations and its implications in the MNC context is Hofstede's (1980) classic study.

However, the culture construct remains poorly defined or, to be more precise, continues to be defined in a myriad of ways. The prevailing understanding has been that culture was something 'out there', external to the individual, often nurturing an 'us versus them' logic. Most studies followed the positivistic ontology where culture was viewed as *etic* or universal, objective, measurable and relatively static (Schaffer and Riordan, 2003; Brannen and Doz, 2010; Usunier, 2011). Culture was primarily treated as a group-level construct (i.e. nation, organization), although culture is created by individual behaviors. Brannen and Doz (2010) point out that significant differences *within* cultures have been found, yet still are overlooked on aggregated levels.

Obviously, national cultures also impact entrepreneurial behaviors; therefore culture becomes interesting to entrepreneurship researchers. While cross-cultural studies emerged as a separate area of interest among entrepreneurship researchers towards the end of the 1980s (McDougall, 1989), interest in the impact of culture on entrepreneurial activity is much older (Hayton et al., 2002). Culture as an important element was acknowledged by Schumpeter (1934) and McClelland (1961). Oviatt and McDougall (2005: 540) identified two streams of international entrepreneurship (IE) research: 'one focusing on the cross-national-border behavior of the entrepreneurs and one focusing on the cross-national-border *comparison of entrepreneurs, their behaviors and circumstances in which they are embedded*' (emphasis added).

While research in IE has grown tremendously over the last three decades (Terjesen et al., 2013), we argue that entrepreneurship researchers have not taken their IE research beyond 'border-thinking' into what we term 'cross-cultural research'. While there are numerous studies comparing entrepreneurial behavior in different countries, most notably the Global Entrepreneurship Monitor (GEM) studies, most do not adequately address differences that are culturally embedded. To state it specifically: most studies, even GEM, use country or nationality as a proxy for culture (e.g. Hayton et al., 2002; Autio et al., 2013). However, this is incorrect as many countries – including the USA – are multicultural in nature. Studies that compare responses or observations across different cultural samples are usually considered cross-cultural studies. But, as pointed out by Schaffer and Riordan (2003), a single-cultural study could be considered cross-cultural 'if it in some way accounted for differences between cultural settings' (p. 171). However, this requires a broader conceptualization of culture than is customary in entrepreneurship research.

As we will argue in this chapter, cross-cultural studies are not just translation–back-translation exercises based on lexical and mechanical translations, but rather involve semantic and semiotic considerations to capture cultural differences (Brannen, 2004; Usunier, 2011). Some differences are subtle while others are more obvious. Important issues include whether culture is defined properly with respect to developing research questions, the establishment of equivalence in sample selection and instrument equivalence (Coviello and Jones, 2004), operationalization of constructs across different cultural groups and validation of scales (Knight, 1997; Antoncic and Hisrich, 2001), and assessing measurement invariance (Runyan et al., 2012). If these issues are ignored, the results may be meaningless, inconclusive or misguiding (Schaffer and Riordan, 2003).

Among cross-cultural studies, an important but frequently overlooked issue concerns language. Linguistics scholars have long explored how language impacts perception and behavior (Whorf, 1956) and language is increasingly acknowledged in the area of marketing and especially within consumer behavior and advertising (Puntoni et al., 2009) and economics (Chen, 2013). Human language is a complex signaling structure that consists of words, or signs, that are combined to provide a meaning for the interpreter (Saussure, 1970). While different languages have many features in common and certain words may even look identical, languages may vary in meaning to such a degree that mere translation will not be sufficient to convey the true meaning of the word. Therefore aspects of language become important in cross-cultural, cross-national comparative studies studies where research instruments are used in multiple countries. Sometimes surveys are translated into the native language, but not always. When they are not, the explanation often offered is that it was assumed that most respondents possess sufficient English-language skills. As any English speaker knows, English speakers are a people divided by a common tongue, a comment often attributed to Winston Churchill when talking about the British and American uses of the language.

Within entrepreneurship research, most findings are published in English, and native English North American scholars have dominated the field (Aldrich 1992, 2000; Davidsson, 2013; Terjesen et al., 2013). The field is indeed international, as is demonstrated by the founding of the International Council of Small Business in 1955, although the organization was long dominated by Americans in its first 30 years of existence. With the launch of the Global Entrepreneurship Monitor (GEM) in 1999, the field clearly became international in more than name. GEM now provides annual cross-national data on approximately 80 countries. GEM has substantially contributed to the increased international nature of entrepreneurship through its consortium of over 500 entrepreneurship scholars and freely available data at www.gemconsortium.org. Furthermore, a quick review of any of the top-tier entrepreneurship journals reveals that recent issues have at least one article written by non-native English scholars. With increasing requirements for academic scholars to publish internationally, the proportion of non-native English contributors is likely to increase. Thus the issue of language and culture becomes even more important in the field.

This chapter therefore provides an overview of cross-cultural, language-related issues that are pertinent to entrepreneurship research. The next section outlines the *emic* and *etic* perspectives of culture. We then describe how language is both instrumental and problematic in any cross-cultural research, but with a special focus on issues observed in entrepreneurship research. We then discuss the role of semiotics. The point of taking this approach is that, by using insights from semiotics we have way of going beyond mere definitions. As most researchers are aware, definitions of key concepts are sources of major debates in most areas of business research. Consider, for example, how one defines 'family' within a family business context. 'Family' has wide cultural differences. Work in entrepreneurship research is no exception. In this chapter we provide examples from various research experiences where language has indeed caused problems.

CULTURE: EMIC AND ETIC PERSPECTIVES

The origins of the 'culture' concept date back to classical antiquity – *cultura* means cultivation or the process of improvement mainly in the context of agriculture. Some 200 ago the concept started to be used in the context of individual improvement, via education – that is, the process of cultivating the mind. In the early twentieth century, the concept of culture was extensively explored in the field of anthropology to describe different symbolic representations, including language, and to describe differences in learned human behavior, which was largely due to the fact that people lived in different parts of the world, had different languages, different religions and various traditions that impacted behaviors.

Modern cross-cultural research usually makes a distinction between two perspectives on culture: *emic* and *etic*. The *emic* perspective acknowledges that attitudes and behaviors are unique in each culture and language. *Emic* studies seek to describe thoughts, actions and sense-making, typically making use of qualitative methods such as ethnographic fieldwork, observations and interviews. The *etic* perspective assumes no differences, that attitudes and behaviors are more or less 'culture free' (Morris et al., 1999; Usunier, 2011). Studies using this approach seek to isolate particular components, state hypotheses and study distinct causal relationships based on large surveys, cross-sectional comparisons or comparative experiments (Morris et al., 1999). As stated earlier, one of the best-known studies embracing the etic perspective is Hofstede's (1980) study of cultural dimensions. Taking the *emic* approach to its extreme, no cross-cultural comparison is possible.

The *emic* approach represents an insider's perspective of culture and acknowledges that certain frames of references may not exist across cultures. By contrast, the *etic* approach takes a distant, outsider's view where constructs apply equally well to different cultures and languages. The focus in *etic* studies is on structured, external and measurable features that can be assessed in parallel in different cultural settings or even experimental settings. Many view *emic* and *etic* as opposites, and it is common for researchers from either perspective to dismiss insights from the other. In an analysis of 210 studies, Schaffer and Riordan (2003) found that only 6 (12 percent) studies used the *emic* approach. While Schaffer and Riordan (2003) argue that a researcher will have to decide which approach to use, we tend to support the views of Morris et al. (1999) and Usunier (2011), who argue that the two approaches should be viewed as complementary and that researchers should integrate them. One way of integrating the two approaches is to apply either perspective, depending on the stage of the research. That is, at the exploratory phase, the *emic* perspective would be more useful, whereas the *etic* approach is more useful at a later stage, for example for testing hypotheses. This is not unlike the mixed-methods approach to research often found in entrepreneurial work. In addition, Usunier (2011) suggests a semantic or cultural approach rather than a lexical approach. He argues that while dictionaries show that various languages indeed have a great deal in common, there are numerous instances when dictionaries are limited, especially regarding subtle differences in terms and usage. While aspects of words may be similar, there may be some that differ *emically*. Failing to take certain *emic* factors into account is called *imposed etics* or *pseudo etics* (Schaffer and Riordan, 2003, p. 174).

We concur with Morris et al. (1999) and Usunier (2011) that, to allow for a richer understanding of culture we should encourage entrepreneurship researchers to adopt a hybrid *emic–etic* approach, where language is at the core (Usunier, 2011) and where culture is assessed based on simultaneously collected culture-specific data rather than using Hoefstede's index (Schaffer and Riordan, 2003). We also suggest that researchers should broaden their methodological toolbox to apply multi-method research designs, including qualitative methods (Brannen and Doz, 2011; Birkinshaw et al., 2011; Welch et al., 2011).

The concept of entrepreneurial passion is a good example here. Research has shown that passion is at the heart of entrepreneurship (Cardon et al., 2013); passions have been shown to fuel motivation and provide meaning for everyday work (Brännback et al., 2006), impact fundraising ability (Cardon et al., 2009b), motivate key employees (Cardon, 2008), to be a key element in entrepreneurial effort (Cardon et al., 2009a) and to impact entrepreneurial teams (Drnovsek et al., 2009).

It is perfectly appropriate to ask an entrepreneur if s/he is passionate about her/his venture activity in most native English-speaking countries. Especially in the USA, it is common to express publicly one's passion about some activity that takes up most of one's time (and mind). It has become highly interesting to explore how entrepreneurs 'live' the influence of passion (Cardon et al., 2013). Most will perceive passion as if the person is really fired up by 'it', really into 'it'. However, in Swedish, while the word is *passion* and spelt identically, there is also an *emic* connotation to the word, which is primarily associated with deep desire, love and even lust (sinful). In Finnish, the word for passion is *intohimo*; it also implies not being rational and very serious, but highly emotional, especially if it is expressed in connection with professional behavior. Thus *intohimo* is almost the opposite of the English meaning of being 'seriously into something'.

What might happen if a researcher asks a Finnish scientist or an engineer (who takes great pride in being professionally serious) if he/she is passionate about their venture or their professionally pursuit? The Finnish respondent might think that the researcher is crazy, and will likely be offended for not being taken seriously by the researcher. There is a risk that if a question were asked in the following manner: 'Are you passionate about your business?' (answer on a 7-point Likert scale), the respondent might stop answering the questionnaire (having taken some time to give answers and then feel mocked). So, how do you study entrepreneurial passion in these countries and compare this with studies conducted in the USA or the UK? Clearly language and culture must be addressed here, but how remains to be seen. For example, recently a scale to measure entrepreneurial passion has been developed and validated (Cardon et al., 2013), but using only a US sample. How that scale works in different cultural settings will certainly be of interest, and we suspect any measurement outcome will vary across cultures.

Another example is slightly different but shows how tricky culturally embedded phenomena can be. Two of this chapter's authors were recently involved in a cross-cultural survey-based study in three countries (Canada, Finland and Turkey) (Lin et al., 2013) involving researchers from Finland, the USA, Turkey, Canada and China. One descriptive background question stirred up a considerable debate within the team: the respondent's parent's educational levels. The item was phrased in such a way as to implicitly assume that only one parent (the father) worked or had a career. While it may still be common in Turkey (and many other countries) that women stay home to raise children (even if they are highly educated), this is certainly not the case in Sweden or Finland (or throughout most of Scandinavia). Sweden and Finland have extensive daycare systems that allow both parents to work. Even in the USA and Canada, a large portion of women work. In this particular case, most (if not all) of the Finnish respondents represented a generation that has spent their pre-school days in daycare (roughly five or six years). This means that most of the Finnish respondents would have been forced to reply that one of the parents worked when in fact both were at work. And yet phrasing the question differently would not have properly reflected the cultural reality in the other two countries.

The above example illustrates that cross-cultural studies can indeed be challenging. As pointed out by several researchers (Harzing, 2005; Aycicegi and Harris, 2004; Puntoni et al., 2009; Keysar et al., 2012), language is problematic in cross-cultural studies. In the aftermath of globalization, business has in essence become monolingual; that is, the lingua franca of modern business is English (Tietze and Dick, 2012). This is not a conundrum typical for large corporations only, but also a reality for highly specialized small technology companies such as biotech start-ups where key scientific knowledge may come from a team of highly specialized international researchers. Even small and medium-sized firms in the wine industry can have vineyards in a number of countries. In the above example concerning the comparison of entrepreneurial cognitions and intentions across Turkey, Canada and Finland (Lin et al., 2013), the survey instrument was not translated in Finland and Canada, but was translated into Turkish for the respondents in Turkey. The respondents in Canada and Finland completed the survey in English and the researchers applied an *etic* approach to culture, although explicitly expecting cultural differences in the results. The respondents were university students, and it was assumed that their knowledge of English was good, thus enabling this approach.[1] This decision certainly saved the researchers time and effort; however, significant insights may have been lost.

Harzing (2005) points out that problems may especially occur when a study analyzes phenomena that are influenced by cultural norms and values. The same can be said with respect to studies seeking to delve into respondents' cognitive processes, such as the above example of entrepreneurial passion or the one on entrepreneurial cognitions and intentions. Studies show that respondents accommodate their answers to the language in question and a seeming *etic* meaning is imposed on the respondents. Back-translation provides a 'quasi-capture' of cultural differences as 'the *emic* meaning from the source language is neither fully transferred nor properly understood while the *emic* meaning from the target language cannot emerge from the data collection process' (Usunier, 2011, p. 315). But research results here are inconclusive. Recent research indicates that response bias will be significantly different when respondents are not responding in their native language (Keysar et al., 2012).

Usunier (2011) also argues that studies that adopt an *emic* approach are stronger with respect to reliability, and data show greater internal validity. Usunier builds on insights from cross-cultural management literature and proposes a cultural rather than just a mechanical approach to translation. A cultural approach means going beyond the dictionary, and is inclusive of contextual differences and sensitive to semantic and experiential issues. The texts may therefore be different. As language and culture are interrelated, it is assumed that, unless researchers are sensitive to these issues, they may use an instrument with lower reliability and internal validity. The following section investigates the language issue in depth and describes why language is important. We argue that cross-cultural researchers in entrepreneurship and small business need to pay attention to language as an issue.

ON LANGUAGE AND SEMIOTICS

Knowledge creation within the social sciences is based on the use of language. Social science researchers must possess expertise in using verbal language more than, for example, a physicist who must be an expert in mathematical formulae as the common language. The use of language is not only vital for disseminating our research results – new knowledge – in writing. Language is also a vital vehicle for conducting social science research by way of collecting data, be it interviews (structured or not) or surveys.

As pointed out by Tietze and Dick (2012), most contemporary scientific knowledge is shared in the English language. Consequently business language in theory and practice is largely monolingual. Little attention is paid to the possible consequences that this situation may have for knowledge creation, especially if the knowledge creators are non-native speakers of English. The use of English shapes the meaning in a way that promotes a certain worldview of English-speaking groups, which omits alternative systems of meaning and practice, thus potentially losing data and overlooking important insights (Tietze and Dick, 2012).

In line with this, we argue that epistemological and methodological dilemmas may arise, which may be rooted in the use of a verbal and written language. We argue that the use of language may impact research design, analysis of results and the conclusions reached, to the point where language could be a limitation of the study. While some entrepreneurship researchers pay considerable attention to validating scales (see examples and discussion in Knight, 1997; Antoncic and Hisrich, 2001; Hayton et al., 2002; Kreiser et al., 2002; Mitchell et al., 2002; Liñán and Chen, 2009; Runyan et al., 2012), the dominating approach is *etic* and most researchers fail to address the impact of culture or language altogether. Language and culture are inferred by country.

In consumer research, a phenomenon known as 'code-switching' has been identified, as impacting consumer persuasion processes. Code-switching refers to mixing language within one sentence, which is highly common among bilingual consumers (Luna and Peracchio, 2005).[2] Studies have also found that memory for second language is inferior to first-language memory (Luna and Peracchio, 2005). While one would assume that responding to surveys in one's native language would increase the reliability and validity of research results, recent research shows that the opposite may in fact be the case. Studies show that a foreign language has a distancing effect, reducing the possibility of intuitive decision-making. A foreign language may function as an emotional barrier (Aycicegi and Harris, 2004; Puntoni et al., 2009; Keysar et al., 2012). Similarly, reduced fluency leads to more analytic decision-making. Keysar et al. (2012) found in their experimental study that using a foreign language reduced decision-making biases, reduced loss aversion and increased the acceptance of both hypothetical and real bets with positive expected value (Keysar et al., 2012). Thus the nature of the language has a systematic effect and in cross-national studies it will be important to know whether respondents use a native language in order to interpret the results accurately.

Language is a complex signals or sign structure, created by humans, of words or signs that are combined into a meaning for the interpreter (Saussure, 1970). In order to deal with the fact that words may have different meanings, not just across cultures, but also within cultures, help may be found in the area of semiotics, the study of signs. In semiotics, 'signs' may be anything from which meaning is generated, such as words, images, photographs, gestures, sounds and objects (Chandler, 2007). The meaning of words is created and expressed by *signs and therefore semiotics has been referred to as the study and structure of meaning.*

In fact, semiotics can be used in analyzing a text or specific words, as it provides the tools to search for the (hidden) meaning of the obvious definition and interpretation. Semiotics also provides an opportunity to understand the conditions under which the signs are formed. It examines the communication of meaning in its indirect, direct, unintentional and intentional form (Echtner, 1999); 'To decline the study of signs is to leave to others the control of the world of meanings which we inhabit' (Chandler, 2007, p. 11), which can be particularly useful for an *emic* approach to cross-cultural research.

Language is a social institution and cannot therefore be developed or modified by an individual. Language is in essence a collective understanding that individuals must accept in its entirety if they wish to communicate a certain meaning to a certain audience (Barthes, 1967). Consequently, the language used in a survey or any other tool used in acquiring new knowledge and information should consider the social institution and culture in which the questionnaire is used (Usunier, 2011). The sign/word system used must therefore be developed in accordance with the collective understanding of the text or words used in its context (signs).

Semiotics

Ferdinand de Saussure is viewed as the founder of modern structural linguistics. His research was focused on the search for linguistic laws that could help in the understanding and development of the science of linguistics. Saussure was particularly interested in the structure of language and its relationship to meaning (Echtner, 1999), and his standpoint of thought was shaped around the dyadic meaning of the signs:

$$Sign = signifier + signified$$

In Saussure's (1959) view, the two components – the signifier (in this case a word: 'entrepreneur') and the signified, which is the concept that the signifier represents, the meaning of a word – defines the sign. Saussurean theories were developed based on the assumption that the understanding of the sign did not work as a direct link between a thing and a name, but instead between a concept (signified) and a sound pattern (signifier) (Saussure, 1970). In Saussure's view, a sign must have both a signifier and a signified to give the sign (or word) a meaning, as no sign (or word) makes sense to the interpreter on its own, but only in relation to other signs (Morris, 1964). In English, a good example is *there* and *their*, as the meaning of the sounded word depends on the context. Saussurean theory therefore implies that the development of a questionnaire where the words are the signifier and the signified is a mental construction within the system of the language and that this is based on the definition of the words and sentences used at a given moment.

It should be noted in the above examples that some words can provide different meanings depending on the reader's understanding. Therefore some words are easier to find a meaning for, for example a 'tree', 'motor-cycle' or 'sailing boat', as they define and describe a physical object, whereas words such as 'experience', 'smell', 'family' or 'culture' are more difficult to define with a shared meaning by all readers, as the meaning is a result of the reader's worldview, experience overall situation in life and the like. This could therefore be viewed as a personal mental definition of the written word or sign. Consequently, no direct relationship can be identified in advance between, for example, the word 'entrepreneur' and its meaning. This suggests that the sign is by definition (i.e. on Saussure's view) a social and historical phenomenon, or a social convention.

For example, the word 'entrepreneur' provides different (mental) associations depending on the meaning that the reader associates with the word and the circumstances (or situation) in which the word occurs. Note that the understanding of the word may also vary over time as the reader develops new meanings of signs or words when experiencing new situations or aging, providing a new life situation in which signs or words have a different denotation and connotation. In this case, this variation gives the word 'entrepreneur' a multiple meaning, which will therefore be applied according to the time, situation and interpreter. In 2005, Bengt Johannisson published a book in Swedish with the title *Entreprenörskapets väsen*, which translates as *The Essence of Entrepreneurship*. At the beginning of the book, Johannisson provides a lengthy discussion of the meaning of the word 'entrepreneur' in Swedish, which goes beyond a regular 'definition of the concept exercise'. The Swedish word is *företagare*, but the word *entreprenör* (pronounced like the English word) also exists. A decade ago the preference would have rested with the former. Most entrepreneurs identified themselves as *företagare*, but not as *entreprenör*. Johannisson (2005) also observes that the word *företagare* conveys a greater sense of dynamism, being constructed from the verb *att ta sig för*, to undertake, to do, whereas *entreprenör* is 'a foreign word' with no corresponding meaning in Swedish.

The use of words within a specific language changes over time, but that timespan does not have to be centuries or decades. Today, the use of *entreprenör* in Swedish is rather common and much more accepted. It is in fact difficult to say which of the two words is used more than the other. Policy-makers are more inclined to use *entrprenör* and speak readily of taking all possible measures to promote *entreprenörskap* (entrepreneurship) in society.

But it is not only within the common spoken language where the use of words changes. It is also how the word is conceptualized by scholars – how the meaning changes and evolves. The evolution of the definition of 'entrepreneur' over time is an example (see Hébert and Link, 1988 for a more detailed overview). The original term 'entrepreneur' is often attributed to Irish-French economist Richard Cantillon (1755), who referred to this individual as a risk-bearer. French economist Jean-Baptiste Say utilized the term 'entrepreneur' in the early 1800s to describe an individual who created value by shifting resources from less productive areas to more productive areas. Later, in the mid-1800s, British economist John Stuart Mill used the term to describe an individual who assumes both the risk and the management of a business enterprise. The next major development in the understanding of the term came from the Austrian economist Joseph Schumpeter (1942), who describes the entrepreneur as an economic actor who distorts equilibria and brings forward the production frontier as part of the process of creative destruction. The American economist Israel Kirzner, also of the Austrian school of economics, describes the entrepreneur as one who discovers previously unseen profit opportunities.

The emphasis on discovery is elaborated in more recent definitions such as Shane and Venkataraman's (2000) focus on three entrepreneurial components: opportunity identification, resource mobilization and opportunity exploitation. English speakers who are not entrepreneurship scholars might best identify with the common dictionary definition: 'one who organizes, manages, and assumes the risks of a business or enterprise' (Merriam-Webster, 2013). The most recent (August 2011) domain statement of the Academy of Management's Entrepreneurship division reads: '(a) The actors, actions, resources, environmental influences and outcomes associated with the emergence of entrepreneurial opportunities and/or new economic activities in multiple organizational contexts, and (b) the characteristics, actions, and challenges of owner-managers and their businesses.' This statement was considerably broadened from an earlier one: 'the creation and management of new businesses, small businesses and family businesses, and the characteristics and special problems of entrepreneurs ... [major topics include] ... new venture ideas and strategies, ecological influences on venture creation and demise, the acquisition and management of venture capital and venture teams, self-employment, the owner-manager, management succession, corporate venturing and the relationship between entrepreneurship and economic development' (AOM, 2013).

Taken together, the above suggests that there is some convergence among the community of entrepreneurship scholars around the world. This should not be surprising as AOM is dominated by English-speaking academics and its journals are in English. However, based on surveys of individuals who are non-native English speakers (and not entrepreneurship scholars) living and working around the world, there is no unified perspective of the terms entrepreneur and entrepreneurship. Thus what academic research means by an entrepreneurial term may not be what respondents to their survey mean when using that term.

BEYOND DEFINITIONS – ANALYZING THE MEANING OF WORDS

The starting point for all stakeholders in a research project is to learn how to read and understand the text (i.e. signs that form specific codes) as 'Codes are interpretive frameworks which are used by both producers and interpreters of text' (Chandler, 2008). In order to develop a text/questionnaire, the researcher should use familiar codes, which are restricted to the most appropriate signifier of the sign.

By including insights from semiotics, we want to 'go beyond' definitions. We strongly believe that this is necessary when conducting research across cultures. Most of us are painfully aware of the difficult and sometimes highly frustrating exercise of defining key concepts. Yet it is one of the fundamental steps at the start of any research endeavor.

In order to develop a research format/instrument to use in cross-cultural entrepreneurship research, semiotics provides a starting point for integrating both *emic* and *etic* perspectives. Fiske (1990) proposes that semiotics could be used to study three main areas:

- *The sign itself*: how the signs are defined and what meaning they stand for, for the interpreter, and the ways in which the sign communicates the meaning to its audience and finally how they stand in relation to those who use them.
- *The codes or systems in which the codes are organized*: this analysis includes how the codes have developed to meet intercultural demands, and/or the communication channels transmitting the codes.
- *The codes and signs developed within a culture*: analyses are dependent on the use of the signs and codes for their existence and form within the specific context.

Signs and codes form the content that develops the meaning of a message. Two factors that play an important part in the result of the interpretation of signs and codes are denotation and connotation. These two factors explain the relationship between the signifier and the signified. They define the meaning to the interpreters of the signs (and codes) used in a survey or interview questions. The meaning, or definition (signification), of the sign is therefore formed as a result of the combination of interpretation between the two.

Denotation is described by Chandler (2007, pp. 137–8) as 'the definitional, literal and obvious or common-sense meaning of a sign. In the case of linguistic signs, the denotative meaning is what the dictionary attempts to provide', and is the first level of signification of the sign. The denotative meaning could therefore be seen as the common definition or signification of a sign, which is recognized by an intercultural audience. The phenomenon could be exemplified by, for example, the image of the Red Cross or a traffic stop sign. These represent signs that are recognized by 'all' viewers and signify in this case an organization and its activity, and, in the second case, the action that needs to be taken as an effect of the sign.

The second level of signification (see, e.g., Emmison and Smith, 2000) or definitions – connotation, facilitates a deeper understanding of the sign and refers to the personal (emotional, ideological etc.) but also the social–cultural associations (Chandler, 2008). Connotation is developed when the denotative meaning interacts with the dominant cultural values associated with the sign, but also with the feelings, attitudes and emotions of the audience/interpreter (Emmison and Smith, 2000). Factors such as the interpreter's age, class and ethnicity affect the connotative association and interpretation of the sign (Chandler, 2007). Understanding both the denotative and connotative meaning (signification) of a sign is vital in developing a research instrument that provides the researcher with the intended and trustworthy result.

As well as the example in the previous section, with the words 'entrepreneur' and 'entrepreneurship', which have various connotations and denotations within the English language, we can once again take a closer look at the word 'passion' across different languages. If we paid attention only to the denotation of passion, a lexical translation would be sufficient. But, as described above, the word in both Swedish and Finnish has particular additional connotations that renders the concept highly problematic. This occurs in other languages as well, such as Spanish.

While the Finnish word for passion is *intohimo* (dictionary translation), which signifies a different meaning from the English word, we could almost solve the problem by using the first part of the word, *into* (which means that you are 'into something' with head and heart). Back-translating *into* into English would give 'excitement' or 'zeal', and we see a difference in connotation. The second part of into*himo* is the problematic bit, as that word literally means 'lust', and that becomes the connotative explanation for our problem in studying entrepreneurial passion in a cross-cultural context.

As discussed above, given that signs contain different layers of meaning, the development of a research specific language, carrying the strategic intent of the researcher and the research agenda, could fill an large gap in the research process. Semiotics provides an 'interpretation beyond the obvious, direct and intentional levels to reveal the obscure, indirect and unintentional communication of meaning' (Echtner, 1999, p. 50). A semiotic approach could help to develop a research-specific system that takes into consideration all the above-mentioned issues.

Barthes (1967) finds that a language is a social institution and is formed based on the collective understanding of the signs and codes used in communication. Therefore a language has to be accepted, in its entirety, by individuals and cannot be developed solely by an individual. Consequently, a research-specific language should consider the social institution and intercultural context in which it is communicated. It must also add to the collective understanding (such as scientific definitions, even those that are not universally accepted, but used by many) of the sign and codes used in forming the message. The language or linguistic system explains the systems and rules that create a language (Saussure, 1970). In order to create a clear and strategically intended and effective communication process, several issues needs to be taken into consideration. For example, Saussure (1970) argues that communication is affected by (a) the psychological effect, for example views and notions; (b) the physiological effect, for example phonation and perception; and (c) the physical process, for example sound waves. The result of these effects and processes is formed based on how the individual acts or the individual's communication process. In order to form a research-specific language, Barthes (1988) presents some general operational principles and arrangements for the semiotic analysis process that could form the starting point for such a process. Barthes (1988, p. 229) anticipates three operations: text segmentation, inventory of codes in the text, and coordination.

- *Segmentation of the text*, that is, of the material signifier. According to Barthes (1988), this segmentation can be entirely arbitrary. This is a way of making a grid of the text by providing fragments of the text upon which to work.
- *An inventory of the codes cited in the text*: this is where the inventory of the text is carried out, or in Barthes's words, 'creamed off'. In this part, the inventory of the meaning is sought and analyzed sentence by sentence.
- *Coordination*: this establishes the correlations of units or of identified functions, which are often separated.

Barthes (1967) points out that a language can only be used when a learning process has been followed and where the signs and codes of the language have been explained. This also applies when forming a research-specific language. According to Saussure (1970), the social side of communication emerges when people interact and communicate, and through this process norms are produced. If these are repeated (not necessarily the exact words) by involved stakeholders, the signs used can be connected to a specific meaning and notion. This suggest that the person communicating interprets the message based on their own knowledge and understanding of the specific subject. The practical use and establishment of the research-specific language among the stakeholders will decide the result of the development and formation of a homogeneous and defined language. In this, the researcher must also take into consideration how the message is communicated – for example through speech or writing – as this will determine how the communication should be developed.

A good example of this can be found in family business research. As noted by Carsrud (2006) and Carsrud and Brännback (2012), 'family' is rarely defined within family business research. It is implicitly assumed that we all share an understanding of what comprises a family: man, woman and two children. This assumption is taken for granted even when we know that what comprises a family will vary considerably across cultures. Even if the intact nuclear family is the most familiar form, it is no longer the most common form. In fact, today dual families have become the norm (Carsrud, 2006). We have reconstituted families with one parent widowed or most likely divorced, with a new spouse and children from prior unions. We have families with unmarried spouses and we have same-sex marriages forming a family (legal in some cultures and illegal in others). In some cultures, siblings or relatives (aunts, uncles, cousins), grandparents, in-laws and ex-spouses are very much part of a family. Here we need both a formal definition of family, but also a culturally embedded explanation. Moreover, it will be necessary to accommodate variations when planning a study as well as when analyzing and interpreting the results.

In Figure 8.1 we present a model for integrating the *emic* and *etic* perspectives based on Eco's (1976) semiotic communication model. This model includes the sender's use of codes and sub-codes in order to develop a coded message, the use of proper channels to communicate the message, the message as a source of information, and finally the context/ circumstances in which the message is interpreted and the interpretation of the message by the addressee. All aspects of the communication process affect the effectiveness of the communication process and the ability to send the intended message to the receiver. From a research perspective, for the development of an instrument that carries the intended message/questions to be interpreted by the interviewee or addressee in accordance with the strategic intent of the researcher, an understanding of receiver's intercultural factors is necessary.

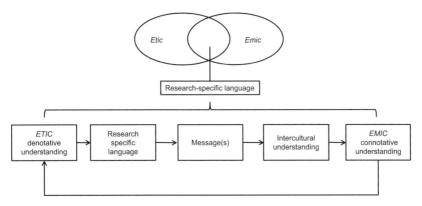

Figure 8.1   *Model for integrating* emic *and* etic *perspectives in research: noting research-specific language*

1. Etic *understanding*: the researcher's knowledge and understanding of the research-specific subject/area of knowledge, for example how is 'entrepreneur' or 'entrepreneurship' defined in an academic text? (see below)
2. *The researcher*: the semiotic understanding of signs and codes forming the research-specific language carrying the strategic intent of the research project and then communicated to the 'audience' or stakeholders. The audience may be multiple: practicing entrepreneurs with their understanding of what it takes to be an entrepreneur, or policymakers with their view of what a 'real' entrepreneur is.
3. *The message*: for example a survey instrument, which has been developed based on 1 and 2.
4. *The intercultural understanding of the target group*: their intercultural platform for defining and interpreting the signs and codes of the message; the questionnaire/interview questions – and their possibility of understanding the message in accordance with the strategic intent of the message. That is, does the target group share the same understanding across cultures or even within cultures?
5. Emic *understanding*: when the researcher is able to capture the specific nuances and connotations as perceived within different cultures and by different target groups.

If conducting a study using the *etic* approach, the researcher would settle with using English-language questionnaires only – arguing that most people seem to speak and understand English these days. This approach is quite common because so many organizations use English as 'company language'. So, for example, when studying the entrepreneurial orientation (EO) in a high-technology start-up, the researcher(s) may conclude that it is appropriate to use an English-language questionnaire. While the EO scale has been *etically* validated in cross-cultural research and shown to be both valid and reliable in French and English settings (Knight, 1997) and in a larger study based on a six-country study (Kreiser et al., 2002), the scale is still problematic.

Then, when the researcher decides that it is necessary to create a survey instrument in the respondents' native language, an easy way to resolve this is to rely on translation and back-translation. However, while this approach may sometimes be the best available, it assumes that language (and culture) is neutral and merely instrumental: *etic*. Translation is certainly easiest on the researcher, as the other approaches require quite a bit of extra effort. We will argue here that for the sake of a good research result it is worth every effort to pursue an approach and develop instruments that will integrate the *emic* and *etic* perspectives (Morris et al., 1999; Schaffer and Riordan, 2003; Usunier, 2011).

IMPLICATIONS FOR RESEARCH AND CONCLUSIONS

The issues discussed in this chapter are relevant to those doing both qualitative and quantitative research, especially in a cross=cultural or transnational context. In addition, the issues raised here can also be applied within any multi-ethnic country when looking at immigrant population, urban versus rural, or where local use of words can differ from that in other parts of the country. Even English words spoken in the USA can carry different meaning to different groups, as anyone who has attempted to do work within ethnic communities will confirm. What this chapter aimed to do was to increase awareness of the role that language and words have in the study of entrepreneurship and that, as academic researchers, we must bear in mind sensitivity to potential issues around language and word usage when designing surveys or conducting interviews.

Specific 'canned' recommendations on how to deal with language issues are not easily provided. It is clear that simple translation and back trans-lation alone will not deal with language issues. Each case will depend on the goals of the research, the subjects of interest and the languages in question. What has been attempted in this chapter is to suggest to researchers that they should be sensitive to meaning within languages and careful when making generalizations from their research, especially any cross-cultural compari-sons are implicit or explicit in their studies.

This chapter has outlined extensive evidence for the need to pay close attention to language in the context of entrepreneurship research. This applies to research conducted within the English language, where words vary in meaning between scholars and laymen or ordinary entrepreneurs, but also in cross-cultural entrepreneurship research. We urge scholars to consider both *emic* and *etic* perspectives in their research and to be aware of the impact of semiotics, and the meaning of words. We hope that this brief introduction to an important component of research provides a foundation for further discussion and development in the field of entrepreneurship.

NOTES

1. Finland has two official languages Finnish and Swedish. Approximately 6 percent of the population speaks Swedish as their mother tongue. These are usually also fluent in Finnish, whereas the Finnish-speaking population is rarely fluent in Swedish. There are cultural differences between these population groups, but it is important to understand that the Swedish-speaking Finns are born in Finland; they are Finns not Swedes. The

situation is somewhat similar to the one in Canada. In this particular study the participants were Swedish-speaking Finns and therefore if the survey instrument had been translated it should have been translated into Swedish.
2.   Code-switching is very common among Swedish-speaking Finns in daily talk. Swedish-speaking Finns will use Finnish words or complete idiomatic expressions in otherwise Swedish sentences.

REFERENCES

Aldrich, H. (1992), 'Methods in our madness? Trends in entrepreneurship research', in D.L. Sexton and J.D. Kasarda (eds), *The State of the Art in Entrepreneurship Research*, Boston, MA: PWS-Kent, pp. 191–213.
Aldrich, H. (2000), 'Learning together: national differences in entrepreneurship research', in D.L. Sexton and H. Landström (eds), *The Blackwell Handbook of Entrepreneurship*, Oxford: Blackwell Business, pp. 5–25.
Antoncic, B. and Hisrich, R.D. (2001), 'Intrapreneurship: construct refinement and cross-cultural validation', *Journal of Business Venturing*, **16**: 495–527.
AOM (2013), www.aomonline.org.
Autio, E., Pathak, K. amd Wennberg, K. (2013), 'Consequences of cultural practices for entrepreneurial behaviors', *Journal of International Business Studies*, forthcoming.
Aycicegi, A. and Harris, C.L. (2004), 'Bilinguals' recall and recognition of emotion words', *Cognition and Emotion*, **18**: 977–87.
Barthes, R. (1967), *Elements of Semiology*, New York: Hill and Wang.
Barthes, R. (1988), *The Semiotic Challenge*, Oxford: Basil Blackwell.
Birkinshaw, J., Brannen, M.Y. and Tung, R. (2011), 'From a distance and generalizable to up close and grounded: reclaiming a place for qualitative methods in international business research', *Journal of International Business Studies*, **42**(5): 573–81.
Brännback, M., Carsrud, A.L., Elfving, J. and Krueger, N.K. (2006), 'Sex, [drugs], and entrepreneurial passion', paper presented at Babson College Entrepreneurship Research Conference, Bloomington, IN.
Brannen, M.Y. (2004), 'When Mickey loses face: recontextualization, semantic fit and semiotics of foreigness', *Academy of Management Review*, **29**(4): 593–616.
Brannen, M.Y. and Doz, Y.L. (2010), 'From a distance and detached to up close and personal: bridging strategic and cross-cultural perspectives in international management research and practice', *Scandinavian Journal of Management*, **26**: 236–47.
Cardon, M.S. (2008), 'Is passion contagious? The transference of entrepreneurial emotion to employees', *Human Resource Management Review*, **18**: 77–86.
Cardon, M.S., Sudek, R. and Mitteness, C. (2009a), 'The impact of perceived entrepreneurial passion on angel investing', in A.L. Zacharakis (ed.), *Frontiers of Entrepreneurship Research: Proceedings of the Babson College Entrepreneurship Research Conference*, Vol. 29, Wellesley, MA: Babson College.
Cardon, M.S., Wincent, J., Singh, J. and Drnovsek, M. (2009b), 'The nature and experience of entrepreneurial passion', *Academy of Management Review*, **34**: 511–32.
Cardon, M.S., Grégoire, D.A., Stevens, C.E. and Patel, P.C. (2013), 'Measuring entrepreneurial passion: conceptual foundations and scale validation', *Journal of Business Venturing*, **28**(3): 373–69.
Carsrud, A.L. (2006), 'Commentary: "Are we family and are we treated as family? Nonfamily employees' perceptions of justice in the family firm": it all depends on perceptions of family, fairness, equity and justice', *Entrepreneurship Theory and Practice*, **30**(6): 855–60.

Carsrud, A.L. and Brännback, M. (2012), 'Where have we been and where we should be going in family business research', in A.L. Carsrud and M. Brännback (eds), *Understanding Family Business Research: Undiscovered Approaches, Unique Perspectives, and Neglected Topics*, New York: Springer, pp. 1–7.

Chandler, D. (2007), *The Basic Semiotics*, Abingdon: Routledge.

Chandler, D. (2008), http://www.aber.ac.uk/media/Documents/S4B/sem10.html, 2.5.2013.

Chen, M.K. (2013), 'The effect of language on economic behaviour: evidence from savings rates, health behaviours, and retirement assets', *American Economic Review*, forthcoming.

Coviello, N.E. and Jones, M.V. (2004), 'Methodological issues in international entrepreneurship research', *Journal of Business Venturing*, **19**: 485–508.

Davidsson, P. (2013), 'Some reflection on research "schools" and geographies', *Entrepreneurship & Regional Development*, **25**: 100–110.

Drnovsek, M., Cardon, M.S. and Murnieks, C.Y. (2009), 'Collective passion in entrepreneurial teams', in A. Carsrud and M. Brännback (eds), *The Entrepreneurial Mind*, New York: Springer, pp. 191–218.

Echtner, C.M. (1999), 'The semiotic paradigm: implications for tourism research', *Tourism Management*, **20**(1): 47–57.

Eco, U. (1976), *A Theory of Semiotics*, Bloomington, IN: Indiana University Press.

Emmison, M. and Smith, P. (2000), *Researching the Visual*, London: Sage.

Fiske, J. (1990), *Kommunikationsteorier – en introduktion*, Borås: Wahlström & Widstrand.

Harzing, A.-W. (2005), 'Does the use of English-language questionnaires in cross-national research obscure national differences?', *International Journal of Cross Cultural Management*, **5**(2): 213–24.

Hayton, J.C., George, G. and Zahra, S.A. (2002), 'National culture and entrepreneurship: a review of behavioral research', *Entrepreneurship Theory and Practice*, **26**(4): 33–52.

Hébert, R.F. and Link, A.N. (2006), 'Historical perspectives on the entrepreneur', *Foundations and Trends in Entrepreneurship*, **2**(4): 261–408.

Hofstede, G. (1980), *Culture's Consequences: International Differences in Work-Related Values*, Beverly Hills, CA: Sage.

Johannisson, B. (2005), *Entreprenörskapets väsen*, Lund: Studentlitteratur.

Keysar, B., Hayakawa, S.L. and Gyu An, S. (2012), 'The foreign-language effect: thinking in a foreign tongue reduces decision biases', *Psychological Science*, **23**(6): 661–8.

Knight, G.A. (1997), 'Cross-cultural reliability and validity of scale to measure entrepreneurial orientation', *Journal of Business Venturing*, **12**: 213–25.

Kreiser, P.M., Marino, L.D. and Weaver, K.M. (2002), 'Assessing the psychometric properties of the entrepreneurial orienatation scale: a multi-country analysis', *Entrepreneurship Theory and Practice*, **26**(4): 71–94.

Lin, X., Carsrud, A., Brännback, M. and Koçak, A. (2013), 'From parental role models to entrepreneurial intentions: key mediating factors across three cultures', Babson College Entrepreneurship Research Conference, Lyon, 5–8 June.

Liñán, F. and Chen, Y.-W. (2009), 'Development and cross-cultural application of a specific instrument to measure entrepreneurial intentions', *Entrepreneurship Theory and Practice*, **33**(3): 593–617.

Luna, D. and Peracchio, L.A. (2005), 'Advertising to bilingual consumers: the impact of code-switching and language schemas on persuasion', *Journal of Consumer Research*, **31** (4): 760–65.

McClelland, D.C. (1961), *The Achieving Society*, Princeton, NJ: D. Van Nostrand.

McDougall, P.P. (1989), 'International versus domestic entrepreneurship: new venture strategic behavior and industry structure', *Journal of Business Venturing*, **4**: 387–400.

Merriam-Webster (2013), www.merriam-webster.com.

Mitchell, R.K., Smith, B.J., Morse, E.A., Seawright, K.W., Peredo, A.M. and McKenzie, B. (2002), 'Are entrepreneurial cognitions universal? Assessing entrepreneurial cognitions across cultures', *Entrepreneurship Theory and Practice*, **26**(4): 9–32.

Morris, C. (1964), *Signification and Significance: A Study of the Relations of Signs and Values*, Cambridge, MA: MIT Press.

Morris, M.H., Avila, R.A. and Allen, J. (1999), 'Individualism and the modern corporation: implications for innovation and entrepreneurship', *Journal of Management*, **19**(3): 595–612.

Oviatt, B. and McDougall, P.P. (2005), 'Defining international entrepreneurship and modeling the speed of internationalization', *Entrepreneurship Theory and Practice*, **29**: 537–53.

Puntoni, S., de Langhe, B. and van Osselaer, S.M.J. (2009), 'Bilingualism and the emotional intensity of advertising language', *Journal of Consumer Research*, **35**(6): 1012–25.

Runyan, R.C., Ge, B., Dong, B. and Swinney, J.L. (2012), 'Entrepreneurial orientation in cross-cultural research: assessing measurement invariance in the construct', *Entrepreneurship Theory and Practice*, **36**(4): 819–36.

Saussure, F. de. (1959), 'The linguistic sign: the object of linguistics', in R.E. Innis (ed.) (1985), *Semiotics: An Introductory Reader*, London: Hutchinson & Co., pp. 24–46.

Saussure, F. de. (1970), *Curso de Lingüística General*, 8th edn, Buenos Aires: Losada.

Schaffer, B.S. and Riordan, C.M. (2003), 'A review of cross-cultural methodologies for organization research: a best-practice approach', *Organizational Research Methods*, **6**(2): 169–215.

Schumpeter, J. (1934), *The Theory of Economic Development*, Oxford: Oxford University Press.

Schumpeter, J. (1942), *Capitalism, Socialism and Democracy*, 3rd edn 1950, New York: Harper Perennial.

Shane, S.A. and Venkataraman S. (2000), 'The promise of entrepreneurship as a field of research', *Academy of Management Review*, **25**(1): 217–26.

Terjesen, S., Hessels, J. and Li, D. (2013), 'Comparative international entrepreneurship research: a review and research agenda', *Journal of Management*, forthcoming.

Tietze, S. and Dick, P. (2012), 'The victorious English language: hegemonic practices in the management academy', *Journal of Management Inquiry*, **XX**(X): 1–13, available online at http://jmi.sagepub.com/content/early/2012/04/29/1056492612444316.

Usunier, J.-C. (2011), 'Language as a resource to access cross-cultural equivalence in quantitative management research', *Journal of World Business*, **46**(3): 314–19.

Welch, C., Piekkari, R., Plakoyannaki, E. and Paavilainen-Mäntymäki, E. (2011), 'Theorising from case studies: towards a pluralistic future for international business research', *Journal of International Business Studies*, **42**: 740–62.

Whorf, B.L. (1956), *Language, Thought, and Reality: Selected Writings of Benjamin Lee Whorf*, edited by J.B. Carroll, Cambridge, MA: MIT Press.

9. Fighting a rearguard action? Reflections on the philosophy and practice of qualitative research in entrepreneurship[*]

Richard T. Harrison and Claire M. Leitch

INTRODUCTION

'What is entrepreneurship?' is a question of abiding interest to entrepreneurship scholars. In the apparent absence, to date, of agreement on a unique core of theoretical or methodological propositions, the answer to this question is most commonly to be found in elaborations of the subject matter (the topic of study) of the field, but this may create more problems than it resolves (Harrison and Leitch, 1996). This is evident from, for example, the recently agreed domain statement of the Entrepreneurship Division of the Academy of Management, which defines entrepreneurship as '(a) the actors, actions, resources, environmental influences and outcomes associated with the emergence of entrepreneurial opportunities and/or new economic activities in multiple organizational contexts and (b) the characteristics, actions, and challenges of owner-managers and their businesses' (Academy of Management, August 2011; www.aomonline. org).

While the breadth of this definition is permissive, in that it allows researchers to define entrepreneurship in a manner that fits their research (Brush et al., 2008; Davidsson et al., 2001), it also dissipates the focus of entrepreneurship research into a fragmented *potpourri* field (Gartner, 2001; Harrison and Leitch, 1996). In consequence, while the field has developed substantially over the past 25 years (Cornelius et al., 2006), there is no clear sense of progress (Aldrich, 1992; Aldrich and Baker, 1997; Brush et al., 2008) and it is still seeking legitimacy (Bruyat and Julian, 2001; Busenitz et al., 2003). In attempting to establish this, in addition to some agreement on the subject of study of the field, it is necessary to develop theory, to determine the boundaries of the discipline, and develop methods, to facilitate the testing of theory and communication within and across disciplines. However, according to Dean et al. (2007), most of the discussion of progress in entrepreneurship research has been on theory development and they argue for a greater focus on method. While not implying that qualitative methods are not valuable, they focus 'on quantitative data analytic techniques because the appropriate use of and sufficient sophistication in the use of analytical techniques is a critical component to the advancement and legitimacy of the entrepreneurship field' (Dean et al., 2007, p. 602).

While we agree that there is a need for more analyses of method in entrepreneurship, a number of studies have already demonstrated that contemporary entrepreneurship research is dominated by statistical analysis within a broadly positivistic framework. For example, Chandler and Lyon (2001) found that 395 of the 418 articles they reviewed in the 1990s used statistical analysis, and 78 per cent of these used multivariate techniques; McDonald et al. (2004), in their review of over 2200 articles, demonstrated the dominance of positivist approaches and research methods; and Dean et al. (2007) identified 354 of their sample of 582 articles published in *Journal of Business Venturing* and *Entrepreneurship Theory and Practice* as employing quantitative data analysis, a proportion that is higher for more recently published papers.

Despite this emphasis in practice on quantitative research, there have been calls at regular intervals for more entrepreneurship research based on qualitative methods (Bygrave, 1989; Huse and Landström, 1997; Gartner and Birley, 2002; Hindle, 2004; Neergaard and Ulhøi, 2007b). In part, these calls reflect the wider adoption of qualitative methods in management and organizational research more generally in response to the expansion of variety and plurality of research domains and questions within the field (Buchanan and Bryman, 2007; Knudsen, 2003). Unlike entrepreneurship, where it appears that the use of qualitative methods is at the margin of the field, in management and organizational research 'the range of types and forms of qualitative methods is, depending on your perspective, exhilarating or exhausting' (Easterby-Smith et al., 2008: 420; see also Page, 2000).

In part, these calls for more qualitative entrepreneurship research reflect the diversity of subjects and hence research questions in the field. In the absence of agreement on the object of study and on theoretical constructs, there is a need for methodological pluralism to capture the breadth and richness of understanding that entrepreneurship requires (Jennings et al., 2005). Indeed, there are many substantive issues in entrepreneurship research that are rarely addressed in the extant quantitative-based literature and 'many of the important questions in entrepreneurship can only be asked through qualitative methods and approaches' (Gartner and Birley, 2002, p. 387). This means that calls for more qualitative research may actually be calls for better-quality and more robust qualitative research rather than for more such research *per se*. While it may be that qualitative entrepreneurship research *is* undertaken, a perception of variable quality and lack of rigour is believed to underlie a 'liability of legitimacy' (Neergaard and Ulhøi, 2007a, p. 1) from mainstream journal editors that 'selects out' such research from the published canon. However, in a survey of the perceptions of board members of *Organizational Research Methods*, the leading methods journal in management studies, one of the strengths of entrepreneurship research identified was the relative richness of data and in particular the potential of qualitative research to develop insights into entrepreneurial processes (Short et al., 2010). Against this, the analysis also highlighted the general lack of a systematic approach to these data.

We argue here that qualitative research can make valuable and unique contributions to the scholarly study of entrepreneurship. We also recognize that these 'knowledges' are of different things: these approaches differ in the ways in which experience is highlighted and how it is sifted (Thorpe and Holt, 2008, p. 4). Our central claim is that qualitative work, if done properly, creates knowledge of an equal validity to that created by objectivist social science, and that this equivalence is not properly recognized in entrepreneurship research.

We justify this claim in two ways. First, we present the case for qualitative research in terms of three themes: the issue of scientific truth and epistemology, that is whether positivist conceptions of objective truth arrived at through hypothetico-deductive method are more or less valid than alternative conceptions; the relationship between the implicit purpose of entrepreneurship research (as, for example, a practical or professional discipline rather than a social science *per se*) and the relative status of quantitative and qualitative research methods; and the pragmatic issue of methodological competence, that is, the determination of 'quality' in qualitative research. We couch this debate in a more general discussion of the distinction between foundationalism and non-foundationalism: foundationalism is predicated on the analysis of an objective reality independent of the researcher, whereas non-foundationalism is based on the argument that knowledge is theory and value laden and that an objectivist social science is impossible (Amis and Silk, 2008; Guba and Lincoln, 2005). Second, we illustrate how codified methodological processes can be developed that will allow a qualitative researcher to signal the goodness of their approach within the range, variety and richness of perspectives subsumed under the label 'qualitative research'.

EPISTEMOLOGY AND ENTREPRENEURSHIP: THE CASE FOR NON-FOUNDATIONALISM

There is a developing view in entrepreneurship that the systematic adoption of a research paradigm characterized by a commitment to theory building and testing in a hypothetico-deductive framework using quantitative methods to analyse large-scale datasets and establish generalisable findings is both necessary and desirable to confirm the maturity of the field (Davidsson, 2003). This is consistent with the argument that the majority of research in entrepreneurship is already firmly grounded in the functionalist paradigm (Burrell and Morgan, 1979) and is based on a set of meta-theoretical assumptions that define the objectivist perspective (Jennings et al., 2005). In this context qualitative research assumes the status of a necessary transitional phase that reflects the relative youth of the field and the consequent lack of time to become familiar with all aspects of the 'entrepreneurial phenomenon' and to develop relevant theory (Davidsson, 2004). In other words, qualitative research is perceived to be a condition of youth and adolescence; quantitative research is a sign of maturity. Consequently, in the face of these arguments for convergence around an agreed methodology, an ongoing commitment to qualitative research bears many of the characteristics of fighting a rearguard action against the unassailable tide of 'science' within the discipline.

For the most part, entrepreneurship researchers undertake their research concerned more about the definition of their object of study (e.g. new venture creation, opportunity recognition, entrepreneurial cognition, venture capital, growth) and the choice of data collection protocols (e.g. secondary data analysis, survey research, interpretivist case studies) than the philosophical assumptions that underlie the way they go about their work. However, these assumptions can and do shape the choices of methods, such as the individual techniques used for data collection and analysis, and methodology, the combination of techniques used to investigate a specific situation. Awareness of these is important in undertaking defensible research:

> The relationship between data and theory is an issue that has been hotly debated by philosophers for many centuries. Failure to think through philosophical issues such as these, while not necessarily fatal, can seriously affect the quality of management research, and they are central to the notion of research design. (Easterby-Smith et al, 2002: 27)

It follows that all researchers are inherently methodological, in that their choice of approaches, methods, techniques, goals, criteria, measurement scales and so on 'presuppose conceptions of scientific or proper method' (Lawson, 2008, p. 44).

In other words, all research rests on beliefs about what constitutes an explanation of social phenomenon, in entrepreneurship as in other realms of social enquiry (Keat and Urry, 1982). As Shapiro and Wendt (2005) have asked, should explanations of social life be deduced from observable facts (the empiricist or positivist position), should they be grounded in people's self-understandings (the interpretivist position) or should they be based on whatever enables us to change the state of affairs in the world (which reflects both an instrumentalist position and a deductivist position based on the generation of effectively predictive theories)? Central to the debate between positivism and interpretivism is a difference in ontology. On the one hand, positivism is based on a realist ontology that observation is theory neutral and that the role of scientific research is to identify law-like generalizations that account for these observations. On the other hand, interpretivism is based on a life-world ontology that argues that all observation is theory laden and that science is not and cannot be the pursuit of detached objective truth. In this context, calls in entrepreneurship for more scientific research, in these terms (e.g. Davidsson, 2003), follows what currently constitutes a mainstream approach to social science research:

> of (unthinkingly) adopting methods assumed to be successfully utilized in the natural science or somehow thought, on an a priori basis, to characterize proper science. Fundamental to the mainstream position is an insistence on working with formalistic models. (Lawson, 2008, p. 443)

This distinction between the positivist and the interpretivist position has been recast in terms of foundationalist and non-foundationalist research (Amis and Silk, 2008; Guba and Lincoln, 2005; House, 2005). Foundationalist research is predicated on the attempt to uncover, analyse and interpret some aspect of an objective reality, that is, a reality 'that can be uncovered, documented and not contaminated by a researcher' (the classic positivist position) or an independently existing external reality 'that it is almost impossible to perfectly realize ... although the researcher and the research site cannot be completely separated, steps can be taken by conscientious researchers to minimise the effects of the researcher on the findings' (the post-positivist position) (Amis and Silk, 2008, p. 475; see also Guba and Lincoln, 2005).

Non-foundationalist research, on the other hand, is predicated on the argument that all knowledge is theory and value laden, and that there is no possibility of uncovering neutral social facts. Therefore there is no possibility of arriving at absolute truths independent of the 'context in, and the researcher by, which they are constructed. In this formulation, there can be no hypotheses to be tested, proven, disproven, or retested, as there are no objective facts to uncover' (Amis and Silk, 2008, p. 457). The distinction between the foundationalist and non-foundationalist perspectives can be captured in a broader characterization of modern Western social beliefs about science, in which objectivity, separation, logical consistency, individual accomplishment, mathematics, abstraction, lack of emotion and indeed 'science' itself have been associated with rigour and hardness, whereas subjectivity, connection, intuitive understanding, cooperation, qualitative analysis, concreteness, emotion and 'nature' have often been associated with weakness and softness (Nelson, 2008, p. 456).

In other words, from a non-foundationalist perspective the objects of social enquiry are essentially different, in an epistemological sense, from everyday things. Social objects are identified by the descriptions, classifications or explanations of the disciplines of social enquiry. The objectivity of these descriptions, classifications or explanations 'entails finding out what procedures (theoretical, practical) are used to produce [them]. This should allow us to say that the objects so described, classified or explained are at least partly "constructed", or produced by, those procedures themselves' (Montuschi, 2003, p. 118). Consequently, objectivity in social research is not and cannot be a prescriptive concept in empirical social science research, nor is it a standard of correctness set out in advance of enquiry: 'talking of objectivity only makes sense in the concrete context of an assessment of a described objective inquiry' (Montuschi, 2003, p. 119).

Law (2004) has recently taken these issues further: his starting point is that methods do not just describe social realities but also help create them: 'we too have our instruments of research. We too reflect on and work within the obdurate realities produced by the hinterland of those realities' (p. 39) (see also Hacking, 1990 and Porter, 1995). In other words, the hinterland of methods enacts realities (Latour and Woolgar, 1986) and those realities in turn 'enact the conditions of possibility of further research' (p. 38). Accordingly, if realities are enacted, then many of the methodological certainties of the social (and natural) sciences are eroded. In the development of an 'ontological methodology' (Law, 2004, p. 154) the *procedural* issue is how to conduct research studies well; that is, how do we reflect and enact particular commitments, for example, to truth, politics or elegance, in an investigation? What does it mean, for example, to investigate well the experience of enacting entrepreneurial intentions (Krueger et al., 2000), to ask the 'why?' and 'how?' and 'how was the experience?' type questions?

These questions open the door to considerations that are both broader and more constrained than traditional questions of methodology. They are broader, in that the concern is not just to 'make truths' but to ask what other realities are being made manifest in the conduct of the research (what does it mean, the 'why'? – in other words, what is the reflexive practice of the researcher in a non-foundationalist search for meaning grounded in research participants' experiences?). They are narrower, because the outcome of these methodologies is to arrive at particular conclusions in particular locations for particular studies, instead of general rules and universal methodologies (the Holy Grail of the foundationalist project),

> there are only specific and enacted overlaps between provisionally congealed realities that have to be crafted in a way that responds to and produces [the] particular ... The general, then, disappears, along with the universal ... But if the universal disappears then so too does the local – for the local is a subset of the general. Instead we are left with situated enactments and sets of partial connections, and it is to those that we owe our heterogeneous responsibilities. (Law, 2004, p. 155)

The implication for entrepreneurship research methodologies is not, however, to throw out accepted methodologies – the so-called standard, often quantitative, methodologies have been instrumentally effective in a number of domains. Rather, the challenge is to recognize that the hegemony of the traditional approach to methods is neither absolute nor desirable. These methods are, in practice, 'badly adapted to the study of the ephemeral, the indefinite and the irregular' (Law, 2004, p. 4). These are the very characteristics of entrepreneurship research that have in more limited discussions been held to justify, if not require, the adoption of qualitative methods (Neergaard and Ulhøi, 2007a).

METHODOLOGICAL STANCE IN ENTREPRENEURSHIP

While Aldrich and Baker (1997) have recognized that entrepreneurship research may adopt multiple paradigms, reflecting competing interests and approaches, and demonstrating a concern with practical relevance, from a normal science perspective progress has been limited. This is the case both in comparison with past research in the field and with more general high-quality organizational research. Specifically, they have argued that convergence in entrepreneurship research, 'the idea that as an intellectual field matures, it becomes increasingly characterized by a set of codified theories, models, methods, and/or measures' (Grégoire et al., 2006), should in part focus on the research designs, samples and methods used. This very quickly may lead to an argument that, to paraphrase Feyerabend (1970), the recipe for a successful science is to restrict criticism, reduce the number of comprehensive theories to one, create a normal science that has this one theory (and its associated methodological strictures) as its paradigm, and 'provide a historico-scientific justification for the ever growing need to identify with some group' (p. 222).

This argument that progress in entrepreneurship research requires, in some sense, convergence will necessitate agreement on research methods and techniques. This is problematic for two reasons. First, it makes the assumption that all disciplines do or could follow a Kuhnian pattern of the evolution of paradigmatic 'normal' science. This appears to ignore Kuhn's own care to insist that the human sciences (as he described them) have not yet reached the stage where there is a dominant paradigm within which normal science progresses; hence his description of them as pre-paradigmatic. Indeed, from an epistemological standpoint, the state of the human sciences may better be described as non-paradigmatic because 'I claim no therapy to assist the transformation of a proto-science to a science, nor do I suppose that anything of the sort is to be had' (Kuhn, 1970, pp. 244–5).

Second, the argument for convergence in entrepreneurship research is predicated on a belief that entrepreneurship is a science in which knowledge is constituted as it is in other sciences. The attractions of foundationalist approaches (reflected in, *inter alia*, Davidsson's (2003) and Aldrich and Baker's (1997) appeal to the natural sciences as an ideal type) arise from this belief. This reflects the situation in management more generally, where early management thought adopted a largely positivist position as it sought to apply the traditions of applied engineering in the natural sciences to the social sciences (Clegg, 2008, p. 156; Shenhav, 1999). This lean towards positivism was reinforced in the early decades of the twentieth century by the subsequent influence of economics, sociology and psychology on the evolution of the discipline. As a result, in both management research in general and in entrepreneurship research in particular, it was possible (and, in contemporary entrepreneurship, still desirable) to lay claims to the natural sciences virtues of rationality, universality, objectivity and value-free knowledge. As Locke (1989) has argued, the establishment of the first university-based business schools adopted scientific management as essential to remove business education from its vocational roots and give it the status necessary for recognition as an academic discipline (Clegg, 2008).

However, there is a view, most recently articulated by Bygrave (2007), that entrepreneurship as an academic pursuit should take as its starting point the status of entrepreneurship as a practical professional discipline in which the fundamental questions are 'What should entrepreneurs do?' and 'How can we improve entrepreneurial practice?' These of course are not questions unique to entrepreneurship within a business-school context (Schatzki et al., 2001; Whittington, 2006), but they do raise a fundamental issue about the nature of entrepreneurship as a discipline and the implications of this for our choice of methodology:

> we have behaved as if we were researchers in liberal arts departments, especially natural sciences, rather than members of a professional school … It seems to me that we suffer from, far too much, physics envy. In our craving for the respect of our academic colleagues we are squandering the opportunity to build a new paradigm with imaginative research methods that are appropriate to a profession instead of a pure science … We can still publish in 'A' journals; we could still, if we wanted to, romp in the fields of sociology, psychology and economics to develop theoretical arguments; but it would not be a pre-requisite and above all else, we would keep our eyes on improving the practice of entrepreneurship. (Bygrave, 2007, pp. 25; 27)

As such, entrepreneurship may be better understood as a design science rather than an analytical science (van Aken, 2004), oriented to the production of knowledge relevant to understanding and interpreting the world according to some criterion or criteria rather than to understanding it in the form of validated propositional knowledge, and serving, as a Mode 2 approach to research, a broader constituency of interests than just the researchers who produce that knowledge (Gibbons et al., 1994). In other words, the status of entrepreneurship as a practice-based discipline (Gherardi, 2006; Schatzki, 2001) suggests that its knowledge is bounded by its contextual nature in a way that suggests other concerns, notably the ethical stance of the researcher and issues of 'power, fairness, efficiency, and the other contested domains of organizational life, that are routinely found in the broader social sciences but seem so often to be filtered out of management' (Clegg, 2008, p. 157).

From both the philosophy of science argument and the debate over the nature of entrepreneurship as a discipline there are significant implications for our choice of methodology in the field. Specifically, the adoption of qualitative research methods is a necessary reflection of both the nature of the object of study and the types of questions to be asked. This reflects the longstanding questioning of the use of natural scientific methods to study human phenomena that can be traced back to Dilthey's (1883/1991) argument that 'the reductive simplification required for experimentation and causal explanation is inappropriate to the goals of understanding and interpretation required for the study of human experience' (Angen, 2000, p. 385). This establishment of an interpretive approach to knowledge (Bernstein, 1995) is predicated on the argument that there can be no understanding without interpretation (Johnson, 1997).

In other words, from a non-foundationalist perspective, in the social sciences qualitative research represents a move away from *erklären*, the

deterministic explanation of human behaviour by establishing causal relationships between variables. Rather, it is concerned with *verstehen*, the
understanding of human behaviour that entails 'capturing the actual meanings and interpretations that actors subjectively ascribe to phenomena in
order to describe and explain their behaviour' (Johnson et al., 2006, p. 132).
Qualitative enquiry, therefore, attempts to embrace the complex and
dynamic quality of the social world. It allows the researcher to view a
research problem in its entirety, get close to participants, enter their realities
and interpret their perceptions as appropriate (Hoepfl, 1997; Shaw, 1999;
Bogdan and Taylor, 1975). It does so by generating thick and rich descriptions of actual events in real-life contexts that uncover and preserve the
meanings that those involved ascribe to them (Gephart, 2004).

However, this recognition of the importance of qualitative methodology
is not intended to argue that only qualitative research matters. If we view an
academic discipline, such as entrepreneurship, as a community of scholars
(Harrison and Leitch, 1996), then the challenge for them is to bring together
insights from multiple disciplines to investigate a set of phenomena that are
'neither so broad as to defy the notion of intellectual community, nor so
narrow we lose sight of our goal' (Davidsson et al., 2001, p. 7). The
implication of this is that the diversity of phenomena studied, and reliance
on methodological practices from multiple disciplines, imposes the need for
methodological pluralism: 'the breadth and richness of understanding is
surely enhanced by acceptance of the need for pluralism' (Jennings et al.,
2005, p. 148). The choice of methodology, therefore, becomes a matter of
methodological aptness: different types of research questions are best
answered by different types of study using different methods. As such, it is
more important to focus on the question being asked than to squabble over
'the best method' (Sackett and Wennberg, 1997). One consequence of this
focus on methodological aptness with respect to research questions is that it
is inappropriate to classify various research approaches under the single
categorization 'qualitative': 'there is no single set of theoretical or
methodological presuppositions to underpin a qualitative paradigm, nor is
there an uncontested collection of methods and research exemplars' (Atkinson, 1995, p. 118). As such, the determination of the 'goodness' (or,
alternatively, rigour, quality, standard) of qualitative research can only be
determined with reference to each particular example of such research
(Emden and Sandelowski, 1998, 1999).

For these reasons there has been renewed interest in the potential of
qualitative research in entrepreneurship (Neergaard and Ulhøi, 2007b;
Leitch et al., 2010; Neergaard and Leitch, forthcoming; Bruton et al.,
forthcoming). Indeed, Gartner and Birley (2002) have suggested that many
important entrepreneurship questions can only be asked (and answered)

through qualitative methods and approaches. They are careful, though, not to enter a debate on whether qualitative research is more 'truthful' than quantitative research; rather, they argue that use of both approaches by researchers is likely to mean that a wider range of questions may be addressed. This argument is developed further by Ulhøi and Neergaard (2007), who assert that there is no one superior methodology for researching entrepreneurship; rather, the approach chosen must be determined in light and the context of the question to be answered.

Notwithstanding the desirability of pluralism, there is a necessary relationship between epistemological position and methodological stance. Non-foundationalism, with its focus on interpretivism and the understanding of the life-world of the research subjects, necessarily implies the use of qualitative methodologies as the foundationalist assumptions of the quantitative approach are incommensurable. However, not all qualitative research will necessarily be non-foundationalist. As Gephart (2004) notes, both quantitative and qualitative research can be undertaken from a foundationalist standpoint, and he demonstrates that the majority of qualitative research he has reviewed is firmly set within a positivist or post-positivist objectivist position. As such, foundationalist qualitative research is subject to evaluation according to the traditional criteria of internal and external validity, reliability, objectivity and generalizability. The pragmatic challenge for non-foundationalist, qualitative research in entrepreneurship is to determine the appropriate criteria for evaluating and signalling the quality of that research (Leitch et al., 2010).

QUALITY IN ENTREPRENEURSHIP RESEARCH

In the context of entrepreneurship research, this issue, though it has not been explicitly articulated, underlies the debate on the adoption of qualitative methodologies. The generally low adoption of, and regard given to, qualitative research in entrepreneurship has been attributed primarily to a perceived lack of methodological rigour and attention to detail in those studies that have been undertaken (Gartner and Birley, 2002; Neergaard and Ulhøi, 2007a). It is, of course, possible that qualitative studies in entrepreneurship are of intrinsically poor quality (although the definition of quality and the indicators of quality are matters for debate: Easterby-Smith et al., 2008). Equally, as Gephart (2004) and Locke (2001) have suggested, in different contexts, researchers may have undertaken robust qualitative research but failed to describe the research process in sufficient detail. We argue that the debate on quality in qualitative entrepreneurship research has been predicated on the assumption of foundationalist approaches. From a non-foundationalist perspective the issue of quality can only be addressed by viewing it as intrinsic to the research design; that is, it is internalized within the underlying research philosophy and orientation.

We have already demonstrated that there is a drift in value systems among researchers, reviewers and editors that favours quantitative over qualitative research (Easterby-Smith et al., 2008; Pratt, 2008). In other words, it remains the case in practice that the continued advocacy of qualitative research more often than not has the feel of fighting a rearguard action against the hegemony of objectivist social science research. Fundamentally, this reflects the fact that the traditional and still dominant method of assessing quality in research is the quantitative theory-driven approach central to the 'scientific method'. This relies on a commitment to the objective discovery of the truth underlying the relations among facts, discovered using research characterized by the traditional criteria of internal and external validity, reliability, objectivity and generalizability (Amis and Silk, 2008). Pragmatically, this drift reflects the fact that all researchers must provide signals of their methodological rigour. It is easier for quantitative researchers to provide a relatively straightforward, transparent methodological account within a standardized set of procedures. For the qualitative researcher the task of providing detailed justification of methodological rigour falls victim to the range, variety and richness of the methodological approaches available.

Reversing this drift, and establishing that research quality is fully consistent with the adoption of qualitative methods, is not easy. For example, van Maanen (1979) argued that it was necessary to reclaim qualitative methods for organizational research to portray more closely 'the meaning, not the frequency, of certain more or less naturally occurring phenomena in the social world' (p. 539). Despite this, Amis and Silk (2008) nonetheless 'contend that traditional and still dominant methods of assessing research quality, founded on a positivistic understanding of the social world, are inherently unsuited to producing the variety of scholarship necessary for a vital, dynamic organizational studies' (p. 456). That said, as Fielding and Fielding (1986, p. 12) have argued, in the context of advocating a mixed-methods approach to management research, all methods of data collection are ultimately analysed qualitatively, in that all analysis is interpretation based on the selective rendering of the 'sense' of the available data: in both qualitative and quantitative research, the 'warrant for their inferences must be confronted'. This same issue has been identified as a potential constraint on the development of the field of entrepreneurship: indeed, Hindle (2004, p. 577) has cautioned that,

> Unless entrepreneurship ... begin[s] to embrace higher volumes of higher calibre qualitative research, the relevance and potency of the entrepreneurial

canon will be severely compromised by a lack of the methodological variety that is so strongly displayed in other social sciences.

This has significant implications for the determination of quality in non-foundationalist research. If there can be no 'appeal to the facts', the external (or objectivist) basis for determining quality, the theory-ladenness of observation requires the internalization of quality within the research philosophy underlying the project. In essence, quality is determined by the purpose and positioning of the research rather than 'being something to be tested at the completion of the research or an outcome of the application of robust methods' (Amis and Silk, 2008, p. 458). The issue for debate is not the legitimacy of qualitative research, for that follows from a non-foundationalist epistemology, but its robustness and internalized quality. It is the researcher's responsibility to provide sufficient information so that the reader may determine whether or not the findings are transferable to a different context and/or situation (Hoepfl, 1997). Ontologically, as Cope (2005) explains, with this type of research no assumptions are made about what is and is not real – descriptions of phenomena begin with people's experiences of them. Thus the research aim is not to confirm or disconfirm prior theories, 'but to develop "bottom-up" interpretive theories that are inextricably "grounded" in the lived-world' (Cope, 2005, p. 167).

Lincoln and Guba (1985) have partially addressed the issue of establishing rigour in qualitative research, albeit from a quasi-foundationalist perspective, by arguing that the onus is on qualitative researchers to demonstrate the neutrality of their interpretations of the data gathered, by adopting a 'confirmability audit'. This would present an overview of the analysis and interpretation process, comprising presentation of the raw data, the researchers' analysis notes, reconstruction and synthesis products based on this analysis, notes on the conduct of the research and analysis process, personal notes and preliminary developmental information. Davidsson (2004), writing from a foundationalist standpoint, emphasizes the importance of showing the development of rigour throughout the entire process: 'with rigor I then mean, roughly, well-founded motivations for the selection of cases or the like; systematic and transparent procedures for data collection and analysis etc' (pp. 58–9).

Gephart (2004, p. 458) elaborates this by indicating that researchers often fail to describe the research process in sufficient detail and to articulate 'how research practices transform observations into data, results, findings and insights'. Thus, for rigour to be achieved, the use of qualitative methods requires 'carefully, and thoroughly capturing and describing how people experience some phenomenon – how they perceive it, describe it, feel about it, remember it, make sense of it and talk about it with other' (Patton, 1990, p. 104). This requires both a sound understanding of the research approach adopted as well as experience and skill in the use of qualitative data-gathering and analysis techniques. The responsibility of qualitative researchers is, therefore, to provide their audience with sufficient information on the design and conduct of the research to allow them to assess the intrinsic goodness of the research process.

In so doing, it will be necessary to reconfigure the concept of the validity of a piece of research (Maxwell, 1992; Johnson, 1997). From a non-foundationalist perspective, Angen (2000, p. 387) has suggested that new configurations of validity depend on qualities inherent to the researcher and to the research process. Accordingly, she recommends that the term 'validation' rather than 'validity' is used to emphasize the way in which 'a judgement of the trustworthiness or goodness of a piece of research is a continuous process occurring within a community of researchers ... Maintaining an antifoundationalist stance on epistemology implies the need for an ongoing open dialogue on the topic of what makes interpretive research worthy of our trust' (ibid.; see also Mischler, 1990; Lather, 1993).

As a basis for assessing the goodness of qualitative research, this emphasis on the process of validation is reflected in three core elements. First, as value-free science is considered an impossibility (Smith, 1990), ethical validation of any qualitative research study requires that we provide 'practical, generative, possibly transformative, and hopefully non-dogmatic answers to the questions we pose as researchers' (Angen, 2000, p. 389; see also van Mannen, 1990). Consistent with Bygrave's (2007) argument that entrepreneurship research should be useful, Unger (1992) suggests that the ethical validation of a piece of research should involve asking if the research is helpful to the target population, if there are alternative explanations to those presented, and if we are aware of or more enlightened about the human condition (or at least that part of it falling within the scope of the research problem) because of the research.

Second, given that methodology *per se* cannot be the basis for establishing validity in non-foundationalist research, validation arises from the substance of the enquiry. Accordingly, the substantive validation of a piece of research must be thought through carefully from the inception of the enquiry through to the completion of the research process. For a number of commentators (Bergum, 1991; Angen, 2000) this requires assessing one's biases at an earlier stage of the process, reflecting on how these are changed through engagement with the research topic and context, through to providing an account of this in the final output. Accounts of such research should, therefore, provide compelling, powerful and convincing evidence for the intended audience (van Mannen, 1990; Smith, 1990).

In this, it is important that the research account is persuasive. As the economist Kenneth Arrow described the criteria for judging competing theories, the key is persuasiveness:

> does it correspond to our understanding of the economic world? I think it foolish to say that we rely on hard empirical evidence completely. A very important part of it is just our perception of the economic world. If you find a new concept, the question is, does it illuminate your perception? Do you feel you understand what is going on in everyday life? Of course, whether it fits empirical and other tests is also important. (Feiwel, 1987, p. 242)

This resonates with the earlier comment by the physicist Niels Bohr, who argued: 'it is wrong to think that the task of physics is to find out what nature is. Physics concerns what we can say about nature … We are suspended in language' (quoted in McCloskey, 2008, p. 418).

Third, and following from the second point, the validation of qualitative research fundamentally depends on the characteristics and abilities of the researcher, and it is the responsibility of the researcher to develop a valid interpretation of their research topic expressly because, unlike foundation-alist research, no specific standard method exists that will 'save the researcher from having to chose how to proceed … we have a human moral obligation to take up topics of principal value; and we must do everything in our power to do them justice' (Angen, 2000, p. 391).

This represents a shift from validity as an outcome (something supported by sound and convincing evidence) to validation as the process of confirmation, of signalling goodness in non-foundational research. Seale (2004) has emphasized the importance of addressing two issues indicating goodness in qualitative research. First, it is important to explain the aim and rationale for the research, to set this in the context of prior knowledge of the topic, to justify the choice of qualitative methods as the most appropriate, to explain the research process in terms of case selection, gaining access and data recording, and to set out the process of data analysis and clearly identify the implications of the findings. Most of these elements apply with equal force to the majority of quantitative studies. Second, and more distinctive to non-foundationalist, qualitative research, is the signalling of openness to emergent issues, the paying of attention to negative and deviant (i.e. outlier) cases, the separation of evidence and interpretation, the communication of transparency and reflexivity in the methods used, the adoption of an approach that is both faithful to and critical of the data, and the exploration of the possible relevance or utility to interest groups. Collectively, these are important, but they do not easily stand the test of practice (Easterby-Smith et al., 2008, p. 425).

The first of Seale's themes can be represented as the process of validation in research design and data collection, data analysis and interpretation, while the second can be reconceptualized in terms of Angen's (2000) distinctions among ethical validation, substantive validation and researcher quality (Table 9.1). Goodness in non-foundationalist, qualitative research requires the clear and coherent signalling of validation in all stages of the research process while recognizing that the detailed manner of this will vary from specific study to specific study: in Gadamer's (1994, p. 184) terms, 'coming to an understanding ... is always coming to an understanding about something'. To reiterate, context matters and the detailed articulation of the validation of any particular qualitative research study will necessarily be *sui generis*.

Table 9.1   Validation of the process of undertaking empirical interpretivist research

	Research design and data collection	Analysis	Interpretation
Ethical validation	Moral stance Practical value Understand meanings Research process	Give voice to participants Choice of method	Generative potential Transforms actions Addresses 'so what?' question
Substantive validation	Intersubjectivity Self-reflexivity Popular and personal understandings Researcher's paradigm and pre-understandings Access	Record own transformation Present disconfirming cases Theoretical candour Transparency	Self-reflexivity Record own transformation Evidence of conceptual development Dynamic research process Transparency
Researcher quality	Characteristics and attributes Indicators of credibility Moral stance Purpose of research	Personal involvement Visibility of researcher's work	Craft-work Rhetoric and persuasion

Key to terms:

Ethical validation

Moral stance: thoughtful, caring and responsible approach to the study of the human condition (Angen, 2000).

Practical value: practical answers to the 'so what?' question; not divorced from real-life context (Sandelowski, 1995); transformative potential, disrupts received notions of how research is formulated, carried out and written up (Angen), alternative explanations presented; explanation of possible relevance or utility to interest groups (Easterby-Smith et al., 2008; Angen, 2000).

Understand meanings: generative potential (raise new possibilities, open up new questions and stimulate dialogue) (Gadamer, 1994); signals openness to emergent issues (Easterby-Smith et al., 2008).

Research process: promotes an equitable context in which diverse voices may be heard, no one's voice is excluded or demeaned (Haraway, 1988; Lather, 1986; Flax, 1990; Caputo, 1987); egalitarian relationship between researcher and participants, researcher not a 'privileged possessor of expert knowledge' (Lather, 1986); creates meaning through discourse.

Choice of method: adoption of approach that is both faithful to, and critical of, the data (Easterby-Smith et al., 2008).

Substantive validation

Intersubjectivity: shared meanings constructed by people in their interactions to understand social and cultural life; vigilant self-critical reflection (Alcoff, 1994) understanding influences on researcher's pre-judgements and pre-understandings.

Theoretical candour: conceptual development evidencing how conclusions were reached (Morse, 1994; Sanjek, 1990).

Record own transformation: articulate process intelligibly and coherently so that the reader may judge the trustworthiness of the arguments made (Madison, 1988).

Dynamic research process: dynamic process of creation of meaning and production of knowledge.

Transparency: dissemination and publication of research; thorough and comprehensive documentation of process undertaken so others can judge the trustworthiness of the meanings presented (Nielsen, 1995; Madison, 1988).

Present disconfirming cases: paying attention to negative or deviant (outlier) cases (Easterby-Smith et al., 2008).

Researcher quality

Characteristics and attributes: good people skills; resilience; patience and persistence; versatility; flexibility; meticulousness; creative and persuasive writer; passion for topic; ethical stance and integrity of researcher (Angen, 2000).

Personal involvement: intensive and personal involvement in the process (Sanjek, 1990) and ability to minimize distance between self and others (Creswell, 1998).

Source: Leitch et al. (2010).

Using the framework developed by Leitch et al. (2010), non-foundationalist qualitative researchers will be able to signal the validation of their research in a way that is consistent with both their own intentions as researchers and the situation and expectations of the researched. However, none of these signals will be effective if the researchers themselves do not indicate their own skills and personal qualities (Morse, 1991). These include possession of good interpersonal skills, including resilience, patience, persistence in the face of ambiguity and setbacks, versatility and flexibility, and meticulousness in carrying out the research. These can be signalled by clearly articulating what was done and how it was done at all stages of the research process. In the creation of intersubjective understanding within both the community of researchers and the community of researched, the ability to communicate persuasively – to use rhetoric, in the Aristotelian sense of the ability to see the available means of persuasion (McCloskey, 2008) – is paramount. In this respect the responsibility and moral integrity of the researcher is fundamental in developing valid interpretations within well-founded research projects. If non-foundationalist research in entrepreneurship is to meet required standards of validation, it will do so because its practitioners are accomplished craft-workers (Kvale, 1996; Mischler, 1990), learning the skills of interpretative research through exemplars, experiential training and practice.

CONCLUSION

Entrepreneurship research, as an emerging field of study, is characterized by considerable methodological diversity, not necessarily accompanied by an equivalent level of methodological sophistication. A number of commentators have argued that the field is still characterized by an over-reliance on naïve descriptive analyses of imprecisely articulated research questions based on samples of convenience. On to this has been grafted an increasingly sophisticated and more rigorously specified multivariate quantitative analysis oriented to hypothesis testing and theory development. However, the field as a whole still shows very few examples of thorough, rigorous and robust qualitative analysis.

We have responded to recent calls for more and better qualitative research in entrepreneurship by elaborating the justification for, and procedures followed in, such research. With due care and attention, qualitative research is capable of producing a rich set of data through which respondents' experiences, perceptions and beliefs may be accessed. This allows both depth of understanding and detail of illustration, and the adoption of such an approach can add significantly to our understanding of entrepreneurial behaviour.

Our discussion has also been set within an argument that the real issue concerning choice of methodology in entrepreneurship is not, as conventionally represented, that between qualitative and quantitative research. It is, rather, the more fundamental choice between foundationalist and non-foundationalist perspectives. We have argued here for non-foundationalism. Following Amis and Silk (2008) and others, all observation is theory laden. In the consequent absence of external reference points against which to compare research design, research execution and the data themselves, the issue of quality can be addressed only by viewing quality as intrinsic to the research design: 'it becomes *internalized* within the underlying research philosophy and orientation rather than being something to be "tested" at the completion ... or during ... the research' (Amis and Silk, 2008, p. 466).

In this chapter we have started a dialogue about reconsidering the nature and purpose of research methodology in entrepreneurship. Our focus has deliberately been on the articulation of the issues involved in establishing and signalling the validation of qualitative entrepreneurship research, but this raises more wide-ranging questions. From a non-foundationalist perspective we conclude that quality – the goodness of the research – has to be established, not through some *ex post* assessment of the truthfulness of the research findings (and their correspondence with the 'facts'), but intrinsically through the validation of the design and execution of the research itself. More importantly, our argument has been that the differentiation between quantitative and qualitative methods disguises a more important distinction between foundationalist and non-foundationalist research. Research undertaken in the spirit of non-foundationalism recognizes that, as we live in conditions of uncertainty, the old gold standards and guarantees proposed by and for methods (in the foundationalist sense) will no longer suffice – we need, as Law (2004) concludes, to 'discover ways of making methods without accompanying imperialisms' (p. 15).

NOTE

* This chapter provides an epistemological and methodological justification for the adoption of qualitative methods in entrepreneurship. It complements an earlier paper that provides more detail on and an illustration of the operationalization of our argument: Leitch et al. (2010).

REFERENCES

Alcoff, L. (1994), 'The problem of speaking for others', in S.O. Weisser and J. Fleischner (eds), *Feminist Nightmares: Women at Odds: Feminism and the Problem of Sisterhood*, New York: New York University Press, pp. 285–309.

Aldrich, H.E. (1992), 'Method in our madness? Trends in entrepreneurship research', in D.L. Sexton and J.D. Kasarda (eds), *The State of the Art in Entrepreneurship Research*, Boston, MA: PWS-Kent, pp. 171–213.

Aldrich, H.E. and Baker, T. (1997). 'Blinded by the cites? Has there been progress in entrepreneurship research?', in D.L. Sexton and R.W. Smilor (eds), *Entrepreneurship 2000*, Chicago, IL: Upstart Publishing, pp. 377–400.

Amis, J.M. and Silk, M.L. (2008), 'The philosophy and politics of quality in qualitative organizational research', *Organizational Research Methods*, **11**(3): 456–80.

Angen, M.J. (2000), 'Evaluating interpretive inquiry: reviewing the validity debate and opening the dialogue', *Qualitative Health Research*, **10**(3): 378–95.

Atkinson, P. (1995), 'Some perils of paradigms', *Qualitative Health Research*, **5**: 117–25.

Bergum, V. (1991), 'Being a phenomenological researcher', in J. Morse (ed.), *Qualitative Nursing Research*, rev. edn, Newbury Park, CA: Sage, pp. 55–71.

Bernstein, R.J. (1995), *Beyond Objectivism and Relativism: Science, Hermenutics, and Praxis*, Philadelphia, PA: University of Pennsylvania Press.

Bogdan, R. and Taylor, S.J. (1975), *Introduction to Qualitative Research Methods: A Phenomenological Approach to the Social Sciences*, New York: Wiley.

Brush, C.G., Manolova, T.S. and Edelman, L.F. (2008), 'Separated by a common language? Entrepreneurship research across the Atlantic', *Entrepreneurship Theory and Practice*, **32**(2): 249–66.

Bruton, G., Si, S. and Suddaby, R. (forthcoming), 'Special Issue: Entrepreneurship through a Qualitative Lens', *Journal of Business Venturing*.

Bruyat, C. and Julian, P.A. (2001), 'Defining the field of research in entrepreneurship', *Journal of Business Venturing*, **16**: 165–80.

Buchanan, A. and Bryman, A. (2007), 'Contextualising methods choices in organizational research', *Organizational Research Methods*, **10**(3): 483–501.

Burrell, G., and Morgan, G. (1979), *Sociological Paradigms and Organisational Analysis*, London: Heinemann.

Busenitz, L.W., West, G.P. III, Shepherd, D., Nelson, T., Chandler, G.N. and Zacharakis, A. (2003), 'Entrepreneurship research in emergence: past trends and future directions', *Journal of Management*, **29**: 285–308.

Bygrave, W.D. (1989), 'The research paradigm (I): a philosophical look at its research methodologies', *Entrepreneurship Theory and Practice*, **14**(1): 7–26.

Bygrave, W.D. (2007), 'The entrepreneurship paradigm (I) revisited', in H. Neergaard and J. Parm Ulhøi (eds), *Handbook of Qualitative Research Methods in Entrepreneurship*, Cheltenham, UK and Northampton, MA, USA: Edward Elgar Publishing, pp. 17–48.

Caputo, J. D. (1987), Radical Hermeneutics, Bloomington, IN: Indiana University Press

Chandler, G.N. and Lyon, D.W. (2001), 'Issues of research design and construct management in entrepreneurship research: the past decade', *Entrepreneurship Theory and Practice*, **25**(4): 101–13.

Clegg, S. (2008), 'Positivism and post-postitivism', in R. Thorpe and R. Holt (eds), *The Sage Dictionary of Qualitative Management Research*, London: Sage Publications, pp. 155–7.

Cope, J. (2005), 'Researching entrepreneurship through phenomenological inquiry', *International Small Business Journal*, **23**(2): 159–83.

Cornelius, B., Landström, H. and Persson, O. (2006), 'Entrepreneurial studies: the dynamic research front of a developing social science', *Entrepreneurship Theory and Practice*, **30**(3): 375–98.

Creswell, J. W. (1998), Qualitative Enquiry and Research Design: Choosing among Five Traditions, Thousand Oaks, CA: Sage.

Davidsson, P. (2003), 'The domain of entrepreneurship research: some suggestions', in J.A. Katz and D.A. Shepherd (eds), *Advances in Entrepreneurship, Firm Emergence and Growth*, Vol. 6, Oxford: Elsevier/JAI, pp. 315–72.

Davidsson, P. (2004), *Researching Entrepreneurship*, Boston, MA: Springer.

Davidsson, P., Low, M.B. and Wright, M. (2001), 'Editor's introduction: Low and McMillian ten years on: achievements and future directions for entrepreneurship research', *Entrepreneurship Theory and Practice*, **25**(4): 81–100.

Dean, M.A., Shook, C.L. and Payne, G.T. (2007), 'The past, present and future of entrepreneurship research: data analytic trends and training', *Entrepreneurship Theory and Practice*, **31**(4): 601–18.

Dilthey, W. (1883/1991), *Selected Works, Volume 1: Introduction to the Human Sciences*, edited by R.A. Makkreel and F. Rodi, Princeton, NJ: Princeton University Press.

Easterby-Smith, M., Thorpe, R. and Lowe, A. (2002), *Management Research: An Introduction*, London: Sage.

Easterby-Smith, M., Golden-Biddle, K. and Locke, K. (2008), 'Working with pluralism: determining quality in qualitative research', *Organizational Research Methods*, **11**(3): 419–29.

Emden, C. and Sandelowski, M. (1998), 'The good, the bad, and the relative, Part 1: Conceptions of goodness in qualitative research', *International Journal of Nursing Practice*, **4**: 206–12.

Emden, C. and Sandelowski, M. (1999), 'The good, the bad, and the relative, Part 2: Goodness and the criterion problem in qualitative research', *International Journal of Nursing Practice*, **5**: 2–7.

Feiwel, G.R. (1987), *Arrow and the Ascent of Modern Economic Theory*, Basingstoke: Macmillan.

Feyerabend, P. (1970), *Against Method*, London: New Left Books.

Fielding, N.G. and Fielding, J.L. (1986), *Linking Data: The Articulation of Qualitative and Quantitative Methods in Social Research*, Beverly Hills, CA: Sage.

Flax, J. (1990), Thinking Fragments: Psychoanalysis, Feminism and Postmodernism in the Contemporary West, Berkeley, CA: University of California Press.

Gadamer, H.G. (1994), *Truth and Method*, 2nd edn, New York: Seabury.

Gartner, W.B. (2001), 'Is there an elephant in entrepreneurship? Blind assumptions in theory development', *Entrepreneurship Theory and Development*, **25**(4): 27–40.

Gartner, W.B. and Birley, S. (2002), 'Introduction to the Special Issue on Qualitative Methods in Entrepreneurship Research', *Journal of Business Venturing*, **17**: 387–95.

Gephart, R.P. (2004), 'From the editors: qualitative research and the *Academy of Management Journal*', *Academy of Management Journal*, **47**(4): 454–62.

Gherardi, S. (2006), 'Practice-based theorizing on learning and knowing in organizations', *Organization*, **7**(4): 211–23.

Gibbons, M., Limoges, C., Nowotony, H., Schwartzman, S., Scott, P. and Trow, M. (1994), *The New Production of Knowledge: The Dynamics of Science and Research in Contemporary Societies*, London: Sage.

Grégoire, D.A., Nöel, M.X., Déry, R. and Béchard, J.-P. (2006), 'Is there conceptual convergence in entrepreneurship research? A co-citation analysis of *Frontiers of Entrepreneurship Research*, 1981–2004', *Entrepreneurship Theory and Practice*, **30**(3): 333–63

Guba, E.G. and Lincoln, Y.S. (2005), 'Paradigmatic controversies, contradictions, and emerging confluences', in N.K. Denzin and Y.S. Lincoln (eds), *The Sage Handbook of Qualitative Research*, 3rd edn, Thousand Oaks, CA: Sage, pp. 191–215.

Hacking, I. (1990), *The Taming of Chance*, Cambridge: Cambridge University Press.

Haraway, D. (1988), 'Situated knowledges: the science question in feminism and the privilege of partial perspective', *Feminist Studies*, **14**(3), 575–99.

Harrison, R.T. and Leitch, C.M. (1996), 'Discipline emergence in management: accumulative fragmentalism or paradigmatic science?', *Entrepreneurship, Innovation and Change*, **5**(2): 65–83.

Hindle, K. (2004), 'Choosing qualitative methods for entrepreneurial cognition research: a canonical development approach', *Entrepreneurship Theory and Practice*, **28**(6): 575–607.

Hoepfl, M.C. (1997), 'Choosing qualitative research: a primer for technology education researchers', *Journal of Technology Education*, **9**(1), http://scholar.lib.vt.edu/ejournals/JTE/jte-v9n1/hoepfl.html, downloaded 28 February 2006.

House, E.R. (2005), 'Qualitative evaluation and changing social policy', in N.K. Denzin and Y.S. Lincoln (eds), *The Sage Handbook of Qualitative Research*, 3rd edn, Thousand Oaks, CA: Sage, pp. 1069–82.

Huse, M. and Landström, H. (1997), 'European entrepreneurship and small business research: methodological openness and contextual differences', *International Studies of Management and Organization*, **27**(3): 3–12.

Jennings, P.L., Perren, L. and Carter, S. (2005), 'Guest editors' introduction: Alternative perspectives on entrepreneurship research', *Entrepreneurship Theory and Practice*, **29**(2): 145–51.

Johnson, P., Buehring, A., Cassell, C. and Symon, G. (2006), 'Evaluating qualitative management research: towards a contingent criteriology', *International Journal of Management Reviews*, **8**(3): 131–56.

Johnson, R.B. (1997), 'Examining the validity structure of qualitative research', *Education*, **118**: 282–92.

Keat, R. and Urry, J. (1982), *Social Theory as Science*, 2nd edn, London: Routledge and Kegan Paul.

Knudsen, C. (2003), 'Pluralism, scientific progress and the structure of organization studies', in H. Tsoukas and C. Knudsen (eds), *The Oxford Handbook of Organization Theory*, Oxford: Oxford University Press, pp. 262–86.

Krueger, N.F. Jr, Reilly, M.D. and Carsrud, A. (2000), 'Competing models of entrepreneurial intentions', *Journal of Business Venturing*, **15**: 411–32.

Kuhn, T.S. (1970), *The Structure of Scientific Revolutions*, Chicago, IL: Chicago University Press.

Kvale, S. (1996), *Interviews: An Introduction to Qualitative Research Interviewing*, Thousand Oaks, CA: Sage.

Lather, P. (1993), 'Fertile obsession: validity after poststructuralism', *Sociological Quarterly*, **34**(4): 673–93.

Latour, B. and Woolgar, S. (1986), *Laboratory Life: The Construction of Scientific Facts*, 2nd edn, Princeton, NJ: Princeton University Press.

Law, J. (2004), *After Method: Mess in Social Science Research*, London: Routledge.

Lawson, T. (2008), 'What has realism got to do with it?', in D.M Hausman (ed.), *The Philosophy of Economics: An Anthology*, 3rd edn, Cambridge: Cambridge University Press, pp. 439–54.

Leitch, C.M., Hill, F.H. and Harrison, R.T. (2010), 'The philosophy and practice of interpretivist research in entrepreneurship: quality, validation and trust', *Organizational Research Methods*, **13**(1): 67–84.

Lincoln, Y.S. and Guba, E.G. (1985), *Naturalistic Inquiry*, Beverly Hills, CA: Sage.

Locke, R. (1989), *Management and Higher Education Since 1940*, Cambridge: Cambridge University Press.

Locke, K. (2001), *Grounded Theory in Management Research*, Thousand Oaks, CA: Sage.

Madison, G. (1988), *The Hermeneutics of Postmodernity: Figure and Themes*, Bloomington, IN: Indian University Press.

Maxwell, J.A. (1992), 'Understanding and validity in qualitative research', *Harvard Educational Review*, **62**: 279–300.

McCloskey, D. (2008), 'The rhetoric of this economics', in D.M. Hausman (ed.), *The Philosophy of Economics: An Anthology*, 3rd edn, Cambridge: Cambridge University Press, pp. 415–30.

McDonald, S., Gan, B.C. and Anderson, A. (2004), 'Studying entrepreneurship: a review of methods employed in entrepreneurship research 1985–2004', *Conference Proceedings RENT XVIII*, Copenhagen.

Mischler, E.G. (1990), 'Validation in inquiry-guided research: the role of exemplars in narrative studies', *Harvard Educational Review*, **60**: 415–40.

Montuschi, E. (2003), *The Objects of Social Science*, London: Continuum.

Morse, J. (1991), 'Designing funded qualitative research', in N.K. Denzin and Y.S. Lincoln (eds), *Handbook of Qualitative Research*, Thousand Oaks, CA: Sage, pp. 138–57.

Neergaard, H. and Leitch, C.M. (eds) (forthcoming), *The Handbook of Qualitative Research Techniques and Analysis in Entrepreneurship*, Cheltenham, UK and Northampton, MA, USA: Edward Elgar Publishing.

Neergaard, H. and Ulhøi, J.P. (2007a), 'Introduction: methodological variety in entrepreneurship research', in H. Neergaard and J.P. Ulhøi (eds), *Handbook of Qualitative Research in Entrepreneurship*, Cheltenham, UK and Northampton, MA, USA: Edward Elgar Publishing, pp. 1–14.

Neergaard, H. and Ulhøi, J.P. (eds) (2007b), *Handbook of Qualitative Research in Entrepreneurship*, Cheltenham, UK and Northampton, MA, USA: Edward Elgar Publishing.

Nelson, J.A. (2008). 'Feminism and economics', in D.M. Hausman (ed.), *The Philosophy of Economics: An Anthology*, 3rd edn, Cambridge: Cambridge University Press, pp. 454–75 (originally published in *Journal of Economic Perspectives*, **9** (1995): 131–48).

Nielsen, H.B. (1995), 'Seductive texts with serious intention', *Educational Researcher*, **24**, 4–12.

Page, R. (2000). 'The turn inward in qualitative research', in B. Brizuela, J. Stewart, R. Carrillo and J. Berger (eds), *Acts of Inquiry in Qualitative Research*, Cambridge, MA: Harvard Educational Review, pp. 3–16; Reprint Series No. 34.

Patton, M.Q. (1990), *Qualitative Evaluation and Research Methods*, 2nd edn, Newbury Park, CA: Sage.

Porter, T.M. (1995), *Trust in Numbers: The Pursuit of Objectivity in Science and Public Life*, Princeton, NJ: Princeton University Press.

Pratt, M.G. (2008), 'Fitting oval pegs into round holes: tensions in evaluating and publishing qualitative research in top-tier North American journals', *Organizational Research Methods*, **11**(3): 481–509.

Sackett, D.L. and Wennberg, J.E. (1997), 'Choosing the best research design for each question', *British Medical Journal*, **315**: 1636–7.

Sandelowski, M. (1995), 'Qualitative analysis: what it is and how it began', *Research in Nursing and Health*, **18**, 371–5.

Sanjek, R. (1990), *Fieldnotes: The Makings of an Anthropology*, Ithaca, NY: Cornell University Press.

Schatzki, T.R. (2001), 'Introduction: Practice turn', in T.R. Schatzki, K. Knorrcentina and E. Savigny (eds), *The Practice Turn in Contemporary Theory*, London and New York: Routledge, pp. 1–14.

Schatzki, T.R., Knorrcetina, K. and von Savigny, E. (eds) (2001), *The Practice Turn in Contemporary Theory*, London and New York: Routledge.

Seale, C. (2004), 'Quality in qualitative research', in C. Seale, G. Gobo, J. Gubrium and D. Silverman (eds), *Qualitative Research Practice*, London: Sage, pp. 409–19.

Shapiro, I. and Wendt, A. (2005), 'The difference that realism makes: social science and the politics of consent', in I. Shapiro (ed.), *The Flight from Reality in the Human Sciences*, Princeton, NJ: Princeton University Press, pp. 19–50.

Shaw, E. (1999), 'A guide to the qualitative research process: evidence from a small firm study', *Qualitative Market Research: An International Journal*, **2**(2): 59–70.

Shenhav, Y. (1999), *Manufacturing Rationality: The English Foundations of the Managerial Revolution*, Oxford: Oxford University Press.

Short, J.C., Ketchen, D.J. Jr, Combs, J.G. and Ireland, R.D. (2010), 'Research methods in entrepreneurship: opportunities and challenges', *Organizational Research Methods*, **13**(1): 6–15.

Smith, J.K. (1990), 'Goodness criteria: alternative research paradigms and the problem of criteria', in E.G. Guba (ed.), *The Paradigm Dialogue*, Newbury Park, CA: Sage, pp. 167–87.

Thorpe, R. and Holt, R. (eds) (2008), *The Sage Dictionary of Qualitative Management Research*, London: Sage.

Ulhøi, J.P. and Neergaard, H. (2007), 'Postscript: Unresolved challenges?', in H. Neergaard and J.P. Ulhøi (eds), *Handbook of Qualitative Research in Entrepreneurship*, Cheltenham, UK and Northampton, MA, USA Edward Elgar Publishing, pp. 477–80.

Unger, R.K. (1992), 'Through the looking glass: no wonderland yet!', in J. Bohan (ed.), *Seldom Seen, Rarely Heard: Women's Place in Psychology*, Boulder, CO: Westview, pp. 147–70.

van Aken, J.E. (2004), 'Management research based on the paradigm of the design sciences: the quest for field tested and grounded technological rules', *Journal of Management Studies*, **41**: 219–45.

van Maanen, J. (1979), 'The fact of fiction in organizational ethnography', *Administrative Science Quarterly*, **24**(4): 539–50.

Whittington, R. (2006), 'Completing the practice turn in strategy research', *Organization Studies*, **27**: 613–34.

10. Ethnographic approaches to entrepreneurship and small-business research: what lessons can we learn?
Karin Berglund and Caroline Wigren

PROLOGUE

I'm looking down the stairs and almost feel a sense of giddiness. Balancing the plates of food requires concentration – in particular considering the steep and narrow stairs. After a few days, however, I'm starting to experience 'the firm' within me: a study of a small firm running a café and restaurant, a bakery, a bed and breakfast and a farm shop in a rural area.

It was high season and an extra employee was much appreciated, so it didn't take long to be accepted and become one of the staff. I started to work in the café: serving lunch, clearing tables, and standing at the counter in the café when needed. During lunchtime the guests ordered lunch at the counter and thereafter they found a table, either inside or outside. The café was situated in an old mill located by a small river. The building consisted of three floors, and a terrace by the river. The tables were scattered all over, which meant that it took some walking to find those who had ordered lunch.

My feet were aching and I felt warm after running up and down the stairs. With food stains on my blouse I somehow had a feeling of satisfaction: having worked hard physically and contributed to serving the customers, I felt like one of the group. I realized that this was knowledge about the firm that I never would have got through conducting interviews.

INTRODUCTION

Professor Paul Reynolds said in a speech that entrepreneurs quickly learn how to tell the polished stories about their journeys when they are asked by researchers and journalists about what they have done and achieved. The notion of polished stories is also recognized by William Gartner (2007) in a special issue on narrative, reflecting upon the fact that he can name dozens of entrepreneurs, and he has several logico-scientific descriptions, explanations, categories, concepts and hypotheses about entrepreneurs, but he cannot say much about their stories. Consequently, it has been argued that the field of entrepreneurship studies needs new concepts if it is to take seriously the ambition to understand entrepreneurs, entrepreneurship and entrepreneuring (e.g. Hjorth et al., 2003; Johannisson, 2011; Steyaert, 2007; Gartner, 2007; Huse and Landström, 1997). In this chapter we will show how entrepreneurship and small and medium-sized enterprises (SMEs) can be researched through the ethnographic method, focusing on understanding the social context of a certain phenomenon or person. Specifically, four ethnographic studies are introduced, which will be discussed as themes: *context*; *the role of the researcher*; *the research process*; and *lessons learned*.

Following these four studies, entrepreneurs and their actions are understood in the sociocultural context (e.g. Johannisson, 2010; Welter, 2010), and entrepreneurship is depicted as mundane and part of everyday doings, sometimes dull and boring (e.g. Steyaert, 1997; Bill et al., 2010). Arguably, it is of importance for entrepreneurship research to make use of a broader variety of methods for understanding the phenomenon of entrepreneurship. So far, the ethnographic method has been only marginally used in the field of entrepreneurship research, which is a loss for the field since ethnography offers knowledge and understanding of the phenomenon that are rarely part of mainstream studies (Aldrich, 1992; Grégoire et al., 2002). While there are few qualitative studies in mainstream entrepreneurship and SME studies, even fewer apply the ethnographic method. Johnstone (2007) concludes that a subgroup in this field uses ethnographic methods and tends to publish in books or in non-entrepreneurship journals.

In the various publication sources, which make up a tributary of mainstream entrepreneurship, there is a multiplicity of accounts, as well as experiments in ethnographic methods, involving direct and sustained social contacts with those who are studied, and rich recordings of these encounters. Examples of those are Ram, who has done several ethnographic studies on small firms (cf. Ram and Holliday, 1993) and Down and Reveley (2004), who examined how generational encounters shape entrepreneurial identities. Taylor et al. (2002) studied managerial legitimacy in small firms and Watson (2009) investigated how entrepreneurial identity was constructed in a family-firm setting. Moreover, O'Connor (2006) took us 'inside' an entrepreneurial process, following the birth of a business, and Bruni et al. (2004) showed how gender and entrepreneurship are enacted as situated practices in their study of small enterprises in Italy.

These accounts all deepen our understanding of why entrepreneurs do particular things, and tell particular stories. Ethnography thus invites us to come closer to the studied phenomena, and beyond polished stories and logico-scientific explanations. The prologue tells us, for instance, a kind of story different from the usual successful and elegant stories of entrepreneurs. This story, narrated by a researcher who 'went entrepreneur' for a couple of days and became part of the daily activities in a small business, illustrates well the richness of stories available when one gets subsumed in mundane activities. These non-polished stories are often disregarded as unimportant and trivial in quantitative research approaches. Moreover, they are difficult to get by 'just' doing interviews as the respondent often provides the answers she or he thinks the researcher expects. Accordingly, these stories are offered by, in one way or another, observing and thus 'becoming part of' the mundane, trivial and dull part of entrepreneurship and the everyday life of small businesses. Methodologically this is referred to as ethnographic work, which will be accounted for in this chapter by four different research studies that the authors have been involved in.

Illustrating these four different ethnographic studies aims to explain how ethnography can be applied in entrepreneurship and SME research. Moreover, we hope to make ethnography seem less ambitious than it may appear at first glance. Sometimes, just observing can add a great deal of information to an interview study. At other times, the researcher can draw upon experience from, for example, having been part of starting someone's own business, or gaining insights from friends who have been through the process, or from being on the board of an SME. With an ethnographic 'eye' we see several instances of 'data' that normally are disregarded. So, in this chapter we hope to inspire a search within our own closets, as well as to slightly adjust the way that qualitative research is conducted. By providing the four ethnographic studies in this chapter, we hope to use the 'ethnographic eye' to tell new, and alternative, stories of entrepreneurship.

The chapter is structured as follows. First, ethnography is introduced, including an account of how ethnographic studies have been conducted historically and how it has been developed, empirically and theoretically. Furthermore, we elaborate on how to do ethnography and give some examples of how it has informed entrepreneurship research then and now, and possibly in the future as well. Thereafter the four ethnographic studies are presented and elaborated according to analytical themes. This chapter is summarized by a discussion of how an ethnographic approach can contribute to developing the fields of entrepreneurship and SME studies.

ETHNOGRAPHY THEN AND NOW

The term ethnography refers to the process of accomplishing the fieldwork and deriving cultural interpretations from it. The concept itself is built upon the Greek word εθνος (ethnos), which means folk/people, and γράφω (grapho), which simply means 'to write'. Thus, in short, ethnography refers to describing 'the worlds' of those who are studied through writing. To get to know the meaning/s people bring to certain phenomena, the ethnographer focuses on different types of texts, oral and/or written (Cassell and Symon, 1994), which has been described as trading in linguistic symbols in order 'to reduce the distance between indicated and indicator, between theory and data, between context and action' (Van Maanen, 1979, p. 520).

At the beginning ethnography was used to denote the study of foreign cultures, with several classical works that have impacted social studies in many ways. Bronislaw Malinowski (1884–1942), who studied the inhabitants of the Western Pacific, focused on gift culture and the gift economy. Margaret Mead (1901–78), who conducted research in the Western Pacific, highlighted how femininity, masculinity and the human was constructed differently in so-called primitive societies. And Claude Lévi-Strauss (1908–2009), who spent years in the rainforest of Brazil in the 1930s, wrote about us, as human beings, creating relations with each other. Lévi-Strauss's studies have had an impact on organization studies in general and subtopics such as the gift economy, the microeconomy and leadership in particular. Hence ethnography is about understanding cultures, and the ethnographic method is about creating understanding, which positions the ethnographer as a learner of the culture through the eyes and ears of the natives. Metaphorically this can be understood as 'coming closer and closer to the lived realities of other people' (Alvesson, 1999, p. 2).

Ethnography is thus typically related to the study of fieldwork of one particular place, people or organization, applying a holistic worldview of 'getting it together' by observing, talking to the 'inhabitants' and writing about it. Often ethnography is simply referred to as 'making observations' or 'conducting field studies'. Two frequently used methods in ethnographic research are interviews and participant observation. These methods are not unique to ethnographic studies. However, applying them in ethnographies entails specific advantages, and vice versa: getting to know the ethnographic perspective entails advantages in 'traditional' qualitative case studies when conducting interviews and observations (cf. Eisenhardt, 1989).

Regardless of label, these approaches signify attempts to come close to the studied phenomena in order to create new knowledge, but also to learn about what we should study (Draft, 1983, p. 539). Simply, 'real-world contacts' are at the center in ethnographic approaches. There are many ways to describe the modes of inquiry in ethnographic research. According to Evered and Louis (1981), there are two modes of inquiry: from the outside and from the inside. While creating understanding from the inside implies that the researcher takes on the role as an actor, to experience the daily life of the studied phenomenon, creating understanding from the outside implies that the researcher takes on the role as an onlooker. According to the first mode the data (or empirical material) is not seen to be logical since it is based on experiences, but in the other mode of inquiry it is seen as logical since it is based on measurements and rationality. Similar dichotomies have been invented, for example thick and thin descriptions (Geertz, 1973), high context and low context (Hall, 1976), and emic and etic (Pike, 1967). While thick descriptions, high context and *emic* represent the type of knowledge and understanding originating from everyday-life situations and is achieved through close contact with those studied, thin descriptions, low context and *etic* represent the type of knowledge and understanding developed and conceptualized by the scientific world.

In recent decades, ethnography, like many other approaches and research fields in the social sciences, has been part of the postmodern turn. This can be described as leaving the grand narrative of a coherent story in favor of acknowledging the many stories that shape cultures. This can be illustrated by moving from the work of Clifford Geertz (1973), where culture is explored through being part of it, to the work of James Clifford and George Marcus (1986), where culture is seen as something that continuously unfolds, and where the ethnographer her- or himself is called into question as a political actor writing certain stories (while leaving others untold).

This turn thus has implications for the role of the researcher, no longer seeing the ethnographer as someone discovering or reflecting culture, but someone who is as much part of making and producing culture (Clifford and Marcus, 1986; Marcus, 1995; Willis and Trondman, 2000). Furthermore, this move has implications for theory, where a more theoretically informed ethnographic writing has a role to play in reshaping existing theories. Willis and Trondman (2000) explain that 'the "nitty gritty" of everyday life cannot be presented as raw, unmediated data, ... nor can it be presented through abstract theoretical categories' (p. 12). Instead they suggest an engagement with the 'real world' to bring 'surprise' to theoretical formulations, as well as to bring about alternative stories about particular phenomena. This can be seen as a process of shifting back and forth, between empirical material and theory, creating distance to both and reflecting on their interrelationships.

While the traditional ethnographic eye views culture as something quite stable, the postmodern eye acknowledges and tries to deal with ambiguities. Marcus's (1995) idea of a 'multi-sited ethnography' implies, for instance, tracing how emerging cultural phenomena unfold in different settings. This way of conducting ethnography opens up to not only following a people, but also to following a thing, a plot, a story/allegory, a life/biography, or to following a conflict. Hence the multi-sited approach encourages ethnographers not only to focus on one 'site' – whether it is one place, one organization or one particular group – but also to follow how a phenomenon unfolds. Moving from its conventional single-site location also implies leaving behind macro-constructions of a larger social order to acknowledge how different sites of observation and participation together cross-cut taken-for-granted dichotomies such as the local/global, public/private and social/individual (Willis and Trondman, 2000; Marcus, 1995), as well as question the misleading dichotomy between 'the entrepreneur' and 'non-entrepreneurs' (Sarasvathy, 2004; Bruni et al., 2004; Berglund and Johansson, 2007).

This way of doing ethnography – by following how 'the new' unfolds and by seeking to create 'Ah-ha' effects in the meeting between social science theory and the ethnographer's eye – echoes the need to understand entrepreneurship as a process. Lately it has been proposed that entrepreneurship needs to be understood – and researched – as a verb, 'entrepreneuring', rather than as the noun 'entrepreneurship'. Entrepreneuring thus makes up a promising concept to create theory from new perspectives in entrepreneurship research, where the phenomenon is not delineated beforehand, but where the researcher is open to the actions and events taking place in particular contexts (cf. Johannisson's 2011 discussion of entrepreneurship as practice or Steyaert's 2007 overview of entrepreneurship as process). Hence, from this perspective, entrepreneurship does not have a particular residence or actor, but emerges from a series of actions that unfolds between sites and people, which fits well with the postmodern eye of the ethnographer. Adopting this 'eye' invites the researcher to understand entrepreneurship as entrepreneuring and to ask questions of an emergent object of study whose contours, sites and relationships are not known beforehand. Since entrepreneuring highlights the emergence of entrepreneurial processes, the postmodern 'eye' in general and multi-sited ethnography in particular seems appropriate to use in order to study the 'becoming of entrepreneurship'.

DOING ETHNOGRAPHY

Doing ethnography is about living, learning and writing about 'the routine, daily lives of people' (Fetterman, 1998b, p. 473) by studying the natives – to have 'been there', as Alvesson (1999, p. 5) stated. Ethnography thus requires gaining access to participation in daily-life activities in order to learn about how people live their lives – in our case entrepreneurs. The researcher does this by taking on the role of an observer as well as a participant. As ethnography is about acknowledging the role of culture, doing ethnography is about trying to be part of a culture or cultures to create an understanding of the different meanings that construct the culture/s. This might not be grasped through snapshot visits in the field or interviews. Applying an ethnographic approach implies that several techniques might be used. While observations, field notes and interviews are common techniques, taking photos, making movies and gathering material of interest may also be useful. This section will briefly introduce the analytical themes that form the four ethnographies: context, the role of the researcher, the research process, and lessons learned.

The research process of ethnography comprises both observations and interviews, and aims at coming closer to the context. In traditional qualitative studies an interview is a constructed social situation where most of the information given by the respondent and interpreted by the researcher is taken out of its context. In such a situation the researcher has his or her social representations of what life is like and who the people being interviewed are, and so has the respondent. A consequence is that both parties might read too much information into the interview. The researcher may end up studying the construction of the talk about a certain phenomenon, rather than how the respondents are relating to the phenomena of interest in their daily lives. Practice is thus taken out of its context and talked about but not actually experienced. In an ethnographic study the researcher continually develops an understanding of the context, which facilitates the interview situation and also guides the questions. The interviewer and the interviewee turn into two people who know about each other and come to share an understanding of the context /phenomenon of interest. This makes it possible to ask more direct questions and sometimes to challenge the interviewees in a way that would not happen in a single interview.

It is when people are in a certain context that they can actually describe what they are doing (Balogun et al., 2003), which means that the small conversations and chats that take place outside the interview context are of great importance for creating understanding of the process. Many times the interview takes on the character of a conversation rather than an interview. A consequence of relying solely on interviews is that ambiguities and inconsistencies are easily overlooked. Working with ethnography has an advantage since it gives the researcher the opportunity to check issues that have been brought up earlier in the process, during meetings and in conversations.

The closer the link between the researcher and the respondent, the more prominently emotions feature in the interview, with the researcher taking on the role of participant. When trust is developed it is easier to ask questions of a more sensitive character. Doing ethnographic research results in several conversations and chats; stories and information that come to hand during those occasions are also of importance for understanding the process. Moreover, knowledge and understanding of the process are often developed through participant observations, which cut across interviews.

While ethnography offers many new insights into the context/ phenomenon of interest, the ethnographer may easily get caught up in the espoused 'grand story' of the field, for example about an entrepreneur or a successful company. On the other hand, the interviewee may well give the answers s/he believes that the researcher wants, and also convey the espoused story to the surrounding world. Moreover, it is argued that researchers probably rely too much on interviews when it comes to understanding situations outside the domain of the interview (see Alvesson, 1999). Using different techniques can therefore help to remain reflexive to the 'truths' constructed during the fieldwork.

A vital part of the research process is writing it up, which starts from the very beginning. Doing ethnography might imply that the researcher cannot tape and transcribe interviews, but s/he can take notes, photos and systematically document daily interactions with the field. Spending more time in the empirical world helps a researcher to broaden his/her understanding of the field by interacting with different people and participating in different arenas. Being present in the field, observing and participating, the researcher becomes involved in everyday social life, and commitment to the field increases over time. A consequence is that it may later take some time and effort to create a distance from the field, and thereby to process stories from it, employing a critical focus. With increased distance, a more balanced view is developed, but being 'caught up' is an unavoidable part of the process. According to Salzer (1994), it is impossible to reach objectivity, but in the best case, we, as researchers, can strive to create intersubjectivity.

Another important part of the research process is reorganizing the material in order to make it presentable, and to create understanding of the study in relation to theory (cf. Willis and Trondman, 2000). Moving into theory is a good way of creating distance from the field and of generating knowledge about the context/phenomenon of interest. This is what we will refer to as 'lessons learned' in the coming review of the four studies. This part of the process is about formulating the results of the fieldwork in a convincing way. Conducting an ethnographic study implies that the researcher takes the responsibility to participate in the continuing dialogue in order to define and redefine it both as a process and as a product (Wolcott, 1995). Leaving out this step means that we risk delivering answers without asking questions.

Summing up, these four themes are of interest when applying an ethnographic approach. First, the social context, the culture studied, is central since it indicates and expresses the mode of indeterminacy in human life. Taking context into account, entrepreneurship cannot be reduced to economic and social conditions, but is part of both. Second, the role of the researcher is important, since s/he uses her/his ethnographic eye to mediate the impressions from the fieldwork, and to find ways to mediate with theories. Third, the research process in general should be accounted for, including both the fieldwork and the writing, and how both lead to new knowledge. Besides these three themes we suggest a fourth to capture the kind of knowledge that is created by entrepreneurship and SMEs through ethnography, which we call 'lessons learned'.

APPROACH TO ETHNOGRAPHIC ENTREPRENEURSHIP STUDIES: INTRODUCING FOUR CASES

In this section we will illustrate four ethnographic approaches to entrepreneurship research. The first, the 'Gnosjö study', gives a traditional view of how ethnography was applied to understanding the culture of a successful industrial district. The second study is made up of three cases of rural entrepreneurs, one of which is quoted in the prologue. The third study shows how the technique of making observations, and the ethnographic eyes of the researchers, can be useful in a research project that is not approached as an ethnographic study, but is more a participative action research project. The fourth study tells of the researcher invited to take part in a large EU project with the aim of creating a more entrepreneurial region, which gives access to different places and contexts where entrepreneurship is conducted differently.

The presentations of the studies are organized by the four themes previously discussed. Thus each study is situated by its context, the research role taken by the ethnographer/s, the research process and how the research was conducted, and by the lessons learned – that is, the knowledge produced by each study.

Traditional Ethnography: Learning about Everyday Life in an Industrial District

Context
The context of the study (Wigren, 2003) is a well-known industrial district in Sweden, called Gnosjö. This district is known for its local entrepreneurial culture. We argue that traditional ethnography here is carried out in one physical place, which makes it possible for the researcher to attend unexpected situations. Even though the study is conducted within the field of business administration and the district is best known for its small and medium-sized locally owned businesses, the decision is made to not only spend time with and in local firms, but also to include other local contexts,

such as local churches, sports clubs, the local Rotary club and so on. The research journey is quite grounded, in the sense that the researcher arrives in the district with an open mind, and with an open research question to learn about the culture. This can be compared with the next story about extended case studies: when that project was initiated the research area and questions had already been addressed.

The role of the researcher

As the district is situated about 80 km southwest of the hometown of the researcher, it could be argued that she would be familiar with the environment, and that she would not be considered an outsider. Before arrival she had not been thinking about herself as an outsider. It became clear, however, that she was. The industrial structure of the region is oriented towards production, and the CEOs who run the companies are men. Being a female academic with a southern accent made her an outsider. Lacking training in the field of engineering, she had little knowledge of technology and machinery. Being quite young, and always with a notebook in her hand, she was often addressed as a 'secretary'. Being young and a woman, however, offered the opportunity to ask different types of question, even naive ones.

The research process

This ethnographic process can be divided into four phases: (1) the time in the field; (2) making sense of the time in the field, and creating distance; (3) writing ethnography; and (4) communicating the findings. During the time in the field the researcher participated in different local arenas. Initially interviews were conducted and a lesson was learned: the respondents expressed an institutionalized story about the district – its grand narrative. Having experienced this, it became obvious that it was important not only to conduct interviews but to try to understand what the people in the field actually did and what they said. For example, did they 'walk the talk' or was there an inconsistency between the stories told and their daily lives? Time in the field was spent not only in firms, but also in other organizations and meeting places, for example the local Rotary Club, local business networks, churches and so on.

During the time in the field the researcher, perhaps because she was young or perhaps because of her personality, became 'hooked' on part of the field: she merged into the field. Creating a mental and physical distance from the field was vital – she started to see things that she had neglected and overlooked while being part of the field. Ambiguities emerged, uncertainties and small stories suddenly started to play more significant roles; so far the grand narrative of the district had dominated the story. When the small stories became dominant, it was possible to understand everyday life in the district. Now it was possible to identify value sources playing roles in the construction of the local cultures. It was suddenly possible to start to write ethnography. One reason why this was an important phase might be that the processes were grounded, in the sense that the research questions were quite vague.

Lessons learned

From this research study new perspectives on the local district were unveiled. The historical story of the district had primarily been voiced by local owner-managers. And this story was shared by many, but as it only was voiced by people in the district with a certain power, alternative stories had been silenced and excluded. Creating space for those stories also implied that a new story was framed and articulated. The contributions to entrepreneurship theory here are several. First, the study shows the importance of taking context into account in creating understanding of entrepreneurs and entrepreneurship. Second, it teaches us something about industrial districts – how easy it is to be caught up in their success stories. During a conversation with Professor Walter Powell it became clear that, because of the ethnographic method, an alternative understanding and reading of the district was possible. From previous research studies on industrial districts we know a good deal about networking in industrial districts, for example, but the focus has been on the positive side of networking. How networks might exclude people has not been much emphasized, as shown by the Gnosjö study. Nor has the focus been on gender structures in industrial districts, which was another contribution of the study. As the aim was to understand the cultures in the district, the focus came to be on norms and values – and by unveiling norms and values, taken for granted by the locals, new knowledge could be created.

Extended Case Study: Understanding Lifestyle Entrepreneurship

Context

The research study reported here is about creating further understanding of rural, lifestyle and entrepreneurial family businesses. It includes three case studies. All three firms have managed to create sustainable development, socially as well as economically, in the countryside. Since 2009 the Swedish Rural Network, organized by the Swedish Board of Agriculture, has nominated a firm as winner of the 'wool-ram' prize. The winner is a firm that can work as a role model for other companies located in the countryside. All the firms in this study have been winners of this prize, which implies that secondary data on the firms exist – that is, texts related to the nomination, stories told in the media about them, and informative web pages. One firm had diversified its dairy farm by producing ice-cream with the milk from their alpine cows; the second had set up a theatre, and the third had rebuilt an old saw mill into a café and restaurant and thereafter developed a bed and breakfast, a bakery and a farm shop.

The role of the researcher
Before arriving at the firms, the researcher had searched for secondary data about them, in order to gain an understanding of the business. During her days at the firms she participated in a variety of activities. When not so engaged, she observed. To be able to understand the culture of a group, one needs to 'be there', to take on the roles of its members. By changing clothes, dressing like them and participating in their activities, it was possible to get an understanding of their daily life that would not have been possible through interviews.

The research process
To learn about the firms, on-site visits with participant observation were conducted. Three to four days were spent in each firm. The method was inspired by ethnography, but as the time on site was quite limited it would not be fair to describe the method as fully ethnographic. The inspiration from ethnography relates to trying to understand the culture of the firm and family from their perspective, for example how they draw boundaries between private and public spheres of life when the physical space is a shared one; and how the physical circumstances influence how this type of firm does family business – how are roles in the family and in the business constructed and created? Such understandings are difficult, if not impossible, to obtain from snapshot visits in the field or through interviews. Instead, this is achieved by being there, and studying the family members in the firms and the employees working with them in their firms.

But by being there the researcher also learned about everyday practices: how the two founders producing ice-cream, for example, had together decided how the production line could be improved, step by step. For example, when tapping the ice-cream they placed the machines and tables in such as way as to get the optimal flow.

Participating in everyday life implied that it was not possible for the researcher to tape or to take notes constantly. The main advantage of not taping is that a familiar atmosphere is developed, which is an advantage for the sharing of stories and experiences. Not all stories will be used in the final academic text, but they all contribute to a holistic understanding of the case.

Lessons learned

This study contributes to the field of entrepreneurship and to family business as it helps us understand the concept of lifestyle entrepreneurship: business processes are followed in which private and public spheres of life overlap. Life is truly organized around the physical space where the families involved live and organize their lives, and run their businesses. From the cases it becomes obvious that the entrepreneurial processes are the result of certain personal and private decisions. In all cases the choice of a certain lifestyle guides the entrepreneurial processes. So far, this has not been acknowledged in the field of entrepreneurship literature, even though we know that entrepreneurs tend to engage in entrepreneurship when they are facing changes in life. Furthermore, in family business literature the family and the business tend to be perceived as two separate systems, and not as one integrated system. It becomes clear when interacting with the families that there are no clear-cut boundaries between the family and the business: the boundaries are vague, floating and in constant flux – and renegotiated over time.

The cases offer a unique context for helping us to create understanding and make sense of questions such as: is it possible to draw boundaries between private and public spheres of life when the physical space is shared; and how do the physical circumstances influence how this type of firm does family business – that is, how are roles in the family and in the business constructed and created?

The Smithy Think Tank – Learning about Societal Entrepreneurship through Participant Observation

Context

The context of this study is a national think tank, 'the Smithy', with the aim of identifying and implementing actions for societal entrepreneurship (SE), to change what is missing or does not work in public structures with the ultimate goal of an inclusive and sustainable society (Berglund and Wigren, 2012; Berglund and Wigren-Kristoferson, 2012). The starting point for the Smithy was a national program of SE initiated by the Knowledge Foundation in 2008. In total the think tank had 18 members, consisting of ten municipality commissioners, three societal entrepreneurs, two researchers (the authors of this chapter) and three civil servants. The civil servants represented two governmental bodies (the Knowledge Foundation and the Swedish Association of Local Authorities and Regions) and one public–private sector partnership, called Arena for Growth (owned by a Swedish bank, a Swedish grocery chain, and the Swedish Association of Local Authorities and Regions). The main issue for the Smithy was to find out how municipalities could support societal entrepreneurs, and eventually identify impediments to increased SE at a local level. The focus in the Smithy was not only on 'thinking', but also on doing. An important task for the participants was therefore to put their thoughts into practice by discussing and granting five projects to effectuate SE 'on the ground', that is, in their municipalities.

The role of the researchers
In 2009 we, the two authors of this chapter, were invited to participate in the think tank. As researchers we were invited to follow the process by participating in and contributing to the think tank's work and to create knowledge from the process. However, we not only participated as 'researchers', but also as equal members of the think tank. Since we observed some vagueness when it came to how the concepts social/societal entrepreneurship were used during the first meetings, we took the decision to intervene in the process by asking the members to take to one of the meetings pictures of their local context relating to societal entrepreneurship, and to bring to another meeting an artifact representing societal entrepreneurship. We asked the members to do this, explaining that it would make us less focused on the definitions of particular concepts and more aware of how societal entrepreneurship was conceptualized in our local contexts. We also illustrated, with some pictures from previous research projects, how a picture sometimes says more than a 'thousand words'. After reflecting on this, the members in the Smithy agreed to participate.

The research process
The process consisted of five one-day meetings, a study trip to the UK and London to learn how the UK was dealing with social enterprises, and a final conference. The study trip lasted two-and-a-half days during autumn 2009. We thus interacted with the participants over a one-year period. Sometimes we took roles as passive listeners – as observers, and sometimes as co-producers of the stories performed – as participant observers. Besides studying the construction of SE from our ethnographic notes, meeting protocols, and the pictures and artifacts that the participants had been asked to bring, we also focused on the five projects that received grants from the Smithy. They themselves told stories on the subject. During the process we also listened to multiple voices, to micro-stories, to the grand narrative and to ante-narratives, in order to highlight what and whom had previously been neglected or silenced (Freire, 1970/1996). The reason for paying attention also to ante-narratives, expressed through micro-stories, was 'to reclaim the

stories of the "little people"' (Boje, 2001, p. 61), those doing the work and making things happen.

Lessons learned

This study contributes to the field of entrepreneurship in several ways. First of all, it contributes to challenging our understanding of profit-oriented entrepreneurship. Applying the conceptual framework of Burke's pentad (used by Berglund and Wigren, 2012, to analyze how the five terms – actors, arenas, means, actions and goals – were constructed in the stories of 'traditional' entrepreneurship and societal entrepreneurship), it is shown that the grand narrative of entrepreneurship consists of the heroic entrepreneur (agent) who creates a kingdom (act) by way of establishing a company (agency) in the market in order to make a profit and contribute to growth (purpose).

However, analyzing the projects launched in the Smithy, it is obvious that they were cast as 'an other', stressing the importance of community, of non-economic values; for example, artisan craftsmanship is stressed, but also how societal structures must be changed. Applying the concept of Tamara (Boje, 2001), we further illustrate how the grand narrative of entrepreneurship emphasizes capitalism, rationality and hierarchy in line with the epoch of industrialization, while the ante-narrative of societal entrepreneurship gives priority to both premodern and postmodern discourses. This study thus adds to knowledge by which the story of entrepreneurship is told differently. If we understand in what ways micro-stories of entrepreneurship can be, and are, told differently, the dominating grand narrative can be re-narrated in a more multi-voiced text, one that includes the tragic as well as the heroic, romantic and comic.

Creating 'Diversity of Entrepreneurship': Following Different Ways to Voice Entrepreneurship in a Regional Context

Context

A region, consisting of three municipalities in mid-Sweden, made up the context of this study. The industrial community culture in the region of this study was characterized by an enterprise discourse, which emphasized companies as productive apparatuses in which a few competent people – often men – were in charge (Berglund and Johansson, 2007). The excluding culture was also an argument for initiating the project 'Diversity in Entrepreneurship' (DiE), which followed this research project (Berglund, 2007). The aim of DiE was ultimately to create a more equal society by developing new strategies, methods and practices to include people in general in entrepreneurial activity. To make the region become this diverse arena for entrepreneurship, four target groups were identified: women from ethnic minorities; school-leavers; disabled people; and cultural workers. By means of the project DiE, an equality discourse was introduced that challenged the enterprise discourse in the region. This discourse emphasized entrepreneurship as a means of battling discrimination and the exclusion of particular groups in relation to the labor market. Thus the idea of egalitarianism is central to equality discourse, which gives prominence to the notion that 'many little things' count.

The role of the researcher
In DiE the researcher was independent of the day-to-day activities of the project, since she was invited to be part of the project but was not expected to carry out evaluation, which was done by an external evaluator instead. This meant that the researcher had access to all activities, but could decide herself what to follow. For instance, as matters became more intense – conflictual – in the midst of the project, she chose to follow these conflicts. This resembles the idea of multi-sited ethnography as outlined by Marcus (1985).

The research process
This project was followed over the course of three years. At the start of the project the researcher visited the involved organizations, and in particular those that were the main partners in the project. In order to get to know more actors, she introduced focus-group interviews, from which she learned about different ways to talk about the DiE project. The main research activities consisted of participant observation, ethnographic interviews and focus-group interviews. This research approach also resulted in the researcher becoming intensively involved in interactions and, at the same time, acting as a sounding board. The set-up of this project thus laid the ground for the researcher to move quite freely within the project and gain access to the involved actors, organizations and project activities.

By following how the project was talked about in the partner organizations, on the one hand, and among the target groups, on the other hand, the researcher started to discern the different meanings ascribed to entrepreneurship. As time passed, tensions and conflict became part of the project, whereby the researcher started to 'follow' situations where the two discourses might collide. That meant paying particular attention to meetings and situations in the project that, at the time, were tense. From following the tensions and conflict a new theoretical perspective of entrepreneurship and regional development could be developed, where conflicts were put forward as constructive.

Lessons learned

The theoretical perspective applied was based upon discourse theory in combination with Freire's ideas on 'conscientization', which refer to a type of learning focused on perceiving and exposing contradictions – social, political or economic – and to take action against the oppressive elements of reality (Berglund and Johansson, 2007). By using equality discourse, the target groups could provide knowledge concerning what it meant to be excluded and what kind of practices were excluding them from the local business support system. Thus, from this perspective, the target groups became experts from whom the actors in the support system could learn. However, by using the enterprise discourse, the target groups were seen as untapped resources for battling unemployment by introducing self-employment as an alternative to sustain the growth of the region. Using this reasoning, the actors became the experts who could advise appointed groups on how they could start a company.

From a Freirean perspective, the encounter of these two discourses can be seen as positive since many people have been made aware of the social, political and economic contradictions that prevent some groups in society from creating a (working) life (Berglund, 2007). Hence the contradictions have enabled the inhabitants to see themselves, and others, as entrepreneurs in regional development processes. Openings have thus emerged to view entrepreneurship from a broader perspective that includes people, and to create practices through which a diverse working life is becoming discernible.

LESSONS LEARNED ABOUT ENTREPRENEURSHIP AND SMES FROM ETHNOGRAPHY

In our illustrations of the four research studies we have highlighted four themes: context; the role of the researcher; the research process; and lessons learned. We now elaborate on these themes, pointing to how ethnography contributes to entrepreneurship and SME studies.

Context

The four studies presented above show that it is possible to draw boundaries around the studied phenomenon in different ways. The first, about Gnosjö, is a study of a phenomenon in a defined geographical physical space, constituting the context of the study. In the extended case studies the contexts are the three family firms, including the families. At the same time, this is a study about the phenomenon of rural entrepreneurship. In the third study about the Smithy, we are able to visit different local contexts through the stories told by the participants; at the same time it is a study of how societal entrepreneurship, as a new concept, has gained a foothold in Sweden. In the fourth study the context is, as in the first study, a regional setting. However, since this context is also a particular EU project, it is linked to national, regional as well as local organizations, which gave the researcher access to a variety of milieus by which she could follow how entrepreneurship is voiced and how entrepreneuring has unfolded over time.

Generally speaking it could be said that context is often overlooked in entrepreneurship research (Welter, 2010), even if several researchers have emphasized the importance of taking context into account in understanding entrepreneurship. Steyaert and Katz (2004, p. 186), for example, write:

> Entrepreneurship is not a unitary or static concept, nor is it one that exists independently of the locale where it emerges. Often entrepreneurship's conception in a particular setting depends on integrating two or more discourses – one economic and one cultural and possibly one environmental or social. The question is: which is the discursive mix through which entrepreneurship becomes socially constructed?

Revisiting the four stories above, it can be concluded that they shed light on different discourses as well as on other mixes of discourses in the four studies. Those discourses could not necessarily be ascribed to the studied phenomenon from the beginning, but came to light through the ethnographic eye – by spending time in the field. The Gnosjö story sheds light on the industrial district discourse: how networking has been taken for granted as a positive aspect of understanding industrial districts. It also shows the difficulty of drawing boundaries between business life and private life in a small community such as Gnosjö. How the private and public discourses overlap and mix has been shown by Granovetter and others, but is not actually taken into account that often in entrepreneurship research focusing primarily on the firm as the arena. In the study on lifestyle entrepreneurship the discourse on rural entrepreneurship emerged while all three firms were consciously and unconsciously telling stories illustrating how they, in different ways, overcame challenges and achieved success in their businesses. The role and high number of stories would have been difficult, if not impossible, to access if the researcher had relied only on interviews. Often, it is in the small conversations that the stories emerge, or as part of the business itself; entrepreneurs tell stories in everyday life without necessarily reflecting upon them as stories. When the think tank, the Smithy, took off, members had no common understanding of the meaning of the concepts of entrepreneurship and societal entrepreneurship. Over time and through the process of meetings, dialogues and a study trip, they started to talk about entrepreneurship as one thing and societal entrepreneurship as another. The meaning-making and the meaning ascribed to the concepts of entre-preneurship and societal entrepreneurship thus brought about different discourses. Likewise, the fourth study illustrates how the equality discourse emerged during the project, and came into conflict with the historical norms and traditions of entrepreneurship in this particular region. In making this conflict open, the community could reflect upon how they included/excluded particular groups from the business arena.

Even if context is emphasized, surprisingly few studies take the role of context into account. By focusing on context, it has been shown that it can vary – for example it can be an analytical means by which the researcher can train her or his ethnographic eye. Besides, getting to know contexts (and seeing how they are linked together) also leads to getting to know 'new', or alternative, stories.

Role of the Researcher

The different stories also exemplify different research roles: what you allow yourself to be in the context and how you decide to approach it. Stewart (1998) notes that when it comes to ethnography, there is one 'focal research instrument', that is, 'the ethnographer's own inquiring experience, in joint, emergent exploration with people who once were called natives' (p. 6). In the stories above the researchers use themselves in different ways. What an ethnographic study ends up being depends on how the research process is set up. Rosen (1991, p. 16 based on Nelson, 1969) writes: 'only by "direct participation" in the affairs of a social group can the ethnographer come to understand the actions and meanings of those who constitute the group'. This is, to be able to understand the ethnography of a group, one needs to be what the members are. That might of course not be entirely possible, but will be to a certain degree. In the four studies presented above the research-ers decide to try to be what the members are: in the Gnosjö study by living on site and spending time there; in the lifestyle study by acting as an employee (see the prologue); in the Smithy by being two of the people in the process, not acting as distanced researchers but as equal members of the group contributing to the project, which simultaneously gave us new insights into entrepreneurship as a process (Berglund and Wigren, 2012); and finally in the DiE project by being one of the project members who could choose what to participate in. Thus the researcher could be informed about the different things that happened (and were voiced) and discern the emerging conflict.

There are advantages and disadvantages of being a direct participant or an observer (Rosen, 1991). The different roles can be related to working knowledge, organizational secrecy, trust and role definition. Working knowledge is knowledge that can only be transformed when engaged 'in the social relations in which the task is embedded' (ibid., p. 16); this is well illustrated in the prologue. Depending on the type and purpose of the study, there can be reasons why the researcher decides to detach her- or himself from the organization/s. One reason may be to avoid being 'located in the same political arena' as the people who are part of the research study (ibid., p. 17). However, from a postmodern point of view, using theory can distance one from a particular political context. Travelling between different contexts (as in the DiE project), the researcher came to know different political contexts and could, thereby, also gain distance and tell an alternative story of how entrepreneurship was intertwined with the political aspects.

The illustrations above used different approaches. While the Gnosjö study is an example of a study in which the researcher was more distanced, the Smithy is an example of a process when the researchers were highly involved. It all depends on how the research process is set up, especially if the process is an interaction between different actors, as the Smithy was. But it also depends on the perspective of the researcher: if he or she is acting in a more traditional ontological role by being the fly on the wall, or if he or she acknowledges the political role of the researcher in making up stories from the given contexts. Hence the approaches range from the more 'traditional' role of the ethnographer in the Gnosjö study to the more 'postmodern' role of the ethnographer in the DiE study.

Research Process

In ethnographic studies it is of great importance that trust is established between the researcher and the 'native' people. When trust is established, the interaction and dialogue between the ethnographer and the 'natives' take on more sensitive and deeper aspects. In this manner, different meanings can be emphasized and the ethnographer goes from being an outsider to becoming almost an insider. An *emic* understanding (Fetterman, 1998a) of the cultures is created, and different meanings are emphasized. *Emic* terms are those terms that are specific to a language or a culture, and they refer to first-order concepts, that is, concepts or ways of expression used by members of a particular group, organization or community. In contrast, *etic* terms refer to second-order concepts, that is, concepts used by scientists. These concepts were originally used by cognitive anthropologists, but are today used more broadly. Geertz (1973) refined the *emic–etic* distinction and introduced the concepts experience-near and experience-distant, and argued that experience-near concepts are those that the 'natives' use and understand, while experience-distant are those concepts used by specialists.

In all of the studies presented above, trust has been of great importance. In the Gnosjö study this became obvious at the end of the research process, when the study was presented. It was a critical study of a well-known industrial district and the author conducting it often felt that, if she had not spent so much time on site, the message of the study would probably have been perceived in a different way by the members of the society. Because she had been there, they knew that she knew – it had a symbolic value. The lifestyle study shows that it is possible to create trust in quite short periods of time; over time the character of the stories in each of the three firms changed in nature. From focusing on business to sharing life experiences, a friendship was developed. The researcher reflected that whatever happens in your own life influences what you bring with you into the field. When visiting the first firm, an elderly relative was at death's door. This of course influenced the days at the firm. In the Smithy both researchers experienced the importance of trust from the very beginning of the project. When it was established, the organizers listened to their input and redefined the project in line with the suggestions from the researchers, probably because trust had been built up through dialogue. Finally, in the DiE study, which lasted longer, trust was established over time. This study was about challenging patriarchal structures in the region, which was challenging in terms of trust. The researcher had to act as a circumstantial activist (Marcus, 1995), positioning herself in the discourse of the particular event during the conflictual period in order to learn about and trace the conflict. As time passed, she could eventually bring up the conflicts from a new, more distanced research perspective, which made people listen since this perspective was not judgmental. From that point, trust could be regained from the people involved, since it was agreed that the project focused on learning about established norms in order to challenge them.

The stories above show that trust can also be created in quite short periods of time, depending on the attitude and approach of the researcher. In all four studies trust was of overriding importance.

Lessons Learned

Regardless of our ontological and epistemological position, a first and crucial step in ethnography is to pose a problem about 'the world of people'. In our field we call them entrepreneurs. However, focusing only on the entrepreneur may leave out many important aspects of entrepreneuring, considering how entrepreneurship takes shape in different contexts in society. While most entrepreneurs, sooner or later, seem to become skilled storytellers, offering glossy stories of their endeavors, ethnography points to how these glossy stories are composed. Moreover, ethnography points to the fact that there are stories other than the glossy ones; we can call them alternative stories. These are the stories about what is going on in everyday life and are in contrast to the logico-scientific explanations that Gartner (2007) initially referred to.

The stories accessed in the studies presented above are not only about success. The study about the well-known industrial district was a critical one, where challenges were highlighted through the voices of local members. In the study about lifestyle entrepreneurship the researcher not only learnt about the 'successful journeys' each firm had made, but was also exposed to the discourse on the rural and the urban: how rural areas are fighting for survival at a time when urban settings all over the world are expanding. One of the three firms had a noticeboard covered in pictures and articles from the media. A few of the articles focused on the family's experience of the tsunami in Thailand, and how they had assisted tailors from Thailand to come to Sweden to sell their services so that they could to rebuild their businesses. Another firm, the one making ice-creams, told stories about their cows. In a big poster they told the story about a cow called Älva (the Swedish word *älv* means river), who got her name because she fell into the river and was rescued. Generally speaking, the themes in the stories were of courage and survival, of taking action and making things happen, and mixed discourses in a way that made these firms stand out.

In the Smithy story the discourse on societal entrepreneurship was contrasted with the discourse on more traditional profit-oriented entrepreneurship, but highlighted community, non-economic values, artisan craftsmanship and how societal structures must be changed (Berglund and Wigren, 2012). In their way of telling stories of societal entrepreneurship human agency was decentered, highlighting the social interaction of entrepreneurship and inviting 'non-entrepreneurs' to take part in these processes. In the DiE study an important contribution was to shed light on how norms and values were challenged throughout a process that can be seen as entrepreneurial in itself. New organizations were founded to encourage entrepreneurship among particular groups in this community, and new networks were built around issues that hitherto had been silenced.

Finally, this theme – lessons learned – touches on questioning norms and values – those in the context we study, but also those in the scientific community. The tricky thing is that norms and values are taken for granted, and can be difficult to discern as well as hard to question since it may upset the status quo. As William Foote Whyte wrote, 'It is said that the most important things to know about a group of people are the things they themselves take for granted. Yet it is precisely those things that the people find most difficult to discuss' (Whyte, 1961, p. 57).

To sum up, even if the four studies differ in many ways, they have one common thread: they bring about alternative stories of entrepreneurship and SMEs. Arguably, it is the time in the field and the ethnographic eye that help to uncover what the people in the fields take for granted. Doing this develops new knowledge and understanding about how people are involved in constructing entrepreneurial situations in life, making some stories glossy while moving others into the background.

Ethnography is not just one 'thing', but takes many different forms, thus pointing to the variety of ways to apply ethnography to entrepreneurship and SME, as well as showing how it may contribute to telling new stories about the phenomena of interest to all of us.

CONCLUSIONS

Applying ethnographic methods implies interacting with entrepreneurs, listening to their stories and reconsidering the terminology that it is appropriate to use. In short, as ethnographers we learn by seeing new things in the cultures that we visit. In this chapter we have responded to the call for new perspectives, new methods and a new terminology by using four ethnographic studies that show the many ways entrepreneurship is enacted in contemporary society. It should, however, be emphasized that we do not argue that any qualitative study can be perceived as ethnographic. In this chapter we have proposed and discussed four themes that we consider to be valuable and important when talking about a qualitative study as ethnographic: context; the role of the researcher; the research process; and lessons learned.

Common to them all the studies is the ethnographic eye, an eye that observes and registers, not for direct analysis, but to collect observations as pieces of puzzles that can bring about new perspectives for social science theory. In all four studies the researchers entered into the research process with an open mind, which has created space for the unexpected. This shows that good research is about serendipity, things we cannot plan for, which is in line with Draft's (1983) reasoning that significant new knowledge is nothing we can plan for, and that research is about ambiguity. Sometimes it is about asking the obvious question, as Mintzberg once did in relation to the question of what managers do (Mintzberg, 1973, p. 4). Quality of work, according to Draft (1983, p. 540), is 'measured by intensity of surprise' and 'it changes how we see things' (ibid., p. 541; cmp. Willis and Trondman, 2000 on the 'ah-ha'-effects).

We argue that there are several similarities between an ethnographic research approach and an effectuation approach (Sarasvathy, 2001). Effectuation, according to Sarasvathy, means that an entrepreneur is taking action instead of planning; he or she is making use of his or her networks, using the resources available. Through trial and error the entrepreneur moves step by step. A researcher applying an ethnographic approach is acting in a similar way. This parable fits especially well when it comes to applying an ethnographic approach for understanding entrepreneurs, entrepreneurship and entrepreneuring. We agree with Steyaert (1997), who reasons that entrepreneurs are different and it is important that research does not overlook this issue: entrepreneurship is 'a creative process enacted through everyday practices: It is never done, and always going on, a journey with more surprise than with predictable pattern' (p. 15). Based on this, it is important that the field tries to make use of a broader variety of methods for understanding the phenomenon of entrepreneurship, with all this implies, than it does today. We argue that being in the field with an open mind and using the ethnographic eye make it possible to follow this journey.

Throughout the chapter we have made use of the themes discussed above. It should be noted that all four studies presented here were conducted in Sweden; this is important in understanding the institutional context, from regulative and normative forces to cultural and cognitive forces (Scott, 2001). Many entrepreneurship researchers emphasize the importance of taking context into account (e.g. Welter, 2010), but it is rare that contexts are given space in entrepreneurship.

Moreover, as has been illustrated by the four studies, ethnography does not come with a particular package of ontological and epistemological assumptions, but can be applied in more 'traditional' as well as more 'postmodern' ways. Regardless of standpoint, ethnography problematizes norms and makes us question taken-for-granted assumptions about 'glossy stories' by paying attention to practices and the alternative stories that make it possible to tell those the glossy versions.

Finally, 'to have been there' – out in the field – is not merely to tick off a number of questions, but to continuously pose new ones, and to face unplanned situations. It is a journey with more surprise than predictable patterns, which results in new questions that can be mediated through theory and tell more stories about entrepreneurship than we can imagine.

REFERENCES

Aldrich, H.E. (1992), 'Methods in our madness? Trends in entrepreneurship research', in D.L. Sexton and J.D. Kasarda (eds), *The State of the Art of Entrepreneurship*, Boston, MA: PWS-Kent Publishing, pp. 191–213.

Alvesson, M. (1999), 'Methodology for close up studies – struggling with closeness and closure', Institute of Economic Research Working Paper Series, 4. Lund: University of Lund.

Balogun, J., Huff, A.S. and Johnson, P. (2003), 'Three responses to the methodological challenges of studying strategising', *Journal of Management Studies*, **40**(1): 197–224.

Berglund, Karin (2007/2012), *Jakten på Entreprenörer – om öppningar och låsningar i Entreprenörskapsdiskursen* [*The hunt for entrepreneurs – on openings and closings in the entrepreneurship discourse*], Stockholm: Santérus Academic Press.

Berglund, Karin and Johansson, Anders W. (2007), 'Entrepreneurship, discourses and conscientization in processes of regional development', *Entrepreneurship & Regional Development*, **19**(6): 499–525.

Berglund, Karin, Dahlin, Maria and Johansson, Anders (2007), 'Walking a tightrope between artistry and entrepreneurship – the stories of Hotel Woodpecker, Otter Inn and Luna Resort', *Journal of Enterprising Communities: People and Places in the Global Economy*, **1**(3): 268–84.

Berglund, K. and Wigren, C. (2012), 'Societal entrepreneurship: the shaping of a different story of entrepreneurship', *Tamara Journal of Critical Organization Inquiry*, **10**(1–2): 9–22.

Berglund, K. and Wigren-Kristoferson, C. (2012), 'Using pictures and artifacts to disclose new wor(l)ds of entrepreneurship', *Action Research Journal*, **10**(3): 276–92.

Bill, F., Jansson, A. and Olaison, L. (2010), 'The spectacle of entrepreneurship: a duality of flamboyance and activity', in F. Bill, B. Bjerke and A.W. Johansson (eds), *(De)mobilizing Entrepreneurship – Exploring Entrepreneurial Thinking and Action*, Cheltenham, UK and Northampton, MA, USA: Edward Elgar Publishing, pp. 158–76.

Boje, D. (2001), *Narrative Methods for Organizational and Communication Research*, London: Sage.

Bruni, A., Gherardi, S. and Poggio, B. (2004), 'Doing gender, doing entrepreneurship: an ethnographic account of intertwined practices', *Gender, Work and Organization*, **11** (4): 406–29.

Cassell, C. and Symon, G. (1994), 'Qualitative research in work contexts', in C. Cassell and G. Symon (eds), *Qualitative Methods in Organizational Research*, London: Sage, pp. 1–13.

Clifford, J. and Marcus, G.E. (eds) (1986), *Writing Culture: The Poetics and Politics of Ethnography*, Berkeley, CA: University of California Press.

Down, S. and Reveley, J. (2004), 'Generational encounters and the social formation of entrepreneurial identity: "young guns" and "old farts"', *Organization*, **11**(2): 233.

Draft, R.L. (1983), 'Learning the craft of organizational research', *Academy of Management Review*, **8**(4): 539–46.

Eisenhardt, K.M. (1989), 'Building theories from case study research', *Academy of Management Review*, **14**(4): 532–50.

Evered, R. and Louis, M.R. (1981), 'Alternative perspectives in the organizational sciences: "inquiry from the inside" and "inquiry from the outside"', *Academy of Management Review*, **6**(3): 385–95.

Fetterman, D. (1998a), *Ethnography: Step by Step*, 2nd edn, Thousand Oaks, CA: Sage.

Fetterman, D. (1998b), 'Ethnography', in L. Brickman and D. Rog (eds), *Handbook of Applied Social Research Methods*, Thousand Oaks, CA: Sage, pp. 473–504.

Freire, P. (1970/1996), *Pedagogy of the Oppressed*, London: Penguin Books.

Gartner, W.B. (2007), 'Entrepreneurial narrative and a science of the imagination', *Journal of Business Venturing*, **22**: 613–27.

Geertz, C. (1973), *The Interpretation of Cultures*, New York: Basic Books.

Grégoire, D., Meyer, D.D. and De Castro, J.O. (2002), 'The crystallization of entrepreneurship research DVS and methods in mainstream management journals', in W.D.

Bygrave et al. (eds), *Frontiers of Entrepreneurship Research,* Proceedings of the twenty-second annual entrepreneurship research conference, Boulder, CO: Center for Entrepreneurial Studies, Babson College, pp. 663–74.

Hall, E.T. (1976), *Beyond Culture,* New York: Doubleday.

Hjorth, D., Johannisson, B. and Steyaert, C. (2003), 'Entrepreneurship as discourse and life style', in B. Czarniawska and G. Sevón (eds), *The Northern Lights – Organization Theory in Scandinavia,* Liber, Astrakt: Copenhagen Business School Press, pp. 91–110.

Huse, M. and Landström, H. (1997), 'European entrepreneurship and small business research: methodological openness and contextual differences', *International Studies of Management and Organization,* **27**(3): 3–12.

Johannisson, B. (2011), 'Towards a practice theory of entrepreneuring', *Small Business Economics,* **36**: 135–50.

Johnstone, B.A. (2007), 'Ethnographic methods in entrepreneurship research', in H. Neergaard and J. Parm Ulhøi (eds), *Handbook of Qualitative Research Methods in Entrepreneurhsip,* Cheltenham, UK and Northampton, MA, USA: Edward Elgar Publishing, pp. 97–121.

Marcus, George. E. (1995), 'Ethnography in/of the world system: the emergence of multi-sited ethnography', *Annual Review of Anthropology,* **24**: 95–117.

Nelson, R.K. (1969), *Hunters on the Northern Ice,* Chicago, IL: University of Chicago Press.

O'Connor, E.S. (2006), 'Location and relocation, visions and revisions: opportunities for social entrepreneurship', in Daniel Hjorth and Chris Steyaert (eds), *Entrepreneurship as Social Change,* Cheltenham, UK and Northampton, MA, USA: Edward Elgar Publishing, pp. 79–96.

Pike, K.L. (1967), *Language in Relation to a Unified Theory of the Structure of Human Behavior,* 2nd rev. edn, The Hague: Mouton.

Ram, M. and Holliday, R. (1993), 'Relative merits: family culture and kinship in small firms', *Sociology,* **27**(4): 629–48.

Rosen, M. (1991), 'Coming to terms with the field: understanding and doing organizational ethnography', *Journal of Management Studies,* **28**(1): 1–24.

Salzer, M. (1994), *Identity Across Borders: A Study in the 'IKEA-World'.* Doctoral Thesis No. 27, Linköping Studies in Management and Economics, Linköping University, Sweden.

Sarasvathy, Saras D. (2001), 'Causation and effectuation: toward a theoretical shift from economic inevitability to entrepreneurial contingency', *Academy of Management Review,* **26**(2): 243–63.

Sarasvathy, S.D. (2004), 'The questions we ask and the questions we care about: reformulating some problems in entrepreneurship research', *Journal of Business Venturing,* **19**: 707–17.

Scott, W.R. (2001), *Institutions and Organizations,* 2nd edn, Thousand Oaks, CA: Sage.

Stewart, Alex (1998), *The Ethnographer's Method,* Qualitative Research Methods, Vol. 46, Thousand Oaks: Sage.

Steyaert, C. (1997), 'A qualitative methodology for process studies of entrepreneurship', *International Studies of Management and Organizations,* **27**(3): 13–33.

Steyaert, C. and Katz, J. (2004), 'Reclaiming the space of entrepreneurship society: geographical, discursive and social dimensions', *Entrepreneurship and Regional Development,* **16**: 179–96.

Taylor, S., Thorpe, R. and Down, S. (2002), 'Negotiating managerial legitimacy in smaller organizations: management education, technical skill, and situated competence', *Journal of Management Education,* **26**(5): 550–73.

Van Maanen, J. (1979), 'The fact of fiction in organizational ethnography', *Administrative Science Quarterly,* **24**(4): 539–50.

Watson (2009), 'Entrepreneurial action, identity work and the use of multiple discursive resources: the case of a rapidly changing family business', *International Small Business Journal*, **27**(3): 251–74.

Welter, F. (2011), 'Contextualizing entrepreneurship – conceptual challenges and ways forward', *Entrepreneurship Theory and Practice*, **35**(1): 165–84.

Whyte, W.F. (1961) *Men at Work*, Homewood, IL: Dorsey-Irwin.

Wigren, C. (2003), *The Spirit of Gnosjö: The Grand Narrative and Beyond*, doctoral thesis, JIBS Dissertation Series, no. 017, Jönköping.

Willis, Paul and Trondman, Mats (2000), 'Manifesto for ethnography', *Ethnography*, **1**(5).

Wolcott, H.F. (1995), 'Making a study "more ethnographic"', in J. Van Maanen (ed.), *Representation in Ethnography*, Thousand Oaks, CA: Sage, pp. 79–111.

11. The practice approach and interactive research in entrepreneurship and small-scale venturing

Bengt Johannisson

1. INTRODUCTION – RESEARCHERS AND PRACTITIONERS PARTNERING FOR KNOWLEDGE CREATION

Beginning at the turn of the millennium late Professor Erik Johnsen at the Center for Applied Management Studies (CAMS) at Copenhagen Business School (CBS) ran a fascinating project. As a pioneering leadership scholar in Scandinavia he asked retired executives in all three sectors constituting the Danish welfare economy – the private, the public and the non-profit/ voluntary – to reflect upon their leadership practices. The project generated more than 30 books authored by more than 100 'senior researchers'. This legacy of reflected practice was condensed by Erik Johnsen into a few brief statements. Three of them are especially relevant beyond Denmark in the context of entrepreneurship and small-scale venturing: (1) leadership is an organic process; (2) hands-on operations are the focus; (3) like all Danes, their leaders unconsciously submit to the Lutheran interpretation of the Ten Commandments.

The lessons from this unique Danish project are also relevant for general studies in entrepreneurship and small-scale venturing. Naturally, all sectors in society accommodate entrepreneurship (Berglund et al., 2013). Small-scale venturing dominates the business community and today it also appears in the public sector in Scandinavian welfare economies. The majority of social enterprises, staffed to a great extent by volunteers, are small organizations. It would certainly be exciting to copy the Johnsen project for such ventures. However, entrepreneurs are more interested in reporting what they have achieved than in how they did it and, furthermore, owner-managers of small firms practise paperless leadership. Accordingly, it is difficult to make entrepreneurs and owner-managers reflect in writing on their practices as entrepreneurs, leaders and managers, the three hats that those in charge in organizations may wear (Czarniawska-Joerges and Wolff, 1991). A possible resolution of this dilemma, which I want to present here, is to create partnerships between practitioners and researchers. Such a pact means that the practitioner does most of the hands-on work and the researcher most of the writing, while reflection comes out of a genuine dialogue between the two.

To deal properly with the creation of a shared platform for knowledge creation between practitioners and researchers calls for a review of ontological and epistemological assumptions. The suppositions held by contemporary research into organized activity about how social reality is constructed promote an ontology of becoming. By linking to rediscovered systems and chaos theories, this view produces the effect that organizations become increasingly 'impermanent' (Weick, 2009). Images of the environment as being unknowable have more or less revolutionized strategy research, not least by inviting the practice framework (Chia and Holt, 2006, 2009). This general trend in organization studies links neatly to already established understandings of entrepreneurship as generically processual (Steyaert, 2007) and as creative organizing of everyday practices (Steyaert, 2004). Entrepreneurship is also presented as the process where coincidences are turned into opportunities that are realized hands on through collective action (Hjorth et al., 2003; Johannisson, 2003).

Turning to what epistemology would be feasible to apply when co-producing knowledge between researcher(s) and practitioner(s) offers some sources of inspiration. The importance of interactive knowledge-creating processes was pointed out early on by Nonaka and Takeuchi (1995). Later Adler et al. (2004) and Van de Ven (2007), for example, contributed to this discourse. The practice turn in organization studies has instigated a more thorough review of epistemological assumptions, including relating paradigm, theory and phenomenon to each other (Orlikowski, 2010). As practices often originate in unconscious insights, producing tacit knowledge, refining and making this explicit must be seen as a major objective in the dialogue between practitioners and researchers. It marks the importance of 'being close, being there' when an event interrupts the ongoing flow of (inter)activities, enforced through decisive intervention, freezes them into a temporary pattern: the emerging venture.

Three further points of departure have to be stated. First, although entrepreneurship and small business/venturing are both constantly challenged by a reality in flux, it is assumed that ventures can be envisioned, enacted and sustained. Maintaining this view makes me disloyal to the practice turn whose adherents see actors as constituted by social practices. Second, I argue that entrepreneurial processes may be enacted in empirical settings of any kind. In Sweden even the public authorities explicitly recognize entrepreneurship as commercial, social and/or cultural venturing.

Third, size does matter within a practice approach, as it is only in small-scale settings, whether a business or social venture, that it is possible to practise the spontaneity and immediacy that entrepreneurship thrives on and practice theories ideally preach.

The purpose of this chapter is thus to propose a practice approach for enquiring into entrepreneurship and small-scale venturing and within that view present and illustrate different ways of doing interactive research.

The chapter is outlined as follows. In the next section I briefly present the practice turn applied to entrepreneurship and small-sale venturing as an appropriate ontological/epistemological frame for an interactive research methodology. Section 3 positions this way of doing research, and in the subsequent section I first present a general way of structuring different interactive approaches and then apply it to four empirical settings in the Swedish context, two commercial, one social and one cultural. In the last section I discuss issues concerning the quality control of interactive research, including some ethical considerations.

2. INVITING THE PRACTICE APPROACH INTO ENTREPRENEURSHIP AND SMALL-BUSINESS RESEARCH

Entrepreneurship researchers provide, as in any social science, a plethora of definitions of the phenomenon, while small-scale operations can be more easily demarcated using quantitative criteria. Searching for an understanding of entrepreneurship within a practice approach is best done by positioning it against another image of the phenomenon. The much-quoted definition by Shane (2003, p. 4) is: 'Entrepreneurship is an activity that involves the discovery, evaluation and exploitation of opportunities to introduce new goods and services, ways of organizing, markets, processes and raw materials through organizing efforts that previously had not existed.' This definition is very close to that by Schumpeter (1911 [1934]). Shane's (2003, p. 9) supplementary comment that 'entrepreneurship can be explained by considering the nexus of enterprising individuals and valuable opportunities' reveals that he considers entrepreneurship as a rationalistic phenomenon realized by capable individuals who know what opportunities are around, what resources to use to enact them and what the environment is like.

Many European images of entrepreneurship present it as a social phenomenon (Steyaert and Katz, 2004), where those involved are slaves to the circumstances. Dominating discourses and strong institutions are assumed to reduce considerably the potential space for revolutionary initiatives.

Entrepreneurship then becomes close to the art of 'making do' (Sarasvathy, 2001), dealing with change in mundane settings (Steyaert, 2004) often by way of imitation (Johansson, 2010). In this perspective, entrepreneurship is an ongoing process (Hjorth et al., 2003), rightly addressed as entrepreneuring (Steyaert, 2007). The individual is reduced to an instigating person who acts driven by existential needs to make a difference and crafts his or her own entrepreneurial identity, sometimes also with the ambition to change the world for the majority (Johannisson, 2011).

Although the entrepreneurial phenomenon has not yet been much discussed in a practice perspective, strategy has. Its point of departure is how we can make the world intelligible. The literature, using a constructivist view (Weick, 2009) or an approach inspired by chaos and complexity theories (Chia and Holt, 2009), comes to the conclusion that more detailed observations of the contemporary world reveal soon enough that it is unknowable. This implies that any attempt to foresee future events, whether guided by rational plans or visions strongly believed in, is futile. What then remains 'in practice' is nearsighted coping. Although I sympathize with this view, I think that its adherents overlook the fact that an ambiguous world opens up for those who can mobilize concerted (inter)action in order to actualize an idea. This is possible because those who may oppose it are simply not ready to mobilize resistance. Still, this entrepreneurial perspective is not adopted in the strategy-as-practice literature. How come?

Turning to literature that searches for the origins of the practice approach to find an answer, I here focus on the work by Theodore Schatzki (1996 [2008]). Reflecting on previous writers on practice, such as Bourdieu and Giddens, he identifies 'practice [as] a temporally unfolding and spatially dispersed nexus of doings and sayings' (p. 89) that puts 'the do-ing, the actual activity and energization, at the heart of action' (p. 90). This is a view that is obviously in stark contrast to Shane's image of entrepreneurship! Elsewhere Schatzki argues that a practice 'embodies materially mediated arrays of human activity centrally organized around shared practical understandings' (Schatzki, 2001, p. 2). Schatzki's images of practice are very appealing when applied to entrepreneurship and small-scale venturing. First, they offer a view that provides an alternative to both the rationalistic view and the often linguistically biased alternative definitions. Action dominates talk, and action rationality (Brunsson, 1985) rules over decision rationality. Second, the notion of practice underlines the importance of hands-on action and the embodied tacit knowledge that it calls for. We know that entrepreneurial ventures and small-business operations become more action oriented as the future becomes increasingly unknowable (Johannisson, 2008). This insight has also reached strategy scholars; see Golsorkhi et al. (2010). Third, the practice approach invites all human faculties in the

crafting of the venture, or as Reckwitz (2002, p. 249) puts it: 'A "practice"... is a routinized type of behaviour which consists of several elements,
interconnected to one another: forms of bodily activities, forms of mental
activities, "things" and their use, a background knowledge of understanding, know-how, states of emotion and motivational knowledge.'

Adopting a practice approach in order to make phenomena that we
associate with entrepreneurship and small business intelligible has considerable face validity. Knowledge is embodied, thus intuitive and tacit, which
means that action is as much guided by emotion as by intention. In
entrepreneurship and small business alike personal networking and com-
municative action are crucial, just as timing in changing environments calls
for belief in serendipity and immediacy. This means that embodied, actionable knowledge (Jarzabkowski and Wilson, 2006) is used and social
capabilities mobilized to build the trust that makes it possible to turn
coincidences promptly into opportunities and attract needed resources
accordingly. Using everyday language avoids confusion caused by translation from/into a professional vocabulary. It is also congruent with the
image of entrepreneurship as a mundane activity and helps to maintain
the bridge between private and public lives, so important in family businesses.

Thus, as regards entrepreneurship, the practice turn as, for example,
applied in the strategy literature, appears as oversocialized, meaning that
the significance of will, vision and determinate (inter)action is depreciated.
In line with chaos theory, many practice researchers thus equate human/
social systems with natural systems, where subjects act purposively but not
purposefully. However, using intuition, a human faculty indeed, making
choices is definitely different from acting instinctively, a feature that we
ascribe to zoological systems. Will and vision guide, and arousal and
sociability energize humans as subjects/actors so that they can practise
'logical incrementalism' (Quinn, 1978) and do not just have to 'muddle
through' (Lindblom, 1959).

People may be differently endowed with the human characteristics that
enable them to deal with an ambiguous environment as a potential and not
an uncontrollable and paralysing space. These contrasting views are often
used to differentiate between entrepreneurial and small-business phenomena. While entrepreneuring is associated with accepting change as a natural
state and incessantly exploring ambiguous environments for potentialities,
small-business operations are assumed to be caught in a straitjacket tailored
by institutional norms and values. As demonstrated by Haag (2012), a
practice approach also lends itself to a balanced view when explaining how
the successful family firm is able to navigate between the Charybdis of

enactable opportunities and the Scylla of (self-)imposed norms and institutional forces in the environment. This makes the practice approach a promising frame for enquiries using an interactive methodology.

3. POSITIONING INTERACTIVE RESEARCH AS A METHODOLOGY

Interactive research is founded on the conviction that knowledge creation about social reality benefits from a genuine dialogue, that is interaction, between those who permanently inhabit that reality and the researchers who visit it. In order to make such an encounter constructive, the parties must pay mutual respect to each other's realities. However, adopting Orlikowski's (2010) trichotomy of modes of engaging practice in research, it becomes obvious that what makes practices a phenomenon, a theory or an ontology, depends on who owns the definition. To the practitioners themselves, practices have an ontological status because they are reality. For researchers, creating understanding through conceptualization is (a professional) practice. Philosophers are expected to reflect on ontology as part of their everyday doing, that is, their practice. Considering the relativity of the proposed modes, what remains as characteristic of practice-based research is a general concern for the details of everyday doings and close-up studies. Catching the infinitesimal and momentary (inter)activities that combine into the practices that build entrepreneurial processes calls for contextual insight and legitimacy that only long-term acquaintance with, or dwelling in, a field can generate. As underlined by Chia and Rasche (2010, p. 40), the intelligence needed is 'internalized predispositions' that cannot be instrumentally learnt but follow from socialization.

The focus on fine-grained social processes within the practice turn makes interactive research approaches feasible. They represent close-up studies that not only invite the researcher to become a participant observer or observing participant. They also expect the researcher to make a hands-on contribution, that is, not just providing a diagnosis, but often bringing change to the phenomenon being studied. But it is when it is changing that a social system reveals its secrets. Such requests for experimenting can more easily be met in research into small-business or entrepreneurial venturing than in more complex settings. In small organizations discursive and embodied interactions are tightly entangled. Besides, the limited scale and scope of operations offer an overview that not only reveals interdependences but also the systemic effects of change in some parts of the organization (Gibb and Scott, 1985). The intertwining of academic and hands-on knowledge means that reflexivity on the part of the researcher, as elaborated upon by Alvesson and Sköldberg (2000), must be reconsidered in the context of interactive research. In the collaborative setting of such research, scholars also share the responsibility to enact joint learning experiences. Accordingly, reflected interactive approaches should rightly be labelled 'constructive' (and not (only) critical) studies.

With Habermas's notion of 'communicate action' and the saying that a genuine dialogue calls for the ability to 'speak the same language', interactive research obviously signals a need for building an epistemological platform on which researchers and practitioners can meet and launch their joint venture to explicate and further refine tacit knowing. Chia and Rasche (2010) have taken on the challenge to create such a platform. Adopting Aristotle's terminology, they state that researchers with a 'building' worldview usually apply *episteme* or *techne* to generate generalizable truths about a disguised world. Adopting a 'dwelling' worldview, practitioners, in contrast, use tacit and situated knowledge guided by *phronesis* and *mētis* in order to cope with ambiguous realities. *Phronesis* 'is the tacit form of prudent practical intelligence and wisdom, acquired through experience, that accounts for the ability to perform expediently and appropriately in defined social circumstances' (Chia and Rasche, 2010, p. 39). *Mētis*, so far seldom referred to in social research, represents an internalized disposition that 'is characterized by agility, suppleness, swiftness of action and the art of dissimulation (seeing without being seen or acting without being seen to act)' (ibid., p. 40). Having said that, Chia and Rasche add little about the implications of a dwelling worldview for the hands-on doing of empirical research. Founded on a dwelling epistemology, different ways of applying an interactive methodology provided here have the ambition to contribute to the filling of this gap.

For two additional reasons I think that adopting interactive research makes the academic enquiry into a challenge, into a(n) (ad)venture, and not into a traditionally administered well-designed (research) project. First, a conventional (research) project assumes the existence of a (research) objective that has usually been designed by the researcher. In action research the needs of the practitioners are expected to guide the enquiry, but the researchers are usually in charge of it; see, for example, Reason and Bradbury (2001). In interactive research, collaborative new knowledge to the benefit of all parties involved is paramount. Second, a project is guided by a plan with a clear-cut demarcation in time and space. Interactive research must, in contrast, and like any venture, be open to new ways of jointly creating knowledge, since the dialogue between those involved in itself offers new openings for gaining insight. Accordingly, interactive methodology resembles playing with Lego rather than puzzle-solving, as suggested by Morgan (1980). Neither the way of joining the pieces nor the outcome is determined beforehand. Furthermore, while a puzzle is two-dimensional, Lego adds a third dimension that catches the creative act.

According to Chia and Rasche (2010, p. 39), a dwelling approach sees '[a]ctors as non-deliberate, relationally constituted nexus of social activities'. In a socially constructed world it is reasonable to assume that these activities are part of currents that cross the fuzzy boundary between the phenomenon and its context; compare for example Czarniawska (2004). In order to be able to deal with such fluent boundaries, the researcher has to be close to the very construction of social phenomena, in this case practices. To my mind, traditional ethnographic research, including 'shadowing', will not suffice, since it aims at uncovering routines and other existing cultural imprints. The act of creation, however, is beyond the reach of the researcher. It is important to 'be there' when change processes are being instigated. Only then will it be possible to grasp how (inter)activities unfold over time and crystallize into an event. This has great implications for researching entrepreneurial venturing within a practice approach.

In the field of entrepreneurship and small-business research there is an increasing concern for the role of context; see for instance Welter (2011). However, the context is then usually considered as a contingency, an intervening variable, and can thus be controlled by adopting a proper research design. Within a 'dwelling epistemology' (Chia and Rasche, 2010), the researcher, in contrast, must (also) get an insight into the context of the phenomenon by attending to everyday activities and interactivities that produce the fuzziness and mobility of its boundary. In addition to being informed about the phenomenon, researchers must thus also be familiar with its context. Only then will they be able to team up on equal terms with practitioners for joint knowledge creation, because practitioners use their overview of the context to navigate in an unknowable world. Elsewhere I elaborate on the need among entrepreneurs and small-business owner-managers to build an 'organizing context' that on one hand enforces and on the other challenges their practices; see, for example, Johannisson (2000a, 2011). Familiarity with the context is important for one more reason. Without the insight and associated legitimacy that familiarity provides, the researcher will be considered as a stranger, or possibly as a tourist, and as such will not be invited to participate in conversations with practitioners. It is also important to understand that contextual knowledge cannot be achieved intentionally and used instrumentally. Creative and improvizing musicians typically 'hang around', that is share a community, for no specific reason see, for example, Barrett (1998). The building of contextual familiarity must thus be as open-minded as the quest for insight into the phenomenon must be focused. Being visible in the context, signalling availability for dialogue, is hence important for interactive researchers.

Table 11.1   Contextual familiarity in interactive research

		Modes of gaining familiarity	
		Refer to earlier involvement	*Demonstrate commitment during the research process*
Familiarity with context	Indirect	(A) Stage an experiment with practitioners, aiming at disclosing hidden agendas	(C) Construct dialogues with practitioners in order to reveal local practices
	Direct	(B) Challenge existing practices through a dramatized intervention	(D) Enact your own venture in order to gain insight into the practices of entrepreneuring

Note: The text in the cells refers to cases that illustrate familiarity tactics.

In Table 11.1 I structure different ways of becoming familiar with the context of the phenomenon concerned in interactive research. The different familiarity tactics are illustrated by the cases elaborated on next. Generally, the context can be demarcated in both time and space. The researcher's familiarity with the context may in the temporal dimension be either accumulated over time, often over quite a long period, as in cases A and B, or developed in parallel with the realization of the event. Sometimes researchers then join an ongoing venturing process (case C) and sometimes they trigger and energize an event themselves (case D). In the first case (C) the involvement began after initiation of the ventures, but in case D it was the researcher that instigated the process. Only then will it be possible to track the original implications of the concrete (inter)activities that enact the venture. The spatial demarcation of the boundary may be mental, social or physical (Hernes, 2003). The familiarity with the context may also be either directly related to the specific phenomenon being studied (cases B and D) or indirectly (cases A and C), that is, to the general field to which it belongs, according to practitioners.

4.   REPORTS FROM THE FIELD

In this section I present the four cases in the field of entrepreneurship and small-scale venturing that illustrate each of the four proposed modes of carrying out interactive research according to Table 11.1. As indicated, the researcher's (my own) familiarity with the context is given special attention. An overview of the four cases is provided in Table 11.2.

Table 11.2   Four cases – an overview

(A) Disclosing hidden agendas in public support of small businesses	**(C) Organizing anarchy – sense-making in a social enterprise**
Purpose: Reveal potential effects of public small-business policy	*Purpose*: Track strategic coping in a social enterprise
Time period: 1975–2007 – present	*Time period*: 1980–2009/11 – present
Acquaintance with the context: – Organizing students' internships in local small businesses for two decades – Visibility as a debater in the local media – Permanent residence in the region	*Acquaintance with the context*: – Action research in societal venturing in the 1980s – Organizing five annual conferences on local economic development – Chairing the board of a regional organization supporting local cooperatives
Interactive involvement: – Recruiting the participants – Staging the event on site – Adapting during the event	*Interactive involvement*: – Reflective daily mail dialogues during two periods (in 2010 and 2011) – Member of the cooperative – Member of a supportive network (later chairing its board)
(B) Warning Icarus – enlightening a local small-firm cluster	**(D) Catching entrepreneurship – in search of practices**
Purpose: Trigger reflexivity in a self-centred industrial district	*Purpose:* Gain insight into the practices of entrepreneuring
Time period: 1975–1995–present	*Time period*: 1981–1999–2011
Acquaintance with the context: – Research in the district for two decades – Repeated reporting of research – Students' internships in the district	*Acquaintance with the context*: – Networking in the regional cultural community – Researching and publicly debating regional economic development – Permanent residence in the region
Interactive involvement: – Simultaneous publication of newspaper articles with contradictory messages – Confronting the small-business community – Dealing with delayed condemnation	*Interactive involvement*: – Instigating the event – Leading everyday organizing – Carrying out multiple reporting

(A) Disclosing Hidden Agendas in Public Support of Small Businesses

The background and purpose of the study

Small firms are often considered to need public support, and many pro-grammes are designed for that purpose. However, there is little scientific evidence that such support actually facilitates firm growth and prosperity; see, for example, Lambrecht and Pirnay (2005). Some studies even propose that the management's positive attitude towards support programmes reduces the likelihood that the firm will become involved in entrepreneurial activities (Greene and Storey, 2004). These studies are, however, supported by overly rationalistic assumptions as regards both the implementation structure and the recipients of the support. Loosening these suppositions, there are several explanations why small-business owner-managers are reluctant to recognize the need for and usefulness of public support. As much of the business venture emerges from the personal network of its initiator, significant contributors are invited because the businessperson trusts them (Johannisson, 2000a). As a construct from above, today largely originating from the European level, the mental maps guiding the support system are dominated by urban values and give preference to formal competences. The areas targeted in the support programmes are usually located outside metropolitan areas and dominated by low-tech businesses, which means that they adopt a contrasting rationale; see Johannisson and Lindholm-Dahlstrand (2009).

The purpose of the research was to deal with the paradox that support programmes are both offered and demanded by small-business owner-managers despite the minimal effect ascribed to the programmes by both the businesspeople and external evaluators.

Familiarity with the context

The municipality concerned is located in the same region as Linnaeus (then Växjö) University. For two decades – 1975–96 – I was in charge of a small-business undergraduate programme that aimed at training the students to become employable as administrators in SMEs. To bridge the academic and business communities and help the students learn about entrepreneurial and small-business practices, every week for two years they spent two days as trainees in a regional small company. Assignments designed in collaboration with the firms and reported on site to the manage-ment of the firm with the teacher being present formed the main examin-ation. For a more detailed report on the programme, see Johannisson (1991). The commitment of the students and the academic staff to the development of small firms in the region probably helped the university in general and me personally gain the confidence of the overall business community. The fact that I have been living in the region for four decades, doing research on entrepreneurship and regional development and regularly appearing in the local media as an academic debater, probably helped to develop trust in the internship programme.

The enquiry – phenomenon, methodology and outcome

The research challenge, the paradox, made a traditional design irrelevant. We realized that we needed to adopt an imaginative, yet not speculative, approach to get the insight needed to dissolve the paradox. Based on the focus-group method, five regional owner-managers were invited in 2007 to a role play, staged as a board meeting in a fictitious SME. The board members were asked to evaluate a number of candidates for the position as the new CEO without any interference from the researchers. After the board meeting we initiated a follow-up conversation on how the meeting had evolved. For a more detailed report on the method used, see Bill et al. (2009); Bill and Olaison (2009).

A focus-group interview is a 'research technique that collects data through group interaction on a topic determined by the researcher' (Morgan, 1996, p. 130). The goal of a focus-group interview is not, as in the case of the general group interview, to gather data from individuals in a group. The idea is that the individuals, through the method's interactive design, should be stimulated to reflect on issues they have knowledge about but are not aware of and therefore cannot articulate (Pearce, 1998; Morgan, 1996). The approach may produce new insights, both for the practitioners and for the researchers. In the focus-group session the participants are outside their normal everyday lives, hopefully relaxed and thus interacting spontaneously. The role of the moderator in the focus-group interview is obviously to facilitate the discussion without 'contaminating' it with his or her own views.

Since as the senior researcher I was familiar with all participants and recruited them (they all immediately accepted the invitation), I could legitimatize the encounter and the study at large. This created a favourable atmosphere and unprompted interaction during the meeting. The five invited SME owner-managers had all, in one way or another, participated in public support initiatives and came from the same municipality. Hetero-geneity ruled with respect to age (40–70 years), experience (from the manufacturing industry to privatized public health) and sex (three women [one of them immediately taking on the role of chairperson] and two men).

During the focus-group interview and auxiliary activities the three research-ers took on the different roles of moderator, secretary and participant observer.

The focus-group interview started by asking the participants to introduce themselves by telling a brief life story. Then the assignment was introduced: Act as if you constitute a board! This board meeting had just one item on the agenda: to hire a new CEO for the small company that was presented in a two-page text. The group members also got a half-page CV for each of the four candidates for the CEO position. The candidates had quite different track records, one for example including work experience from the regional Swedish support agencies and one having spent time at the EU in Brussels. As a board our 'actors' were expected to evaluate each of the final applicants and then rank them. We gave the group participants time to read the material and told them that it was up to them to run the board meeting. When the group 'closed' the board meeting, the moderator initiated and led a discussion. Only then did the moderator ask questions regarding both the CEO candidates' presentations and the conversation during the 'board meeting'.

We had constructed a focus-group conversation with different stages in order to have multiple arenas for discussion. First of all, we wanted to see if the participants in their presentation mentioned their experiences with support initiatives. Second, in the material for the board meeting we had given several clues as to initiating discussions about support. These two sections were meant to mirror the importance the participants give to support initiatives when describing themselves and discussing a specific SME and its context. Third, the final discussion, with direct questions from the moderator, initiated reflection and explanations. Here the participants were able to motivate their statements and, for example, explain why some issues were not dealt with. Since the board meeting paid little attention to potential support for the firm when reconfiguring with a new CEO, many of the questions concerned different aspects of the participants' previous 'real-life' experiences from dealing with support programmes.

The whole meeting lasted for two hours, one of which concerned the board meeting itself. The presentation round took about 20 minutes, and thus 40 minutes were devoted to the more general discussion, to which everyone in the room was invited.

During the session the board members/owner-managers expressed some hard feelings towards the EU bureaucracy, but did not accuse the support agents of malevolence. Rather, they expressed the general feeling that the agents have their own agenda and perhaps also a limited understanding of the business world and the realities facing SMEs in their everyday activities. Neither did our board members accuse the support system of representing a waste of public money. They stated only that its bureaucracy, whether on the European, national or regional level, represented an alien social construct to businesspeople. The outcome of the exercise, that is, our interpretation and coping with the paradox, was thus that SME support programmes offer a rationale for businesspeople who wish to make a contribution to society, in particular to their local community in so far as securing financial resources for its businesses. They also provide small-business owner-managers with an arena where it is possible to offer their expertise, make new acquaintances and refine the crafting of their own identity. It was obviously not just about money for their own business.

(B) Warning Icarus – Enlightening a Local Small-firm Cluster

The background and purpose of the study
Originating in ideas originally explicated by Marshall (1920 [1979]), the logic, practices and functionality of 'industrial districts' have for several decades been debated in the literature on spatial organizing of economic activity (see Becattini et al., 2009). In an industrial district the networked small-(family)business community is deeply embedded, historically, culturally and socially. The industrial district as a highly institutionalized setting provides advantages such as flexible specialization in focused industries and a favourable business climate. Nevertheless, it hides disadvantages. The viability of the specialized interrelated firms is limited to the industry to which they belong. This means that local embedding creates a lock-in effect when there is a radical environmental change (cf. Grabher, 1993). Besides, with a successful track record the business community easily becomes complacent. This reduces the perceived need for change as well as the collective absorptive capacity of the local business community when external impulses indicate dramatically changed conditions.

The Gnosjö region in southern Sweden possesses manufacturing traditions that go back several centuries. It is considered to be the only fully fledged industrial district in Sweden (Johannisson, 2009). The local accumulation of social capital has on the one hand benefited the creation and maintenance of a viable small-business structure (Johannisson, 1983), but on the other hand it has institutionalized a paternalistic culture that marginalizes immigrants in general and new Swedes in particular, and also discriminates against women as entrepreneurs (Wigren, 2003). Still, in the 1980s the Gnosjö industrial district was the economically most successful region in Sweden, outperforming even the capital region of Stockholm. Since then the development of low-cost economies, first in Europe and later in South East Asia, has considerably increased the competition in the low-technology fields where the Gnosjö business community is located.

Regional adaptation to this structural change has been a long and burdensome journey because of the low level of education in the region. Resistance to higher education had accumulated over the years, in parallel with the commercial success of the firms. Only in the mid-1990s were more systematic measures taken to accelerate the move of the business community into the emerging knowledge economy. Soon enough the municipality and a technology centre started to organize training and technology transfer activities. These were considered very effective when compared to similar initiatives in other parts of Sweden. However, the business community remained sceptical, sometimes for good reasons, as the external interventions paid little respect to the informal/tacit knowledge of owner-managers and employees (cf. Johannisson, 2000b).

The organizing and success of the Gnosjö region offered an exemplary case to bring up in an academic educational setting. As part of the European Doctoral Programme in Entrepreneurship and Small Business Management (Johannisson and Veciana, 2008), the students at Linnaeus (then Växjö) University studied the role of small business in local and regional development. The doctoral students' major assignment was to review the potential of the Gnosjö region, located about 100 km from the university, as a socioeconomic phenomenon. The students were divided into groups of three or four, and each group was provided with a different theory to apply in interpreting the structures of and ongoing processes in the business community. During a two-day visit to the region the students interviewed owner-managers as well as representatives of the municipality, trade unions and the industrial development centre. The questions asked operationalized the different conceptual frameworks that had been elaborated by the student groups. The reports from the field research accordingly provided quite different images of the future potential of the industrial district. For details concerning design of the field assignment, see Johannisson et al. (2007).

After the formal examination of the student reports, I proposed to the two groups, using diametrically contrasting conceptual frameworks – and accordingly providing opposite visions about the future of the region – that each group should write an article on the findings and submit it to one of the daily newspapers in the region. Since all groups included a Swede, this appeared to be a feasible suggestion. My rationale for initiating this experiment was that the region and its over-confident business community would be awakened by the contradictory publications and be urged to reconsider its view as regards non-local and formal knowledge. However, both groups declined my suggestion. Then I decided to organize and enact the challenge myself.

The purpose of the study was thus to trigger a sustainable change in a self-centred region by launching an experiment that would enlighten its business community and enhance its learning capacity.

Familiarity with the context
Since the mid-1970s I have repeatedly done research in the Gnosjö region (see, e.g., Johannisson, 1983; Johannisson et al., 1994). Besides reporting back research findings to the business community at special meetings, I have frequently been invited to local business associations to give present-ations on different subjects. On one occasion I also organized a local 'Starting your own business' course. Some of my undergraduate students have been apprentices in local firms. I know several local owner-managers personally, many of them also having (had) leading positions in local politics and/or religious communities. At the time of the interactive study I had thus accumulated trust for two decades. This meant that I put consider-able social capital at stake when provoking the dominant discourse by means of the media.

About a decade earlier I had collaborated with a local newspaper with another provocative initiative, albeit not as radical as this case reports. I wanted the local owner-managers participate in a meeting that I had arranged in order to inform them about the findings from one of my studies in the region. On the very day of the meeting I thus published in one of the local newspapers an article in which I argued that the region should establish a local wage-earners' fund. The Swedish parliament had recently decided that part of the profits generated by Swedish firms should be deposited to build funds controlled by employees for them to invest in equity and accordingly gain influence in the firms concerned (cf., e.g., Johannisson, 1987). National protests against this proposal originated in the Gnosjö region and the argument I put forward in the article was that a local fund would make the 'confiscated' money stay in the region. The local businesspeople of course opposed the idea, but the debate that followed my presentation revealed my concern for the regional business community. I wanted to highlight the need to be alert not only to technological and economic, but also to social change. When I had stated my honest intent I made some new friends among influential owner-managers and community leaders.

The study – phenomenon, methodology and outcome
At the time of the study with the doctoral students the business community of Gnosjö industrial district was, as indicated, about to invite formal knowledge to complement existing practices. However, the counterforces to

the much-needed change seemed to dominate. Considering the low legitimacy of academics in the region, a traditional knowledge-transfer approach by a formal presentation of my reflections seemed futile. A different, more radical and dramatic mode of enlightening the business community was called for.

Since the student groups did not want to get involved, I summarized the two contrasting student reports in two articles in two regional newspapers, both signed by me. I managed to persuade both editors to publish them the very same day (without informing them about my experiment). Accordingly, one article/newspaper stated that the days when the Gnosjö region was economically successful were definitely gone, while in the other article I argued that the Gnosjö way of doing business should be used as a role model by other regions. The initiative upset the editors but even more so, of course, the regional owner-managers. They seem only to have read the negative article. Their dismay triggered a local debate that lasted for several months. My attempt to explain the intention of the provocation in a third article was disregarded by the business community. Instead I was more or less forced about six months later to accept an 'invitation' to a meeting arranged by the regional trade associations.

Walking diagonally through the large dinner hall where the local businesspeople had gathered to reach my 'electric chair' was like running the gauntlet. With the chairman of the local trade association (whom I knew well), a consultant and a representative of the county administration as bodyguards, I was cross-examined by the well over 100 owner-managers concerning my statement about the emerging crisis in the region. Only after two hours did one of the local business leaders suggest that, after all, my message that there seemed to be an increasing knowledge deficit in the region might be worth listening to. Not surprisingly, he was an academically trained technician who had immigrated to the region. After his intervention the accusations became less intensive, but when the meeting ended the majority of the participants in the meeting were still upset because I had questioned their ability to cope with contemporary and upcoming challenges in their business environment.

It is difficult to estimate the long-term effect of my provocation because, as indicated, other initiatives to enhance training and education, generated regionally as well as nationally, were launched in the region (see Johannisson, 2000b). But I was reminded of my initiative when, five years later, I took doctoral students to the region. This time the study trip included firms where I was not personally acquainted with the management. When I called the owner of one of these firms in order to arrange a meeting, he yelled at me: 'I don't want to see you in my company! Because of your article customers who approach us ask if we will be able to deliver considering the problems in the region!' Having discussed the matter for some time, the owner-manager reluctantly welcomed us to his factory. Once there, we had very constructive discussions in a relaxed atmosphere. And when I was invited in the years after the upsetting experiment to give presentations at local trade associations, the participants expected me to be provocative. To me this signalled a more reflective business community.

(C) Organizing Anarchy – Sense-making in a Social Enterprise

The background and purpose of the study

Social enterprises, with objectives beyond the economic ones and with means that are not always available on the market, appear as very complex and dynamic organizations if compared with traditional small family businesses. Social enterprises are often involved in practices that run across sectoral boundaries. In other words, they organize resources originating in the voluntary sector as well as in the public and private sectors (see Berglund et al., 2012). Social and commercial enterprises also have many features in common. Aimed at making local, national and international communities socially and ecologically sustainable, individual social enterprises must also be economically sustainable. Just as any firm today needs to demonstrate social responsibility, studying social enterprises may provide useful lessons for (small) commercial firms operating on the market.

The study reported here concerns Macken, a small social enterprise in Växjö, a university town in southern Sweden. Växjö is (inter)nationally recognized as a 'green city' but also presents itself as a multicultural town. Many of the new Swedes, though, live in a special residential area with its own private and public service centres, including schools – and Macken. Several other social enterprises operate in Växjö, but most of them organize a considerably narrower range of activities than Macken. This social venture was launched in 2005 by a journalist and environmental activist. As a social entrepreneur, he initiated a local debate on the necessity to recycle limited resources. A local politician was intrigued and her involvement triggered the unique political decision that everything that was possible to recycle/recondition, for example furniture, bikes or textile fabrics, could be taken away from the local dump by the Macken people. (For more detailed accounts regarding this case, see Johannisson, 2012.)

In Macken user-value is thus recreated by reconditioning such items in 'language workshops', staffed by teams consisting of physically disabled or socially marginalized native Swedes and not-yet-integrated new Swedes. This arrangement helps individuals in both groups to gain self-respect. The new Swedes are introduced to a new language in a working context that is familiar to them and the native Swedes can use their knowledge about the trade and Sweden in a way that is meaningful to both themselves and society. Macken's products are distributed through its own second-hand outlets and the enterprise also provides services such as courses in Swedish and in how to run your own company, in collaboration with public organizations and institutions. In 2012 Macken established a business development centre and in 2013 it adopted a social-franchising concept, helping new Macken cooperatives to emerge in other municipalities.

The purpose of the study was to outline a conceptual roadmap for empirical journeys into the practices of societal entrepreneurship. This is achieved by tracking emergent patterns concerning the way societal entrepreneurship is enacted as creative organizing.

Familiarity with the context
In the early 1980s I was involved in an action-research project in a small community in a region close to Växjö and my university. There, people, led by a charismatic community entrepreneur, mobilized in order to launch new ventures that would create local jobs and save existing public services (see, e.g., Johannisson and Nilsson, 1989.) My contribution included 'translating' and putting into practice the lessons learnt from the original research in the Gnosjö industrial district; cf. case B. The societal venturing turned out to be very successful. Within five years the local glassworks, rescued by the mobilization from a close-down by being turned into a cooperative (that included far more community people than the workers at the glassworks), had become the financially most successful company in the industry. Formally, the research project had ended by then, but I have been in touch with that community ever since. I have also carried out further studies of local mobilization, including a similar action-research project in an adjacent region. At the beginning of the 2000s I organized five consecutive annual national conferences at Linnaeus University on local economic development. The conferences established a temporary cluster among the local activists, often organizing cooperatives. The fifth conference was organized in collaboration with Coompanion, a partially publically financed regional agency that supports the creation and development of cooperatives. One of these cooperatives is the social enterprise Macken.

The enquiry – phenomenon, methodology and outcome
To gain the needed insight into the practices of Macken I adopted a threefold dialogical mode. The first stage involved qualitative interviews, conversations, with key actors. These interviews included the social entrepreneur and two more leaders, as well as one of two business angels who volunteered in Macken. The second set of accounts consisted of two e-mailed daily dialogues between the social entrepreneur and myself for

one month in 2010 (October) and for one week in 2011 (March/April). While the dialogue in the autumn may be characterized as a reflective conversation about the conditions for running Macken, the spring dialogue reported the everyday doings of the entrepreneur, on which I commented only briefly. The third set of accounts reflects my dwelling in Macken and its spatial and social context. Part of that 'hanging around' experience directly concerned (and still concerns) the social enterprise and includes intense and interactive participant observation/observing participation in a number of formal and casual meetings with (part of) the organization members during 2009–11.

The enquiry into the practices of entrepreneurship as appearing in the Macken social enterprise highlights, among other things, two generic features. The first is the ongoing arranging of embodied needs and resources, people and relations, which I associate with the core of entrepreneuring as a process and with 'bricolage' as a certain kind of organizing (see Baker and Nelson, 2005). The second involves the temporal features of the of social-venturing process, that is, its regularities and disturbances in the flow of activities that produce a certain rhythm.

The notion of 'bricolage' has to be qualified as 'social bricolage' in the context of social venturing. This takes it beyond 'bricolage' as originally presented by Lévi- Strauss (1962 [1966]), meaning recycling artefacts at hand to form new patterns (see also Didomenico et al., 2010). To begin with, social bricolage appears as an ongoing process, rightly referred to as 'bricolaging', or as a practice. Second, the aim of bricolaging, that is, 'making do', is not just meant to instrumentally solve a problem involving artefacts or, as elaborated on by Sarasvathy (2001), to start a journey with unclear ends and means (but with optional routes) to cover individual needs. It is social bricolaging because it is about social value creation and production, which is especially challenging organizationally. Third, it is social, because it is about bringing people into new constellations (often across sectoral borders).

The variety in terms of objectives, projects and membership in the social enterprise furnishes social bricolaging with a dynamic dimension where one 'thing', resource or opportunity follows upon another. Thus in Macken, for example, a textile workshop was carefully planned and enacted in order to facilitate the integration of female new Swedes. When it turned out that one of the participants was also an artist, one outcome of the project was an art exhibition. A similar social ambition encouraged a woman in a neighbouring small community, who was a trained florist, volunteer to organize immigrant women in a workshop in her field of interest. Many more operations are triggered in a casual way. For example, visitors to the local dump who met with Macken's people asked for help with transportation, and that activated the establishing of a special logistics unit in Macken.

'Amplified immediacy' is a concept generated out of the experiences gained in the Macken studies. This concept tries to capture the genuinely processual, dynamic features of social entrepreneuring. The stabilizing and institutionalized forces in the environment of the social enterprise together generate a dynamic tension which in turn produces what I associate with the basic rhythm of social entrepreneuring. This immediacy can be further qualified in five respects. First, it emerges as a temporal feature linked to spontaneity based on the belief that every moment is or can be made into the 'right' one, a feature that is related to *kairos* and synchronicity, that is, to different aspects of timing (in contrast to chronological time). Second, the immediacy communicates that a sensation does not have to pass any filter of time-consuming reflection in the cognitive space, which often makes the feeling of the 'right moment' disappear. Reflection happens rather in or after action (see Schön, 1983). Third, since action, experimenting, is instantly triggered, road blocks can quickly be excluded, creating space for trying out new, possibly more appropriate, options. Fourth, the inspired actor spontaneously searches for partners in an existing personal network with the proper attitude and resources who can realize an enactment. Fifth, immediacy itself mobilizes intense involvement, a feeling of urgency and responsibility to complete what has been initiated.

Researching a social enterprise and its ways of coping by adopting an interactive mode also improves, to my mind, our general understanding of organizational challenges in entrepreneurship and small-scale venturing. It reveals the complexities of everyday doings and sayings, the adopted practices, and how they have emerged.

(D) Catching Entrepreneurship – In Search of Practices

The background and purpose of the study

To state that the world has become more complex in the digital era is close to a platitude. What is important is how such environments are dealt with – as threats or as opportunities. They represent 'unknowability', which is far beyond what is associated with risk and uncertainty. Contemporary environments are ambiguous. Still, or rather because of that, entrepreneurial ventures are invited. Facebook today (2013), with more than one billion users, has in less than half a decade both undermined existing global structures and enacted a new one. This magic has been possible because an ambiguous environment has correctly been treated as a potential space by the corporation and its entrepreneurs. Envisioning a road to the realization of a vision and practising flexibility and learning down that road obviously makes it possible to enact ventures even in an unknowable, emerging world.

Tracking the trajectory of a venture within this view, however, makes it especially important to be well informed about the initial conditions of the venturing process, as its further development is sensitively dependent on those conditions. Within a practice approach these conditions are closely linked to the moments when the ideas and commitments of the instigator for the first time materialize and 'go public', appearing as a new venture. This suggests that only the entrepreneur, the one who triggers the entrepreneurial process, is able to make sense of the evolving events by which the venture becomes enacted.

For two main reasons we know little about the practice of entrepreneurship and small-scale venturing, especially about its early phases. First, the staging of a new venture is very laborious and intense, and allows little time for reflection. Intense action orientation (Johannisson, 2008) and ongoing interaction (Johannisson, 2000a) call for incessant attention, which means that it is difficult for the practitioner to mobilize reflection. Second, the original 'act of creation' is often hidden even from the entrepreneur, which means that the reconstruction of the venturing process is storied into one logic or another (cf. Sarasvathy, 2001). What is then left for the researcher to initiate and process entrepreneurially is to enter the driver's seat. This calls for an auto-ethnographic approach (see, e.g., Young, 1991; Alvesson, 2003).

The purpose of the study was to personally enact entrepreneurship in order to track its generic practice features by launching a venture in a familiar context.

Familiarity with the context

Vesper (1980 [1990]) states that those who successfully launch ventures have previous experience from the field they enter. Throughout my 25 years (at the time when I launched the venture) of living in the region I have also regularly participated in, and sometimes organized, different debates on economic, social and cultural issues. This fairly active citizenship has over the years created public visibility and a broad personal network among different regional stakeholders. Considering that I had argued from the position of a 'traditional' researcher that new ventures sediment out of the personal network of their initiators (Johannisson, 2000a), it was only 'natural' for me to staff my venture team with personal associates in my regional network involving university colleagues as well as members of other constituencies, such as the public administration and the cultural community. 'Natural' is surrounded by quotation marks because the teaming up with personal acquaintances was not the outcome of rational choice but of spontaneously including people I trusted and felt might be able to contribute to the realization of my venture. In fact the staffing appeared as a self-organizing process, where people who were concerned spontaneously joined the project, while the indifferent ones denounced it. For example, although I invited all the personnel at the university to contribute to the writing, only two people ended up as active contributors.

The enquiry – phenomenon, methodology and outcome

The proposed 'enactive' approach states that the phenomenon, here the entrepreneurial event, has to be both initiated and extensively reflected upon by the researcher. In that respect the (research) venture appears as a quasi-experiment. The enactment of a double identity – acting as an entrepreneur while keeping the identity of a researcher – has an impact on the making of the venture/phenomenon that remains throughout the enquiring process. It is also the entrepreneur/researcher who puts an end to the directed (entrepreneurial) process.

The event concerned, for reasons presented below termed the Anamorphosis project, was launched in January 1999 and lasted for nine months. It has been extensively reported in Johannisson (2005). The original venture concept was to demonstrate that regional development can be realized if representatives from the research and fine-arts communities can manage to collaborate. In order to test this idea I built an arena where researchers and artists could meet and hold conversations. This platform, physically located in a building just outside the university campus, was constructed of three elements. First, the project group was staffed by artists/curators and researchers along the lines presented above, with original artists/curators directly chosen from my personal network and subsequent ones on recommendation from those already engaged. As indicated above, the university staff was approached more generally, albeit with very modest success. Second, by inviting Sweden's most established artist in the anamorphosis genre, an audience could be attracted. Anamorphosis is a form of art that combines creativity and formal (mathematical) construction. It creates distorted (two-dimensional) images of (three-dimensional) artefacts that by way of for example, cylindrical mirrors can be reconstructed to the eye. Thus, in itself, the genre combines art and science. Accordingly the event was called the Anamorphosis project. Third, during the exhibition 30 seminars were organized on different aspects of how the interface between art and science might benefit regional development. Several of the speakers were known to the national Swedish public. The events, both the exhibition and the seminars, attracted large audiences. However, only a small portion of the targeted researchers/students and business representatives attended.

The main report from the project (Johannisson, 2005) organizes the ethnographic accounts according to the three kinds of 'tales' that van Maanen (1988) suggests: the realist, the impressionistic and the confessional. The auto-ethnographic approach embedded the realist and impressionistic tales into the confessional tale. The realist report provided a straightforward story about the venturing process as it evolved chronologically. The impressionistic tale, in contrast, adopted a *kairos* logic, which means that it reported incidents that I experienced as critical of the enactment process. Like entrepreneurs passionately engaged in their venturing, I was emotionally triggered both when initiating the project and throughout its course, but especially so when the critical incidents happened. The irrationalities that this involvement may have triggered reflected, to my mind, not only an intrinsic feature of the entrepreneurial process. They also forced me to immerse myself in the process and helped me to silence, even abandon, my previous taken-for-granted understandings of entrepreneurship, thus creating space for new interpretations of the phenomenon.

The lessons learnt about entrepreneurship from the enactment included first and foremost generic features of the phenomenon as an emergent and not fully controllable process. I experienced the process as guided by intuition and 'make do', and yet supported by the espoused vision of an exhibition and seminars that would attract large audiences. As revealed by Brytting (1990) in his grounded approach to organizing in small firms, a dualistic order of spontaneity and planning ruled. The images of cultural entrepreneurs as thriving on chaos and academics on institutional order were revealed as outcomes of wishful thinking. The artists who were involved rather appreciated the order that was provided by regular and formal meetings. The researchers on their part valued, in contrast, the 'anything goes' atmosphere that (also) characterized the venture. The study also revealed the fuzziness between what should be considered as the phenomenon/the project and what belongs to its context. Throughout the process the boundary between venture and context was constantly and unrestrainedly renegotiated in order to effectuate what was considered necessary. In that coping mode resistance played an important role in identifying alternative routes to a realized vision. In order to tap its energizing potential resistance, I in some cases even constructed situations in which resistance would reveal itself and make me justify my own efforts to prove myself and the relevance of the project.

5.   CONCLUSIONS: INTERACTIVE APPROACHES AS RESPONSIBLE RESEARCH

Inspired by Chia and Rasche (2010), I have argued that research into entrepreneurship and small-scale venturing seen as practices calls for a epistemology that is based on a dwelling worldview. This invites an interactive methodology aimed at joint knowledge creation, and in order to make a genuine dialogue possible the researcher must dwell in the context of the venture and immerse him/herself in its becoming on terms similar to those of the practitioners. This means that the researcher is also expected to be able to practise *mētis*, that is, by concrete action and experimenting, contribute to the everyday activities that the actualization of a venture calls for. This hands-on involvement raises a number of questions that relate to what I call 'responsible research', encompassing issues of quality control as well as moral concerns.

In contrast to the majority of qualitative approaches within social-constructionist ontology and epistemology, interactive methods not only interpret what others are doing, but they also support others, hands on, to do whatever has to be done. This means that the elaborate reflexivity toolbox that Alvesson and Sköldberg (2000) offer is not appropriate, since it is closely related to phenomena that present themselves as written or oral texts. Declining a proven way of practising reflexivity of course invites criticism. It may present interactive research as speculative and trying to legitimize a researcher's guesswork that can easily and literally be 'made' into a self-fulfilling prophecy. However, making sense of social phenomena within a linguistic turn, for example by using narrative approaches, equally easily leads to speculation through different kinds of literary tropes such as metaphors. It just happens to be more legitimate in the academic community, where a professional discourse is dominated by words. In that perspective it is not surprising if enactive approaches using auto-ethnography, as adopted in case D, are looked on with scepticism, to some extent for good reasons. Using interactive approaches, especially auto-ethnography, for theorizing practice means that the researcher must spend a great deal of time contributing to intense processes where change is incessant. This in turn entails that the researcher will have less time for taking notes, let alone for reflection.

Phronesis, which also practises a dwelling epistemology, explicitly incorporates, in contrast to *mētis*, a moral dimension to interactive research. On the one hand, you may argue that researchers who become personally and hands-on involved in ventures pretentiously and irresponsibly go far beyond the capabilities that they have achieved in their academic training. With this in mind, the risks associated with having researchers who contribute in this way, and sometimes even instigate ventures themselves, should be considered. The mutual trust between practitioners and researchers that is a generic condition for high-quality interactive research may be misused by researchers who have not yet gained the insight associated with practical wisdom and prudence.

Above I proposed that interactive research should be guided by a constructive critical ambition. Criticism should thus be accompanied by a responsibility to not only propose alternative measures but also to contribute hands on to their enactment. Hence, if scholars involved in traditional critical analyses are content with revealing the misuse of power by some and/or the marginalization of others, interactive researchers should feel responsible for contributing to enacting the change that the research has revealed as needed. This does not necessarily mean direct involvement in the change itself but may imply a 'conscientization' of those concerned (see Berglund and Johansson, 2007).

As already stated, the context of a research phenomenon can and should be both temporally and spatially framed. Even if familiarity with the context beforehand is important for proper and responsible knowledge creation, the moral responsibility for the phenomenon that was interactively researched does not end with the closing of the research project. Rather, it is transferred to its context. Thus, after the experiment in case A I published several articles in the regional newspaper that concerned issues relevant to the local business community. In case B, concerning the industrial district, within a couple of weeks I, as indicated, supplemented the two contradictory articles by a third (published in only one of the newspapers, however). There I informed the readers about my ambition to create awareness within the regional business community about the need for considering formal knowledge in addition to local (tacit) knowledge. As indicated in the case report, I have also contributed in other ways to the industrial district. In case C, the Macken social enterprise, I have since the publication of the original research remained involved as a volunteer, both hanging around and taking on formal positions. In 2012 I became the chairman of the supportive network 'Macken's Friends' and I also coach nascent entrepreneurs. In addition, I have become involved in a new interactive research project involving Macken. In case D I remained in the artist's community for 12 years as a member of its board, including holding positions as its accountant and chairperson. For two years I also moved my (research) office to the premises that hosted the Anamorphosis project. These different involvements in the wake of the research ventures provided many opportunities to repay the trust and time that the practitioners so generously shared with me.

My point is that quality issues in interactive research are strongly associated with the knowledge-creation processes themselves, as well as with how the researchers commit themselves not only to the project, but also to its embedding context. Alvesson and Sköldberg (2000) also underline that there are different understandings of what kind of 'truth' research may aim at, which accordingly decides what research quality is. In interactive research a pragmatic image of truth applies: true is that which can be tried in concrete action and whose consequences turn out to be sustainable. Adopting this truth criterion means that for the researcher it is not only a moral obligation to remain in the context of the researched phenomenon but also a way of enhancing the quality of the research by contributing to the sustainability of its findings.

From a moral and pragmatic perspective, interactive research is especially challenging to small firms and organizations. They usually lack the absorptive capacity in terms of employees who are themselves academically trained, which is required to fully benefit from a dialogue with researchers. Usually the development of a shared 'language' between researchers and practitioners is then recommended. This would obviously imply the shared use of a vocabulary that is very close to everyday language. However, even if the researchers are able to translate their academic jargon into a plain vocabulary, this will not do. The dwelling epistemology needed is, according to Chia and Rasche (2010), an internalized disposition that cannot be instrumentally built but may only sediment out of sharing a context with the practitioners concerned. If researchers are not prepared to invest the time required to engage in appropriating such a contextual insight, small firms had better enhance their capabilities by using consultants.

Nevertheless, it is feasible to apply interactive approaches to other empirical phenomena besides entrepreneurship and small-scale venturing. Not only do they effectively reveal the difficulties of finding and keeping a dividing line between phenomenon and context, a challenge that generally applies in social research. It also reveals the challenges of distinguishing between commercial and non-commercial orientations in venturing processes in modern welfare economies. Both in the social venture (Macken – case C) and the cultural event (the Anamorphosis project – case D) discourses on financial issues were constructive not only for legal–technical reasons but also because they brought order to an anarchic organizing process. In addition, the tension between *phronesis* and *mētis* easily reveals itself in entrepreneurial small-scale settings. In Macken the social ambitions were guided by the moral concern that can be associated with *phronesis*, while the daily hands-on operations called for situated sensemaking and associated enactment that used the kind of knowledge that only the *mētis* kind of knowledge can provide. These lessons should inspire researchers to engage in further studies using interactive approaches.

REFERENCES

Adler, N., Shani, A.B. and Styhre, A. (eds) (2004), *Collaborative Research in Organizations: Foundations for Learning, Change and Theoretical Development*, Thousand Oaks, CA: Sage.

Alvesson, M. (2003), 'Methodology for close-up studies – struggling with closeness and closure', *Higher Education*, **46**: 167–93.

Alvesson, M. and Sköldberg, K. (2000), *Reflexive Methodology. New Vistas for Qualitative Research*, London: Sage.

Baker, T. and Nelson, R. (2005), 'Creating something from nothing: resource construction through entrepreneurial bricolage', *Administrative Science Quarterly*, **50**(3): 329–66.

Barrett, F.J. (1998), 'Creativity and improvisation in jazz and organizations: implications for organizational learning', *Organization Science*, **9**(5): 605–22.

Becattini, G., Bellandi, M. and De Propris, L. (eds) (2009), *A Handbook of Industrial Districts*, Cheltenham, UK and Northampton, MA, USA: Edward Elgar Publishing.

Berglund, K. and Johansson, A.W. (2007), 'Entrepreneurship, discourses and conscientization in processes of regional development', *Entrepreneurship & Regional Development*, **19**(6): 499–525.

Berglund, K., Johannisson, B. and Schwartz, B. (eds) (2012), *Societal Entrepreneurship – Positioning, Penetrating, Promoting*, Cheltenham, UK and Northampton, MA, USA: Edward Elgar Publishing.

Bill, F. and Olaison, L. (2009), 'The indirect approach of semi-focused groups', *Qualitative Research in Organizations and Management: An International Journal*, **4**(1): 7–26.

Bill, F., Johannisson, B. and Olaison, L. (2009), 'The incubus paradox: attempts at foundational rethinking of the "SME support genre"', *European Planning Studies*, **17**(8): 1135–52.

Brunsson, N. (1985), *The Irrational Organization. Irrationality as a Basis for Organizational Action and Change,* New York: Wiley.

Brytting, T. (1990), 'Spontaneity and systematic planning in small firms – a grounded theory approach', *International Small Business Journal*, **9**(1): 45–63.

Chia, R.C.H. and Holt, R. (2006), 'Strategy as practical coping: a Heideggerian perspective', *Organization Studies*, **2**: 635–55.

Chia, R.C.H. and Holt, R. (2009), *Strategy without Design. The Silent Efficacy of Indirect Action*, Cambridge: Cambridge University Press.

Chia, R.C.H. and Rasche, A. (2010), 'Epistemological alternatives for researching strategy as practice: building and dwelling worldviews', in D. Golsorkhi, L. Rouleau, D. Seidl and E. Vaara (eds), *Cambridge Handbook of Strategy as Practice*, Cambridge: Cambridge University Press, pp. 34–46.

Czarniawska, B. (2004), *Narratives in Social Science Research*, London: Sage.

Czarniawska-Joerges, B. and Wolff, R. (1991), 'Leaders, managers, entrepreneurs on and off the organizational stage', *Organization Studies*, **12**(4): 529–46.

Didomenico, L. Di, Haugh, H. and Tracey, P. (2010), 'Social bricolage: theorizing social value creation in social enterprises', *Entrepreneurship Theory and Practice*, July: 681–703.

Gibb, A.A. and Scott, M. (1985), 'Strategic awareness, personal commitment and the process of planning in the small business', *Journal of Management Studies*, **22**(6): 597–622.

Golsorkhi, D., Rouleau, L., Seidl, D. and Vaara, E. (eds) (2010), *Cambridge Handbook of Strategy as Practice*, Cambridge: Cambridge University Press.

Grabher, G. (1993), 'The weakness of strong ties: the lock-in of regional development in the Ruhr area', in G. Grabher (ed.), *The Embedded Firm. On the Socioeconomics of Industral Networks*, London: Routledge, pp. 255–77.

Greene F.J. and Storey, D.J. (2004), 'An assessment of a venture creation programme: the case of Shell LiveWIRE', *Entrepreneurship & Regional Development*, **16**(3): 145–59.

Haag, K. (2012), *Rethinking Family Business Succession. From a Problem to Solve to an Ongoing Practice*, Dissertation series No. 082, Jönköping: Jönköping International Business School.

Hernes, T. (2003), 'Organization as evolution of space', in B. Czarniawska and G. Sevón (eds), *Northern Light: Organization Theory in Scandinavia*, Malmö: Liber, pp. 267–89.

Hjorth, D., Johannisson, B. and Steyaert, C. (2003), 'Entrepreneurship as discourse and life style', in B. Czarniawska and G. Sevón (eds), *Northern Light: Organization Theory in Scandinavia*, Malmö: Liber, pp. 91–110.

Jarzabkowski, P. and Wilson, D.C. (2006), 'Actionable strategy knowledge. A practice perspective', *European Management Journal*, **24**(5): 348–67.

Johannisson, B. (1983), 'Swedish evidence for the potential of local entrepreneurship in regional development', *European Small Business Journal*, **1**(2): 11–24.

Johannisson, B. (1987), 'Entrepreneurship in a corporatist state: the case of Sweden', in R. Goffee and R. Scase (eds), *Entrepreneurship in Europe: The Social Processes*, London: Croom Helm, pp. 131–43.

Johannisson, B. (1991), 'University training for entrepreneurship: Swedish approaches', *Entrepreneurship & Regional Development*, **3**(1): 67–82.

Johannisson, B. (2000a), 'Networking and entrepreneurial growth', in D. Sexton and H. Landström (eds), *Handbook of Entrepreneurship*, London: Blackwell, pp. 368–86.

Johannisson, B. (2000b), 'Modernising the industrial district: rejuvenation or managerial colonisation?', in E. Vatne and M. Taylor (eds), *The Networked Firm in a Global World: Small Firms in New Environments*, Aldershot: Ashgate, pp. 283–308.

Johannisson, B. (2003), 'Entrepreneurship as a collective phenomenon', in E. Genescà, D. Urbano, J. Capelleras, C. Guallarte and J. Vergès (eds), *Creación de Empresas – Entrepreneurship*, Barcelona, Spain: Servei de Publicacions de la Universitat Autònoma de Barcelona, pp. 87–109.

Johannisson, B. (2005), *Entreprenörskapets väsen (The Esssence of Entrepreneurship)*, Lund: Studentlitteratur.

Johannisson, B. (2008), 'The social construction of the disabled and unfashionable family business', in V. Gupta, N. Levenburg, L.L. Moore, J. Motwani and T.V. Schwarz (eds), *Culturally-Sensitive Models of Family Business in Nordic Europe: A Compendium Using the Globe Paradigm*, Hejderabad: ICFAI University, pp. 125–44.

Johannisson, B. (2009), 'Industrial districts in Scandinavia', in G. Becattini, M. Bellandi and L. De Propris (eds), *A Handbook of Industrial Districts*, Cheltenham, UK and Northampton, MA, USA: Edward Elgar Publishing, pp. 521–34.

Johannisson, B. (2011), 'Towards a practice theory of entrepreneuring', *Small Business Economics*, **36**(2): 135–50.

Johannisson, B. (2012), 'Tracking the everyday practices of societal entrepreneuring', in K. Berglund, B. Johannisson and B. Schwartz (eds), *Societal Entrepreneurship – Positioning, Penetrating, Promoting*, Cheltenham, UK and Northampton, MA, USA: Edward Elgar Publishing, pp. 60–88.

Johannisson, B. and Lindholm-Dahlstrand, Å. (2009), 'Bridging the functional and territorial rationales – proposing an integrating framework for regional dynamics', *European Planning Studies*, **17**(8): 1117–34.

Johannisson, B. and Nilsson, A. (1989), 'Community entrepreneurship – networking for local development', *Entrepreneurship & Regional Development*, **1**(1): 1–19.

Johannisson, B. and Veciana, J.M. (2008), 'The internationalization of postgraduate entrepreneurship education: the case of EDP', in H. Frank, H. Neubauer and D. Rössl (eds), *Beiträge zur Betriebswirtschaftslehre der Klein- und Mittelbetriebe. ZfKE- Zeitschrift für KMU und Entrepreneurship*, Special issue 7.

Johannisson, B., Alexanderson, O., Nowicki, K. and Senneseth, K. (1994), 'Beyond anarchy and organization: entrepreneurs in contextual networks', *Entrepreneurship & Regional Development*, **6**(4): 329–56.

Johannisson, B., Caffarena, L.C., Cruz, F.D., Epure, M., Pérez, E.M., Kapelko, M., Murdock, K., Nanka-Bruce, D.N., Olejárová, M., López, A.S., Sekki, A., Stoian, M.-C., Tötterman, H. and Bisignano, A. (2007), 'Interstanding the industrial district – contrasting conceptual images as a road to insight', *Entrepreneurship & Regional Development*, **19**(6): 527–54.

Johansson, A.W. (2010), 'Innovation, creativity and imitation', in F. Bill, B. Bjerke and A.W. Johansson (eds), *[De]Mobilizing the Entrepreneurship Discourse. Exploring Entrepreneurial Thinking and Action*, Cheltenham, UK and Northampton, MA, USA: Edward Elgar Publishing, pp. 123–39.

Lambrecht, J. and Pirnay, F. (2005), 'An evaluation of public support measures for private external consultancies to SMEs in the Walloon Region of Belgium', *Entrepreneurship & Regional Development*, **17**(2): 89–108.

Lévi-Strauss, C. (1962 [1966]), *The Savage Mind*, Chicago, IL: University of Chicago Press.

Lindblom, C. (1959), 'The science of muddling-through', *Public Administration Review*, **19**: 79–88.

Marshall, A. (1920 [1979]), *Principles of Economics*, 8th edn, London: Macmillan.

Morgan, D.L. (1996), 'Focus groups', *Annual Review of Sociology*, **22**: 129–52.

Morgan, G (1980), 'Paradigms, metaphors and puzzle solving in organization theory', *Administrative Science Quarterly*, **25**: 605–22.

Nonaka, I. and Takeuchi, H. (1995), *The Knowledge-Creating Company*, Oxford: Oxford University Press.

Orlikowski, W.J. (2010), 'Practice in research: phenomenon, perspective and philosophy', in D. Golsorkhi, L. Rouleau, D. Seidl and E. Vaara (eds), *Cambridge Handbook of Strategy as Practice*, Cambridge: Cambridge University Press, pp. 23–33.

Pearce, M (1998), 'Getting full value from focus-group research', *Ivey Business Journal*, **63**(2): 72–7.

Quinn, J.B. (1978), 'Strategic change: Logical incrementalism', *Sloan Management Review*, Fall: 1–28.

Reason, P. and Bradbury, H. (2001), 'Introduction', in P. Reason and H. Bradbury (eds), *Handbook of Action Research. Participative Inquiry and Practice*, Thousand Oaks, CA: Sage, pp. 1–14.

Reckwitz, A. (2002), 'Toward a theory of social practices. A development in culturalist theorizing', *European Journal of Social Theory*, **5**(2): 243–63.

Sarasvathy, S.D. (2001), 'Causation and effectuation: toward a theoretical shift from economic inevitability to entrepreneurial contingency', *Academy of Management Review*, **26**(2): 243–63.

Schatzki, T.R. (1996 [2008]), *Social Practices. A Wittgensteinian Approach to Human Activity and the Social*, Cambridge: Cambridge University Press.

Schatzki, T.R. (2001), 'Introduction: practice theory', in T.R. Schatzki, K. Knorr Cetina and E. von Savigny (eds), *The Practice Turn in Contemporary Theory*, London: Routledge, pp. 1–14.

Schön, D. (1983), *The Reflective Practitioner. How Professionals Think in Action*, New York: Basic Books.

Schumpeter, J.A. (1911 [1934]), *The Theory of Economic Development*, Oxford: Oxford University Press.

Shane, S. (2003), *A General Theory of Entrepreneurship: The Individual–Opportunity Nexus*, Cheltenham, UK and Northampton, MA, USA: Edward Elgar Publishing.

Steyaert, C. (2004), 'The prosaics of entrepreneurship', in D. Hjorth and C. Steyaert (eds), *Narrative and Discursive Approaches in Entrepreneurship*, Cheltenham, UK and Northampton, MA, USA: Edward Elgar Publishing, pp. 8–21.

Steyaert, C. (2007), 'Entrepreneuring as a conceptual attractor? A review of process theories in 20 years of entrepreneurship studies', *Entrepreneurship & Regional Development*, **19**(6): 453–77.

Steyaert, C. and Katz, J. (2004), 'Reclaiming the space of entrepreneurship in society: geographical, discursive and social dimensions', *Entrepreneurship & Regional Development*, **16**(3): 179–96.

Van de Ven, A.H. (2007), *Engaged Scholarship. A Guide to Organizational and Social Research*, New York: Oxford University Press.

Van Maanen, J. (1988), *Tales of the Field. On Writing Ethnography*, Chicago, IL: University of Chicago Press.

Vesper, K.H. (1980 [1990]), *New Venture Strategies*, 2nd edn, Englewood Cliffs, NJ: Prentice-Hall.

Weick, K.E. (2009), *Making Sense of the Organization. The Impermanent Organization*, Vol. 2. Chichester: Wiley.

Welter, F. (2011), 'Contextualizing entrepreneurship – conceptual challenges and ways forward', *Entrepreneurship Theory and Practice*, **35**(1): 165–84.

Wigren, C. (2003), *The Spirit of Gnosjö. The Grand Narrative and Beyond*, dissertation, Jönköping: Jönköpings International Business School.

Young, M. (1991), *An Inside Job*, Oxford: Oxford University Press.

Index

Abdel-Khalek, A.M. 129
Academy of Management
    Entrepreneurship Division 56, 167,
        177
    symposium (2009) 10
Academy of Management Journal
    (AMJ) 1, 2, 61, 62, 64, 71, 85
    control variables 136, 142
action research 234
Adler, N. 229
Administration Science Quarterly
    (ASQ) (journal) 61–2, 64, 85, 142
advocacy research worldview 6
agency theory 27, 43
Aguinis, H. 99, 113, 114, 115, 116, 118,
    119, 120, 121, 122, 128
Akerlof, G. 43
Alcoff, L. 193
Aldag, R.J. 128
Aldrich, H.E. 56, 57, 58, 59, 60, 61, 62,
    63, 64, 76, 80, 81, 158, 177, 183,
    184, 202
Alpert, M. 48
Alvarez, S.A. 10, 56, 81
Alvesson, M. 204, 206, 208, 234, 252,
    254
Amabile, T.M. 107
American Psychological Association
    (APA) 114
Amis, J.M. 3, 179, 181, 182, 188, 189,
    195
Amit, R. 27
amplified immediacy 248
Amundson, S.D. 41
analysis of variance 101
analytical procedure 63
Anamorphosis project 250, 254
anarchist approach to science 46
Anastasi, A. 130
Anderson, D.J. 128, 129
Angen, M.J. 185, 190, 191, 192, 193
ante-narratives 214, 215
Antoncic, B. 157, 163

applied research program (ARP) agenda
    35–9
    alternative explanations, eliminating
        39
    controllable variables 38
    cost-effective solutions 39
    how and why questions, addressing
        38
    practical outcomes/significance 36,
        37
    replicability, evidence of 36
    unexpected findings 37–8
Arena for Growth (Swedish public–
    private sector partnership) 213
Aristotle 234
Armstrong, J.S. 34, 37
Arnold, J. 152
Aronson, E. 90, 95
Arrindell, W.A. 122
Arrow, K. 43, 191
Atinc, G. 136, 139, 142, 143, 144, 148,
    150, 151, 153
Atkinson, P. 186
Austin, J.T. 136, 139
Autio, E. 157
auto-ethnographic approach 249
Aycicegi, A. 161, 163

Babson College Entrepreneurship
    Research Conference, Lyon
    (2013) 1, 7
background theory 4
Bagby, R. 88
Bagozzi, R.P. 113, 115
Baker, T. 57, 58, 59, 61, 62, 63, 64, 76,
    79, 80, 81, 177, 183, 184, 247
Balogun, J. 207
Bandura, A. 149
Bansal, P. 2
Barley, S.R. 44
Barney, J.B. 56, 81
Baron, R. 56
Barrett, F.J. 235

Barthes, R. 164, 169–70
Bauer, C. 38
Becattini, G. 241
Becker, G.S. 43, 45
Becker, T.E. 136, 139, 142, 144, 148,
    149, 150, 151, 153
'behavioroid' measures 92
benchmark journals 61, 65, 66, 71, 76
Bergkvist, L. 126, 128, 129
Berglund, K. 8, 206, 213, 215, 217, 219,
    222, 228, 245, 253
Bergum, V. 190
Bernstein, R.J. 185
best practices 12
    control variables 148–51
Bettis, R. 78
between-subjects design 102, 103
Bezos, J. 93
bias 13, 30
    avoiding 95–6
Bill, F. 202, 239
biotechnology ventures 15–16, 18
Birch, D.L. 34, 36
Bird, B.J. 8, 112, 119, 123, 130, 139
Birkinshaw, J. 160
Birley, S. 178, 186–7
Blaug, M. 21, 23, 28, 33, 43
Boal, K. 56
Bogdan, R. 186
Bohr, N. 191
Boje, D. 215
Bonnett, C. 124
Bono, J.E. 2
Bourdieu, P. 231
Bradbury, H. 234
Brännback, M. 8, 160, 170, 170–1
Brannen, M.Y. 156, 157, 160
Brannick, M.T. 136, 137, 139, 142, 144,
    145, 147, 148, 149, 150, 151, 153
Branson, R. 48
Breaugh, J.A. 136, 139, 142, 145, 146,
    147, 148, 149, 150, 152, 153
Brettel, M. 116
bricolage 247
Brief, A.P. 128
Brin, S. 93
Brockner, J. 107

Bruni, A. 202, 206
Brunsson, N. 231
Brush, C.G. 8, 22, 56, 57, 59, 63, 79, 81,
    89, 177
Bruton, G. 186
Bruyat, C. 177
Bryant, F.B. 122
Bryk, A. 104
Bryman, A. 178
Brytting, T. 251
Buchanan, A. 178
Burmeister-Lamp, K. 99
Burrell, G. 24, 58, 180
Busch, A. 43
Busenitz, L.W. 57, 59, 79, 177
Butler, J.E. 27
Bygrave, W.D. 26, 27, 28, 88, 178, 184,
    185, 190

Campbell, D.T. 89, 90, 92, 113, 114,
    115–16, 118, 119, 123, 130, 145,
    152
Campbell, J.P. 128, 129
Campbell-Hunt, C. 47
Canada
    cross-cultural survey 161, 162, 174
    doctoral business programs 25–6
Cantillon, R. 166
Caputo, J.D. 193
Cardon, M.S. 115, 117, 118, 121, 160,
    161
Carlson, K.D. 136, 142, 143, 145, 148,
    149, 150, 151
Carnap, R. 28
Carsrud, A.L. 8, 170, 170–1, 171
Carter, S. 80
Caruana, A. 24
Carver, R.P. 37
case studies 216
Cassar, G. 116
Cassell, C. 204
Cattell, R.B. 114, 117, 125
causal modeling 116
causal predictor variables 139
causal relationships, experimental
    methods 92–3
Chandler, D. 164, 167, 168, 169

Chandler, G.N. 27, 57, 59, 79, 88–9, 114, 116, 121, 130, 178
Chave, E.J. 121
Chen, C.C. 117, 124
Chen, M.K. 157
Chen, Y.-W. 163
Chia, R.C.H. 229, 231, 233, 234, 235, 252, 254
chi-square tests 63, 66
Chua, W.F. 58, 60
Churchill, G.A. 113, 114, 115, 116, 118, 119, 120, 130
Churchill, W. 158
CITI (Collaborative Institutional Training Initiative) 98
Clegg, S. 184, 185
Clifford, J. 205
C-OAR-SE procedure, measurement development 123
codes, and language 168, 170, 171
code-switching 163, 174
coding of data 62–3
coefficient alpha method, internal reliability 119, 122, 123
coefficient of stability (test–retest reliability) 118, 130–1
Cohen, J. 32, 37, 137, 142, 149, 152
Cohen, M.D. 22
Cohen, P. 137
Cohen's kappa statistics 63, 81
Collaborative Institutional Training Initiative (CITI) 98
Colquitt, J.A., George, G. 2
communicate action notion (Habermas) 234
company language 172
composite reliability 119–20
computer simulation/modeling 85
conceptual replication 105
conferences 1, 17, 78, 246
confirmation bias 30
confirmatory factor analysis (CFA) 117, 125
confounding variables 141
conjecture, philosophy (Popper) 23
Conklin, B. 144, 151
Connelly, B.L. 32, 37

Conner, K.R. 44
connotation 168–9
conscientization 217, 253
consensus theory of truth 22–3, 24
constructivism 6, 231
constructs 113–14
    construct validity 89, 93, 114, 123
    culture 156
    job satisfaction 127–8
content validity 114, 115, 121–2, 123
    versus face validity 130
context 2, 5, 12, 15, 18, 192, 235, 236
    ethnography 202, 207, 208
        case studies 209–16
        lessons learned 217–19
    familiarity with 238–9, 243, 246, 249–50
control variables 136–55
    best practices 148–51
    contamination issues 145–6
    generalizability of results 146–7, 148, 188
    inclusion without theoretical justification 137, 142–3, 148
    measurement and use 149–50
    in non-experimental entrepreneurship research 137–8, 148, 151
    parental role model and intention to start new business venture, hypothesized relationship 139–41
    purification principle 144, 145, 148
    reporting 150
    results interpretation 150–1
    selection 148–9
    statistical control 138–42, 144, 151
    use 142–8
    Venn diagram 140, 141, 147
    see also predictor variables
convergent validity 114, 115
Cook, T.D. 89, 90, 92, 113, 114, 115, 116, 130
Coompanion (regional agency) 246
Cooper, A.C. 27, 30, 31
coordination, in language 170
Cope, J. 189

Corley, K. 2
Cornelius, B. 30, 48, 177
Cornforth, C. 43
correlations 116
correspondence theory of truth 22, 24
Cortina, J.M. 119
cost-effective solutions 39
Coviello, N.E. 157
Covin, J.G. 121
Craig, E. 22
Creswell, J.W. 193
criterion variables 139, 142, 145
criticism 253
Cronbach, L.J. 113, 114, 115, 119, 126, 130
Cronbach's alpha estimation method 119, 120, 123, 125, 130
cross-cultural studies 156–76
    challenges of 161–2
    emic and etic perspectives 158, 159–62, 168, 171, 172, 173
    language 157–8, 163–7
    research implications 173
    semiotics 157, 164–7, 168, 169
    see also culture
'crud factor' 31, 32
culture
    construct of 156
    and ethnography 206, 223
    impact on entrepreneurial activity 156–7
    origins of concept 159
    see also cross-cultural studies; ethnography
Czarniawska, B. 235
Czarniawska-Joerges, B. 228

Dalton, D.R. 47
Darley, J.M., Jr 104
data analysis 192
data coding 62–3
data collection 61–2, 162, 180, 192
    experimental methods 94, 96
databases
    lack of publicly available 14–15
    public 84
David, R. 27, 44, 47

Davidsson, P. 56, 57, 58, 59, 63, 80, 158, 177, 180, 181, 184, 186, 189
Davis, P. 43
Dean, M.A. 56, 57, 59, 81, 177–8
Deeds, D. 8
Delgado-García, J.B. 143, 144, 151
Delmar, F. 56
denotation 168
Department of Health and Human Services (DHHS), Office for Human Research Protections 98
dependent variables 31, 112
    experimental methods 89, 90, 91, 92, 96, 100, 105, 107
    open- or closed-ended 96
descriptive statistics 150
DeVellis, R.F. 115, 118, 119, 120–1, 122, 124
Dewald, W.G. 36
Dick, P. 161, 163
Didomenico, L. 247
Dilthey, W. 185
dimensionality, and reliability 117–20
discipline of entrepreneurship 185
discourse theory 217
discriminant validity 114, 115
divergent validity 93
'Diversity in Entrepreneurship' (DiE) project 209, 215–17, 219, 220, 221, 222
doctoral business programs 25–6
Donaldson, J. 43
Donaldson, L. 44
Doucouliagos, C. 43
Dow, Gregory, K. 44
Down, S. 56–7, 78, 202
Doz, Y.L. 156, 160
Draft, R.L. 204, 223
Drnovsek, M. 160
Drolet, A.L. 127, 128
dual families 171
Duhem–Quine problem 29
dust-bowl empiricism 46
'dwelling' worldview 234, 235, 254

Easterby-Smith, M. 178, 180, 187, 188, 191, 193

Echtner, C.M. 164, 165, 169
Eckhardt, J.T. 56
Eco, U. 171
Edelman, L. 8
Eden, D. 36
EDGAR database 18
Edwards, A.L. 88, 90
Eisenhardt, K.M. 8, 204
Emden, C. 186
emic and *etic* perspectives
    cross-cultural studies 158, 159–62,
        168, 171, 172, 173
    ethnography 205, 220–1
Emmison, M. 168
empirical replication 105
empirical research challenges in
        entrepreneurship 10–19
    dust-bowl empiricism 46
    lack of agreed-upon definitions in
        field 13–14
    lack of established and readily
        available outcome variables 14
    lack of publicly available databases
        and secondary data for firms
        14–15
    multi-industry 13
    nature of entrepreneurial action
        12–13
    reasons for undertaking empirical
        research 11–12
    solid sample frame, difficulty in
        finding or creating 15
    strategies for successful research
        asking interesting questions 17–18
        embedding oneself in chosen study
            area 17
        focus 15–17
        footprints, looking for 18–19
        natural experiments, seeking out
            19
    validation of process 192
England, P. 43
English language 158
entrepreneurial action, nature of 12–13
Entrepreneurial Attitude Questionnaire
        (EAQ) 96, 97
entrepreneurial orientation (EO) 172

entrepreneurial phenomenon 180, 231
    versus small-business phenomena
        232
entrepreneurial process, characteristics
        88
entrepreneurship
    definitions 177–8
    entrepreneurship theories, as
        non-scientific 27
    and epistemology 180–3
    as idiosyncratic and context-specific
        12, 15, 18
    macro level versus venture level 10
    as multidisciplinary 2–3
    pre-paradigmatic field 11, 23
    research *see* empirical research
        challenges in entrepreneurship;
        research, entrepreneurship
    terminology 166–7, 169
*Entrepreneurship & Regional
        Development* (journal) 61, 85
*Entrepreneurship Theory and Practice
        (ET&P)* 1, 61, 81, 86, 178
    control variables 136–7
    experimental methods 89, 90
episteme 234
epistemology 163, 184, 235
    and entrepreneurship 180–3
errors 118
    Type II 149
Essence of Entrepreneurship, The
        (Johannisson) 165–6
ethical validation 193
ethnographic approaches
    case studies *see* ethnographic case
        studies
    definition of ethnography 84
ethnography 201–27
    'Ah-ha' effects 206, 223
    auto-ethnographic approach 249
    case studies
        'Diversity in Entrepreneurship'
            (DiE) project 209, 215–17,
            219, 220, 221, 222
        lifestyle entrepreneurship (rural
            entrepreneurs) 209, 211–13,
            218

participative action research
project ('Smithy think tank')
209, 213–15, 218, 221
traditional ethnography (Gnosjö
industrial district, Sweden)
209–11, 217, 220, 221
conducting 206–9
context 202, 207, 208
case studies, description 209–16
lessons learned 217–19
and culture 206, 223
definition 203–4
development 204–6
emic and *etic* perspectives 205, 220–1
field studies 204, 208
lessons learned 208, 209, 217–23
case studies 211, 213, 214–15, 217
summary 221–3
modes of enquiry 204–5
multi-sited 205
participant observation 212
research process 202, 210–11, 212,
214–15, 216
lessons learned 220–1
researcher role 205, 207, 210, 212,
214, 216
lessons learned 219–20
techniques 207
traditional 205, 209–11, 235
see also cross-cultural studies;
culture
European Doctoral Programme in
Entrepreneurship and Small
Business Management 242
European research tradition in
entrepreneurship 56–7
European entrepreneurship journals
61, 65, 71, 77, 78
evaluation apprehension 94
Evered, R. 204
Everitt, B.S. 122
exogenous theory assessment model 42,
43
experimental methods 88–111
biases, avoiding 95–6
causal relationships 92–3
control group 101

factorial designs 92, 101–4
'how' and 'why' of entrepreneurial
action 108
independent check on the
manipulations 97
measurement 91–2
motivational orientations toward
cognitive activity 106–8
operationalization 91, 97, 105, 108
procedures and reservations 104–6
quasi-experimentation 90
random assignment 99–101, 108
reactivity 94–7
responsible conduct of research 98–9
social psychology 90, 92, 97, 101,
105–6
standardization 96, 108
validity 89, 92–3
'what' of entrepreneurial action 108
experimenter expectancy 94
exploratory factor analysis 117, 122
external validity 89, 116, 188
extraneous nuisance variables 136, 139,
140, 146

Fabrigar, L.R. 117, 125
face validity 123, 130, 232
Facebook 248
face-to-face interviews 94, 95
factor analysis 115, 117
factorial designs 92, 101–4
fractional 104
family business research 158, 170–1,
241
Feigenbaum, S. 36
Feiwel, G.R. 191
Ferratt, T.W. 128
Fetterman, D. 206, 220
Feyerabend, P. 46, 183
field notes 207
Fielding, J.L. 188
Fielding, N.G. 188
Fiet, J.O. 32, 93, 99, 105
Finland 160, 161, 162
languages 173–4
Finn, A. 130
Fischhoff, B. 48

Fiske, D.W. 114, 115, 123, 145
Fiske, J. 168
Flax, J. 193
Fletcher, D.E. 24
Fligstein, N. 44
focal theory 4
focus group interviews 216, 239, 240
focusing 15–17
Foo, M. 99
footprints, looking for 18–19
Forbes, D.P. 59
Ford, H. 48
Forscher, B.K. 31
foundationalist research 181, 182, 187, 189
  see also non-foundationalist research
Freire, P. 214, 217
Frey, B. 44
Friedman, H. 116
Fuller, S. 24
Fuller, T. 24
functionalist perspective 57
Furnham, A. 124
Furubotn, E. 44

Gadamer, H.G. 192, 193
Ganzach, Y. 131
Gardner, D.G. 129
Gartner, W.B. 1, 56, 57, 59, 78, 79, 81, 91, 116, 124, 177, 178, 186–7, 201, 202, 222
Gatewood, E.J. 96, 98, 99
Geertz, C. 79, 205, 220–1
Geletkanycz, M., 2,
GEM (Global Entrepreneurship Monitor) studies 1, 157, 158
gender factors, random assignment 100
generalizability 146–7, 148, 188
generalization theory 130
Gephart, R.P. 186, 187, 189
Gerbasi, K.C. 122
Gergen, K.J. 105
Geyskens, I. 44
Gherardi, S. 185
Ghoshal, S. 27, 44
Gibb, A.A. 233
Gibbons, M. 185

Giddens, A. 231
gift culture/economy 204
Gilbert, D.T. 90
Global Entrepreneurship Monitor (GEM) studies 1, 157, 158
Glorfeld, L.W. 117
Gnosjö industrial district (Sweden)
  ethnographic case study 209–11, 217, 220, 221
  and small scale venturing 241–5
Golsorkhi, D. 231
Google Scholar 2
Gordon, R.A. 149, 150
Gouldner, A.W. 30, 34, 38
Grabher, G. 241
Graham, J.M. 119
grand narrative 214
Granovetter, M. 44, 218
Grant, A.M. 2
Grant, P. 57, 60
Green, D.P. 41
Greene, F.J. 238
Grégoire, D.A. 183, 202
Guadagnoli, E. 122
Guba, E.G. 60, 179, 181, 189
Guttman, L./Guttman scaling 121

Haag, K. 232
Habermas, J. 234
Hacking, I. 182
Hackman, J.R. 127
Hair, J.F. 122, 130
Hall, E.T. 205
Han, S. 27, 44, 47
Handbook of Social Psychology (Lindzey) 90
Haraway, D. 193
hard sciences 23
Harris, C.L. 161, 163
Harrison, R.T. 3–6, 8, 177, 186
Harzing, A.-W. 161, 162
Haynie, J.M. 99
Hays, W.L. 32
Hayton, J.C. 157, 163
Hébert, R.F. 166
Hernes, T. 236
Herron, L. 88

hierarchical linear modeling (HLM) 104
Higgins, E.T. 106–7
Hindle, K. 178, 188–9
Hirsch, P.M. 44
Hisrich, R.D. 157, 163
Hjorth, D. 202, 229, 231
Hobbs, D. 38
Hoepfl, M.C. 186, 189
Hofer, C.W. 27, 28, 33, 88
Hofstede, G. 156, 159, 160
Holliday, R. 202
Holmes, C.B. 128, 129
Holst, E. 43
Holt, R. 179, 229, 231
Honig, B. 56
Horn, J.L. 117
House, E.R. 181
Hsu, D.H. 56
Hubbard, R. 34, 36
human capital theory (HCT) 27, 43
    micro-level and macro-level 45
    testing 23, 30, 45–8
    variants 46
    see also testing of theories; theories
human resources (HR) 13
Hunter, J.E. 137, 138
Huse, M. 178, 202
hypothesis testing *see* testing of theories
hypothetico-deductive method 5, 179, 180

imposed etics 160
increasing human experience model (IHEM) 45
independent variables 112
    experimental methods 92–3, 100, 105, 108
in-depth interviews 106
Institutional Review Board (IRB) 98, 99
intellectual community 186
interactive research 230, 252
    'dwelling' worldview 234, 235, 254
    Lego analogy 234–5
    as methodology 233–6
    as responsible 252–4
intermediate-strength theories 28, 29

internal reliability 118–19, 120
internal validity 89, 92, 162, 188
international business (IB) 156
International Council for Small Business (ICSB) 87, 158
international entrepreneurship (IE) 157
International Small Business Journal (ISBJ) 61, 86
    experimental methods 89
interval scales 121
interviews
    in-depth 106
    ethnographic 207, 216
    face-to-face 94, 95
    focus group 216, 239, 240
IRB (Institutional Review Board) 98, 99
Ironson, G.H. 127, 128

Jarzabkowski, P. 232
Jennings, P.L. 24, 178, 186
Jensen, M.C. 43
job creation 36
job satisfaction, single- versus multiple-item measures 127–8
Johannisson, B. 8, 24, 165–6, 202, 206, 229, 231, 235, 238, 241, 242, 243, 244, 245, 246, 249, 250, 251
Johansson, A.W. 206, 215, 217, 253
Johnsen, E. 228
Johnson, P. 186
Johnson, R.B. 185, 190
Johnstone, B.A. 202
Jones, M.V. 157
Journal of Applied Psychology 136, 142
Journal of Business Venturing (JBV) 61, 81, 86, 89, 137, 178
Journal of Experimental Social Psychology 90
Journal of Management and Strategic Management 136
Journal of Small Business Management (JSBM) 1, 61, 81, 86–7, 89, 90, 137
journals, entrepreneurship 1, 22, 34, 40, 45
    benchmark 61, 65, 66, 71, 76
    control variables 136–7, 142, 143

European-based 61, 65, 71, 77, 78
experimental methods 89–90
mission statements 85–7
and progress measurement *see*
    progress measurement in
    entrepreneurship research
qualitative research 178, 179
SSCI rankings 56, 61
top-tier management 77
US-based 65, 66, 71, 76, 77
see also specific journals
Julian, P.A. 177

Kahneman, D. 102
kairos 248, 251
Kaiser, H.F. 117, 125
kappa procedure, data coding 63
Katz, J. 56, 218, 230
Kauffman Foundation 12
Kayande, U. 130
Keat, R. 181
Kelley, H.H. 37
Kenny, D.A. 152
Kenworthy, A. 8, 81
Ketchen, D. 47
Keynes, J.M. 21–2
Keysar, B. 162, 163, 164
KI rule (eigenvalue-greater-than-one
    rule) 117
Kim, P. 56
Kirchhoff, B.A. 34
Kirk, R.E. 32, 34, 37
Kirzner, I. 81, 166
Klimoski, R.J. 139
Knight, G.A. 157, 163, 172
knowledge
    academic and hands-on, intertwining
        233–4
    creation of
        researchers and practitioners
            partnering for 228–30
        in social sciences 163
    embodiment 232
    interactive research 233–4
    practical, developing 35–9
        applied research program (ARP)
            agenda 35–6

replicability 33–4
Knowledge Foundation 213
Knudsen, C. 178
Kotowitz, Y. 43
Kreiser, P.M. 163, 172
Krueger, N.F. 182
Kuder, G.F. 119
Kuhn, T.S. 11, 21, 22–3, 24, 29, 39, 58,
    60, 184
Kvale, S. 194
Kwan, K.M. 33, 36

Lakatos, I. 22, 23, 28, 29, 39
Lambrecht, J. 238
Landström, H. 178, 202
Lang, S. 8
Langlois, R.N. 44
language 157–8, 163–7
    back-translation 162, 169, 172
    and codes 168, 170, 171
    everyday 232
    Finnish 173–4
    meaning of words, analyzing 167–73
    research-specific 169, 170, 172
    and semiotics 164–7, 168, 169
    signs 164, 165, 168
    as a social institution 169–70
    structure, relationship to meaning
        164–5
    Swedish 166, 173
    translation 172
Larson, J.R. 127
Latané, B. 104
Latham, S. 8
Lather, P. 190, 193
Latour, B. 182
Law, J. 182, 183, 195
Lawal, S.O. 99
Lawson, T. 181
Leitch, C.M. 3, 8, 177, 186, 187, 193,
    195
Lévi-Strauss, C. 204, 247
Levy, D.M. 36
Lewin, A.Y. 44
lifestyle entrepreneurship, case study
    209, 211–13, 218
Likert, R. 92, 121

Likert scaling 121, 124
Lin, X. 161, 162
Liñán, F. 163
Lincoln, Y.S. 60, 179, 181, 189
Lindblom, C. 232
Lindholm-Dahlstrand, Å 238
Lindsay, D.S. 37
Lindzey, G. 90
linguistics 157
Link, A.N. 166
Linnaeus (formerly Växjö) University,
    Sweden 238, 242, 246
literature reviews 59–60, 62
Locke, E.A. 127–8
Locke, K. 187
Locke, R. 184
lock-in effect 241
locus of control 124
logical incrementalism 232
logical positivist research tradition 3,
    22, 28
logical probability 28
longitudinal studies 138
Louis, M.R. 204
Lounsbury, M. 44
Low, M.B. 57, 58, 60, 78, 81
Lubart, T.I. 34–5
Lumpkin, G.T. 106
Lumsden, J. 115
Luna, D. 163
Lykken, D.T. 31, 32–3
Lyon, D.W. 27, 57, 59, 79, 88–9, 130,
    178

Machlup, F. 20
Macken (small social enterprise),
    Sweden 245–8, 253
MacMillan, I.C. 57, 58, 60
Madison, G. 193
Maglen, L.R. 28, 43
Malinowski, B. 204
Manolova, T. 8
Marcus, G.E. 205, 206, 216, 221
Marshall, A. 241
Martín-Cruz, N. 143
Marxism 27
Maxwell, J.A. 190

Mayer, K.J. 2
McClellan, M. 39
McClelland, D.C. 157
McCloskey, D. 191, 194
McDonald, S. 178
McDougall, P.P. 156–7, 157
McDougall, W. 90
McKinley, W. 58
McMullen, E. 8
McNamara, G. 2
Mead, M. 204
measurement
    of constructs 113
    control variables 149–50
    developing a measure 120–4
    experimental methods 91–2
    multi-item measures
        developing (example) 124–6
        information inaccuracy 127
        job satisfaction 127–8
        respondent fatigue 127, 128
        respondent refusal 127
        versus single measures 114, 126–9
    pool of items, generating 120–1
    purpose of measure, determining 120
    validity *see* measurement validity
    see also progress measurement;
        progress measurement in
        entrepreneurship research
measurement validity 112–35
    characteristics of valid measurements
        114–17
    critical role 112–13
    dimensionality and reliability 117–20
    improvement requirements 130
    within-individual variation 116
    psychometric perspective 113, 122,
        130
    reliability 114, 117–20
    unidimensionality 114, 117–20, 122
    and validation 113–14, 122
    see also measurement
Meehl, P.E. 20, 24, 26, 27, 28, 29, 31,
    32, 37, 38, 40, 41, 114, 115, 137,
    138, 139, 144, 146, 147, 149, 150,
    152, 153
metaphysics 22

meta-theory, 26, 57
methodological falsification (Popper) 26
methodology, research
  analytical procedure 63
  choice, in entrepreneurship research 194–5
  data coding 62–3
  data collection 61–2, 94, 96
  defined 20–1
  experimental *see* experimental methods
  interactive 230, 233–6
  philosophy of science 24–6
  problems 26–35
    practical research requirements 33–5
    statistical testing 32–3
    theory 26–8
    theory testing 28–31
    variables and related measures 31–2
  progress measurement 57, 61–4
  qualitative research 183–7
  rigour 188, 189
  sample description 64
  survey-based 64, 66–7, 84, 94
mētis 234, 252, 254
Meyer, G.D. 22
Milgram, S. 105
Mill, J.S. 166
Miller, M.B. 130
Mincer, J. 45
Miner, J.B. 27
minimum average partial (MAP) approach 117
Minnesota Center for the Philosophy of Science 24
Minnesota Satisfaction Questionnaire (MSQ) 131
Mintzberg, H. 223
Mischler, E.G. 190
Mises, L. von 20
Mitchell, J.R. 104
Mitchell, R.K. 57, 60, 79, 163
mixed-methods research 160
Mone, M.A. 58

Monllor, J. 107
Montuschi, E. 182
Moran, P. 24, 44
Morgan, D.L. 239
Morgan, G. 24, 58, 180, 234
Morris, C. 165
Morris, M.H. 159, 160, 173
Morrison, D.G. 127, 128
Morse, J. 193, 194
Mullahy, J. 39
Mullen, M.R. 57, 60, 79, 89
multi-item measures
  developing 124–6
  versus single measures 126–9
multinational corporations (MNCs) 156
multiple regression analysis 138, 139, 144
multitrait–multimethod matrix (MTMM) 115
Murphy, K.J. 43

Nagy, M.S. 128, 129
narrative literature reviews (NLR) 30
national cultures 156
National Panel Study, US Business Startups 12
natural experiments, seeking out 19
natural science 184
Neergaard, H. 178, 179, 183, 186, 187
Nelson, J.A. 182
Nelson, R. 247
Nelson, R.K. 219
neo-institutional theory 44
Netemeyer, R.G. 122, 124
networking 17
Newcombe, N.S. 147
Newhouse, J.P. 39
NHST (null hypothesis significance testing) 29, 30
Nickerson, R.S. 30
Nielsen, H.B. 193
Nilsson, A. 246
nominal scales 121
nomological (predictive) validity 114, 115–16
Nonaka, I. 229
non-foundationalist research 179, 195

epistemology and entrepreneurship
  181–3
methodological stance, in
  entrepreneurship 185, 187
quality in entrepreneurship research
  189, 190, 191, 192, 193
  see also foundationalist research
North America, doctoral business
  programs 25
nuisance variables 136, 139, 140, 146
null hypothesis 101
null hypothesis significance testing
  (NHST) 29, 30, 32–3, 37
Nunnally, J.C. 113, 117, 118, 121, 122,
  123, 124, 126, 127, 129

objectivity, in social research 181, 182,
  188
observation 189
O'Connor, E.S. 202
Office for Human Research Protections
  (OHRP), Department of Health
  and Human Services 98
Olaison, L. 239
Oldham, G.R. 127
ontology 181, 182
operationalization, experimental
  methods 91, 97, 105, 108
ordinal scales 121
*Organization Research Methods
  (journal)* 179
organizational behavior (OB) 13
organizational science 27
Orlikowski, W.J. 229, 233
Osgood, C.E. 121
Osterloh, M. 44
Oviatt, B. 157

Page, R. 178
Pahre, R. 39
Panel Study of Entrepreneurial
  Dynamics (PSED I) 1, 97, 124,
  125–6, 135
parallel analysis 117
parametric procedures 33
Parida, V. 146

participant observation, ethnography
  212, 216
participative action research project
  ('Smithy think tank') 209, 213–15,
  218, 221
passion, entrepreneurial 115, 117
  cross-cultural studies 160, 161
Patel, P.C. 93, 105, 144, 151
Patton, M.Q. 189
Patzelt, H. 103
Paulhus, D. 124, 125
Pearce, M. 239
Pearson chi-square test 66
Pedhazur, E.J. 144, 145, 147, 149, 150
Penrose, E. 20
Peracchio, L.A. 163
Perren, L. 57, 60, 79
Perrow, C. 44
Personnel Psychology (journal) 142
Peter, J.P. 112–13, 114, 115, 116, 118,
  119, 122, 127, 128
Pfeffer, J. 41
Phan, P.H. 27
Phillips, B.D. 34
philosophy of science (POS) 185
  conflicts 24
  core curriculum requirements, Ph.D
    program websites 24–5
  importance 20–4
  as meta-theory 26
  methodology 24–6
phronesis 234, 252–3, 254
physics 191
Pike, K.L. 205
Pirnay, F. 238
Platt, J.R. 31
pluralism 187
Pollock, T.G. 2, 79
Popper, K.R. 22, 23, 24, 26, 27, 42
Poppo, L. 44
Porter, T.M. 182
POS *see* philosophy of science (POS)
positivism 60, 77–8, 178, 179, 181
  see also logical positivist research
    tradition
postmodern turn 205
post-positivism 5, 60

Powell, W.W. 44, 211
practical knowledge, developing 35–9
　applied research program (ARP)
　　agenda 35–6
　replicability, evidence of 33–4
practice approach, inviting into
　　entrepreneurship and
　　small-business research 230–3
practice turn 232
pragmatism 6
Pratt, M.G. 188
predictive power of theory, need for
　　41–2
predictive theory *see* scientific
　　paradigms/theories
predictor variables 137, 138, 153
　best practices 149, 150
　and control variables 143, 144, 145,
　　146
　statistical control 139, 142
　see also control variables
pre-scientific theory 22, 23, 26
Priem, R.L. 27
primitive societies 204
progress measurement in
　　entrepreneurship research 56–87
　background to study 58–61
　implications 76–80
　limitations/conclusions 80–1
　literature reviews 59–60, 62
　methodology 61–4
　normal science 58, 60, 61, 76, 77, 79,
　　80
　positivism 60, 77–8
　research design 63, 66–71
　research method *see* research
　　methods
　results 64–76
　reviews of field 56–7
　sample response rate and size 63,
　　66–7, 68, 73, 74
　sensitivity analysis 71–6
　single- versus multiple-paradigm
　　approaches 57, 58, 78, 80
　statistical methods 69, 74
　topic area 63, 67–8, 73
　units of analysis 63, 69, 75

see also journals, entrepreneurship
proxies 114
prtesti procedure, STATA 63
PSED I (Panel Study of Entrepreneurial
　　Dynamics) 1, 97, 124, 125–6, 135
pseudo etics 160
Ptolemy, C. 21
Puntoni, S. 157, 161, 163
purification principle, control variables
　　144, 145, 148

qualitative research 11
　context, importance of 192
　demand for, in entrepreneurship
　　178–9
　and drift in favour of quantitative
　　research 188
　epistemology and entrepreneurship
　　180–3
　hypothetico-deductive method 179,
　　180
　methodological stance 183–7
　non-foundationalist 179, 181–3, 185,
　　187, 189, 190, 191, 192, 193,
　　195
　philosophy and practice 177–200
　quality in 187–94
　rigour 188, 189
　validation process 192, 193
quality, entrepreneurship research
　　187–94
Quinn, J.B. 232
Quinn, R.E. 127

Raiffa, H. 48
Ram, M. 79, 202
random assignment, experimental
　　methods 99–101, 108
Rasche, A. 233, 234, 235, 252, 254
ratio scales 121
Raudenbush, S.W. 104
Raykov, T. 119
reactivity, in experimental research
　　94–7
Reason, P. 234
Reckwitz, A. 232
reflexivity 233–4, 252

refutation, philosophy (Popper) 23
regression coefficients 116, 146
Reichers, A.E. 126, 128, 129
reliability 114, 117–20, 188
   classical theory 130
   composite 119–20
   defined 118
   emic perspective, culture 162
   and generalization theory 130
   internal 118–19, 120
   test–retest 118, 130–1
Renko, M. 8, 114, 115, 121
replicability 33–4, 36
   conceptual and empirical replication
      105
   experimental methods 91, 105
reporting 150
research, entrepreneurship
   applied research program (ARP)
      agenda 35–6
   empirical research challenges *see*
      empirical research challenges in
      entrepreneurship
   findings, requirements for 34
   fishing-expedition-style 32
   methodology *see* methodology,
      research
   practical requirements 33–5
   practice approach, inviting into
      230–3
   progress measurement *see* progress
      measurement in
      entrepreneurship research
   qualitative *see* qualitative research
   quality in 187–94
   relevance to practitioners and
      entrepreneurs 79–80
   reliability *see* reliability
   replicability 33–4, 36
   'traits versus non-traits' 80
   twentieth-century challenges 1–9
   validity *see* validity
research design 3–6, 192
   progress measurement in
      entrepreneurship research 63,
      66–71
research methods

experimental *see* experimental
   methods
progress measurement in
   entrepreneurship research 62–3,
   64–6, 72–3
   weighted 72–3, 76
   see also methodology, research
research process, ethnographic
   approach 207, 208
   case studies 202, 210–11, 212,
      214–15
research program concept (Lakatos) 23
researchers 172, 193
   partnering with practitioners for
      knowledge creation 228–30
   reflexivity of 233–4, 252
   role, in ethnographic case studies
      202, 205, 207, 210, 212, 214,
      216
research-specific language 169, 170,
   172
resource-based view (RBV) 27
responsible research 98–9, 252–4
Reveley, J. 202
Reynolds, P.D. 12, 116, 201
Richardson, M.W. 119
Riordan, C.M. 156, 157, 159, 160, 173
Ritzer, G. 59, 78
Robinson, K.C. 33
Rodriguez-Escudero, A.I. 143
Rosen, M. 219, 220
Rosenberg, M.J. 94
Rosenthal, R. 32, 33, 94, 106
Rosnow, R.L. 32, 33
Rossiter, J.R. 122, 123, 126, 128, 129
Rotter, J.B. 124
Rozeboom, W.W. 37
Runyan, R.C. 157, 163
rural entrepreneurs, ethnographic case
   study 209, 211–13

Sackett, D.L. 186
Sackett, P.R. 127
Salanié, B. 43
Salmon, W.C. 28, 35, 37
Salzer, M. 208
samples 15, 63, 64

literature reviews 60–1
random sampling 100
response rates 63, 66–7, 68, 73
size 66, 68–9, 74
Sandelowski, M. 186, 193
Sanjek, R. 193
Sapienza, H. 88
Sarason, Y. 24
Sarasvathy, S.D. 57, 79, 108, 206, 224,
    231, 247, 249
Saussure, F. de 158, 164–5, 169–70
Say, J.-B. 166
scale development studies, in
    entrepreneurship 121
Scarpello, V. 128, 129
Schaffer, B.S. 156, 157, 159, 160, 173
Schatzki, T.R. 184, 185, 231
Schjoedt, L. 8, 112, 114, 121, 123, 124,
    125, 126, 130, 131, 135, 139
Schmelkin, L.P. 149
Schmidt, F. 32, 34, 37
Schmidt, F.L. 137, 138
Schmitt, N.W. 139
Schön, D. 248
Schriesheim, C.A. 47
Schultz, H. 93
Schultz, T.W. 45
Schumpeter, J. 157, 166, 230
Schwab, D.P. 112, 114, 120, 130, 136,
    139, 152
Schwartz-Shea, P. 26
science
    anarchist approach to 46
    hard 23
    natural 184
    normal 58, 60, 61, 76, 77, 79, 80, 184
    organizational 27
    philosophy *see* philosophy of science
        (POS)
    scientific paradigms/theories 21,
        26–7, 28
Scott, M. 233
Scott, W.R. 224
scree plot 117
Seale, C. 191, 192
secondary data 77, 90
    lack of 14–15

Securities and Exchange Commission
    (SEC) 18
Seghers, A. 147
segmentation of text 170
self-efficacy 112
Selznick, P. 44
semantic differential scaling 121
semiotic communication model 171
semiotics 157, 164–7, 168, 169
Semrau, T. 143
Sen, A.K. 43
sensitivity analysis 71–6
Shadish, W.R. 152
Shane, S.A. 27, 31, 36, 56, 57, 81, 106,
    166–7, 230, 231
Shapiro, I. 41, 181
Shaver, K.G. 8, 90, 96, 99, 114, 121,
    124, 125, 130, 135
Shaw, E. 186
Shenhav, Y. 184
Shepherd, D. 56
Shepherd, D.A. 104
Short, J.C. 58, 179
Sigelman, L. 30
signifier 165
signs, in language 164, 165, 168
Silk, M.L. 3, 179, 181, 182, 188, 189,
    195
Sköldberg, K. 234, 252, 254
Slevin, D.P. 121
small and medium-sized enterprises
    (SMEs) 162
    ethnography 202, 203
    hidden agendas, disclosing in public
        support of small businesses
        238–41
    small-business phenomena versus
        entrepreneurial 232
    Small Business Economics (journal) 61,
        71, 81, 87
    experimental methods 89
Smith, J.K. 190
Smith, P. 168
Smith-Cook, D. 88
Snyder, P.A. 32, 34
social bricolage 247
social cognition 106

social facilitation experiment (Triplett)
  90
social media 248
social psychology 90, 92, 97, 101,
  105–6
Social Science Citation Index (SSCI,
  2011) 56, 61
social sciences
  knowledge creation 163
  as pre-paradigmatic 21, 23
  progress measurement in
    entrepreneurship research 58
social-franchising 246
societal entrepreneurship (SE) 246
  participant observation 209, 213–15
Society of Experimental Social
  Psychology 90
soft psychology 27
Sorenson, O. 56
Sparrowe, R.T. 2
Spector, P.E. 136, 137, 139, 142, 144,
  145, 147, 148, 149, 150, 151, 153
Spence, M. 43
split-half method, internal reliability
  119
Staines, G.L. 127
standardization, experimental methods
  96, 108
STATA (statistical software package) 63
statistical conclusion validity 89, 92
statistical control 138–42, 144, 151
statistical significance 37
statistical testing, problems with 32–3
Staw, B.M. 38
Stemler, S.E. 63
Sternberg, R.J. 34–5
Stevens, S.S./Stevens scaling 121
Stewart, A. 219
Steyaert, C. 202, 206, 218, 224, 229,
  230, 231
Stiglitz, J.E. 43
Stinnett, A.A. 39
Stone-Romero, E.F. 136, 137, 139, 147,
  150
Storey, D.J. 238
Strahan, R. 122

Strategic Entrepreneurship Journal 1,
  137
strategic management research 78
strategy-as-practice 231
strong theory 28, 43–4
structural equation modeling 116, 138
Stuart, T.E. 56
sub-codes 171
subjectivity 22
substantive validation 193
Summer, C.E. 22
survey-based methodology 64, 66–7,
  84, 94
  cross-cultural studies 161
Sutton, R.I. 38
Sweden 160, 161
  Arena for Growth (public–private
    sector partnership) 213
  on entrepreneurship 229–30
  ethnographic case studies
    'Diversity in Entrepreneurship'
      (DiE) project 209, 215–16,
      219, 220, 221, 222
    Gnosjö industrial district 209–11,
      217, 220, 221
    lifestyle entrepreneurship 209,
      211–13, 218
  Gnosjö industrial district
    ethnography 209–11, 217, 220,
      221
  and small scale venturing 241–5
  Linnaeus (formerly Växjö)
    University 238, 242, 246
  Macken (small social enterprise)
    245–8, 253
  new Swedes 245
  Swedish Association of Local
    Authorities and Regions 213
  Swedish language 166, 173
  Swedish Rural Network 211
Symon, G. 204

Takeuchi, H. 229
Tamara concept 215
Taylor, S.J. 186, 202
techne 234
Tepper, B.J. 2

Terjesen, S. 8, 157, 158
testing of theories 23, 28–31, 60, 194
    applied research program (ARP)
        agenda 35–9
    exogenous assessment model 42, 43
    ineffective use of theories 30
    lack of coordination in field of
        entrepreneurship 30–1
    narrative literature reviews 30
    null hypothesis significance testing
        29, 30, 32–3, 37
    predictive power, need for 41–2
    theory review studies 47
    weak and strong tests 29
    weak theories 32
    worldview/common-sense notions,
        fitting with 29–30, 37
    see also theories
test–retest reliability 118, 130–1
text segmentation 170
Thailand, tsunami in 222
theories
    agency 27, 43
    background 4
    consensus theory of truth 22–3
    correspondence theory of truth 22
    'damn strange coincidence'
        (Popperian risk) 28, 35
    focal 4
    generalization 130
    human capital theory *see* human
        capital theory (HCT)
    importation of 27, 39–41, 108
        model for 41–4
        most-used theories in top three
            entrepreneurship journals 40
        special concerns 42
    ineffective use 30
    intermediate-strength 28, 29
    meta-theory, philosophy of science as
        26
    neo-institutional 44
    pre-scientific 22, 23, 26
    and research methodological
        problems 26–31
    scientific 22, 26–7, 28
    strong 28, 43–4

testing *see* testing of theories
unvetted 41
verismilitude, possessing 40–1
weak 28, 32
see also entrepreneurship theories
thick description 186, 205
Thompson, B. 32, 34
Thompson, L. 48
Thorpe, R. 179
Thurstone, L.L./Thurstone scaling 121
Tietze, S. 161, 163
Tolbert, P. 44
Tolbert, P.S. 44
trait validity 115, 116
transaction cost economics (TCE) 27,
    44
Trevor, C.O. 131
Triplett, N. 90
Trondman, M. 205, 206, 208, 223
truth
    consensus theory 22–3, 24
    correspondence theory 22, 24
Tsang, E.W.K. 33, 36
Turkey 161, 162
Type II error 149

Ulhøi, J.P. 178, 179, 183, 186, 187
uncertainty 108
Unger, R.K. 190
unidimensionality 114, 117–20, 122
United Kingdom (UK), doctoral
    business programs 25
United States (US)
    journals, entrepreneurship 65, 66, 71,
        76, 77
    passion, entrepreneurial 160
    scholarship published in 80
universities, doctoral business programs
    25–6
unknowability 248
Urry, J. 181
US News and World Report 25
Usunier, J.-C. 156, 157, 159, 160, 162,
    164

validation
    ethical 193

process 192, 193
substantive 193
and validity 113–14, 122
validity
construct 89, 93, 114
content 114, 115, 121–2, 123, 130
convergent 93, 114, 115
discriminant 114, 115
divergent 93
experimental methods 89, 92–3
external 89, 116, 188
face 123, 130, 232
internal 89, 92, 162, 188
measurement *see* measurement
validity
of measures in entrepreneurship
research *see* measurement
validity
nomological (predictive) 114,
115–16
statistical conclusion 89, 92
trait 115, 116
types 113–14
and validation 113–14
van Aken, J.E. 185
Van de Ven, A.H. 229
Van der Ende, J. 122
Van Essen, M. 43
Van Maanen, J. 188, 190, 204, 251
variables
causal predictor 139
confounding 141
controllable 34, 38, 39
control *see* control variables
criterion 139, 142, 145
dependent *see* dependent variables
established and readily available
outcome variables, lack of 14
extraneous nuisance 136, 139, 140,
146
independent *see* independent
variables
methodology problems 31–2
predictor *see* predictor variables
between-subjects 102
within-subjects 102–3
between-subjects 103

uncontrollable 38
Veciana, J.M. 242
Velicer, W.F. 117, 122, 125
Venkataraman, S. 27, 31, 36, 57, 60,
106, 166–7
Venn diagram 140, 141, 147
ventures, small-scale 228–58
biotechnology 15–16
case studies
background and purpose 238,
241–3, 245–6, 248–9
enactment of entrepreneurship
(contemporary environments)
237, 248–51
enquiry (phenomenon,
methodology and outcome)
239–41, 243–5, 246–8, 250–1
familiarity with context 238–9,
243, 246, 249–50
hidden agendas, disclosing in
public support of small
businesses 237, 238–41
local small-firm cluster (industrial
district) 237, 241–5
overview 237
social enterprises, sense-making
237, 245–8
contextual familiarity 235, 236,
238–9, 243, 246, 249–50
and entrepreneurship 10
field reports 236–51
interactive research 230, 252
as methodology 233–6
as responsible 252–4
partnership of researchers and
practitioners for knowledge
creation 228–30
practice approach, inviting into
entrepreneurship and
small-business research 230–3
verisimilitude, theory possessing 40–1
Vesper, K.H. 96, 249
Vetter, D.E. 34, 36
visual analog scales 121

Wanous, J.P. 126, 128, 129
war stories 11–12

Watson, T.J. 202
weak theory 28, 32
Web-based design 97
Weick, K.E. 229, 231
Weiss, D.J. 131
Welch, C. 160
Welpe, I.M. 99
Welter, F. 2, 202, 218, 224, 235
Wendt, A. 181
Wennberg, J.E. 186
Werner, A. 143
Whetten, D.A. 38
Whittington, R. 184
Whorf, B.L. 157
Whyte, W.F. 222–3
Wigren, C. 8, 209, 213, 215, 219, 222, 241
Wigren-Kristoferson, C. 213
Wiklund, J. 56, 57, 59, 63, 80
Williamson, O.E. 27

Willis, P. 205, 206, 208, 223
Wilson, D.C. 232
within-subjects design, experimental methods 102–3
Wolcott, H.F. 208
Wolff, R. 228
Woolgar, S. 182
Wright, M. 57, 79–80
Wu, J. 136, 142, 143, 145, 148, 149, 150, 151

Yarnold, P.R. 122
Yin, R.K.
Young, M. 249

Zahra, S.A. 21, 23, 30, 35, 57, 79–80
Zenger, T. 44
Zhang, A., Shaw, J.D. 2
Zucker, L. 44
Zwick, W.R. 117, 125